PETER MOORE

Damn His Blood

Being a True and Detailed History of the Most Barbarous and Inhumane Murder at Oddingley and the Quick and Awful Retribution

VINTAGE BOOKS
London

Published by Vintage 2013

2 4 6 8 10 9 7 5 3

Copyright © Peter Moore 2013

Peter Moore has asserted his right under the Copyright, Designs
and Patents Act 1988 to be identified as the author of this work

First published in Great Britain in 2012 by
Chatto & Windus

Vintage
Random House, 20 Vauxhall Bridge Road,
London SW1V 2SA

www.vintage-books.co.uk

Addresses for companies within The Random House Group
Limited can be found at: www.randomhouse.co.uk/offices.htm

The Random House Group Limited Reg. No. 954009

A CIP catalogue record for this book
is available from the British Library

ISBN 9780099554677

Typeset by Palimpsest Book Production Limited,
Falkirk, Stirlingshire

Penguin Random House is committed to a sustainable future for
our business, our readers and our planet. This book is made from
Forest Stewardship Council® certified paper.

Printed and bound in Great Britain by Clays Ltd, St Ives plc

DAMN HIS BLOOD

*Being a True and Detailed History of the Most
Barbarous and Inhumane Murder at Oddingley
and the Quick and Awful Retribution*

Peter Moore is a writer and freelance journalist.
Born in Staffordshire in 1983, he studied history
and sociology at Durham University and then
spent six years working in the media in Madrid
and London. He now teaches creative writing
at City University in London.

Damn His Blood is his first book.

To my father

Tis a sad thing to die and know before that they are damned.
None knows the misery of commencing their hell upon earth.

Arian Elwood, wife of an excommunicated man

I fled, and cried out DEATH!
Hell trembled at the hideous name, and sigh'd
From all her caves, and back resounded DEATH!

Paradise Lost, John Milton

Contents

	Author's Note	xi
	Introduction	1
	Prologue: Midsummer Day	5
1	Rev. Mr Parker of Oddingley	15
2	The Gun	32
3	The Easter Meeting	55
4	The Dance of the Jackdaw	62
5	Damn His Blood	74
6	Hue and Cry	93
7	Dead and Gone	109
8	The Man in the Long Blue Coat	113
9	Droitwich	125
10	Seduced by the Devil	134
11	A Dirty Job for Captain Evans	150
12	The Horrors	171
13	The Old Barn	191
14	Extraordinary and Atrocious Circumstances	206
15	In the Words of Thomas Clewes	229
16	Marvel-Hunters and Wonder-Lovers	244
17	The Assize	264
18	Damned	292
	Epilogue	310
	Acknowledgements	321
	List of Illustrations	323
	Notes	325
	Select Bibliography	343
	Index	349

Author's Note

Damn His Blood is a true story. This account is based entirely on contemporary and near-contemporary evidence of events in Oddingley and Worcester during the late eighteenth and early nineteenth century. All speech is drawn directly from source material – court reports, private letters, newspaper articles, printed chapbooks and pamphlets, and witness testimony.

Although written English was fast becoming standardised at this time, there are still variations in the spelling of several characters' names. In particular Richard Heming was often recorded as 'Hemming' and George Banks often written as 'Bankes'. I have chosen to drop one 'm' from Heming and the 'e' from Banks.

Introduction

At the beginning of the nineteenth century the village of Oddingley in Worcestershire was little different to any other of its type in the English Midlands. The problems it faced were typical ones. There was creeping migration as young parishioners drifted north to the industrial heartlands of Birmingham and the Black Country. There were anxieties over the harvest, the scarcity of food supplies and the speed of inflation. In the village there was a lingering dispute between the parish clergyman and local farmers over the tithe, and in the newspapers fears persisted of an imminent invasion, with Pitt the Younger, the prime minister, warning Britons to 'expect the French every dark night'. In a politically divided country, riven by war and taxation, there was little reason to notice Oddingley, with its sloping meadows, airy pear and apple orchards, tangled hedgerows and lonely farmhouses, until the dreadful murder that shook it in June 1806.

The case unravelled slowly over the days and many years that followed. What initially appeared to be a single vicious act transpired, in time, to be something far worse. The crime had been conceived, executed then concealed in such an extraordinary manner that it gained infamy, becoming one of the most compelling of its age. As facts were reported – chiefly through the newspapers – inquisitive Georgians became captivated by the unequalled colour, detail and the ever-twisting, ever-evolving narrative of the case. It was a story of moral corruption, of greed and ruthlessness. It began with a single shot, with the excitement of a chase and then the uneasy thrill of a manhunt. But this initial enthusiasm soon gave way to uncertainty.

The magistrates who were sent to investigate were country gentlemen, thrust into duty because of their geographical proximity to the crime scene rather than for their ability to construct a case or pursue a felon. And there were many questions for them to answer. What should they make of the farmers' curses? What of the clandestine meetings? What of the murder weapon? What of the suspects? It seemed that every little triumph or breakthrough led only to a new strange riddle or another dead end.

In time it became a newspaper sensation. Articles were published in titles as geographically distinct as the *Belfast News Letter* and *Ipswich Journal*. In Edinburgh the *Caledonian Mercury* labelled the crime a 'mysterious conspiracy', while in London the *Examiner* and *Morning Chronicle* both agreed it was a 'strange case'. Journalists detected elements of other crimes in the Oddingley affair: of Eugene Aram's murder of Daniel Clark in Yorkshire, of Richard Patch's killing of Isaac Blight in 1805, of the Red Barn Murder in 1827 and even the Cato Street Conspiracy of 1820. Details from these cases were present as echoes in articles filed by the handful of fortunate journalists who gained access to the Worcester courtrooms. A crime committed in an ill-considered instant left the village's reputation blackened for generations, its name known throughout the land.

The Oddingley case evokes the expressive and uncouth Georgian society that directly preceded Victorian Britain. Here many parishes remained worlds of their own, where little networks of hardy alliances were built on a stiff foundation of family loyalty and respect, where the men drank hard, worked hard, swore oaths and cursed. For many historians this world has remained elusive and opaque, with the Oddingley villagers of 1806 living in a time before determined record keeping began. It is a lost society that is resurrected in this criminal case, as the voices, concerns and culture of a rural parish at the beginning of the nineteenth century come to life. It's the world which years later provided such a rich mine for novelists such as Charles Dickens and Thomas Hardy, and characters such as kindly Joe Gargery the blacksmith, Abel Magwitch the convict, Michael Henchard and Donald Farfrae would have been at ease in the village alongside those who were there in 1806: Captain Evans the retired military officer, parish farmers John Barnett and Thomas Clewes, Richard Heming the tramping odd-job man and Reverend Parker the local parson. For the growing professional classes of late Georgian England, so intent on cleansing society of its ills and excesses, the story was a disquieting tale of a parish astray. More than perhaps any murder before, the crime involved a whole community, and the investigating magistrates' attempts to unearth facts were dogged by questions of who knew what and at what price they were willing to reveal the truth. In time Oddingley gained a reputation as an unhappy place of secrets and lies. It was cursed, wretched, damned.

Beautiful and almost perfectly hidden among the hills and the woods of the Worcestershire countryside, the village was an unlikely setting for a terrible crime. Mary Sherwood, a popular children's author, wrote at the time,

> If ever there was a secluded, humble, quiet-looking village – a village thinly populated, and which, to all appearance, is the domicile of only patient and peaceable sons of the soil – it is Oddingley. Its aspect belies it. It was the scene – and that not many years since – on which were exhibited some of the fiercest passions of man's fallen nature; the spot where the seeds of malice, hatred, and the most determined and deeply seated revenge sprang up and ripened into a harvest of crime – crime most deliberately conceived and delicately executed.

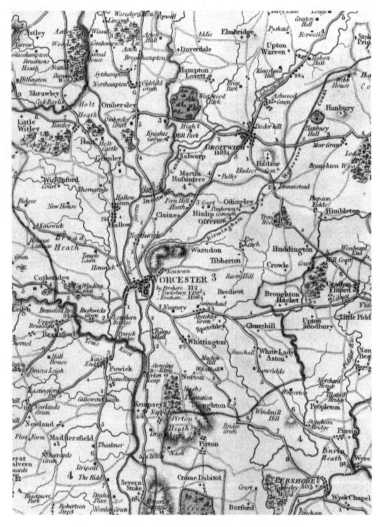

Map of Worcestershire in 1804 by Charles Smith.
Oddingley lies to the northeast of Worcester

PROLOGUE

Midsummer Day

Oddingley, Worcestershire, 24 June 1806

At around four o'clock in the morning on 24 June, Midsummer
Day, John Chellingworth stepped out of his cottage in Oddingley
and set off on a journey south. The clover harvest and haymaking
seasons had arrived and meadowlands across Worcestershire
awaited the reapers who would skim the fields with scythes, cutting
the crops to within an inch of the ground before raking the yields
into rows and turning them again and again beneath the sun.
Chellingworth was a journeyman worker and he had secured three
weeks' work at a farm in Gloucestershire, at least 20 miles and a
full day's walk away. The first shadowy smudges of light had not
yet appeared in the sky when he met Pritchard, another village
farmhand, and the two men struck out on the road together. They
passed St James' Church and Church Farm, and then the drowsing
farmyard at Netherwood – flanked with several old barns and a
tall brick farmhouse – before they rounded a corner and climbed
away up a steady slope towards Crowle, the adjoining parish, and
out of view.

Chellingworth and Pritchard would already have crossed the
parish boundary when the sun rose at a quarter to five. It shone
over a scene of rare quiet in the village, an ephemeral moment
before the day's work began. Within an hour labourers would
be streaming into the yards, lanes and meadows, carrying heavy
tools, jugs of weak beer or perry cider, and pushing handcarts,

wheelbarrows and wagons. Once they reached the mowing fields, the farmhands would start shifts that would stretch until darkness fell or the weather turned. And though the haymaking season had barely yet begun, they had already suffered one scare. On 12 June a violent storm had knifed wildly across the Midland sky. Rain had drenched the pastures and young crops, and 'awful and tremendous' peals of thunder had rung from black clouds overhead, which illuminated the county with 'the most vivid flashes of lightning'.

The storm passed and minds had now turned towards the festival which lay before them. Although it was not an official holiday, Midsummer Day remained a notable date in the calendar, and one which retained its airy, seductive and supernatural allure. In ancient England Midsummer Day was celebrated with Celtic fire festivals that marked the height of summer. Great bonfires were burnt at elevated points across the kingdom and fairs staged in assorted towns. On Midsummer Eve livestock would be dragged by their owners before fires, where they would be blessed by the crackling flames, and men, fortified with alcohol, would line up to leap over the embers in a symbolic ritual which dramatised the perilous and delicate relationship between nature and man. Folklore dictated that the greatest leap determined the height of the year's harvest.

Midsummer was a time of magic and myth, where divisions between one world and the next blurred temporarily. Wise women recounted stories about Robin Goodfellows, elves, spirits and fairies that danced in the woods and flitted across the meadows. A chance encounter with one could bestow on a wanderer the gifts of a bard or the terrors of madness. On Midsummer Day it was traditional for villagers across England to gather St John's Wort, an earthy yellow medicinal herb that was said to be infused with all the mysterious powers of the sun, bringing happiness, comfort and good fortune. In Worcestershire in 1806 this seasonal sense of excitement was increased in the week before

Midsummer by a partial eclipse of the sun, which was sighted across the county.

In Oddingley 24 June held other significance. It was the date by which many of the parish farmers were required to have paid their annual rents to Lord Foley, the local landowner, and for the wider community it was remembered as the day of the popular Bromsgrove Fair. Country fairs were important and much anticipated fixtures in the rural calendar with yeomen, tradesmen and hawking parsons exploiting their popularity as an opportunity to sell produce. Meanwhile, the larger farmers treated fairs as social occasions where they could hire additional labourers from among the crowds, exchange stories with old friends and complain about the weather.

The rich landscape of a typical fair is recreated in the opening scene of Thomas Hardy's *The Mayor of Casterbridge*, when Michael Henchard arrives at the village of Weydon Priors on fair day. He sees the vast field before him bedecked with 'peep-shows, toy-stands, waxworks, inspired monsters, disinterested medical men . . . thimble-ringers, nick-nack vendors and readers of Fate'. Such amusements offered workers a necessary release from the monotonous grind of daily life on the farms, allowing them to act irresponsibly among the lively but unrefined entertainments which included xenophobic plays, drinking stalls and bawdy comedians. William Hazlitt, the contemporary essayist, once observed that labourers used fairs as an excuse to behave like 'a school-boy let loose from school, or like a dog that has slipped his collar', waltzing drunkenly between the jugglers, the roasted hogs and the ginger-bread bakers.

Forty-one different fair days were held annually across Worcestershire, with larger towns such as Worcester, Droitwich, Kidderminster and Pershore boasting two apiece. At Bromsgrove the fair was particularly noted for linen and other cloth, cheese, horses and cattle, and for Oddingley's farmers it was close at hand, little more than an hour away. Despite this, only those who were able to delegate their duties could afford to attend. Thomas Clewes – master of Netherwood Farm – was one of these, and he was seen riding through the village on Midsummer morning by Susan Surman, a dairymaid who worked for farmer John Barnett at Pound Farm. As Clewes passed Pound Farm, Surman heard him say that 'he should be very glad to find a dead parson in Oddingley when he came back'.

Over at Church Farm the clover was being cut and wooden hurdles were being sawn and then blacked in the muddy pool that lay in a dip below the fold-yard – a sheltered area encircled by barns, stables and workshops, where sheep were often penned. Here a second dairymaid, Elizabeth Fowler, saw Richard Heming, a labourer, hauling hurdles out of the pool. He was being helped by a 14-year-old boy called Thomas Langford. Captain Evans – master of Church Farm – was in the fold-yard, and Elizabeth heard him ask the labourer when he thought the job would be finished.

'Not on the morrow,' Heming told Evans. He added that he would come the next day if he could.

Half a mile north John Barnett, master of Pound Farm, had opted to remain in the village. He spent the morning directing tasks from his fold-yard and the hours passed quietly. At about 3.30 p.m. Barnett walked over to a nearby field to meet his 24-year-old carter, James Tustin, who was responsible for hauling crops about the farm. Barnett and Tustin spoke for some minutes, brooding over the sad news that Reverend Harrison of Crowle had fallen from his horse and died. Barnett told Tustin, 'You mark if you don't hear of this one coming to some unfortunate death, dying in a ditch.'

Barnett and Tustin were among scores of parishioners at work in the meadows. Most were preparing for the clover harvest or hacking at thistles and weeds; others were driving back and forth between Oddingley and the mill at Huddington, three miles away. It was a dry day. Two of John Barnett's servants were mowing grass and clover in the village centre, and nearby John Perkins, another farmer, was tending a bonfire outside Oddingley Lane Farm. At this time of year house martins darted through the muggy air, gathering scraps of earth for their nests, and hares raced across the large grassy pastures in the north of the parish. By now, the first wild roses had appeared in the hedgerows and the scarlet poppy and sow thistle had flowered. In the fields farmhands listened for the cuckoo, whose cry changed at midsummer from 'cuck-oo' to 'cuc-cuckoo'.

For Reverend George Parker, Midsummer Day was like any other. Tuesdays brought no official business and he was free to pass the time as he wished, in his study or gardens, with his wife and daughter or friends. There was just one job to distract him. He kept a little herd of four dairy cows which were led up to graze in the north of the parish, in his glebe meadows, each morning by his servant. Every afternoon Parker would fetch them home himself, an easy task entailing little more than a gentle stroll along Church Lane and then perhaps a minute more along an overgrown byway, before he could gather them together and drive them home for milking. Parker was a man of particular custom, and he set off for his glebe at five each afternoon. Usually he took his seven-year-old daughter, Mary, with him, but on 24 June 1806 he left his rectory alone.

By now the narrow lanes that cascaded down through Oddingley from the north, winding from Hadzor or Smite Hill towards Tibberton and Crowle, were dotted with travellers, tradesmen and farmers returning from Bromsgrove Fair. In the village James Tustin saw Parker as he passed Pound Farm. Hardly a minute later Susan Surman, who was bringing down Barnett's cattle, met him further along the lane. Reverend Parker and Surman paused to bid each other good afternoon. It was just a brief exchange, but it was one that the dairymaid would for ever recall with a chill of terror. Surman entered Barnett's Wash Pool Meadows, and Parker turned right into his glebe.

At about five or six minutes past five o'clock, two butchers from Worcester, Thomas Giles and John Lench, were walking through Oddingley on their way north to Hadzor. They had passed Oddingley crossroads and were about 'two stones throws' north of Barnett's Pound Farm when they heard the piercing report of a shotgun from behind a hedge. The butchers stopped and listened. The echo of gunfire had passed in a second. All that remained was the low chatter of birdsong. Lench told Giles that he had seen a hare rush across the lane. Someone must be shooting game.

A split second later came a 'wry, dismal' shout of 'Murder! Murder! Murder!' It was a desperate cry, even heard by James Tustin a quarter of a mile away at Pound Farm. The butchers wheeled around. The shouting had come from a meadow, close by but shielded from view behind a tall, thick hedgerow. Determined to investigate further Lench and Giles ran up the lane 'as hard as they could'.

The butchers soon reached a gate which opened out into Barnett's Middle Wash Pool Field, and they raced across to the adjacent hedgerow, frantically trying to glimpse through the woven briars, holly and hawthorn, but it was impossible 'owing to the thick of it'. Temporarily defeated but with increasing resolve, they then ran up the meadow desperately searching for a stile or a gate.

At the top of Middle Wash Pool Field the hedge dipped down enough for Giles, the taller of the two, to peer over. He saw a short man running down the field. His body was bent, his arms hung low and limp by his side, a spectacle Giles later described as a 'slooping posture'. The man was wrapped in a blue greatcoat, dotted with white buttons. He was wearing an old-fashioned round hat.

Giles dropped to his knees, crawling and scrambling through the undergrowth, as Lench arrived behind him. Spotting the man with the 'slooping' gait, Lench cried out across the field, 'You villain! What have you been doing?'

The man in the blue coat was 'all of a tremble'. He paused for a second, gazing across the meadow at Lench. His body was pulled into a crooked defensive posture. Lench noticed that he looked 'very pale'.

'Me? Nothing at all,' the man called back.

By now Giles had plunged beneath the hedge and entered the field. He rushed straight for the man, who was fumbling with a bag which, as the butcher approached, he threw into the hedgerow. The man turned round just in time to see Giles dashing towards him, and narrowly avoided his swinging arm.

As Giles recovered his footing, his target spun about and raced away towards a gate. It was only then that the butcher had a chance to survey the scene before him. Giles hurried down the middle of the meadow, where he found 'a man in a state of burning, both his clothes and his flesh'. From the long gown, it was clear that the victim was a clergyman. He had been shot from close range, and hit in the midriff. The wadding from the shot had burrowed into his skin and was now beginning to smoke. A minute later and the body would be alight in the tall summer clover.

Other, terrible wounds had been inflicted to the victim's head. On the right side it was horribly clubbed inwards, with large blunt gashes to his forehead and above his right eye from which blood still flowed. As Giles stared down at the body, frozen in horror, he saw the clergyman's leg stir and right fist clench 'as if he was in the act of dying'. He had clearly been the victim of a ferocious attack. Not many yards away, partially obscured by foliage at the foot of the hedgerow, were a thin bag and the broken components of a shotgun.

Only then did Lench join Giles beside the corpse. 'Stop looking at the man that is dead, but run after the one that is living and get him if we can!' he implored. His words had an instant rousing effect on Giles, who lifted himself up and ran off towards the gate in pursuit. John Lench, suddenly alone with the smouldering body at his feet, turned back towards Pound Farm, where he hoped to find help. But before he reached the fold-yard he met Tustin in the lane. Minutes before, Tustin had heard shouts from the glebe meadow, but had thought it was just the shrieks of playing children. Now he saw Lench rushing towards him. 'There's a man shot in the glebe fields! Come along!' the butcher cried.

Several fields to the west of the glebe meadow, Thomas Giles had quickly caught up with the man in the long blue coat. Giles was athletic, could run swiftly and, would later declare, 'was almost level with him within the space of about three grounds'. Once within earshot, he called out for him to surrender.

It was a hazardous situation. Giles was fitter and faster than the man he chased, but to get too close was dangerous. The man had just committed a violent crime and had been disturbed at the scene by more than one person who would be able to iden-tify him. His capture would almost certainly result in a swift trial and subsequent execution. He must have known that he had little left to lose.

Mindful of his own safety above all else, the butcher chose to trail the murderer rather than striking a blow at him. For almost a mile he tracked his target as they snaked westwards, always keeping a hedgerow between them for his protection. At length the man stopped, stooped down beneath the hawthorn and looked the butcher full in the face. He was a short man, Giles recalled, with a thick prominent jaw and a large bald forehead. He was deathly pale.

The murderer thrust his hand into his pocket and whispered to Giles that if he did not stop following him, he would 'blow his brains out'.

This was too much for Giles, who watched as the murderer gath-ered up the skirts of his greatcoat and went off along two fields 'very gently' in the direction of Hindlip, a nearby village.

Rather than follow at a distance, Giles turned back and retraced his steps towards Oddingley. There, about a mile away, all thoughts of the clover harvest had now dissipated. The early-evening sun shone over a scene of growing confusion and outrage in Reverend Parker's glebe meadow. His body lay where it had fallen, his midriff smeared with drying blood, horribly burnt and blackened. Like the hares in the meadows or the house martins in the lanes, his murderer had appeared only for a few moments. And before the last breath had left Reverend Parker's body, he was gone.

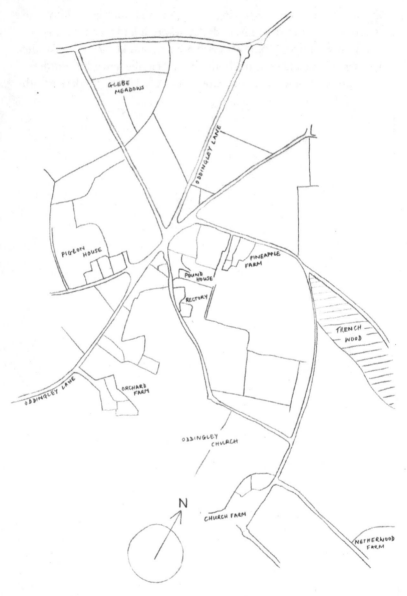

GLEBE MEADOWS

ODDINGLEY LANE

PIGEON HOUSE

PINEAPPLE FARM

POUND HOUSE

RECTORY

TRENCH WOOD

ODDINGLEY LANE

ORCHARD FARM

ODDINGLEY CHURCH

N

CHURCH FARM

NETHERWOOD FARM

Oddingley Village in 1806

CHAPTER I

Rev. Mr Parker of Oddingley

Nine months earlier, September 1805

The parish of Oddingley lay low and inconspicuous, sprawled over a shallow undulating valley in the mid-Worcestershire countryside. It was a picturesque but isolated place, a blend of open fields, twisting lanes, stray oak trees and fruit orchards, which all told measured about a thousand acres. The seven farms at the village's backbone were distinct and self-contained. Their pretty half-timber or red-brick farmhouses stood behind trimmed hedges and wooden gates and were surrounded on all sides by barns, workshops, stables, ricks, muddy pools, old marl pits and, in the fields beyond, the huddled roofs of labourers' cottages. In the summer months the meadows and open pastures rang with the rattle of traps, the moans of livestock being driven from fold-yard to market and the shouts of labourers at harvest. But now, with autumn approaching, the pace of life slackened as the leaves began to yellow in Trench Wood and the cold nights drew steadily in.

Oddingley lay roughly in the centre of Worcestershire, a short distance north of the fertile market gardens of the Vale of Evesham. Just three miles away was Droitwich Spa, where the local market was held each Friday and villagers met to drink and socialise. Further to the south-west, Worcester perched splendidly on the banks of the River Severn, the city's cobbled streets laced with the smouldering chimneys of porcelain factories and the shop windows of its 'forty or fifty master glovers', who brought the city almost as much fame as the quality of its salmon and lamprey – a rusty-coloured eel and a particular local delicacy – that were fished from the moody waters of the river.

Worcestershire attracted businessmen and travellers from all parts of Britain. On his tour of the kingdom the poet Robert Southey remarked rosily that Worcester was 'a fine and flourishing city, in the midst of a delightful county'. His sentiments were echoed by Mr W. Pitt, a surveyor from Birmingham, who was commissioned by the Board of Agriculture in the early 1800s to complete a review of the area with 'observations on the means of improvement'. The land to the north of Worcester, Pitt observed, was 'most beautiful . . . one combination of noble hills, forming, as it were, the frame of a delightful picture . . . diversified with all the beauties of hill and dale, wood and water'.

Oddingley was buried deep in this rural landscape. It was a comely place of fairs, pear cider, religious festivals and the hunt, and it provided a home for some 112 inhabitants including a full cast of likely rural characters: dairymaids, carters, shepherds, stable boys, blacksmiths, farriers, threshers, reapers and drovers. Among these labourers literacy levels were low and traditions strongly kept. Glimmers of the village's cultural past were captured in the names of the farmers' fields: Calves Close, the Old Rickyard, Flax's Close and Nuthill Sling. At work they wore the familiar uniform of flowing smock frocks, beaten corduroy breeches, heavy pairs of leather working boots and handkerchiefs tied at the neck. In winter this costume was supplemented by the greatcoat, often patched and torn or hackneyed with age. The labourers scraped their livings where they could: drawn like moths about a light from one temporary contract to another, occasionally straying out of the parish for two or three weeks at a time on the promise of something better.

By the end of September the pace and industry of the summer months was replaced in Oddingley by a quieter period in the farming calendar. There was also cause for relief. Across the county crops had fared far better in 1805 than in the preceding year. The bad harvest of 1804 had inflated the price of wheat in the Worcester markets by 47 per cent to 89s. 9d. a quarter, kindling memories of famine and unrest. But throughout the summer of 1805 the weather had held, and by the middle of September temperatures were still unusually high – the *Morning Chronicle* in London attributing a plague of wasps in the city parks to the warmth of the season.

There was no such irritation 130 miles away in Worcester, where the county newspapers continued to fill their columns with news of council meetings, notices of farm sales, adverts for patent medicines and reports of the continuing conflict with France. Of all issues, the war remained the driving subject. For the past two years the *Worcester Herald* had speculated about the possibility of Napoleon mounting a successful crossing of the English Channel and had kept a careful diary charting the movements of the Worcester Volunteers – a jumbled assembly of men armed with little more than muskets, knives and pitchforks – who were to form a home guard in the event of a successful attack. Many believed the long-threatened invasion was still imminent and on 17 August the paper reported that three days' gunfire had been heard thundering along the French coast.

This news filtered out from Worcester to the surrounding coun-tryside, where it was absorbed in the farming communities. Of these, Oddingley was a typical parish, only differing from other villages in that it did not have a resident squire. The great local landowner, Lord Thomas Foley, resided at his lavish country seat eleven miles away at Witley Court, meaning there was a gap at the top of the parish hierarchy. Without the customary figurehead, Oddingley parish was instead led by an uneasy amalgam of its leading men, which included the seven village farmers – six of whom leased their properties from Foley – and the clergyman, Reverend George Parker.

As with most of his contemporaries, no physical description of Parker survives. The only clue to his appearance comes from a single woodcut, etched many years later. It depicts Parker in the seconds before his death, a young man wearing a broad hat which is perched loosely back on the crown of his head. The clergyman's face appears strong and determined but also at the same count sunken and starved

This dramatic but untrustworthy depiction of Reverend Parker's murder is
the only surviving image of Oddingley's clergyman

of expression. It is likely that the author did not know his subject, or
that the detail of the piece was bent to serve the drama and required
narrative of the moment. A more vivid image was left by Thomas
Alsop, a local farmhand, who recalled Parker strolling languidly along
the lanes, smoking his pipe and 'tossing up a penny piece'.

It was now more than 12 years since, on Friday 3 May 1793, he had
arrived in Worcestershire to accept Lord Foley's offer of the living
of Oddingley parish and to claim its accompanying salary of £135
per annum and assorted benefits. These included the three-storey
rectory on Church Lane, its accompanying gardens and the right to
keep animals and cultivate the glebe – upwards of ten acres of
meadow to the north of the village centre.

George Parker had been 30 years old when he first set foot in
Oddingley. He was able, principled and worldly, still a bachelor
and quite possibly an instant attraction for the eligible local ladies.
There must have been every hope that the appointment, which

constituted his second ecclesiastical post, would be successful and
enduring. Yet it was a hope that soon faded. By the autumn of
1805 Parker was deeply unpopular with many in the parish. There
had been sparks of violence and a succession of court cases with
John Barnett of Pound Farm. Thomas Clewes from Netherwood
had been heard damning his name in the Droitwich taverns, and
as details of the poisonous quarrel seeped out into nearby parishes,
it was said that opposition to Parker was led by Captain Evans of
Church Farm. It was clear to all across the parish that the feud
cut deep.

George Parker was not a native of Worcestershire. He was born to
Thomas and Jane Parker at a farm in Johnby in the Lake District,
hundreds of miles to the north of Oddingley. Thomas Parker is
recorded as being 'a respectable yeoman, of good connections' and
like many in the locality probably filled his fields with flocks of
Herdwick and Rough Fell sheep, which were traded at the market
in Penrith, seven miles away. George Parker was baptised at
Greystoke Church on 26 June 1762 in the grassy shadows of the
Lakeland Fells.

In the 1760s Thomas Parker and his young family were comfort-
ably set in life. Whereas almost all of his peers leased their slices of
the Cumberland hills from members of the old landed gentry, Parker
held a considerable estate in his own name, something that was a
clear source of independence and pride. A quirk of Parker's acreage
was that a portion lay detached from the rest, intermixed with fields
belonging to the Duke of Norfolk and controlled by his son, the
young Earl of Surrey, who lived just two miles from Johnby at
Greystoke Castle. At some point around the year 1770 Thomas Parker
had approached Surrey, proposing to reorganise these boundaries so
that they could manage their estates more effectively. It proved an
astute move. The result of the ensuing arrangement pleased Parker
and Surrey so much that a friendship was formed. To further express
his gratitude Surrey promised Thomas Parker that he would provide
an education for his son George.

It was an unexpected twist that carried George Parker's life on a new and exciting course. Supported by Surrey, he enrolled in the endowed grammar school at Blencow, just a mile and a half from his family home, where he studied history and the classics alongside the sons of gentlemen. Thereafter, George Parker's bond with Surrey strengthened. The earl was an eccentric politicking Whig famed in high society for his disregard for social and hygienic niceties and for the 'habitual slovenliness of his dress'. Among commoners, though, he was highly popular, a charismatic figure known for his 'conviviality' of spirit, his reformist tendencies and for being something of a provocateur. During the general election of 1774 he supported several local freemen who managed to dislodge the Carlisle parliamentary constituency from the powerful and fabulously wealthy Tory-leaning Lowther family. At the elections of 1780 and 1784 he was himself elected to Parliament, where he instantly joined Charles Fox in fierce opposition to the American war.

How precisely George Parker served the Howard family during these years is unclear, though one theory suggests he was engaged as Surrey's election agent. This fact was later questioned, but it still appears the most plausible explanation. By nature George Parker was ambitious, persuasive and hard-working, traits which displayed themselves in subsequent years and would have served him well while scrambling through the thickets of an eighteenth-century general election campaign. Agents were sent out into the boroughs, charged with cajoling, harrying and pestering the freemen for votes, reminding them of their allegiances and distributing financial incentives when necessary. A trusted knot of energetic lobbyists would have been indispensable for Surrey, who did not just have to trouble himself with his own election campaigns in Carlisle, but also had to orchestrate others intended to plant favoured Whigs in Westminster from constituencies scattered about the country in places like Arundel, Leominster and Hereford. That the young Parker was duly dispatched to such distant outposts of the Howards' vast estates would explain his taste for travel, something that may well have developed in these formative years.

Parker would have been an able candidate for the role. Having concluded his education at Blencow, it is difficult to envisage him returning to labour on the family farm. Rather, as young, erudite and at ease among the gentry, it seems more logical that he would be employed in a sphere where he might use his ability to write and reason. Crucially, too, Parker's loyalty was beyond question. Since his earliest childhood he had been allied to Surrey: he had grown up with Greystoke Castle hidden, symbolically, just beyond the horizon; his family were dependent on the Howards for their social standing and now he was indebted to Surrey for his education. The young protégé was absorbed into his patron's inner circle, and most accounts agree that it was a role in which he thrived. They declared that Parker carried out his duties with such cool reserve and careful professionalism that Surrey recalled his contribution for years after.

In the early 1780s George Parker's life took its most significant turn. Perhaps fired by his travels and his own latent ambitions, he resolved to leave Cumberland and to journey south to the Midlands to study theology. This he did, and for several years afterwards he resided at St John's Academy in Warwick, where he served as classical assistant. The move, however, did not mean a total splintering of his relationship with Surrey – who had now become the Duke of Norfolk following the death of his father in 1786. Indeed, the new duke lay behind Parker's elevation to a curacy in Dorking, one of the Howard family's parishes. Several years later Parker relocated yet again. It is unclear just what lured him to Oddingley. Perhaps it was the prospect of a sedate community and a reasonable income. Or he may have been tempted by its appealing location so close to Worcester Cathedral, a spiritual, intellectual and administrative centre of the Protestant Church.

As with Parker's other appointments, the duke's influence swirled like a current just beneath the surface. The opening at Oddingley came after Norfolk had appointed Reverend Samuel Commeline – Parker's predecessor – to another of his parishes, at Hempsted just outside Gloucester. Commeline's move left Oddingley temporarily vacant and enabled Norfolk to recommend Parker as a replacement to his parliamentary friend and fellow Whig, Lord Foley. It was a typical eighteenth-century transaction, and it concluded in May 1793, when Reverend Parker was presented to his new parishioners by Bishop Hurd of Worcester. George Parker's unlikely rise from yeoman's son to country parson was complete.*

Settling into Oddingley in the summer of 1793 Parker had his best years before him, but to his new parishioners he was unknown and untried and he must have been acutely aware that he was an outsider. In this corner of England the locals spoke with a slow, sloping accent. 'You' was 'thee' or 'yaw'. 'Nothing' was pronounced 'nought' and 'i' became 'oi'. Vowels were short and stunted, leaving 'sheep' as 'ship', and the 'h' was often lost altogether giving 'ighest' and 'ill'. Pitt the surveyor remarked that during his time in the district he experienced many other provincialisms: of these, he explained, 'an occasional visitor can pick up but a few; it requires long residence, and much colloquial intercourse with the middle and lower classes'. It was a new code to master, and one that Parker would never consider his own.

In the years before mass transportation, at least a generation before the railways, Parker's northern roots, his accent and mannerisms, distinguished him from the other villagers like sand from stone. In the 1790s much of the population of rural Britain was born, raised, lived and died within a handful of miles. Until 1795 wandering vagrants could still be sent back to their home parishes if they were suspected of burdening the poor rate, a law which lent some credence to Adam Smith's bleak observation that it was more difficult for them 'to pass through the artificial boundaries of a parish than the arm of the sea or a ridge of high mountains'. And while the poor were repelled, other newcomers were often tolerated uneasily.

Parker's life in Oddingley began quietly but with steady purpose.

---

* Although the £135 stipend was not an extravagant parochial salary, it was still substantial and compared well with other professions. Just a few years later, in 1801, the brilliant young chemist Humphrey Davy would resign his post at the Pneumatic Institute in Bristol to accept the role of director of the Chemical Laboratory at the Royal Institution in London for a far more modest salary of £100 per annum, plus 'coals and candles'.

His appointment signalled a change for the villagers, who had been
so neglected in recent years by their political and spiritual masters.
The records show that Reverend Commeline was an absentee

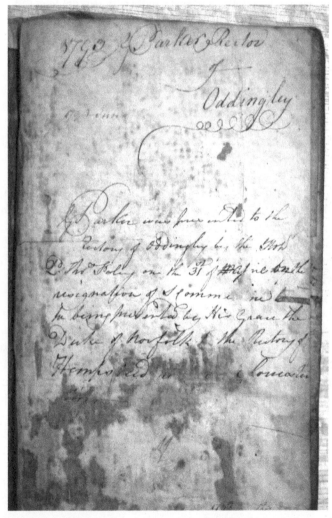

Parker's ornate handwriting across the front of Oddingley's parish records is
one of the few tangible traces of his personality

clergyman, paying clerical deputies to conduct services on his behalf with a portion of his salary. In the years 1780–92 the signatures of five curates fill the pages of the parish marriage register while Commeline's does not appear once. Only with Parker's appointment in 1793 does stability settle on the records.

The Oddingley marriage register comprises one of a tiny number of documents that record life in the parish in the last decade of the eighteenth century. It's a world for the most part lost to history, and observing it at a distance of more than two centuries is like peering into a darkened room lit only by dim chinks of light. Even so, traces of the new Reverend Parker can be found in these frail records. It is clear that he devoted his time and attention to his new parish, his application shown by the fact that he conducted all the important services himself. Parker's relish for the job is also suggested by an odd fragment in the marriage register. Hard against the top of the parchment at the front of the book a careful and florid hand has written, 'The Marriage Register of Oddingley, from 1756.' Underneath, with the ardour of an aspiring professional or of a freshly appointed manager keenly marking his new territory, comes in carefully crafted letters: 'G. Parker, Rector.'

Inside the calfskin cover of the other surviving parish register – a collection of notes tracking the church's business in the parish back into the middle of the seventeenth century – is a more definite sign of Parker. Here the quill begins with the same autograph: 'G. Parker, Rector.' The ink is thin and the P of Parker surrounded by dashing loops. Below is a sliver of autobiography, all composed in the third person with the characters slanting confidently to the left: 'G. Parker was first invited to the rectory of Oddingley by the Ld Tho Foley on the 31 April on the resignation of S Commeline, he being presented by his Grace the Duke of Norfolk to the rectory of Hempstead, Gloucester.'*

It's a curious and enlightening passage. It is the source which reveals the duke's role in his preferment, but it is also a throwaway

---

* Parker muddles the date of his arrival. All other sources agree that he was presented to Oddingley on 3 May, and in any case 31 April is an erroneous date.

scrap – perhaps penned in the idle hours of a lazy afternoon – that allows us to peer into Parker's mind. There is pride and satisfaction at his achievement, which he relives in prose, jotting it down like a little victory. But there's also something more. Why should Parker choose to record it in the parish register? Why should he, so new to the village, affix his signature and several celebratory lines to the head of a book which by then was more than a century old and intended for an utterly different purpose? None of Parker's predecessors had been driven to such a thing, and it reveals either a calculated assertion of his presence or an unintentional slip of vanity.

These traces of Parker stem from his first years in Oddingley, which were seemingly his happiest. He forged several friendships, one with Reverend Reginald Pyndar of the neighbouring parish of Hadzor, a justice of the peace, and another with Oddingley's ubiquitous clerk, John Pardoe. In the mid-1790s Parker met and married Mary, a lady from a humble background, and commenced a happy marriage, which produced a daughter in 1799, also called Mary.

The best account of Parker from this time comes in a memoir written by Benjamin Sanders, a button maker from Bromsgrove who met and befriended him while at Worcester planning his family's emigration to America. The friendship between Parker and Sanders was brief, lasting just six months, but it was one of significant emotional intensity. Sanders' recollections must date to the mid-1790s and they show Parker at his best.

At Worcester I became acquainted with a clergyman, in a singular kind of way; we met merely by chance. It is wonderful how, where congeniality of disposition exists, how soon and firmly friendship gets cemented. Such was the case with the gentleman, the Rev. Mr Parker and myself. He had two livings, one at Hoddingley [*sic*] and another at Dorking, he was a great favourite of the late Duke of Norfolk. We became most confidential friends. He would often hope my wife and I would alter our minds and remain in England, and that he would contribute half his fortune if we would do so, but our minds were fixed. We remained six months in Worcester. I went to Bristol and engaged our passage to New York (Alas! the time was now come for my father and me to part, never to see each other more in this world.) This was a severe trial, it seemed to penetrate to the innermost recesses of my heart; but my friend [Parker] was near me to give me consolation in my present affliction; he was a good and most sincere friend. He proposed to walk with us twelve miles, on the road, he informed me by the way that he should soon get married to a lady after his own disposition – a most amiable one I am certain.

Here we catch a glimpse of Parker and Sanders together at their parting, two figures suspended on the landscape, almost like characters from a Wordsworth poem. The clean south road stretches out before them. There's a cool Midland breeze, a roadside inn with its jutting sign, the fingerpost pointing the way to Bristol, the clatter of horses' hooves, the rattle of the mail or the Birmingham coach with its pack of weary horses pressing on along the turnpike. And among them all this little party of travellers on foot: Parker, perhaps in a cassock or with his Geneva gown billowing, holds a pipe in his right hand and is in deep conversation with Sanders, who is warmly and soberly dressed for the voyage in his greatcoat and heavy leather boots, perhaps gripping a bag of keepsakes or a purse of guineas for the ship's captain. There is a hint of excitement and an element of sadness as Parker confides his plans to marry. They know that they will never meet again.

It's an evocative account and about as close to Parker as one can get. Sanders depicts the young clergyman as a kind-hearted man, easy in the company of friends and capable of inspiring feelings of loyalty and trust. That Parker quickly fashioned a lasting emotional bond with Sanders – a man who was socially beneath him, as a member of the mercantile classes – pleading with him to stay in Worcestershire, comforting him for half a year prior to his departure and then accompanying him on the road for the opening stretch of a journey that would see him cross the Atlantic, evokes the image of a caring, altruistic personality.

Sanders' description tallies with other accounts of Parker. For the poor in Oddingley he was an attentive minister, ready to aid them with a glass of brandy, or to care, advise and comfort. He was compassionate enough to forfeit his tithe of milk to the old or the infirm, prompting a labourer, William Chance, to declare Parker 'was good to the poor, and as good a man that ever lived'. Another farm-hand, William Colley, echoed this sentiment, claiming, 'Parker was as good a master to him as ever he had, and that he had never heard any ill of him except from two or three of the large farmers.'

Such noble qualities manifested themselves in Parker's friendship with Sanders. Perhaps the clergyman felt a kinship with the button maker, who was about to embark on a voyage of hope just as he had done himself 15 years before. Perhaps his motivation for trying to stop Sanders flowed from regret at his own ambition, or even a mournful longing for the quiet farm and settled life that he had left behind.

But subtle evidence of Parker's vanity also escapes from Sanders' account. Parker tells him that he was a parson of 'two livings', one that Sanders incorrectly records as Hoddingley and a second at Dorking. That this was the case is possible. At the turn of the nineteenth century pluralism – the practice of drawing a salary from more than one ecclesiastical living at a time – was rife and a tolerated way for clergymen to top up their annual incomes. There is, however, no evidence that this is the case with Parker, and this detail supports the image of an aspiring man keen to document his successes and perhaps embellish the truth. This suspicion can only be strengthened by Sanders' mention of 'his fortune'. Clearly Parker and Sanders had discussed money during their brief friendship and evidently they shared some traits: they were both young, financially ambitious and willing to surrender the emotional ties of their homes and extended families in pursuit of a better exist-ence elsewhere. But although Parker had certainly fared well in life thus far, talk of a fortune in the 1790s was presumptuous, and the lasting image of the two together, walking south along the turnpike road towards Bristol, is one of a pair of able thinkers driven on by ambition and fixed upon their own self-improvement.

These were the qualities that would shortly drive Parker into a long and exhausting conflict with the Oddingley farmers. For them he had a problem of temperament: a maddening haughtiness that displayed itself at its very worst in his strict collection of the tithe, an 'eternally vexatious subject' which entitled Church of England clergymen to a tenth of the produce of the parish farms and formed the majority of their annual income. The tithe dispute deepened as the years passed, and by September 1805 of the seven ratepayers in Oddingley parish only two of them – Old Mr Hardcourt and John Perkins – could still sustain a conversation with Parker. By the rest he was seen as a rapacious swindler who stretched his powers to their furthest limit. The most militant farmers, Thomas Clewes of Netherwood, John Barnett of Pound Farm and Captain Evans of Church Farm, had come to consider each of Parker's new demands as a test of character they were compelled to resist and challenge at every turn.

The fallout from the quarrel was profound. Parishioners were caught between the factions: forced to choose between their spiritual leader and their employers, whom they were dependent on for subsistence. Previous years had been pockmarked by furious arguments, outbursts of violence and poisonous court cases. The situation had been exacerbated by the absence of a local squire who may have mediated between the parties, by Commeline's absence, which had enabled the farmers to cultivate their independence, and by the fact that Parker was an outsider. The two parties were further separated by politics, with Reverend Parker's ties to the Duke of Norfolk and Thomas Foley connecting him with the Whig cause in a countryside which remained overwhelmingly and staunchly Tory.

Politics mattered during the 1790s. The French Revolution had fed a reformist movement in England which cleaved the country in two, with loyal Church and King enthusiasts, known as scrats, rising in noisy patriotic opposition to revolutionary sympathisers branded either Painites (after Thomas Paine's *Rights of Man*) or Jacobins. This split dominated Parker's first years in Oddingley, and was only soothed when the French Republic veered away from its early ideals and Bonaparte appeared as a common enemy. Divisions and uncertainties endured, however, and since the failure of the Treaty of Amiens in 1803 the Worcestershire countryside had throbbed with news about the renewed French war. Fears of a brutal English revolution had long simmered, with Robert Southey grimly confessing, 'I believe that revolution inevitably must come, and in its most fearful shape.' By the end of September 1805 parishioners in Oddingley were feeling the same anxieties as those in other corners of the United Kingdom. They were determined and nervous, patriotic yet on edge.

Britain had been sustained throughout the war years by the career of Admiral Lord Nelson. His great victories at Cape St Vincent, the Battle of the Nile and the Battle of Copenhagen had become a source of national pride, a symbol of British courage, brazen skill and daring. Excited crowds had swarmed the streets during his brief visit to Worcester in 1802, where he had been granted the freedom of the city and had Copenhagen Street named in his honour. Three years later with Britain once again at war, the *Worcester Herald* had spent the summer months following his pursuit of the French fleet of Admiral Villeneuve across the Atlantic.

Nelson had returned in late August, but there still remained a prospect of the French and Spanish fleets breaking out from their blockaded ports and massing in the English Channel. On Sunday 15 September Nelson was dispatched on what was to be his final mission from Portsmouth in the *Victory*. The newspapers reported that the admiral had sailed before a light breeze and at sunset was off Christchurch, to the west of the needles. At nightfall fog had come down and he was gone.

All England followed developments, but locally there were other concerns. Many believed the country was being subverted by an organised network of French spies and conspirators. In Worcestershire a slew of robberies had been noticed and there were concerns over the rising number of animal thefts. Perhaps the worst indicator that the countryside was becoming more dangerous was the growing number of footpads and highwaymen who worked the county's rural lanes. Particular attention had been given to the fate of a butcher named John Hilcox, who had been apprehended on his way northwards from Bristol the previous year 'by a genteel-dressed man, mounted on a bay horse' who had troubled him for his money and then shot him through the head.

Then, on 28 September 1805, *Berrow's Worcester Journal* carried a piece concerning the discovery of a concealed subterranean den in the Trench Wood, a thick oak and ash wood which sprawled across the long parish boundary between Oddingley and neighbouring Crowle.

> The following extraordinary and interesting discovery was made . . . in Trench Wood, near Oddingley, in this county. As a boy was gathering nuts among some bushes, at that place, his foot suddenly slipped into a hole, and he lost his shoe . . . Not being able to recover it, he informed a person of circumstance, who came to the place, upon searching the hole he found that the sides were covered with soot; this, of course, induced him to search further, and, upon clearing away some moss, he discovered a door in the ground . . . large enough for a man to descend through, and, a few feet further, some clay steps, which led to an apartment being about six feet square; the covering was made of black poles running across, which were closely covered on the outside with moss and bushes: it had also a fireplace and one small seat: in it were found some meat, which appeared to have been lately dressed [and] some cheeses.

Trench Wood was a dwindling relic of the long destroyed Forest of Feckenham and for generations had endured a mean reputation in the area, with one local writer observing wistfully that it had 'inherited all the romantic terrors of the ancient chase'. Children were warned against straying too close to its edge, and many believed it was inhabited by criminals from the murky Georgian underworld: smugglers, poachers and burglars, mythically gaunt and sallow men who lurked in the shadows and waited for their chance. For years there had been suspicions that such criminals operated from a base hidden deep among the trees. Now, it seemed, there was proof.

The discovery was also reported in the *Worcester Herald*, and both publications noted that the hideout had been planned with such 'care and ingenuity' that its detection seemed at once both captivating and disturbing. For how many years had criminals – sheep stealers, petty thieves or worse – slipped unnoticed along the country lanes? Did the den belong to strangers who practised their mischief in the cities and towns or was it a meeting place for, perhaps, familiar faces living in parishes nearby? *Berrow's Journal* concluded it was most probably the work of a single, slinking individual, observing, 'the road which the occupier appeared to have used was not by any regular path, but through a small brook, so that everything was contrived in the most artful manner'. The *Worcester Herald* disagreed, declaring archly, 'There cannot be doubt that this den had been the receptacle for thieves of all descriptions.' They added, 'We trust we shall shortly have to publish their apprehension, and thus put an end to all further depredations which have been seen very frequently committed in this part of the country.'

Whether the work of one man or many, at the moment of discovery all the den's recent occupiers were gone, and little hope was placed on their return and apprehension. For the inhabitants of Oddingley, it must have been a disquieting matter. Both sheep stealing and robbery were capital offences, and those convicted often paid with their lives, a fact that added extra menace to the situation and made fugitives all the more dangerous. Yet the autumn of 1805 had brought signs of a fresh start for the parishioners of Oddingley. The harvest had been a successful one, Napoleon's invasion had still not materialised, and most surprisingly of all there had come a conciliatory offer from the farmers that promised to bring a conclusion to their feud with Parker.

The exact timing of the farmers' offer is not recorded, but it seems likely that it was in the autumn of 1805 when they approached him with a proposal to renegotiate payment of the tithe. The moment would come to represent a crucial turning point in the story, as it was an opportunity Parker would miss. This incident, coupled with the discovery of the den in Trench Wood, marked the definite beginning of a sequence of events that terminated in the terrible attack just nine months later. Reverend George Parker, a precocious child from the distant Cumberland hills, would become the figure at the centre of one of the great criminal cases of the early nineteenth century. The crime was very much of its time: encouraged to its conclusion by a fragile climate of war, of patriotism and revolution, and committed by a terrible concoction of personalities who had been thrown together by fate.

CHAPTER 2

The Gun

Oddingley, Worcestershire, 7 April 1806, Easter Monday

On Easter Monday 1806 Elizabeth Fowler, a 25-year-old dairymaid, was at work at Church Farm in Oddingley. The date was among the most important in the Christian calendar and across the kingdom parishes were celebrating the festival in their own style: playing annual sports or exchanging pasche eggs, hard-boiled eggs dyed in cochineal and inscribed with the end of a tallow candle. At Church Farm, though, Elizabeth Fowler's routine continued uninterrupted. A little after daybreak she stepped out of the farmhouse into the thin morning light and crossed the fold-yard to the cowshed, where the farm's little herd of dairy cattle were housed throughout the winter months. She fed the animals with hay and cake, then prepared to drive them on the mile-long journey to Tibberton.

Over the past few weeks the first signs of spring had settled on the village. The winter of 1805–6 had been cold: icy winds had drifted down through the middle of England from the north, bringing with them snow, hail and sleet. On 9 January a terrific storm had ripped right across the county, tearing up trees by their roots and blowing down chimneys. A few weeks later the River Severn had broken its banks at Worcester after a heavy snowfall upstream in Shropshire, causing a torrent that 'rushed with incredible strength and fury, bearing away everything before it which had not been previously secured'. It was not until the Easter weekend that the frequent showers and dreary clouds that had darkened the skies in February and March gave way to a brighter spell of weather. By the first week of April fields set aside for cultivation had been tilled and crops sown. Cowslips and dandelions skirted hedgerows, lending the lanes a shot of seasonal colour.

Church Farm was a large and handsome property. Its half-timbered farmhouse had perhaps served at some point as the local manor house and it dated back around 200 years. Still grand and imposing, it had nonetheless lost its gleam of perfection and at certain points holes in the outer walls had been filled with restorative patches of brickwork. The building stood three storeys high, was crowned with a fine thatched roof and occupied the most beautiful setting in the parish on the rim of a shallow valley a little distance down from the cool limestone walls of the church. Since 1798 Church Farm had been leased from Lord Foley by Captain Samuel Evans. The Captain – as he was generally known – was a towering figure in the parish. Now aged about 73, he was a clash of conflicting characteristics. To visitors he was polite, formal and welcoming: one remembered him as 'a remarkably fine old man, with hair as white as snow' with manners reminiscent of 'a gentleman of the old school'. But Evans also had a more restless, combative edge, something that seemed to stem from his army days. To his servants he could be short-tempered, keen-eyed and demanding, and at Church Farm he had instilled a work ethic that was unmatched elsewhere in the village. One labourer remembered him as a 'passionate old fellow' who was 'not particular before whom he used violent language'. Another recalled his narrow aquiline features, and the sight of him striding the lanes 'as upright as a lath'.

Most people who met the Captain were left with a strong impression of his personality. One of these was Mary Sherwood, a prolific and successful children's author. A frequent visitor to Oddingley, Sherwood would occasionally meet the Captain on her walks through the country lanes. Later she jotted down a pithy character sketch, describing him as a 'fine person with a superior military air, with the command when it suited his turn, of a manner much superior to that which is met with in general rural life'.

As Sherwood's portrait suggests, the Captain was somewhat

misplaced in the countryside. He had not been born or raised in Oddingley and had spent the majority of his working life in towns or on active duty with his regiment. Over the past decade, though, he had carved out a position for himself at the helm of local politics, merging into the community in a way Parker never had. He was a capable man, trusted for his judgement and engaged in public life as a magistrate in nearby Droitwich. Indeed, the Captain was far more interested in social than agricultural matters. He kept Church Farm more as a country residence to underpin his status as a minor member of the gentry than out of any deep interest or family tie to farming, preferring to declare his occupation as 'gentleman' in the local directories or on official forms. To allow himself to devote time to pleasure and his duties in Droitwich, the Captain delegated the majority of the farm's daily operations to a dependable 23-year-old named George Banks.

In both physique and character George Banks was a contrast to the Captain. Where Evans was old, meddling and acerbic, Banks was young, dutiful and industrious, his tall frame of five feet ten inches a familiar sight in Church Farm's fold-yard. The relationship between the men was close, and it attracted comment in the village. Despite Banks' youth, the Captain had ignored the claims of many more experienced parishioners and appointed him his deputy, with all of the powers of a farm bailiff. As such, Banks was entrusted with the direction of all day-to-day farming matters: setting tasks for the farmhands, organising the fold-yard, driving livestock between the fields and managing the sheds and stables. Meanwhile, the Captain held fort in the farmhouse, attending to his business in Droitwich several times a week and limiting his domestic interests to the collection of money and the payment of servants.

Though the most visible, George was just one member of the Banks family who lodged at Church Farm. His mother Mary, who was around 50, was an old friend of the Captain's and had brought her children to Oddingley from their previous home near Ludlow in Shropshire following the death of her husband. Three children remained at the farm in the spring of 1806. There was George's elder sister Catherine, in her mid-twenties, and the Captain's house-keeper, and a 19-year-old brother named Henry, who was often away at school in a nearby town. The Captain treated the Banks family as his own, and to many there was something strange in the arrangement of the household. Some villagers believed that Mary shared Evans' bed by night and the two lived as man and wife in secret. A sly twist to the rumour, probably borne out of the Captain's tenderness towards his bailiff, was that George Banks was his natural son.

Such whispered tales provided the dramatic background to daily life in insular communities like Oddingley, where any hint of a scandal was something to be seized upon and then discussed avidly around the chimney corners. Indeed, farmyard gossip was both a familiar and sustaining currency in the village, which until the beginning of the nineteenth century had been rarely troubled by outside affairs.

There was a story in Oddingley that the village's name derived from an ancient encounter between two giants. The first, Odd, and the second, Dingley, were said to have met on a heath in the north of the parish to determine who controlled the land. Folklore remembered how Dingley had prevailed and that Odd in defeat had cried out, 'O Dingley, Dingley, spare my breath. It shall be called Od-Dingley Heath.' It was an appealing myth and one that still held currency in the parish, which could more reasonably trace its roots back to around the time of the West Saxons' triumph at the Battle of Dyrham in 577, when the Britons were forced from the land about the lower Severn. The village, had it then existed, would have been lost amid the towering oaks of the vast Forest of Feckenham as the area around Gloucester fell under the influence of Ceawlin of Wessex. Apart from the names of some rivers and hills, the Saxons left few traces in the area, but to Oddingley they gave a name: Oddinga meaning the kin of the people of Odd (a common Saxon name) and Oddinga-lea the clearing or area of open land belonging to them.

Over the next millennium the forest was gradually gnawed at by successive generations and the manor of Oddingley was passed down from the Bishop of Worcester to the Crown before falling into private ownership shortly after the Reformation. By 1661 it was in the hands of the Foley family, who had added the parish to their extensive portfolio of land and henceforth appointed the clergyman and collected rents from the tenant farmers. By the time Captain Evans secured the deeds for Church Farm from Lord Thomas, the Foley family was entrenched as one of the most prominent in all Worcestershire, and the Forest of Feckenham was reduced to splintered fragments. Bow Wood, Thrul Wood, Oakley Wood and Goose Hill Wood were all relics, as was Trench Wood – also known by some as Foley's Wood – which lay across the south-eastern edge of Oddingley parish, crowning the brow of an escarpment.

Geographically the village could be broadly divided into three distinct areas. Most of the 22 listed buildings were ramshackle labourers' cottages hewn from wood and plaster huddled around the junction of Oddingley Lane, Church Lane and Green Lane, which met at a piece of level ground in the centre of the parish. These lanes were little more than heavily rutted bridleways or dirt tracks,

St James' Church and Church Farm today. The Birmingham and Worcester Canal that flows beside the buildings was constructed in the 1810s

pockmarked with the hooves of livestock and the wheels of carts and traps. They were seldom repaired and badly made, and liable to flood during the wettest of the winter months, leaving the villagers stranded in their homes for days at a time. Even in fine weather the farmers struggled to drag their produce along the three-mile trip to Droitwich, and riders knew that even a sure-footed horse might be brought down by a plunge into one of the many potholes if they travelled too fast.

Church Lane swung southwards from the crossroads, down a gentle slope and into the shallow basin where St James' Church and Church Farm stood side by side. These two buildings, heaped almost on top of each other, were a visual representation of the village quarrel: the church sitting on its little knoll being the spiritual centre of Reverend Parker's parish, and the old farmhouse below the home of his great antagonist Captain Evans. Both properties looked south out over the valley floor and the finest of Oddingley's fields towards the quietest corner of the parish, where Trench Wood loomed darkly over a scattered cluster of woodcutters' cottages and the tall red-brick farmhouse of Netherwood Farm, the lonely residence of Thomas Clewes.

At 36, Clewes was a 'bluff-looking labouring man' with dull eyes and a ruddy face. He had been born in the nearby parish of Hanbury, the eldest of a family of six, and had moved to Oddingley while still an infant. Clewes' father, William, had quickly established the family in the village and had served as churchwarden, a responsibility that marked him as respectable and perhaps smoothed the path for Thomas' marriage to Diana Nash, the daughter of an affluent local farming family, in 1798. Clewes' luck had held as he had secured the deeds to Park Farm shortly afterwards. In 1805 he had once again seized an opportunity, moving to the grander property at Netherwood, which had suddenly fallen vacant.

Netherwood Farm lay detached from the remainder of the village, just two lengthy fields and a short slope from the edge of Trench Wood. This was the lowest and dampest corner of the parish, an area said to abound with vipers – known in the local dialect as ethers

– from which, one local author suggested, Netherwood's name came. By 1806 Clewes was fully installed in the property with his wife Diana, who had already given birth to two boys and two girls, and who – at the time of the Easter Festival – was around four months pregnant with a fifth child. Thomas Clewes ran Netherwood Farm with the assistance of his younger brother John, who also lived at the farmhouse. The brothers headed a small workforce of casual labourers and live-in servants, who tended the dairy herd and watched the crops. Like many other households, the Clewes family was guarded at night by yard dogs.* One of their hounds, a villager later remembered, was 'a very cross one'.

Clewes was a successful man, but some of his habits caused his family worry. Villagers knew that he was fond of drink, sometimes brash in conversation and careless with the company he kept at the Red Lion in Droitwich. With his servants at Netherwood Clewes was strict and haughty, and 'one who regarded the cottagers of the parish in the light of serfs created for the benefit of the farmers', one writer later recalled. This disdain for the very class he had risen from marked Clewes as one of the most socially ambitious of all the farmers. And life at Netherwood was not only notoriously tough, but occasionally brutal. Eleven-year-old farmhand Thomas Arden later recalled how John Clewes had once strung him up by the heels in the stable on suspicion of stealing tobacco. '[I] was hung up half an hour or more,' he said.

Thomas Clewes' ascension to master of Netherwood raised him to the social level of, if not financial parity with, Captain Evans and John Barnett of Pound Farm, the village's largest property. Barnett was 32, 'a respectable looking yeoman with a head of slightly greying hair and calm blue eyes'. Hard-working, astute and reticent but with a fiery temper that could flare unexpectedly, John Barnett most closely resembled the classic image of the English agriculturalist. He was

---

* Terriers, bulldogs and spaniels were common breeds of hound in the locality, but for guarding property no breed was more efficient than the mastiff, 'the size of a wolf, very robust in its form and having the sides of the lips pendulous. Its aspect is sullen, its bark loud and terrific.' (*The London Encyclopedia*, Vol 7. 1824. p.389.)

the eldest surviving son of Thomas Barnett, who had died in 1785, and ran Pound Farm with his younger brother William on behalf of their mother, who for more than 20 years following the death of her husband had retained the lease for the property.

Four other agriculturalists controlled the remaining farms, which all lay scattered a short distance from the crossroads. John Perkins, an impetuous single-minded man in his twenties, had lived in the village for the past decade and had recently assumed control of Oddingley Lane Farm; Edward Hardcourt – Old Mr Hardcourt as he was known – kept a small farm of no more than a few fields off Church Lane; Samuel Jones, an unassuming character about whom little is known, also farmed in the parish, as did John Marshall of the colourfully named Pineapple Farm.

Of these seven men all but Hardcourt were tenant farmers who paid annual rent to Lord Foley in exchange for their houses and the right to farm the attached land on leases of eight years. The tenant farm system was well established as the staple form of land management in England at the time, enabling prudent landlords like Foley to appoint businesslike farmers to work the land on their behalf. Tenancies were rarely available and hard to win, with aspiring farmers needing to be diplomatic, forceful, well connected and hard-working to succeed. Life for the Oddingley agriculturalists would have wavered very little from this studious description 40 years before by Oliver Goldsmith in *The Vicar of Wakefield* (1766).

As they had all the conveniences of life within themselves they very seldom visited the towns or cities in search of superfluities. Remote from the polite, they still retained the primeval simplicity of manners; and frugal by habit, they scarcely knew that temperance was a virtue. They wrought with cheerfulness on days of labour, but observed festivals as intervals of idleness and pleasure. They kept up the Christmas carol; sent true love-knots on Valentine's Morning, ate pancakes on Shrovetide, showed their wit on the 1st of April, and religiously cracked nuts on Michaelmas Eve.

Elizabeth Fowler was the only female live-in servant at Church Farm, and after driving the cows to be milked she returned to the farmhouse at midday on Easter Monday. She briefly rested in the kitchen with Catherine Banks, the housekeeper, and Catherine's mother Mary. Snatching a meal – a slice of wheaten bread, perhaps, and a block of Cheshire cheese – there would have been a chance to discuss the latest news. A few hours earlier a traveller had been ambushed by a band of footpads on the turnpike between Worcester and Droitwich, just two miles from Oddingley. Footpads, unlike highwaymen, were poor, worked on foot and killed indiscriminately to eliminate witnesses. They were considered the lowest and vilest class of English criminal and a curse on rural travel. The unfortunate victim, a man named John Williams, had been robbed of 5s. 6d. in silver and a half-crown ticket (about a week's wage) but had escaped alive. The footpads had then vanished from the scene.

The ancient countryside of gentle hills and twisting lanes about Oddingley lent itself well to such dramas. Hedges of hawthorn, ash, elm, hazel, sallow and holly had for centuries been used as much for food as barriers to livestock and were garnished with stray fruit trees – wild cherry, pear and crabapple. The resulting hedgerows were not just woven, oblique shields for the farmland behind, but also cover for cut-throats, highwaymen, thieves and footpads. As Elizabeth Fowler was sent out that afternoon to scour the fold-yard, the sty, stacks and the sheds for eggs, the story must have played strongly in her imagination.

Elizabeth searched the hen houses and the fold-yard and at length came to a rick – a carefully built and protected structure used to store either straw or hay – which stood close to the farm gate. There, she later remembered, something caught her eye. The rick was old – from the previous summer – and to deter rats and other rodents and to keep the straw dry, it stood about three feet clear of the ground, elevated on a number of stone stilts known as staddles. Behind one of these staddles, hidden only partially under a little mound of scattered straw, was something that looked like one of the farm tools but wasn't.

Elizabeth crouched down. It was a long narrow bag, fastened at the top with binding. Picking it up, she found it heavy. Fashioned from stiff leather, it smelt slightly of salt. Carefully she placed the object back on the ground and undid the binding. Inside she discovered the long polished barrel of a shotgun.

When Elizabeth returned to the farmhouse, Catherine Banks told her that the Captain and George had both left for a church meeting and were not expected back until late. It was an anxious and puzzling situation. Guns were not rare in the countryside, but those that did exist were usually stowed safely away in glass cabinets or locked in bedroom cupboards. Why someone should leave such a valuable and dangerous weapon unguarded by the gate of a village farm was a mystery.

'Dare you bring it in?' the housekeeper asked Elizabeth. Fowler fetched the bag from beneath the rick and laid it between them on the servants' table.

Meanwhile Captain Evans and George Banks were passing below the oak porch of St James' Church on their way to the annual vestry meeting. Set for Easter Monday, vestry was the most significant parish meeting: annual accounts were approved by the executive,

Woodcut of St James' Church, Oddingley

and officials – the overseer, constable, vestry clerk and churchwardens – elected for the year ahead. Vestry was attended by all of the parish's leading men and, reflecting its importance, was not held at a local public house or a nearby farmhouse, but at the parish church under Parker's chairmanship.

St James' Church was the oldest building in the parish and badly in need of investment and repair. A local writer would later portray it as a dilapidated structure, ravaged by wind and rain and supported by the type of 'rude timberwork' that might be found 'in a granary or malthouse'. In the damp, badly lit nave, where Parker and the farmers convened, was a mildewed font and an old grinder organ. Above them all, traversing the ceiling, there was a length of wood carved alternately with images of cheerful cusps and inverted vipers – symbols of heaven and hell. The atmosphere of gloom and decay was an accurate metaphor for relations between Oddingley's leading men. For years meetings had been awkward and fractious, damaged by persistent undertones of personal dislike. The vestry of 1806 was no different and brought the sharpest confrontation yet as Parker and his parishioners battled for power in the year ahead.

The meeting began with the election of the parish officers, and, led by Captain Evans, the farmers asserted their weight of numbers by electing John Barnett as overseer and then his younger brother William as constable. These offices were unpaid but carried great prestige and power, with the overseer responsible for the parish finances and the constable invested with power to apprehend offenders, collect evidence on behalf of victims and ensure that the village's militia quota was filled. For Parker the election of the Barnett brothers was a blow. Both of them disliked him, and John had been openly hostile for some years. Perhaps nettled by these decisions and with little forbearance, Parker decided to strike back. He retaliated on a point of order, refusing to approve the annual accounts.

Parker took exception to a subsidised dinner which had been planned and attended by the farmers following the previous year's vestry meeting. His complaint was that the expenditure had not been approved and his inference was that several farmers were indulging themselves with parish money. It was a valid but somewhat unusual objection. As unpaid public servants it was customary for elected officials across the country to compensate themselves with an annual dinner in exchange for their time, skills and commitment. A tacit agreement usually ensured that a slight redistribution of the finances for this purpose was not checked, and the practice was so widespread that Francis Grose the lexicographer had complained some years earlier, 'Every parish officer thinks he has a right to make a round bill on the Parish during his year of power.' Parker's objection inflamed what was already a brittle and tense atmosphere. To the farmers it was a contrived and snide attack. A passionate argument ensued, with the Captain, John Barnett and Thomas Clewes rounding on him. Inevitability they raised the subject of the tithes, and thereafter the meeting descended into chaos. The farmers stalked out, abandoning an event intended to bring parishioners together. John Perkins was the only one who stayed to speak to Parker, perhaps the only farmer he could still count as a friend.

Resentment had characterised the relationship between Captain Evans, John Barnett and Thomas Clewes and their clergyman for years, and above all else the Oddingley tithe dispute was the issue that cleaved them apart. The tithe was a complex and unpopular tax. At the very simplest level a tenth of all parish produce 'or some other things in lieu' was payable by ratepayers to tithe owners – most commonly members of the clergy or landed gentry. The levy had endured without revision since deepest history, and its payment was a symbolic act designed to bind pastors and labourers together in the productive toil of a community in a partnership of earth and faith. In 1806 the tax still comprised the backbone of Parker's annual salary, and it was following his decision to re-fix its value in line with inflation at the turn of the century that clashes had begun.

Reverend Parker was an ambitious man, and though it was clear he intended to serve his parish well, throughout the 1790s it had become plain that he also expected to be paid correspondingly. It was perhaps a logical step for Parker, who had overachieved in his early years, to build on his new position, but whatever designs he had of making his fortune at Oddingley were seriously challenged by the financial climate. Inflation was rampant in the last decade of the eighteenth century, with the price of wheat (and therefore bread) darting up with disarming speed, from 58 shillings a quarter in 1790 to 128 shillings in 1800. Rising prices led to unrest, with bread riots beginning in Wales in the 1780s spilling over the border to Hereford and Worcester in the 1790s, where the city's corporation was forced to help support the poor. A melancholy note received by the editor of *Berrow's Worcester Journal* on 20 April 1801 was evocative of the struggle many families had to make ends meet. It declared people were living in 'an age of extortion' and it lamented, 'The poor, in general, exclaim loudly against the dearness of provisions.'

But it wasn't just the poor who were affected by the increasing prices; the middling classes to which George Parker belonged would have seen their cost of living rise sharply too. With the addition of a wife and a daughter to his household, extra strain would have been placed on Parker's finances, and at some point around the turn of the century he decided to redress the balance by amending the £135 tithe payment that he was owed each year by the village farmers. It was the simplest way of raising his income, but it sparked the quarrel that would define Oddingley's identity for years to come.

Before Parker's arrival the parish had opted to 'compound' the tithe: the £135 fixed sum was paid annually in a single payment on Lady Day, 25 March, thereby sidestepping all the problems of gathering each tithe individually. This was a sensible arrangement as tithe law was so horrifically complex, so riddled with subtleties and ambiguities that it often caused more confusion than it delivered answers. Not only were tithe holders – mostly members of the clergy or landed gentry – entitled to 'great tithes' such as corn, grain and wood, but they were also due many 'small tithes' ranging from fruit, garden herbs, root and other vegetables to honey, flax and a hundred other minor items including activities such as labour – a notoriously awkward asset to quantify.

All of this was overruled by local customs that ensured that the tithes were never calculated in the same way in any two places. Each parish kept a document called a glebe terrier which listed in great detail the tithe holder's right to each different item. These rights had been established over time, in a process of constant negotiation and renegotiation between the tithe holder and the ratepayers. In many instances bargains had been struck between the two parties whereby farmers had achieved exemption from a certain obligation by paying a customary annual or one-off fee, known as a modus. Once recorded in the terrier a modus was very difficult to alter and tithe owners were often shackled to unfavourable agreements settled by their predecessors. In one instance, in Abbots Bromley in Staffordshire, the clergyman had to content himself with just £2 12s. 4d. for an area of 1,390 acres of prime titheable land, from which he should have expected many hundreds of pounds.

A surviving 'true and perfect terrier' for Oddingley from 1714, copied in a measured hand onto a single sheet of parchment, numbers in a pithy list the benefits of the parish. The dwelling house or rectory was accompanied by several barns and buildings, including a house for pigs. The incumbent also had rights to the two orchards that surrounded the property and a portion of meadowland lying across the common in the north. Three distinct moduses applied in the parish. An exception had been negotiated for all the timber and wood taken from Trench Wood, and there had been an agreement relating to 'corn, hay and all other things growing', and likewise for the 'tithes of wool, lamb and piggs [sic]'.

This is very much the same agreement that Parker inherited 75 years later from Reverend Samuel Commeline. In compensation for the above exceptions, the financial equivalent had been set at £135, divided proportionally between the ratepaying properties. But within five years of his arrival Parker had decided the arrangement was unfair and had called a meeting with the ratepayers, informing them he intended to raise the overall value of the tax to a single payment of £150 to reflect rising prices. The farmers, led by Captain Evans, refused Parker's proposal outright.

How justified was Parker in demanding the rise? Certainly £135 in 1800 did not have the purchasing power that it would have done 50 years before, and in every area the cost of living was increasing in a seemingly endless upward spiral. If the price of wheat could more than double between 1790 and 1800, then what might it do in another ten years? Another unnerving reflection of the bewildering rise in prices was noted by Pitt the surveyor, who estimated that the cost of labour had leapt by 20 per cent in the 11 years between 1794 and 1805. The farmers of course were suffering too, having to pay their workforce higher wages, but in other ways they remained somewhat sheltered, as they had the ability to feed themselves and in some cases even make tidy profits from the rising market.

Parker, though, clearly felt the changes keenly. By the start of the nineteenth century it was rare to find livings that supported the comfortable and occasionally extravagant lifestyles country parsons had famously enjoyed. The past 50 years had seen the status of the clergy slip, and in comparison with the rocketing fortunes of the industrialists they now seemed little better than a plebeian class. It was said that for each clergyman who achieved the status of a gentleman, ten others were left as menial servants, condemned to a life of toil in their glebe fields, feeding swine and loading dung carts. Many were forced to supplement their incomes. Some became agriculturalists: keeping livestock, growing crops and raising coppices for timber. In 1806 William Wilberforce informed the House of Commons that he was aware of a curate who augmented his parish income with a job as a weaver.

Parker's temerity, however, was dangerous. There were already many disputes across the country between clergymen and farmers over tithes, with the agriculturalists claiming that the levy discriminated against them disproportionally, while failing to tax the emerging classes in the industrial towns. It seemed unfair that a wealthy London banker should escape the attentions of the taxman while the fields of England remained subject to the full ravages of the law. Parker's annual salary, too, was already much higher than what they could expect to earn from their properties, with an average yeoman farmer's income hovering at around just £100. According to the diary of Richard Miles, a nearby farmer, in 1807 a wagoner could be employed for £12 12s. a year, a manservant for £10 10s., and a dairymaid for £5 or £6. So Parker's proposed rise would have only cost the wages of three dairy-maids shared between all of the seven ratepayers. But without the farmers' agreement, Parker's plans were ruined. He returned angrily to his rectory, only to emerge shortly afterwards displaying what would become characteristic tenacity: he announced his intention to collect the tithe in kind – an unheard-of action in Worcestershire.

Tithing in kind meant visiting each of Oddingley's ratepaying properties assessing the different yields and taking what was owed on the spot. As the acceptance of monetary compound was entirely at the discretion of the tithe owner, tithing in kind remained a fall-back for clergymen willing to undergo the inconvenience of collecting individual yields themselves. The practice, however, was rare and only remained in the north-western counties, where Parker would most probably have seen it as a boy, and in Kent. In Worcestershire tithing in kind had dwindled then disappeared over the centuries, and Parker's decision to reintroduce it was like dragging the village back into the feudal age.

It was a decision mired in difficulties. Parker was forced to hire men to visit farms and collect produce on his behalf. He was compelled to buy barrows and handcarts, and to build a barn to store all the collected items. As Oddingley was such a large and sprawling parish, it became a lengthy and troublesome task with Parker or one of his employees forced to haul carts and drive animals along the twisting lanes. Worst of all he was cast into the demeaning role of taxman and market trader, his decision thrusting him into the very day-to-day situations that the tax was designed to protect him from. A humorous ballad penned in the eighteenth century underlined colourfully the problems associated with tithing in kind. It recounts the story of a parson's attempt to claim his tithe pig – a plan foiled by a characteristically uncooperative farmer.

> Good morning says the parson,
> Oh, good morning sir, to you
> I'm come to claim a sucking pig

You know it is my due
Therefore, I pray, go fetch me one
That is both plump and fine
Since I have asked a friend or two
Along with me to dine

Then in the stye the farmer goes,
Amongst the pigs so small
And chooses for the parson,
The least amongst them all;
But when the parson saw the same
How he did stamp and roar
He stampt his foot and shook his wig
And almost curst and swore

The ballad foreshadowed events at Oddingley, where clashes between Parker and his ratepayers commenced shortly afterwards. The first had occurred four or five years before the vestry meeting, when Parker and Thomas Lloyd, his first tithe man, called at Pound Farm and met John Barnett, who quickly ordered them to leave. Parker refused, declaring that he was there by right. At this, Barnett's temper cracked and he squared up to the clergyman. 'Damn your blood!' he shouted. 'Take that!' And he kicked him sharply on the thigh.

Parker reported the incident and had Barnett successfully prosecuted for assault. It was a warning to the farmers, who knew that if they refused him the tithes he was within his rights to have them hauled before the common law courts. If they were found guilty of failing to pay church rates they could be punished by a fine or, in extreme instances, prison. Parker had a second weapon too. He could report them to the ecclesiastical courts, where wayward parishioners could be admonished openly, suspended from church altogether or forced to do penance. A typical punishment ordered delinquents to stand outside the church porch on a Sunday morning before divine service, dressed in a long frock with bare legs and feet.

Fear of such punishments – financial, spiritual or social – was enough to force most of the farmers to pay without complaint. But the spark of violence at Pound Farm in 1801 was a harbinger of what was to come as litigation between the clergyman and Evans, Barnett and Clewes became, for a time, a feature of village life. Records from Parker's solicitor in Worcester show that the ensuing legal costs alone, which had to be met by the farmers, reached around £100.

In 1803 there was another incident. William Colley, a local farmhand, was working at Pound Farm, just 20 yards from Parker's rectory. Barnett had told him to crop the tops of his apple trees, and shortly after he had finished, Parker appeared to claim his tenth of the clippings. In the farmhouse Colley found John Barnett peering through a window. He muttered he 'would give any man five Guineas who would shoot the parson'.

The sentiment was repeated elsewhere. Shortly afterwards, William Colley heard Captain Evans exclaim that 'there was no more harm in shooting the parson than in shooting a dog'. And when Parker's name was mentioned at Netherwood, Thomas Clewes declared 'it was no harm to shoot such a fellow as that' within earshot of one of his ploughmen, William Chance. The measure of similarity between these expressions hints that the farmers had begun to share their dissatisfaction openly. Their collective wish that he be shot suggests that by 1803 there was already an unsettling degree of collaboration between the men.

The difficulties surrounding Parker's decision to collect the tithe in kind were aggravated by the divisive politics of the age. Parker would have been 27 years old in July 1789 when the French had risen up against Louis XVI and his finance minister Calonne, who had proposed further crippling taxes on salt, land, tobacco and grain. The revolution that followed was initially received with enthusiasm by many Britons, who celebrated the sight of ordinary French citizens casting off the irons of a despotic regime. But as France sank deeper into violence, the majority of British support ebbed away with the mounting horrors of the September Massacre of 1792, the executions of Louis XVI and Marie Antoinette and the Reign of Terror thereafter. By the mid-1790s the British revolutionary cause had gone beneath ground, into murky clubs and secret societies which treasured their radical ideals and were bent on political reform. Pitt's government reacted to the threat by deploying spies, suspending habeas corpus and feeding reports of Jacobin plots to pro-government newspapers.

Meanwhile Pitt's war taxes placed a heavy load on the back of the average Briton, and when the harvest failed, as it did several times in the 1790s, food riots followed. One typical example came in June 1795, in Bristol, when malnourished working families gathered in the city centre, smashed butchers' windows with a hail of stones, carried away all the meat and provoked a confrontation with the militia. Just four months later, after the failure of the harvest, crowds took to the streets of Westminster, haranguing politicians. Outside Downing Street they chanted, 'No war, no Pitt, cheap bread'.

Across the country a whole generation knew nothing but uncertainty and fear for more than a decade. For the young, war and revolution were a familiar backdrop, and few could remember as far back as the brief peaceful interlude of the 1780s, a time when Thomas Clewes and John Barnett were just young men and George Banks no more than a child. For these farmers, their present lives were so tainted by uncertainty that they glamorised the past as a time when everything was ordered and right. Now there were wars, revolutions and tithe disputes, curses that combined and manifested themselves in an increased hatred of the outsider. Just as they learnt to hate the French and the vain ambition of Napoleon Bonaparte, they came in time to despise Parker. To the farmers he was dishonest, draconian, treacherous and snide, with something secretive or mercurial within him. They took to calling him by a new nickname, the Bonaparte of Oddingley.

This was a clever invention that in all likelihood was coined by Captain Evans, who would have understood the power of rhetoric and fearful imagery from his army days. Casting Parker as Bonaparte was a clear signal to the parishioners. It challenged them to choose a side, to act as honest patriots loyal to their parish and country. At the same time it shackled Parker's reputation to that of the most reviled man in the land. Everyone knew about Napoleon. The press and especially the ruthless London caricaturist James Gillray played on ingrained xenophobia, depicting him variously as a posturing dwarf, a spoilt child, a seducer of his sisters, a falcon-eyed predator or an unhinged madman. One chilling nursery rhyme reflected the anxieties of the typical British family.

> Baby, baby, naughty baby,
> Hush, you squalling thing, I say;
> Hush your squalling, or it may be,
> Bonaparte may pass this way,
>
> Baby, baby, he's a giant,
> Tall and black as Rouen steeple;
> And he dines and sups, rely on't,
> Every day on naughty people.
>
> Baby, baby, he will hear you
> As he passes by the house,
> And he limb from limb will tear you,
> Just as pussy tears a mouse.

At the beginning of the nineteenth century there was nobody to compare with Napoleon. Eager students in British towns were marked as young Bonapartes, devouring books, writing bad poems and dreaming of dramatic social success as the young Napoleon had done a decade before. In *The Age of Revolution 1789–1848* the historian E. J. Hobsbawm argues that Napoleon's name became a byword for personal ambition, inspiring those whose fantasy was to replicate the magnificent rise of *Le Petit Caporal*, as a 'Napoleon of finance' or a 'Napoleon of industry'.

All common men were thrilled by the sight, then unique, of a common man who became greater than those born to wear crowns. Napoleon gave ambition a personal name at the moment when the double revolution had opened the world to men of ambition. Yet he was more. He was the civilised man of the eighteenth century, rationalist, inquisitive, enlightened . . . He was the man of the Revolution, and the man who brought stability. In a word, he was the figure every man who broke with tradition could identify himself with in his dreams.

In the English imagination Napoleon was a lowly creature: effeminate, ostentatious and untrustworthy – the antithesis of John Bull, the gritty, no-nonsense farmer. And as Bonaparte had brought misery to Britain, Parker had brought discord to Oddingley on his arrival in 1793 – the very year war had begun. As the rift between the clergyman and his parishioners deepened, reports began to circle that the farmers met at night in secret locations to curse him and plot their revenge. Drunken oaths were sworn; Parker's blood was damned.

Their characterisation of Parker, however, was flawed. He had not set out to destroy the existing order in Oddingley, rather re-establish it. He was not a member of the new enlightened classes – an industrialist, a philosopher, a soldier or an explorer – he was a country parson, the very paragon of English tradition and respectability. Of all the parishioners, Captain Evans was the closest to this vision of Napoleon. He was the self-made military man who had risen against the odds to a position of rank, wealth and power.

The nickname may have been unjust, but it stuck. Parker became the outsider – mischievous, antagonistic and ambitious – while, the farmers, led by Evans, were the opposite: free, independent and right. But while the nickname was a powerful social device it did little to help the farmers in the eyes of the law. The most they could do was to make it as difficult as possible for Parker to collect his taxes.

Captain Evans had his cows milked in the adjoining parish of Tibberton in order to avoid the tithe; others hid their goods in hay ricks, barn corners, outhouses and workshops. Villagers were caught in the crossfire, their loyalty split between Parker, their spiritual leader and kindly neighbour, and the farmers who they relied upon to stay above the breadline. Most calculated that it was better not to anger their employers, and the congregations thinned for Sunday service at St James'. One of Thomas Clewes' workers recalled, 'None of the family or servants ever frequented Oddingley Church; my master told us he would not order us not to go, that we might go if we like, but he had rather we should stop away.'

It seemed that there was no remedy for the quarrel. By 1805 Parker was employing more and more tithe men, so that he did not have to speak to the farmers himself. One of these recalled how 'Barnett, Banks and Captain Evans always abused Mr Parker whenever they met him' and speculated that Thomas Clewes had devised an ingenious strategy to spoil his tithe milk by adding a secret substance to it, causing it to sour as soon as it came from the cow.

That Clewes resorted to skulduggery was possible, but others had less time for such measures and a further incident between Parker and Barnett was more characteristic. Parker had gone to Pound Farm in midsummer 1803 to collect his tithe lamb and met Barnett brooding silently in the fold-yard. Barnett asked Parker which of the animals he would like, and the clergyman responded that Barnett could pick two or three of the lambs out, and from them he would select one. Barnett, exasperated with Parker and livid he was wasting his time, grabbed one of the young animals and thrust it into the parson's arms, shouting, 'Take that or you shall not have any one!' Barnett damned Parker, who fled the fold-yard hurriedly without his lamb. A few weeks later Barnett was prosecuted yet again. The courts were becoming an important check point in a vicious cycle: reaction to Parker, followed by litigation, followed by more reaction – all at an ever-quickening pace.

For the farmers it was an exhausting and futile struggle: they had to submit and Parker was going to make them. Also, after several years it had become clear that they were surrendering far more than £135 a year to Parker by paying in kind. In the autumn of 1805 they backed down and informed Parker that they were willing to pay him £150 a year to compound the tithe and bring an end to the dispute.

The offer satisfied his initial demand, but instead of accepting the proposal outright Parker imposed a precondition to the agreement. Collecting the tithe in kind had been expensive. He had been required to hire staff, to build a tithe barn and fill his tool shed with all the implements of a country farmer. Parker told the farmers that he would only agree to their offer if they paid him £150 in compensation for the inconvenience they had caused.

The farmers were outraged. They had conceded defeat only to be dismissed and embarrassed once again. They flatly refused Parker's proposal. Only Old Mr Hardcourt and John Perkins remained on speaking terms with the clergyman after this, a fact which annoyed their peers and further split the village. In January 1806 Captain Evans' frustration at the situation had flared at Perkins. 'Mr Parker is a very bad man,' the Captain told him. 'Nobody in the parish agrees with him.' When Perkins disagreed, the Captain flew into a rage. 'Damn him!' he swore. 'There is no more harm in shooting him than a mad dog!'

This was more than a throwaway curse; it was the unchecked sentiments of an angry and frustrated man. The Captain's words were redolent with imagery: Parker was a rabid dog – fierce, deranged and unpredictable. Just as a mad hound might fly at an innocent bystander, infecting them with its bite, Parker was doing the same – poisoning Oddingley with his greed, his ambition and ideas.

CHAPTER 3

The Easter Meeting

Tibberton, Worcestershire, 7 April 1806, Easter Monday

God Speed the Plough was a public house a few paces off the main road at the northern end of the village of Tibberton. It was a small two-storey brick building fitted with neat twin dormer windows nestled into the front of its steep sloping roof. The inn was one of two which served the growing population of Tibberton, a parish a mile to the south-west of Oddingley. Tibberton had a quite different appearance to that of its neighbour. It wasn't lost amid sprawling hedgerows or fruit orchards, but properly and deliberately arranged about the road which ran through it like an artery, drawing traffic from all the nearby villages as it wended south towards Worcester. A single row of thatched labourers' cottages lined this route, which on market days teemed with horse-drawn traps, wagons and handcarts, as farmers hauled their goods to market and the drovers urged their stock languidly on.

On the evening of Easter Monday the Oddingley farmers convened at the Plough to celebrate the annual parish dinner. Their own village was too small to support a public house of its own, and Tibberton – with its larger population and busier road – offered the farmers the closest inn of any size. It was now several hours since the argument with Reverend Parker at the vestry, and the farmers' numbers had swollen, with brothers, local tradesmen and friends joining Captain Evans, the Barnett brothers and Thomas Clewes in the parlour. Among the new arrivals was John Clewes, Thomas' brother, and George and Henry Banks, who were there at the invitation of

Evans. The Captain took the seat at the head of the table – a position which should have been reserved for Parker.

An evening of hard drinking followed. Inns such as the Plough sold ale from wooden casks, wine by the bottle or hogsheads of perry, a pear cider that Robert Southey would encounter two years later on his tour through Worcestershire. 'Perry is the liquor of this country,' Southey wrote under the extravagant pseudonym Don Manuel Alvarez Espriella. 'The common sort when drawn from the cask is inferior to the apple juice, but generous perry is truly an excellent beverage. It sparkles in the glass like Champaign, and the people assure me that it had not unfrequently [sic] been sold as such in London.'

Alcohol played an important role in village life. Gallons of weak ale or perry were used to sustain the farmers and labourers in summer, during the exhausting harvest shifts, and drinks were exchanged after hours on market days in the alehouses or in farmhouse parlours late at night, when bottles of claret or brandy were fetched up to toast the latest military victory, profitable sale or stroke of luck. All of the Oddingley farmers drank, Thomas Clewes and John Barnett particularly so, and the men were regulars at a long list of local establishments, of which the Red Lion on the Droitwich road was perhaps the most popular. Like many of these, the Plough at Tibberton was divided into a taproom – a stark space fitted with low stools and floored with beaten sand, where the heaviest of the drinking was done from pewter mugs – and the parlour, which catered for a higher class of clientele, who enjoyed such luxuries as carpeted floors, stuffed leather benches and mahogany tables.

In the parlour of the Plough that evening the farmers, almost all of them united against Parker, had a rare chance to share their grievances in an atmosphere that was close and confessional. As there were no women present, there was no one before whom the men had to moderate their drinking, their language or their behaviour. By the time the meal had drawn to a close and the cloth pulled from the table in readiness for the round of toasts, the mood among the farmers was boorish and excitable.

Toasts were an old English tradition, a vital component of any red-blooded dinner party and often loud, enthusiastic and vulgar. It was customary for each diner to stand and toast a gentleman's name, beginning at the top of society with a member of the royal family and weaving downwards, through a list of landlords and popular local characters, before challenging another member of the table to do the same. Fifteen years before, 18 toasts had been raised at a reformist dinner in Birmingham to celebrate the second anniversary of the storming of the Bastille. The dinner, attended by prominent dissenters and reformists, inadvertently sparked a wave of destructive anti-Jacobin riots in Birmingham; the toasts – to the 'King and Constitution', the 'National Assembly of the Patriots of France' and to the 'Rights of Man' – were perceived as a direct call to arms. The same uneasy passions were present a decade and a half later in Tibberton. In early 1806 patriotic feeling was running high. Nelson's brilliant but tragic victory at Trafalgar was a fresh and stirring memory, as was the defeat at Austerlitz and the death of William Pitt a month later. The *Gentleman's Magazine* remembered the age as 'a time when every newspaper poet, according to his style, exhorted patriots to resist "proud Gallia", [and urged] John Bull to come on and show his fists'.

As head of the table, it fell to Captain Evans to toast first. It was a practice with which he would have been familiar and he took to his feet charging his glass to the King. Other toasts followed to 'some noblemen' and all were returned loudly. At length Evans stood once again and turned towards John Perkins.

For most of the farmers Perkins' friendship with Reverend Parker amounted to a shameful breach of loyalty, and as a result relations between the farmers had soured. The young farmer had only opted to join the dinner a few hours earlier at the insistence of Parker himself, who, anticipating intemperate words or scenes, had urged him to attend to defend his name. Now Captain Evans seized his opportunity to mock them both, inviting him to drink the health of a *friend*. Perkins refused the invitation, sidestepping the obvious challenge to mention Parker's name.

The Captain returned Perkins' stoicism with mockery. He declared

James Gillray's depiction of the infamous Bastille toasts that inadvertently
sparked three days' rioting. Charles Fox toasts with his left hand

Perkins was neglecting his duty to the table and lifted his glass yet
again – this time in his left hand – calling out, 'To the health of the
Reverend George Parker!'

'All drank it but poor Hardcourt and me,' remembered Perkins.

Not only was the Captain's toast designed to humiliate, it was an
ironic and highly symbolic act. For centuries witchcraft and devilry
had been associated with the left hand. It was commonly thought
that Satan used the left hand to baptise his followers, that he whispered his commands into the left ear and lingered behind the left
shoulder of his followers. The left-handed were maligned accordingly,
with shamed mothers demanding that affected children overcome
the disability or at least shield it from public view. The poet Walter
Savage Landor in his *Imaginary Conversations* wrote, 'Thou hast some
left-handed business in the neighbourhood, no doubt,' a euphemism
that was repeated elsewhere for other dishonest or devious deeds:
left-handed favours, left-handed marriages or left-handed alliances.
As such, Captain Evans' toast was laden with imagery. He was openly
suggesting Parker was an aberration: left-handed toasts were reserved
for enemies, the untrustworthy or sinister.

Following the Captain's toast, Perkins was subjected to jeers from around the table. Sensing that Perkins' temper was growing increasingly brittle, George and Henry Banks – the two youngest members of the party – goaded him further still, accusing him of being a Jacobin.

For Perkins this was an intolerable slur. 'Jacobin' was applied to those who supported the French Revolution, political radicals who advocated total democracy, the overthrow of the monarchy and aristocracy and reform of the state and taxation. The Jacobin movement had reached its zenith in England during the 1790s and a new generation of King and Country patriots – to which both George and Henry Banks belonged – had risen up in opposition. For many the merest mention of Jacobinism was enough to stir up images of the bloodiest scenes of the French Revolution: the Reign of Terror, which left thousands dead, the icy eloquence and sanguinary ferocity of Saint-Just, the crazed ruthlessness of Joseph Fouché, of Danton and Robespierre. Historian E. P. Thompson wrote that Jacobins were entrenched 'in every town and in many villages throughout England' for many years, 'with a kist [chest] or shelf full of Radical books, biding their time, putting in a word at the tavern, the chapel, the smithy, the shoemaker's shop, waiting for the movement to revive'.

It is unlikely there was any truth behind the Banks brothers' claim. Perkins was never accused of being a Jacobin again and it is probable their insult was simply designed to sting and humiliate. Their inference was that Perkins had deserted the cause of his peers in the tithe dispute, a parallel act of treachery. But the taunt was not without irony: as a steadfast supporter of Parker and his right to collect the tithe in kind, 'Jacobin' was perhaps the least appropriate insult to hurl at the farmer.

In a flush of temper John Perkins rounded on Captain Evans. He swore loudly, reminding him that as a magistrate he should not be breaking the peace. The young farmer then turned on the Banks brothers. He declared that he was no Jacobin, and that for the slur he was ready to fight the best man among them.

Evans responded angrily to the outburst. 'Damn you!' he swore

from the head of the table. 'You ought to be turned out of the room
for not drinking the toast.'

The Captain and the Banks brothers returned to Church Farm around
midnight, and when Catherine Banks told Evans about the discovery
of the shotgun earlier that day he did not appear surprised. The
following morning he summoned Elizabeth Fowler and the Banks
family into the parlour and ordered George Banks to examine the
weapon. It was an old-fashioned firearm, a flintlock shotgun that
could be broken down into three parts, and most commonly would
have been used in the fields or woods for shooting fowl, foxes or
rabbits. Its barrel was empty. Whoever had hidden it had not done
so in haste. The Captain told them they should treat the matter as
a secret. 'It should stay in the house until enquired for,' he said. 'I
dare say the person that left it will call for it.'

For a week afterwards the gun remained at Church Farm, and as
the days passed, anxieties subsided. No further news of the footpads
was heard, and just as the incident was about to be dismissed as little
more than an unsettling curiosity, a local farmhand appeared to claim
the shotgun. Richard Heming was a jobbing carpenter, wheelwright,
occasional employee of Captain Evans and a sporadic visitor to
Oddingley. Across the village he was well known, and he had a talent
for slipping almost imperceptibly in and out of daily life. Heming
was a short man who walked with an awkward sloping gait, back
on his heels. He usually wore an old blue coat and brown corduroy
trousers. His face was round, his hair dark and bushy. About his neck
he knotted a scarlet handkerchief.

Heming told Evans that the shotgun was his. He had been travelling past Church Farm along the lane towards Crowle, a hilltop
village a mile south of Oddingley, when a rainstorm had struck.
Fearing the gun would be ruined, Heming decided to leave it 'out
of the wet and in the dry'. He had swept some straw over the weapon
and left.

Evans accepted Heming's account without question, although a
gun was a curious instrument for a carpenter to be carrying and

Heming did not disclose his reason for having it. Nor did he state why he had been happy for it to remain unsecured, out of doors, for as long as a week.

The Captain handed the shotgun to the labourer, who, almost as quickly as he had appeared, sloped away up Church Lane and out of sight.

CHAPTER 4

The Dance of the Jackdaw

The Rectory, Oddingley, May 1806

The weather grew steadily drier and warmer in Oddingley as April progressed. The winds which blew lustily into the Midlands from the Bristol Channel, chilling the inland counties of Gloucestershire and Worcestershire throughout the winter, had settled, and as far away as London the *Morning Chronicle* was remarking, 'The grasses, both natural and artificial, have lately improved much, and the Meadows and Pastures in the inland counties . . . appear beautifully thriving, green and luxuriant.' This was the scene in early May as the focus of farm life shifted with the season from the fold-yards, stables, sheds and workshops to the fields, where young crops of oats and barley had begun to break through the stiff cloddy marl that coated the parish like a varnish.

Springtime was vivid and colourful in rural Worcestershire, one of England's greenest counties freckled with thick woods, rolling hills and dashing brooks. In early April bluebells had burst into bloom on the outskirts of Trench Wood, where among the wild flowers, far less obvious and hidden in the long grass, were isolated colonies of tall delicate orchids named twayblades. Beside them the ridged lime-green stalks of adder's tongue fern rose from the wet earth like tiny arrows and the first emerald leaves of toxic meadow saffron shone in the spring sunshine. Lapwings and buzzards wheeled overhead.

Reverend Parker lived with his wife and their young daughter at

Oddingley Rectory, a sallow, dismal building set a little back from Church Lane, a lonely watery track that meandered down in a series of sweeping bends from the crossroads to the church. Although of some size, the rectory was unimpressive and certainly nothing about it befitted the residence of a country gentleman. Many considered Parker's home ugly, devoid of any character. Theodore Galton, a local novelist, recalled the rectory 75 years later, deriding it as a 'hideous, whitewashed, brick structure . . . scarcely worthy of the humblest of suburban villas'.

The rectory stood three storeys high and had been built according to prevailing Georgian instincts. It had a wide facade, a pointed porch, rows of airy sash windows – two either side of the front door at ground level, and three across the upper floors – and a twin set of tall, twirling chimney stacks, a particular local fancy. Ringing the property was a four-foot picket fence which enclosed a thinly populated garden scattered with laurels and other evergreens and carpeted with a gravel drive. At dusk jackdaws would roost on the rectory roof and the row of elms behind the house at the point where the garden disappeared into hedgerows, the hedgerows into orchards and then the orchards away into the rugged farmland beyond.

For 13 years the rectory had been a haven for Parker, away from the Captain, John Barnett, Thomas Clewes and the strains of the tithe dispute. One night in May 1806 this all changed. The first of the disturbances that would shake the household came in the third week of the month. Parker and his wife were asleep in their bed when there was a sharp sound at the window. A shower of jagged objects had hit the glass. Alarmed and frightened, the couple had woken at once. 'Neither of us spoke nor got up to the window,' Mary Parker remembered.

The following morning Parker rose early. He carefully surveyed the garden, pacing deliberately for some time, puzzling over the problem. He then returned indoors. The rectory's grounds would not have been difficult to enter. It was flanked on one side by hundreds of old twisted pear trees which easily comprised the largest orchard in the parish. If someone had wished to approach without being noticed, the picket fence would only have been a slight obstacle and the orchard provided the perfect escape route.

The next night was quiet, and so was the next. But later in the week the couple were woken once again by clattering at the window. Again Parker rose at dawn to comb his garden for any sign that a person may have been concealed there. If he did discover anything he did not tell his wife. Later she concluded someone must have been trying to lure him to the window or out into the garden. She thought the noise may have been made by a person throwing shot or gravel.

The night-time disturbances were yet another anxiety with which the Parkers would have to live. The clergyman took the threat seriously. He stopped walking alone in the parish after dark and by day would often detain friendly labourers to quiz them on the movements of the farmers, wondering aloud what it was that they were saying or doing. The situation must have been equally distressing for Mary Parker, who throughout remained a ghostly figure. Ostensibly the farming community was a man's world, with women reduced to the position of drudges and chattels, but there are hints in the Oddingley story that female villagers played a greater role. For as long as anyone could remember women had worked side by side with men in the fields and in Oddingley many accounts of life on the farms and the movements of the masters were made by female farmhands, dairymaids or housekeepers. In some instances women even held the reins of power, like Old Mrs Barnett, who retained the lease to Pound Farm and effectively employed her sons John and William as her bailiffs.

Little is known of Mary's background, only that she appeared in Oddingley in the mid-1790s, shortly after George, raising the possibility that she may have previously been employed in his household at Dorking or hired to serve at the rectory on his appointment. Within several years they were married and, by contemporary standards, they formed an odd couple. Mary was seven years older than George and furthermore she was uneducated and of lower status – disadvantages that temper somewhat the characterisation of her husband as wildly socially ambitious. She brought no financial benefit to their union, and in an age when marriages could be as much about business as sentiment it seems mutual attraction rather than monetary convenience was the spur for their relationship. In June 1799 Mary gave birth to a daughter at the dangerously advanced age of 45. It was an event that stands out like a milestone in the mist for, on the tithe dispute, the rift between her husband and Captain Evans and the anxious nights of broken sleep, Mary Parker left behind only the slightest of records.

In 1806 Oddingley was part of a society undergoing deep and profound change. Since the 1760s distinct revolutions had occurred in industry, science, landscape, art, politics and agriculture. They had rippled out across Britain, overturning centuries-old boundaries, challenging prevailing attitudes and the status quo. In Worcestershire, situated in the heart of the Midlands, a hotbed of enlightened thought and industrial experiment, these changes were close at hand. Twenty-five miles north of Oddingley was Birmingham, dubbed by Edmund Burke 'the grand toy-shop of Europe'. By 1780 the town was said to be mass-producing an extraordinary half-million items – everything from salt cellars, buttons, buckles, coins and candle snuffs – each year, many of which emerged from the iron gates of Matthew Boulton's famous Soho factory.

The gritty accomplishment of the industrialists were mirrored by the more flamboyant escapades of adventuring pioneers like James Sadler, who on 25 August 1785 became the first man to fly over Worcestershire in a hot-air balloon. The launch of Sadler's 'aerial voyage' was witnessed by a crowd which gathered in Worcester to see him rise briskly into a cloudy sky and a high wind that blew him west of the city for two hours, where he terrified a field of harvest workers during his descent. In 1796 a curious but vital medical breakthrough was made in Gloucestershire, the county south of Worcestershire, with Edward Jenner's development of vaccination. Jenner had discovered that he could protect his patients from deadly or disfiguring smallpox attacks by first exposing them to the less

serious cowpox virus. His experiments were detailed in his mono-
graph *An Inquiry Into the Causes and Effects of the Variolae Vaccinae* in
1798. The year after this the verb 'to revolutionise' – or 'to change
something completely and fundamentally' – was recorded for the
first time.

The most visible changes to the landscape came in pockets of
frantic urban growth, where quiet vistas were suddenly filled with
fire, smoke and activity. Rural parishes like Oddingley were overshadowed by these industrial towns, many of which had risen with
fabulous speed, often from the seed of a single mill or foundry. As
towns like Birmingham grew the population of Oddingley dropped
– from a peak of 173 in 1780 to just over 100 in 1810. It was part of
a wider national trend. In the first three decades of the nineteenth
century the rural population would diminish from above a third to
beneath a quarter of the total, and many of those who left would
not return. They were lured away by the prospect of steady work
and financial rewards, but in reality as many went to subsist as seek
their fortune. The gradual trickle of migrants left deserted cottages,
overworked farmhands and shrinking congregations in their wake.

Those labourers who remained were faced with new challenges.
Successive enclosure acts had been passed in the last decades of the
eighteenth century in a bid to make rural England more efficient.
The laws carved up the commons, amalgamating the land into large
estates – a source of opportunity for ambitious farmers like John
Barnett and Thomas Clewes. Oddingley Heath, a vast common to
the north of the parish, had already been enclosed by 1791 with
villagers stripped of their ancient rights to graze livestock, collect
nuts and berries. The move formed part of policy that would see
740,000 acres of open land enclosed between 1760 and 1810. At the
beginning of 1806 a bill was passed in Parliament concerning land
in Crowle, the adjoining parish. It was another signal that Oddingley's
surviving commons might be next on the list. Reverend Richard
Warner, on a tour of the southern counties, mused, 'Time was when
these commons enabled the poor man to support his family, and
bring up his children. Here he could turn out his cow and pony, feed

his flock of geese, and keep his pig. But the enclosures have deprived him of these advantages.'

In the 1790s uncertainties over land rights mixed with new worries about the rate of inflation. Since the beginning of the French war the British economy had hovered in an endless state of flux: roaring forward one year only to implode spectacularly the next. The effects were magnified in the countryside, where a fraught population worried about the crops and the cruel caprices of nature. The years 1799, 1800 and 1804 were particularly disastrous for Worcestershire's farmers, who saw their crops drowned by a succession of devastating rains. In 1802 a hurricane tore across the county, destroying acres of farmland and leading to a fire at the windmill at Kempsey, just south of Worcester, '[its] sail being whirled around with such great rapidity', it was reported. One local chronicler recalled that the new century had broken amid a 'tempest of war and confusion'.

Tensions from the ongoing war seeped into county life too, provoking a change in mindset at local level. In August 1803, with a French invasion increasingly likely, 722 men assembled at Pitchcroft in Worcester and declared themselves the Worcester Volunteers. Over the following months they dragooned the countryside, drawing recruits from every town, village and hamlet. The degree of enthusiasm for the regiment was displayed the following December, when local ladies 'brought up every particle of flannel that they could lay their hands on, to make flannel dresses [for the men]'. Like the Home Guard of the 1940s, the Volunteers readied themselves for the invaders, marching in nervous enthusiasm from one side of the county to the other. One morning in 1804 the recruits based in Bewdley and Kidderminster were stirred to action, being 'alarmed very early by the beating of the Volunteer drums, in consequence of reports that the French had landed, 50,000 strong'. It transpired to be another false alarm, but not before they had completed a march of some several miles. They returned, it was dryly reported, 'in ire and chagrin'.

The volunteers remained in Oddingley's neighbourhood for several years, serving as a constant reminder of the dangers Britain faced.

The population was unsettled: weapons such as pistols, cutlasses and blunderbusses, clubs and bayonets were in ever higher circulation. There were rumours of spies, and strange men with unfamiliar accents were regarded with suspicion. This was the climate in which Parker strove to collect his tax. Worcestershire, like many other counties, was an uptight, uncertain place. As he maintained his policy of collecting his tithe in kind Parker continued to have the support of the law, but he must also have seen the French Revolution as an example of how laws can suddenly change.

From Oddingley Rectory Parker must have watched as these changes swirled through British society. He could not have foreseen any of it. At some pivotal moment in his early life, among the rolling hills and opaque silver skies of the Lake District, he had decided to leave for clerical school in Warwick. To become a clergyman was an admirable rational ambition. He would be a member of the gentry in his own right. Thereafter, a good position would bring him a healthy income, a country residence, a team of servants, a position at the core of his parish and a moral platform to guide the souls of his congregation.

It was a lifestyle that is perfectly portrayed in the pages of Reverend James Woodforde's diary. Woodforde was a near-contemporary of Parker. He enjoyed a happy life, the majority of it spent at Weston Longville in Norfolk, where he served as the parish parson. Just 20 years Parker's senior and shielded from the industrial upheavals of the Midlands, Woodforde waged war against nothing more than the toads that infested his pond. He fired his blunderbuss to celebrate King George's birthday and passed time playing whist or tending to his garden and animals – on one memorable occasion accidentally getting his pigs drunk on strong ale.

In many ways Woodforde's life was uneventful, but he dutifully recorded his daily routines for more than four decades, documenting with seductive simplicity a benign existence of blithe country walks, occasional sermons and annual holidays, all fuelled by an endless supply of horrifically rich food. This was the archetypal life, the life glamorised by ambitious young curates like George Parker. For Woodforde, living on a generous £400 a year, the tithes were not a divisive tax but an opportunity to knit his community further together. At the end of every year he held a 'tithe frolic' to which the ratepayers were invited. The entry in his diary for 30 November 1784 details one of these affairs.

> They were all highly pleased with their Entertainment but few dined in the Parlour. They that dined in the Kitchen had no Punch or Wine, but strong Beer and Table Beer, and would not come into the Parlour to have Punch. I gave them for Dinner some Salt Fish, a Leg of Mutton boiled, and Capers, a fine Loin of Beef roasted and plenty of plumb and plain Puddings. They drank in the Parlour 7 bottles of Port Wine and both my large Bowls of Rum Punch, each of which took 2 Bottles of Rum to make.

Woodforde was only separated from Parker by two decades in age and a hundred miles in distance, but his experiences could hardly have been more different. Throughout the second half of the eighteenth century Norfolk remained a gentle backwater of rural England, socially and politically stable and deeply patriotic. In the Midlands 20 years later the industrial towns were not ruled by decaying feudal hierarchies, but by a new elite of diligent, rational men, their mounting fortunes generated by machines and manpower rather than ancient laws and custom. And towns like Birmingham did not just create wealthy industrialists, but served as incubators for the reformist and dissenting movements, both of which attacked the establishment of which Parker was an ingrained and immovable part.

By the beginning of the nineteenth century more and more ratepayers were questioning the right of their clergyman to a tenth of their produce, and with Pitt's war taxes mounting, tithe disputes and parochial tensions were becoming increasingly common. Parker was far from suffering alone, and there is a striking parallel between his experiences in Oddingley and Reverend John Skinner's at his parish of Camerton in Somerset. Like Woodforde, Skinner was a diarist, but he differed in almost every other sense. He was meddlesome, irritable and a fierce defender of his rights. For decades he quarrelled with his parishioners, whom he despaired of as insolent creatures. He was ignored, defied and provoked by a hardened group of farmers and labourers, who enraged him by jangling the church bells at night and releasing a screaming peacock beneath his window. A gun was fired at his dog, and when it came to the tithe the farmers were evasive. Once they brought him a broken-back lamb for his share.

Like Parker, Skinner attempted to fight his enemies head on. The results were documented in his diary: stories of petty squabbles in the lanes, sinister goings-on, and the wretchedness of his parishioners, best seen through their drinking and swearing. Skinner became increasingly intolerant with age. He took to distracting himself from the deficiencies of his own life by burying himself in the past. In time he became a noted archaeologist and antiquarian, responsible for excavating many barrows around Camerton, a place that he became convinced was Camulodunum, the capital of the ancient Trinovantes tribe and the most ancient of all Roman settlements in Britain.

This was a faraway, fantasy world to which Skinner clung with all his might. By 1839 he could stand it no longer. An extract taken from the *Bath Chronicle* of 17 October reads, 'On Friday morning, in a state of derangement, he [Reverend Skinner] shot himself through the head with a pistol, and was dead in an instant.'

Both John Skinner and George Parker were men out of time. Oddingley and Camerton would never be their happy fiefdoms in the same way that Weston Longville had been Woodforde's. Dreams that had been forged in the late eighteenth century had vanished by the beginning of the nineteenth. As Parker and Skinner stood fast, the sands shifted around them. They had not anticipated the changes: the industrial and political revolutions, wars and inflation. In Oddingley Parker had certainly not bargained on men like Captain Evans, Thomas Clewes and John Barnett – men who would fight him at every step. Parker had arrived at his post to find the rules were changing, that he had been cheated by society of his inheritance and robbed of his dream.

Almost a century after his death, Virginia Woolf still felt a sense of tragic pity for John Skinner and his futile attempts to salvage the souls of his wretched parishioners. It was a fate that Reverend George Parker of Oddingley shared.

> Irritable, nervous, apprehensive, he seems to embody, even before the age itself had come into existence, all the strife and unrest of our distracted times. He stands, dressed in the prosaic and unbecoming stocks and pantaloons of the early nineteenth century, at the parting of the ways. Behind him lay order and discipline and all the virtues of the heroic past, but directly he left his study he was faced with drunkenness and immorality; with indiscipline and irreligion; with Methodism and Roman Catholicism; with the Reform Bill and the Catholic Emancipation Act, with a mob clamouring for freedom, with the overthrow of all that was decent and established and right. Tormented and querulous, at the same time conscientious and able, he stands at the parting of the ways, unwilling to yield an inch, unable to concede a point, harsh, peremptory, apprehensive, and without hope.

As Reverend Parker puzzled over the night-time disturbances at his rectory in Oddingley, in London the government was announcing new measures that would all but double the existing property tax and lower the threshold of eligibility. It was a bold move from Lord Grenville's new administration, which had been formed following Pitt's death in January and which was being increasingly derided in the press as the 'Ministry of All the Talents'. The tax increases were roundly criticised, with William Cobbett declaring in the *Political Register*, '[it] leaves no man anything in this world that he can call his own'.

On 28 May James Gillray responded with a satirical caricature that captured the national mood. Entitled *The Friend of the People & His Petty-New-Tax-Gatherer, paying John Bull a Visit*, it lampooned Charles Fox, the foreign secretary, and Lord Henry Petty, the new chancellor of the exchequer. The two men are shown rapping impatiently at John Bull's door, with Petty bellowing 'Taxes! Taxes! Taxes!' as he leans on the knocker. As his furniture is carted away on the street behind, John Bull peeps out of an upstairs window, replying, 'Taxes? – Why how am I to get Money to pay them all? I shall very soon have neither a House nor a Hole to put my head

Published on 28 May 1806, James Gillray's *A Friend of the People & his Petty-New-Tax-Gatherer, paying John Bull a visit* shows a worn and irritable country

in.' The corpulent Charles Fox, supporting a vast folio crammed with a list of new levies, calls up, 'A house to put your head in? Why what the Devil should you want with a House?'

Like much of Gillray's work the piece was a searing parody, an intoxicating cocktail of lofty satire and burlesque imagery that tapped into a national mood of gathering frustration and captured dissembling politicians like Fox and Petty riding roughshod over popular opinion. The caricature is suggestive of the brittle atmosphere that was pervading England by the end of May. It was a country worn to the bone. The stoic John Bull is depicted embattled in his garret window, about to snap. It is a neat visualisation of the plight of the Oddingley farmers. Not only were they subject to the increased property tax, but they also had to contend with the extra menace of Parker's tithe. The harvest months now loomed before them, the stones at the rectory window just one harbinger of what was to come.

CHAPTER 5

Damn His Blood

Oddingley, May, June 1806

At about midnight on Saturday 24 May, Sarah Lloyd, a 24-year-old farm worker, was sitting up with her younger sister at their family home, a labourer's cottage, when they were disturbed by a noise from outside. The Lloyds' cottage stood by the crossroads, surrounded by clover fields and an area of open grassy pastures known locally as the Hulls. In the hours since the sun had set at nine o'clock the village had quietened as work had finished for the day and labourers had returned to their homes and beds. The noise was loud and peculiar enough to wrest Sarah's attention from her conversation and draw her outside. She opened the cottage door and stepped out into the night. In the garden she heard the noise again – it was drunken voices, all of them raised and jeering. The sounds came from the direction of the Pigeon House, a squat brick outhouse which was owned by the Barnett family, who used it as a summer-house and a store for their finest cider. Sarah crept through the spring air towards the building. Once within earshot, she hid herself 'under a tree which was nearly down'.

From here Sarah could distinguish the voices of a number of local farmers. 'I heard several toasts drank and several persons named,' she recalled, among whom were Captain Evans, John Barnett, Thomas Clewes, George Banks and Mr Davis of Dunhampstead. She recognised each man distinctly and recalled Thomas Clewes' voice particularly. She heard the master of

Netherwood Farm propose a toast: 'Let us drink damnation to him, he will not be here long to trouble us – and let us drink it left-handed!' Sarah listened as each of the men repeated Clewes' charge. She had 'no doubt' that Reverend Parker was the subject of the toasts, as there was, as she put it, a 'misunderstanding' between the parties.

The toasts continued for some time as Sarah remained concealed 20 yards away behind the collapsed tree, shielded from view in the darkness. But she was not alone in the Pigeon House Meadow that night. A farm dog that belonged to one of the Barnett brothers had been tethered outside the building and, hearing her cough, began to bark. In panic, Sarah scrambled up and started for her cottage, but the moment she moved, the wooden door of the Pigeon House burst open behind her and two men flew out into the night in pursuit. They made after Sarah, who charged desperately through the grass. She reached her cottage before them and pushed the door closed.

'I wish we had catched her!' she heard Davis say to George Banks. 'Damn her blood! We would have mopped her up.'

'Damn her eyes!' Banks replied. 'I wish we had and catched her.'

By now Sarah's father had been roused by the commotion. George Lloyd was well known in Oddingley as a friend of Parker's and a respected labourer. Holding his gun, he called through the door to Banks and Davis, ordering them to leave and threatening that if they did not he would be forced to shoot. At this, the men retreated into the night.

Sarah was terrified by the incident. For several days she refused to leave the cottage, and when she did, on Tuesday 27 May, she hastened directly to Parker's rectory, telling the clergyman exactly what she had heard. Parker listened carefully to Sarah's account and weighed it. 'Girl, I don't care a fig for them altogether,' he replied.

For all Parker's indifference, feigned or not, there were signs throughout May that the farmers' anger was stirring in new ways. Earlier that month a surveyor named George Gilbert Jones had been sent to Oddingley. Jones had no prior connection to the parish, where he spent almost a month researching the land for a new rate form. On his arrival he was instantly forced into an extraordinary situation,

finding all the farmers except Perkins 'at enmity' with Parker – a
fact which forced him to flit like a diplomat between one faction
and the other as he worked his way through the village.

Jones had been forewarned about the tithe dispute by his employer,
who had told him that it was better to lodge outside the parish. But
although he followed this advice, taking rooms at a nearby inn, he
did socialise with both Reverend Parker and the Captain, dining
frequently with them as the weeks passed. Through his work and
these social events, the surveyor gained an unusually full insight into
the feud. On several occasions Jones heard the Captain and George
Banks 'damn the parson's eyes and say that it was no harm to shoot
him'. He detected a similar sentiment at Pound Farm, though he
found John Barnett more guarded. Barnett confessed to being angry
at the manner in which Parker was collecting the tithe in kind, but
was otherwise reticent, reluctant to say anything more. The other
farmers, particularly Clewes, said nothing. Of all of the villagers,
Jones came to spend the most time with young George Banks, who
had been instructed by the Captain to act as his guide. Jones found
Banks an engaging personality, and they met in the evenings to play
cards at Church Farm. But while the bailiff was good company, Jones
also noticed an impatient, vicious streak in his character. 'Banks was
the most violent' in his language, he recalled later. It was a hint that
there was something more to the bailiff than first met the eye: it
was plain he was alert, keen and able, but was he also impetuous,
quietly belligerent and indiscreet?

Jones had completed his survey and left Oddingley by the middle
of May, around a week before the farmers' meeting at the Pigeon
House. It was now less than a month before the clover was ready
to be harvested and the haymaking season was due to begin. In the
valley between the village crossroads and the edges of Trench Wood
crops of wheat, barley and oats were growing tall in the fields. For
the farmers these were anxious days, and for much of the time they
lived by their wits, knowing a single sharp frost, unexpected rainfall
or fierce storm could ruin months of work. As by its nature collection of the tithe in kind closely mirrored the agricultural calendar,

the busy months of May, June and July were natural flashpoints and to the farmhands and local tradesmen there were signs that tempers were already unusually frayed.

An early indication of this came at Church Farm at around the end of May. Captain Evans was sitting in his parlour with Mary Banks one evening when he sent for Elizabeth Fowler, the dairymaid. It was a strange summons, and when she presented herself it became clear that he did not wish to speak about the farm or any of her other duties. Instead he offered her a glass of wine. The dairymaid accepted the drink, but as she took it up he stopped her and challenged her to raise it as a toast against Parker. Elizabeth refused and excused herself, leaving the Captain 'very much offended'.

On Tuesday 10 June Thomas Reed, a cabinetmaker from Worcester, was drinking at the Raven on Droitwich Road – a short distance from the city – when he saw a group of Oddingley men enter and start a boisterous conversation at a table in the taproom. Reed only knew three of the men, the two Barnett brothers and a labourer, John Chance. Soon the men were complaining loudly about Parker and the tithe, and, unusually, John Barnett was the most vociferous of them. He declared that if he had ten children, he was sure that one of them would be claimed as tax. Later they stood up, pulled off their hats and then 'drank damnation' to Parker. One of the men Thomas Reed did not recognise (most likely Clewes or Banks) described waspishly how he had recently cut four and a half cabbages from his garden and then sent for Parker, asking him to take the remaining half. The tone of the conversation, which varied from cruel humour to malice and icy threats, struck Reed strongly. Over the next few years he would tell 'different people [of it] a hundred times'. One detail he remembered above all others was John Barnett's claim that 'he would give £50 for a dead parson'.

This incident was followed, several days after, by another in Oddingley parish. Reverend Parker had walked down Netherwood Lane to Thomas Barber's shop at Sale Green. The two men were friendly and had fallen into a conversation when they were interrupted by Clewes unexpectedly knocking at the door. Anticipating

a confrontation, Parker hurried out of the kitchen door as Clewes
entered, but the farmer caught a glimpse of him as he disappeared
along the lane. Clewes turned to Barber and told him there was £50
for any man 'who would shoot the parson'.

By mid-June there were indications that Parker was growing
uncharacteristically nervous. He cut down on his rambles through
the lanes and he avoided Church Farm, Pound Farm and Netherwood
altogether. Whether he had been cautioned that the farmers were
offering a reward for his murder or not, he had certainly been told
enough by Sarah Lloyd to know they were proposing toasts against
him and meeting by night to vent their anger. Perhaps instinct was
drawing him back from any contact with the men, but it was difficult
to avoid people in a place like Oddingley and from the middle of
June there was a further worry. The Captain, who for so long had
avoided Parker and treated him with contempt, seemed determined
to catch him and was seen on various occasions in Church Lane,
waiting for him to emerge from the rectory.

A chance soon presented itself. The lanes were busiest during
harvest time, with labourers drawing handcarts, fetching supplies
from the cottages and relaying messages back and forth. Much of
the traffic flowed along Church Lane outside the rectory, where on
Tuesday 17 June two labourers from Crowle stopped to speak to
Parker. A minute later Captain Evans appeared on horseback from
around a kink in the lane. He rode towards Parker, and when he
was within earshot called out, 'Stop, sir, do stop! Let me speak to
you once more!'

It was perhaps the first time the two men had encountered one
another since their argument at the vestry meeting ten weeks before.
The image of the two adversaries together is a vivid and enduring
one: the Captain on horseback, advancing at a pace towards Parker.
The clergyman is defiant, resolute and static, the Captain dynamic,
domineering and aggressive. As Evans approached, Parker shouted
to him, 'You are not going to pay the debt of nature – that is the
only debt you will pay.' It was a dismissive riposte with clear implications: that while the Captain might strive to evade his obligations

to God on earth (his payment of the tithes), he would not be able to avoid divine punishment at the Day of Judgement. It was a stinging rebuke to an elderly man.

There was no further conversation. Parker turned his back and retreated into the rectory, leaving the Captain in the lane with John Bridge and Joseph Kendall, the two labourers. Incensed that his attempt at conciliation had been so starkly rebuffed, the Captain damned Parker furiously, concluding his flow of invective with a cry of rhetorical exasperation, asking the men 'which ship *he* belonged to'. It was a moment of unbridled anger, a public spilling-over of many months of simmering frustration in full view of the villagers.

It seemed a final blow that ruined any lingering hope that a compromise might be struck between the parties before harvest, yet, just three days afterwards, the Captain tried again. Catching Parker in Church Lane, Evans pursued him on horseback as he retreated towards the rectory, imploring him to stop and talk. The appeals, though, fell on deaf ears. Once more Parker slipped away before Evans could corner him or impart whatever message it was he was so desperately trying to convey. 'God damn the fellow!' Evans shouted. 'Lord have mercy upon me, what a fellow it is!'

Inside the rectory Parker was comforted by his wife. In a fit of exasperation he told her, 'I will swear my life against them all, for I know not what they want – unless it is my life.'

For years much of the resentment towards Parker had been subsurface. The frustration and anger of the farmers had for the most part festered in the privacy of Netherwood Farm, Church Farm and Pound Farm, only emerging publicly in isolated outbursts. Since the argument at the vestry meeting, however, the mood in the parish had blackened. The farmers' provocations had only led to a strength-ening of Parker's resolve. Every attempt at conciliation had resulted in escalation, and of all the clashes these final two between the Captain and Parker were the most significant. In one sense they can be seen as a microcosm of the whole quarrel – Evans, the reluctant ratepayer, helplessly hemmed in by the law, moving from attempts at compromise to outpourings of anger and abuse, while Parker remains throughout as he always was: infuriatingly steadfast and unswervingly aloof.

The relationship between Evans and Parker cuts to the heart of the Oddingley feud. Behind the wrangles over tithes and control over the parish purse there lay something deeper: a vicious personality clash. Divided by circumstance, the two men were in fact remarkably similar. Both had risen to join the ranks of the gentry, both considered themselves community leaders and both were determined, driven and principled. Had their lives been exchanged, each might have fared well in the other's shoes. But fate had brought them together in conflict. Parker represented the Church, with all of its ancient powers of unyielding authority over the mind and soul, while Captain Evans, the retired military man, symbolised a quite different breed of material and secular power. The feud at Oddingley was a tithe dispute, but it is more clearly seen through the prism of this personality clash between the Captain and the clergyman: two men who could never get on.

Little is known of Samuel Evans' early life. The few surviving sources note that he initially worked as a baker in Kidderminster, a town about 20 miles north of Oddingley, before joining the army. A further source mentions his reputation as 'a wild youth'. A clear biography only emerges with the start of the American War of Independence in 1775, a conflict which caught the British government on the back foot and quickly brought the weakened state of its armed forces into sharp focus. After the opening phases of the fighting it became apparent that what had initially been treated as a local uprising was actually far more serious. Soon the French were embroiling themselves in the conflict alongside the rebels, and opportunistic ships belonging to the Spanish, Dutch and French navies were massing in the Caribbean, eyeing the wealthy British colony of Jamaica. Facing the prospect of war on two fronts, the government was forced to dramatically increase the size of the armed forces, from 48,000 men in 1775 to 110,000 six years later. Most of the new recruits were enlisted in a rash of new regiments raised between 1778 and 1780, and it is at this point that Samuel Evans, then aged about 46, first surfaces – as a recruiting sergeant for the 89th Regiment of Foot. By 1779 the outfit – better known as the Worcestershire Volunteers or Carey's, after its commanding colonel Lucius Ferdinand Carey – was fully operational, and Evans was in the thick of its attempts to recruit men.

This was an important position. The army depended on recruiting sergeants to fill its ranks quickly and efficiently in an age before conscription. Such men were typically determined, ruthless and loyal, capable of seducing, pressuring or bribing men into service and always mindful of the financial rewards available for doing a good job. Traditionally recruits came from two channels: volunteers, who were rewarded with a bounty, and pardoned criminals, who used the

ATTIC MISCELLANY.

MANNING THE NAVY.

Press gangs were a familiar evil in Georgian England. In the late 1770s new legislation opened inland areas as well as coastal towns up to forced recruitment

army as a way of escaping their past transgressions. But by 1778 it had become plain that this system was not yielding sufficient numbers and measures were rushed through Parliament to rectify the problem. By the next year the bounty for volunteers had been increased to £3 3s. a head and, of greater importance, the forced recruitment or 'impressment' of 'able-bodied, idle and disorderly men who were without trade and employment' was legalised. The British army needed soldiers, and the government was willing to give men like Samuel Evans the powers to get them.

Roving press gangs, led by recruiting sergeants and consisting of little bands of soldiers, sprang up in response to the act and they struck terror into the British population. Press gangs were nothing new; they had stalked port towns for years scouring the docks and nearby inns for out-of-work sailors and other seamen who would suit the navy. Such gangs, however, had usually remained in coastal areas, only straying inland occasionally. But by the spring of 1779 the whole of Britain was in effect opened up to forced recruitment and the following months saw a surge of new recruits, with men like Evans able to earn as much as £1 a day. The financial rewards meant that compassion was rarely extended towards loiterers, beggars or the unemployed. Arriving in a town, a press gang would usually establish its headquarters in an alehouse – known colloquially as a rondy – where they slouched away their spare time drinking, plotting and roaming the nearby streets. One source describes a gang as 'a roistering drinking crew . . . never averse from a row'. Typically they were armed with cutlasses, clubs or daggers which they would use without care. One illustration of a press gang at work, depicts five expressionless soldiers dressed in tunics and cocked hats, armed with swords, pistols and truncheons, forcing men into shackles and dragging them away.

Samuel Evans was an active presence throughout the worst months of the recruiting crisis, thriving in this brutish, pragmatic world, where he was judged by his results not his methods. The job, by its nature, was opportunistic and occasionally violent. Street fights and alley scuffles with drunks, robbers and street hucksters were common. Recruiting sergeants were forced to prise information from wily informants and catch out determined men, who would go as far as incapacitating themselves (cutting off their thumbs and forefingers was the most common method) to avoid being ensnared. But it was an environment in which Samuel Evans excelled.

Evans' success was enough to catch the attention of his superiors. A set of stiff entry requirements usually prevented those from the lower orders being appointed officers in the eighteenth century (a candidate for a commission had to hold an annual income of at least £200 – the income of a gentleman – if their commission was not bought, and most of them were), but with resources so stretched and Evans so obviously able, the usual barriers were temporarily relaxed, and on Saturday 30 October the *London Gazette* carried the news that Samuel Evans had been appointed an officer. He had joined the ranks of the gentry and was thrust into a team of regimental officers comprising two majors, seven captains, eleven lieutenants, eight ensigns, a chaplain, an adjutant, a quartermaster and a surgeon at the head of a body of many hundreds of men. It was the single most significant day of Samuel Evans' life and it left him more powerful than ever.

By October 1779 Evans' regiment was ready for duty, and in December it set sail from Portsmouth for the West Indies. The 89th Foot had originally been bound for Jamaica, but it was diverted to the Leeward Islands, where it saw action in Saint Lucia. Afterwards the regiment was stationed in Barbados and Tobago, but as time passed its men were increasingly worn down by what was already known as the 'torrid zone'. This label applied to much of the Caribbean and referred to the ruthless mix of New and Old World diseases that thrived in the humid atmosphere and tore through the constitution of any unadjusted arrival. Yellow fever, which inflicted a sufferer with black vomit, a black tongue and yellow skin, was the most prevalent among the maladies to strike the 89th Foot, but hordes of other diseases thrived with almost equal force, infecting men with high fevers, shivering fits, sores, weeping wounds and other conditions for which there was no known cure. Ten out of the 29 officers fell victim to tropical disease during the tour of the Caribbean, a total which left the regiment desperately short of leaders and precipitated the promotion of Ensign Evans to lieutenant in May 1780.

A year later the 89th Foot was relieved, and it set sail for England on 4 May 1781. Thereafter it spent the summer recruiting afresh, at Hereford, Dudley, Leominster and Ludlow, but by this point the war was drawing to a close and the government's thirst for men was satisfied. Shortly before the Peace of Versailles was signed in February 1783 the government circulated a memorandum stating that 'all men enlisted since 16 December 1775 shall be discharged when peace declared, provided they have served three years'. It was another fortuitous turn of events for Evans, who in May 1782 had received his final promotion – to captain – and in March 1783 he began his long half-pay retirement.

By now he was styling himself as Captain Evans, an evocative identity rich in patriotic overtones which allowed him to transfer an element of military glamour and hierarchy into his civilian life. At the age of 50 he was a gentleman, admired, connected and possibly notorious around Worcestershire. His life had followed an upward trajectory for many years, and by the early 1780s all the trappings of his early days as a commoner seemed rubbed away, leaving the man Mary Sherwood would later encounter. 'Whatever his parentage might have been,' she explained, 'he had an air of a gentleman of the old school, and not in the least of a person suddenly raised from a low estate. He was, when it pleased him, equally polite and courteous in his manners, as well as dignified in his general carriage.' Such a radical transformation as Sherwood suggests, was not easily undertaken, and it exposes Evans both as an ambitious man keen to shake off his past but also able, almost chameleon-like, to adapt to different environments. Two decades later, in Oddingley, he retained his military aura and for many of the parishioners he would have been a towering personality, to be feared and respected in equal measure. In an age when very few travelled beyond the neighbouring counties or as far as London, Evans would have been considered an adventurer, a self-made man of the same generation as James Cook, the son of a Yorkshire day labourer who had entered the navy as an able seaman and risen to the rank of captain.

By experience and nature Evans was a leader. The social boundaries that had stood before him at the opening of his career had been overcome, and there would have been little to suggest that Parker and his demands for the tithe were anything more than another stone to be kicked from his path. Like many others who return from battlefields and are thrown back into society, Evans had a dangerous self-confidence burning inside him. In his dealings with Parker and Perkins, this element is always just beneath the surface.

In his very first publication, *Sketches By Boz*, Charles Dickens caricatures the half-pay captain – a familiar personality in early-nineteenth-century Britain, like an unruly sage full of nuisance and tales of war and with little time for civic niceties. It's a sharp skittish description which in some ways could be applied to Evans.

> He attends every vestry meeting that is held; always opposes the constituted authorities of the parish, denounces the profligacy of the church wardens, contends legal points against the vestry clerk, will make the best tax gatherer wait for his money till he won't call any longer, and then he sends it; finds fault with the sermon every Sunday, says the organist ought to be ashamed of himself, offers to back himself for any amount to sing the psalms better than all the children put together, male and female, and, in short, conducts himself in the most turbulent and uproarious manner.

Captain Evans brought much of this same unruly dominance to Oddingley with him when he arrived at Church Farm in 1798. He demonstrated a flair for organising men, assembling support for a cause, aggressively pursuing a line of argument as well as a willingness to engage to his advantage with awkward situations. In May 1806 Oddingley was visited by the local militia, and eligible villagers who had been drawn by lots to serve were required to present themselves for inspection. George Banks was one of these and was only saved from service by the Captain, who ordered a parishioner named Clement Churchill to stand in his place. It was a clever switch, as Evans knew full well that Churchill would be rejected due to his height (the militia required men at least five feet four inches tall). All the while, Churchill recalled, the real George Banks was at plough in Oddingley.

This little vignette reveals how the Captain was ready and willing to exploit situations for his own benefit or to help out those close to him. It also demonstrates his ability to carry off a bare-faced lie with composure. Perhaps he knew the recruiting sergeants conducting the muster; he certainly knew how the process worked and how best to play it. His status as a magistrate, charged with upholding the law, seems not to have had the slightest bearing on his actions.

A less immediate but equally powerful echo of the Captain's military days comes in the nature and tone of the farmer's language towards Parker throughout the quarrel. The most commonly recorded of their curses was 'damn', a verb which has subsequently lost much of its power but at the time remained potent, bordering on the taboo. In Christian societies damning a person meant wishing them away to hell and the Devil, to a life of eternal punishment, pain and misery. For the outwardly respectable classes it was a profanity best hidden away in private, but it was used openly by the lower orders, especially soldiers and seamen, for whom it was the sharpest insult, reserved for personal enemies, dangerous social deviants and figures of hate.

To be damned publicly was ominous. Shortly before his home was razed to the ground and his effigy burnt by a baying mob in Birmingham on Bastille Day 1791 Joseph Priestley, the notorious dissenting chemist, had to endure the sight of every blank wall in the town centre being chalked with the slogan 'Damn Priestley' by loyalist mobs. In the very same year a definition of the verb was left, inadvertently, in James Boswell's biography of Dr Johnson. Boswell included the following exchange between Johnson and a friend:

Johnson: I am afraid that I may be one of those who shall be damned (looking dismally).

Dr Adams: What do you mean by damned?

Johnson: (passionately and loudly) Sent to Hell, Sir, and punished everlastingly.

Many publishers censored the word from pamphlets, fearful that they might be aiding its spread. Its use provoked an uneasy feeling in the minds of right-minded Christians, who week after week were reminded of the horrors of hell from the pulpit. Some writers used its power to enliven their work. Byron intensified the shock of his poem *Don Juan* by embroidering one verse with the curse 'Damn his eyes', which he referred to as 'that once all-famous oath'. More striking still was Jonathan Swift's haunting poem *The Place of the Damned*, which drew its power from repetition of the word, leaving a bitter sense of anger and hopelessness: 'Damned lawyers and judges, damned lords and damned squires; Damned spies and informers, damned friends and damned liars.'

Swift's was a technique that moderate writers shied away from, and for the century and a half which followed many authors avoided the word altogether and others side-stepped what was increasingly considered offensive by resorting to euphemisms such as 'jiggered' or 'drat', in itself a shortened version of another religious curse 'God rot your bones' or 'God rot.' In newspaper reports 'damn' was rare, and when it did surface it was almost universally linked to the criminal and malicious sectors of society. Dickens reserved it for exceptional moments, such as the rooftop scene at the end of *Oliver Twist* which marked Bill Sykes' grisly end. '"Damn you!" cried the desperate ruffian. "Do your worst! I'll cheat you yet!"'

In Oddingley the word was used openly. The farmers damned Parker at the Easter dinner and in the Pigeon House; Barnett damned him at the Raven; and Captain Evans, boldest of them all, damned him in daylight in the lanes. After being chased to her house Sarah Lloyd was damned by Banks and Mr Davis, and John Perkins was damned for his disloyal and shameful friendship with Parker. The farmers were not just wishing Parker away to hell, they were wishing the same fate on anyone who stood alongside him. The prevalence of the word in the court documents and newspaper reports of the case is striking and somewhat unusual. There is every reason to believe it arrived in the parish with the Captain, a man who would have been exposed to violent or fractious language during his time in the army, his cry to the labourers in Church Lane – 'which ship he belonged to' yet another subtle reminder of his military days.

These angry moments suggest a primitive edge to Oddingley. While the industrial towns all around buzzed excitedly with the ideals of the Enlightenment, driven onwards by the pursuit of science and reason, in the countryside farmers were still offering up toasts to supernatural powers, inviting them to inflict harm or evil on their clergyman. These toasts reflect a lingering belief in word magic – that a person could be blighted or harmed by the force of a ban or a curse. The left-handed toasts, like those offered at the Plough or in the Pigeon House, added yet a further twist to the ritual. They were laced with imagery, addressed directly to the Devil.

Swearing was an evil that the respectable classes recoiled from and railed against, and punishments for those found guilty could be severe. For day-labourers, sailors, common soldiers or seamen there was a fine of one shilling for a first conviction. For farmers, merchants and any other person beneath the rank of gentleman the rate was increased to two shillings, and for gentlemen and those of higher status the fine was five shillings. The amounts were doubled for a second offence and tripled for a third. Furthermore a raft of legislation had been passed by the Pitt government during the 1790s to counter the increasing number of sedtious meetings in the country – which, it was held, was teetering on the brink of revolution. Particularly stiff punishments were meted out to those convicted of taking or administering oaths that bound individuals to mutinous or seditious causes. Hard evidence about the farmers' meeting in the Pigeon House might be difficult to bring before a magistrate, but it was clear the men were acting on the very edge of the law.

Parker did not react to the farmers' curses; instead he brushed them off as best he could. But they were an affront to his reputation he could barely ignore. In 1806 Georgians were still consumed by questions of personal honour, and offended parties would often retaliate to perceived affronts to their dignity by challenging the offenders to fist fights or duels. Such encounters occurred at all levels of society, and even Pitt, the prime minister, had become entangled in an argument that ended in a duel on Putney Heath just a few years earlier. In the Midlands there were many further examples much closer to home, one of which had occurred in the parish of Spondon in Derbyshire, where the local curate had shot and killed the schoolmaster in a duel after the two men had quarrelled over 'a brisk gay widow'.

But instead of returning insult with violence, Reverend Parker reacted to the farmers' provocations with stoicism. Perhaps he was not a fighting man; perhaps he did not want to lower himself to the indignity and fanfare of a public confrontation; or perhaps he planned to seize the moral high ground by acting with decency. Such an approach was probably the best available to him, and it was certainly better than fighting men like Evans, Barnett and Clewes head on. But his unwillingness to defend himself publicly could also be perceived as a weakness. It was a weakness that the farmers sought to exploit throughout the spring and early summer of 1806, and of them all Captain Evans was the man who displayed a talent for using language and rhetoric most effectively.

When Evans summoned Elizabeth Fowler to his parlour at the end of May he was doing more than urging her to swear allegiance to his faction in the village dispute, he was asking her to collude in an oath. This behaviour may well have also stemmed from Evans' military career – he would have understood that popular support was vital in any divisive cause – but his challenge to Elizabeth was clever and pointed.

Since the earliest days of English society the belief had persisted that individuals could be bound by an oath to an employer, a quest or a cause. Such oaths are seldom used nowadays – they are only employed formally in court – but in the early nineteenth century they remained an important method of extracting allegiance or guaranteeing support. An oath was sealed when an individual swore aloud over a sacred object or in the presence of their social superiors. By challenging Elizabeth to swear an oath, Evans was testing her loyalty, trying to bind her to him through the magic of words.

Such magic, akin to a spell, can be found in Thomas Hardy's *The Mayor of Casterbridge*, set in rural England in the first third of the nineteenth century. In the opening scene the novel's tragic hero, a hay-trusser named Michael Henchard, swears a solemn oath to avoid all strong liquor for twenty-one years after a night of terrible drunkenness during which he sold his wife and baby daughter for the sum of five guineas. Henchard's oath is sworn over a Bible at the parish church and its solemnity is reflected in Hardy's prose.

> Hence he reached the church without observation, and the door being only latched, he entered. The hay-trusser deposited his basket by the font, went up the nave till he reached the altar-rails, and opening the gate, entered the sacrarium, where he seemed to feel a sense of strangeness for a moment; then he knelt upon the foot pace. Dropping his head upon the clamped book which lay on the Communion-table, he said aloud –
>
> 'I, Michael Henchard, on this morning of the sixteenth of September, do take on oath before God here in this solemn place that I will avoid all strong liquors for the space of twenty-one years to come, being a year for every year I have lived. And this I swear upon the book before me; and may I be struck dumb, blind and helpless, if I break this my oath!'

Oaths have a long history. For centuries communities had been held together by formal oaths or other invisible bonds of allegiance that helped to dictate their actions, ensuring the political make-up of a village or town remained relatively stable, and important secrets were kept safe. Oaths were also used to bind individuals to a cause. In 1803, when the Despard Plot – a scheme which purportedly involved the assassination of King George III, the seizure of the Tower of London and the Post Office and the proclamation of Great

Britain as a republic – was foiled by the government, many of the alleged participants were discovered to be carrying unlawful oaths in their pockets headed: 'Constitution: The Independence of Great Britain and Ireland'. The importance individuals placed on such pledges is perhaps best demonstrated by the convict Abel Magwitch in Dickens' *Great Expectations*. Magwitch displays a total reliance on a black Bible that he carries everywhere with him and on which he forces successive characters to swear loyalty. To Magwitch, Pip observes, the Bible seems to have powers equal to a 'spell or a charm'. When Pip's friend the hapless Herbert Pocket encounters the convict for the first time, Magwitch flies at him in a flurry of curses that do not abate until a peculiar ceremony involving the Bible has been concluded. 'Take it in your right hand! – Lord strike you dead on the spot, if ever you split in any way sumever! Kiss it!' Magwitch snarls.

Oaths were used in this way to secure loyalty and distinguish friends from enemies, and Fowler was acting bravely in refusing Evans' request. In rural parishes like Oddingley those considered disloyal to a cause could face the wrath of the community and the prospect of being hounded out by ridicule or alienation. Such a fate was a reality for those such as John Perkins, Sarah Lloyd, Old Mr Hardcourt and Elizabeth Fowler who stood by Parker. The two remaining farmers, Mr Marshall and Mr Jones, who stayed neutral throughout the dispute, might well have calculated that it was better to remain quiet rather than take the clergyman's side.

This may have been a wise choice. When a community's will was gathered behind a popular cause its power could be overwhelming. Unpopular villagers could be bullied into submission, ridiculed mercilessly or provoked into embarrassing themselves. There were far cruder ways to settle local scores. In some villages labourers would dress in gaudy, hideous costumes to mock adulterers or debtors. In *The Mayor of Casterbridge*, when the shameful affair between Michael Henchard and Lucetta Le Sueur is exposed, a drunken mob gathers and then roars through the town in a humiliating procession or skimmity-ride ('an old foolish thing that they do in these parts when a man's wife is – well, not particularly his own'). The Casterbridge mob carries effigies of Henchard and Lucetta. The figures are tied back to back at the elbows and processed through the middle of the town on a donkey. It was rough, crude justice, the horror of which was enough to kill Lucetta: '"Tis me!" she said, with a face as pale as death. "A procession – a scandal – an effigy of me, and him!"'

The Oddingley farmers set out to undermine Reverend Parker just as the fictional townsfolk of Casterbridge first undermined then humiliated Lucetta. The farmers characterised Parker as an evil aberration who had abused his position as the village clergyman for his own selfish ends. Parker was not just the Bonaparte of Oddingley, he was the Devil dressed in the clothes of a priest. They damned his soul, damned his eyes, damned his bones and damned his blood.

CHAPTER 6

Hue and Cry

Oddingley, 24 June 1806, Midsummer Day

On Midsummer afternoon John Perkins was at work at his farm a quarter of a mile south of the village crossroads. Oddingley Lane Farm was one of the smaller holdings in the parish. It was connected to the little network of country roads by a wide earthy drive which branched off from the southern part of Oddingley Lane. Perkins' farmhouse lay at the far end of this drive behind a little pool. It was surrounded by a scattered cluster of cow sheds, cart houses and workshops, filled like all the others in the parish with wheelbarrows, handcarts, tongs, weeding hooks, hammers and nails, saws, pincers, scythes and pitchforks. Farmers across Oddingley guarded their tools carefully, knowing they were among their most valuable and vital possessions. Keys to the workshops were kept by the farmers, and into the woodwork of each implement they burnt their initials as a deterrent to thieves.

Midsummer came in the middle of a busy stretch in the farming calendar, and unlike Clewes and Old Mr Hardcourt, Perkins had decided not to travel to Bromsgrove for the annual fair, instead opting to remain in the village. Traditionally the first few weeks of June were devoted to sheep shearing, a task which had to be completed by the middle of the month so attention could shift towards haymaking and the clover harvest – two of the most delicate and important businesses of the year. Both clover and sainfoin grass – typically the variety raised for hay – were highly nutritious foods for livestock, and to harvest and store them well was vital for the future of a farm. Once cut with a scythe, the crops had to be withered beneath the sun until they were dried, sapped of their juices and ready to be carted off and built into ricks.

A short distance north of Oddingley Lane Farm, across a narrow stretch of land known as Cottage Meadow, Perkins' neighbour Samuel Jones was also in his fields that summer afternoon, as was George Banks, a quarter of a mile away near Church Farm. There is no surviving record to show which labourers Perkins had working for him on 24 June. The only other person who can be placed at Oddingley Lane Farm with any certainty is his wife of three years, Betty.

John and Betty Perkins were among the Parkers' closest friends in the parish. Parker had officiated at their wedding, on 16 October 1803, at which Mary Parker had taken the unusual step of signing the register instead of Pardoe, the parish clerk. As Mary was illiterate she could only manage a dog-legged cross in the gap her husband left for her signature, but it was a symbolic act and enough to demonstrate the depth of trust and friendship between the couples. The bond had endured, and they had continued to worship at Parker's services throughout the quarrel and in the face of all the Captain's threats. John and Betty Perkins would have been among the congregation at Parker's final service, two days earlier, on 22 June, where there had been disquieting whisperings in the pews.

Parker had conducted the service dressed in a new set of clothes, something that had caught the eye of several parishioners. During the service Sarah Lloyd, who had recently been so terrorised by Banks and Davis outside the Pigeon House, had been approached by William Knight, one of Captain Evans' servants. Knight had asked Lloyd whether she liked Reverend Parker's new clothes; Lloyd had replied that she did. Knight rejoined, 'Oh, he has got his dying dress on.'

One of John Barnett's servants, the carter named James Tustin, had also been at church that morning. Tustin was one of Barnett's most loyal workers, responsible for keeping the horses and managing the fold-yard when the brothers were away. Tustin had told Lloyd, 'There will something happen in Oddingley in less than a week that never happened before and that will make your hair stand on end.' Lloyd had asked Tustin what he meant, but there was no reply.

It was now two days after the Sunday service and Perkins was working in his fields. Weeding wheat and other crops was a constant battle in spring and early summer. Between late April and the end of June teams of women and children walked the furrows, stabbing at thistles and dock leaves to stop their hardy roots from taking hold. For this they used a spear-like implement called a spud, the blade of which resembled a carpenter's chisel bent to an acute angle and sharpened like a knife.

On Midsummer afternoon Perkins was busy with a similar task. One of his meadows had been blighted by an outbreak of a weed known as cammock or rest harrow, a low-growing but pretty wild-flower, so called because its roots were so thickly knotted they could bring a heavy tool like a harrow to a jolting halt. From the middle of the afternoon onwards, he busied himself in the field, hacking at the plant.

At around four thirty in the afternoon Perkins gathered the cammock into a heap, and at five o'clock he set his little bonfire alight. He did not hear anything unusual. There was just the dim rustle of a harvest scythe, the occasional sweep or creak of a wheel-barrow, and the gentle sound of birdsong: robins, blackbirds, chaf-finches, blackcaps and willow warblers, darting across the fields and into hedgerows where their nests were hidden among the brambles. Unlike James Tustin and the two butchers half a mile away at Pound Farm, he did not hear the blast of a shotgun or Reverend Parker's piercing, desperate cry of murder.

John Lench and Thomas Giles, the two butchers from Worcester, were only a hundred yards away from Parker's glebe on Oddingley Lane when the attack took place. But there was no hope of them reaching the scene quickly. The glebe meadows were contained within a triangular-shaped series of fields rented by John Barnett that were enclosed on all sides by tall hedgerows. A series of gates conducted workers into the heart of these meadows, where the crime scene lay. It was about five or six minutes past five o'clock when Parker was attacked. The hedgerows, full and thick, shielded a place that had clearly been selected for its seclusion. As the gunshot rang out, there were only three people within the little triangle of mead-owland: Parker, his murderer and John Barnett's dairymaid, Susan Surman.

The shot was fired just yards from Surman and the sound terrified her. A second later she heard Parker's cry of murder, and she fled out of Barnett's field into the lane towards the village, flanked by his cattle, who also charged in shock. Thereafter Surman's move-ments are difficult to pin down. It is not recorded where she went or whom she told of the attack. At the trial when questioned she added just one inchoate detail to the butchers' account. 'Looking in the direction from which the report came,' she remembered, 'I saw the Rev. Mr Parker run towards Mr Barnett's hedge.'

Minutes later, Lench and Giles had almost trapped the murderer at the scene. But a moment's hesitation had allowed him to escape, pursued by Giles, into the lanes to the east. Lench then began his desperate search for help. Within a few minutes he had found James Tustin near Pound Farm and had begged him to come after Giles and the murderer. The two men sprinted back towards the glebe, turning into another track to look for Giles. Without any clue as to which of the maze-like paths that branched out to the north, west and south he had taken, they abandoned the chase. It was eight or nine minutes after the gunshot when Lench and Tustin returned to the spot where Parker lay, sprawled helplessly in the grass.

Tustin gazed down at the bloodied body. Just a minute earlier he had told Lench that the victim was definitely not Parker, 'as the parson had just gone up the fields for his cows'. But now, confronted with the body, he was able to confirm that it was the clergyman – a stranger to Lench. As he stared down, Tustin claimed he heard Parker give a final, feeble gasp, as if he could see the last of his life ebbing away. Lench, however, would challenge this account at the inquest, stating that when they returned 'he was quite dead'.

Parker's bloodied corpse cut a frightful picture. The smouldering wadding that had entered his body with the shot had by now ignited into little flames which ran along the seams of his linen breeches and small clothes.* Little puffs of smoke and the sickly stench of burning flesh were 'rising from his right side', which John Lench later described as being 'all of a mooze'. The right side of his head was bludgeoned in and blood oozed from an inch-long gash on his temple. It was not just the corpse that was alight; Tustin noticed 'the grass round the wound was burning'. Nothing could be done to help Parker. The emphasis now lay upon a swift parochial response: in capturing the man responsible and dragging him back to the village for interrogation.

Lench and Tustin left the glebe for a second time, hurrying towards Pound Farm, where they hoped to find John Barnett. Although Barnett's mother held the deeds to the property, he was its de facto master, with the power to instruct the workers and make use of the horses and weaponry. Barnett knew the land well, the slopes of the fields, the gaps in the hedgerows, the bustling or deserted lanes into which a fugitive might retreat or steal himself away. As the overseer, an elected parish official, he also had the moral authority to command the villagers to action.

A quarter of an hour earlier, at about 5 p.m., John Barnett had left Pound Farm for a quick tour of his fields. He called at Mr Jones' barn, which stood a short distance from his gate at the far side of the crossroads, then turned towards the Pigeon House Field, where he checked the work of two farmhands who were mowing grass and cutting thistles. Barnett had not stopped to talk and was back at Pound Farm by 5.15 p.m. 'Two or three minutes afterwards' Lench and Tustin arrived, breathless, in his fold-yard.

---

* Undergarments worn traditionally by clergymen.

Barnett was standing beside his gate when Tustin informed him that 'he had found Mr Parker dead' in the glebe meadows. The farmer made no immediate response and Lench, anxious for his companion Thomas Giles, who had now been gone about a quarter of an hour in search of the murderer, asked him 'if he would please go to the place and look at the body'. Barnett refused. He gave no explanation. He just stood, with no trace of agitation, beside his gate.

Lench must have been confused by Barnett's apparent indifference to the serious crime that had just been committed. The parish clergyman had been hunted down in his own glebe fields, shot and then clubbed to death. Nothing like this had happened in living memory, and already vital minutes had elapsed since Giles had disappeared into the lane after the murderer. With no assistance forthcoming Lench and Tustin left Barnett in his fold-yard and walked down Church Lane towards Oddingley Rectory, carrying the terrible news with them. They 'told the servant girl what had happened', then turned once again back towards the body.

Meanwhile, news of the attack was being carried by word of mouth through the parish: from field to field, fold-yard to farmhouse, by labourers, children and passing travellers through the lanes. Many abandoned their work and started towards Parker's glebe to see for themselves if the story was true or a midsummer hoax. Thomas Langford, a worker at Church Farm, learnt the news from a passing farmer. At the opposite end of the village an 11-year-old boy named Hubert told Sarah Marshall of Pineapple Farm that Parker had been shot dead. She rushed to the glebe alongside a growing number of labourers, but there was little she could do. Her husband, a farmer with the resources and authority to organise a manhunt, was also away from Oddingley at Bromsgrove Fair.

Some reports of Parker's death were horribly distorted. In the Pigeon House Field Thomas Alsop, one of Barnett's farmhands, heard about the murder at around six o'clock when a boy named Thomas Greenhill was sent with the news. Greenhill told Alsop that 'someone had set the parson on fire'. At this, Alsop left his tools and returned to Pound Farm, where he found Barnett 'bringing the cows out of the yard for me to take to Mr Green's of Smite'. These were the same cattle that Susan Surman had milked an hour earlier and Alsop was surprised that Barnett now wanted them driven out of the parish. 'He had not said anything to me before about taking the cows,' the labourer remembered.

As Alsop led the cattle out of the fold-yard and into the lane, he asked Barnett why there was a great number of villagers 'riding up the Rye Grass Field' towards Parker's glebe.

Barnett replied that 'someone has been killing or shooting the parson', but as he spoke did not look Alsop in the eye. Instead he bent his head to the ground. 'He smiled and seemed pleased,' Alsop recalled.

John Perkins learnt of the murder at about half past five. He was still tending to his bonfire when 'a little girl' – perhaps Parker's seven-year-old daughter Mary – appeared in his field. She told Perkins that the Reverend had been shot and Mrs Parker would like to see him 'directly'. Perkins threw down his tools and ran into the lane, leaving the bonfire burning behind him.

At the rectory Perkins found Mary Parker in the garden. She was leaning against a set of milk pails in the yard. 'For God's sake!' she cried when she saw Perkins. 'Go to Mr Pyndar directly, for I have no friend but you and him!'

Two miles away, in the neighbouring parish, Reverend Reginald Pyndar, one of King George's justices of the peace, was haymaking in the meadows near his rectory at Hadzor. It was around a quarter to six when John Perkins entered the field, dismounted and told Pyndar that Parker had been killed in his glebe – shot, and his head beaten in. For a moment Pyndar listened to Perkins' story, trying to absorb it. Pyndar was 51 years old, educated, sure-footed and a well-known member of the local set. He had the authority and personality to restore order to Oddingley in the wake of the murder, and as Perkins turned his horse for his return journey Pyndar called for his mare.

'I will meet you in Mr Barnett's Grounds as soon as I can,' he shouted as John Perkins rode away at the gallop.

In 1806 there was no professional policing system in England to track fugitives, and the best chance of capturing suspected criminals following a violent crime lay in swift action. The further a villain could get from a crime scene, the better their chances of escape. Much then depended on the hue and cry, an ancient social device which ensured that however fast a suspect ran they could never outpace the shrieks and cries ('Murder! Murder!' or 'Stop thief!') that followed them along streets and alleys, through lanes and into market-places, inns and houses as the message was passed from one person to another in a fearful relay of voices. A comic ballad published in 1782 by the poet William Cowper dramatised the raising of a hue and cry.

> Six gentlemen upon the road
> Thus seeing Gilpin fly,
> With postboy scampering in the rear,
> They raised the hue and cry:
>
> 'Stop thief! Stop thief! – A highwayman!'
> Not one of them was mute;
> And all and each that passed that way
> Did join in the pursuit.

The hue and cry was particularly effective in urban areas, where a mass of bystanders, shopkeepers and passers-by could be animated by a single shout. It appears in the famous scene in *Oliver Twist* when the Artful Dodger snatches a handkerchief from Mr Brownlow's pocket as he stands reading outside a bookshop in London. Oliver, the Dodger's unwitting new recruit, is mistaken for the thief by the confused crowd, which rolls and roars behind him as it chases him down.

'Stop thief! Stop thief!' There is a magic in the sound. The tradesman leaves his counter, and the car-man his wagon; the butcher throws down his tray; the baker his basket; the milkman his pail; the errand-boy his parcels; the schoolboy his marbles; the paviour his pickaxe; the child his battledore. Away they run, pell-mell, helter-skelter, slap-dash, tearing, yelling, screaming, knocking down the passengers as they turn the corners, rousing up the dogs, and astonishing the fowls: and streets, squares, and courts re-echo with the sound.

Despite the lower population density, the hue and cry was often similarly effective in rural areas. In one case that was widely reported, in Surrey in 1742, two highwaymen ambushed and threatened to rob a man outside the town of Ripley. The spirited victim quickly sounded a hue and cry, riding after the men crying out 'Highwaymen, highwaymen!' as he went, sparking a pursuit of his assailants which continued for several miles through the country-side. At some point the victim's calls were heard by two bystanders who fetched a brace of pistols, mounted their horses and joined the chase.

The highwaymen were pursued by a growing crowd to Ripley Green, where a cricket match was under way. Here the crowd tightened around them. Their cry changed from 'Stop! Thieves! Highwaymen!' to 'Knock them down, knock them down!' The sportsmen closed on the men with their bats. Helplessly cornered, one of the highwaymen shot and killed a cricketer seconds before he was arrested by the local constable. The second highwayman was taken shortly afterwards, a court scribe recording, 'The town being alarmed, [he was] beset on all sides.'

At Oddingley Reverend Parker's desperate cry of 'Murder!' was a final act that can be interpreted variously: as a flash of bravery, of helplessness or even as a glimmer of the same stoic resolve that had seen him through the painful years of the tithe dispute. Perhaps even as Parker felt the weight of the shot crashing into his middle, he had a second to accept that his life was going to end violently and all that remained was to ensure that his attacker would be captured.

But his attempt to raise a hue and cry failed. The murder scene had been carefully selected, and only Susan Surman, James Tustin, Thomas Giles and John Lench were within earshot. Tustin and Surman failed to repeat Parker's cry, and the butchers, unsure of what was happening, chose to investigate further rather than turn back towards the village, cottages and farmhouses behind them. In the crucial few minutes following the attack not a single person was stirred to action, and the murderer – who evidently knew the surrounding countryside well – was able to escape into the thinly populated fields to the west, away from Oddingley village, away from the hamlet of Dunhampstead and the busy farms and fields which dotted the weaving road north to Hadzor.

By the time John Barnett refused Lench's plea for help ten minutes had passed since the attack and any chance of an effective hue and cry had been dashed. When Perkins left for Pyndar's house at about half past five the likelihood of a quick capture was fading with the afternoon sun.

Betty Perkins had learnt the news of the murder at the same time as her husband and at about 5.30 p.m. had set off for the glebe fields to see Parker's body. On her way through the village she was stopped by a stranger on horseback, who asked her what had happened. This was a farmer, Mr Hemmus, from Woofferton in Shropshire. Hemmus had been to Bromsgrove Fair that day and, like many others in the lanes, was now travelling home. Betty told him that their clergyman had been attacked and murdered, and Hemmus replied that he 'would go after the murderer if anybody would go along with him'.

James Tustin, who was standing nearby, instantly volunteered to join Hemmus 'if anyone would lend him a horse'. Betty Perkins agreed to do so, and the party set off towards Pound Farm, where Tustin left them at the gate to change his clothes. Meanwhile Betty carried on to Oddingley Lane Farm, where she had 'her horse got ready' and brought back up to the gate for Tustin. Betty then continued up to the glebe, where she met Tustin's young son. The boy told her that his father had been prevented from joining Mr

Hemmus by his mistress, Mrs Barnett. Old Mrs Barnett had refused to allow Tustin to leave the farm with a criminal loose in the countryside. If it was not for Mrs Barnett, the boy explained, 'he would have gone in a minute'. Without help, Hemmus had left Oddingley and continued on his journey home.

As frustrated in her attempts to aid the chase as Lench had been before her, Betty Perkins continued to the centre of the glebe, where many villagers were crowded in mute horror about Parker's body. The clergyman's groin was exposed and badly burnt, his head bloodied and battered. Surman, who by now had returned to the scene of the crime, had doused the flames and pulled off Parker's singed breeches and underclothes, exposing the charred and shot-freckled skin below. After initially fleeing the glebe, it seems that Surman had spent some time at Pound Farm during the preceding 20 minutes. She too had witnessed the Barnetts' attempts to disrupt the manhunt. 'Four or five others offered to go with Mr Barnett's servant [Tustin],' she later remembered. 'But Mr John Barnett would not let him go.'

Thomas Giles now reappeared with the news that the murderer had threatened him and had run off toward Hindlip, a neighbouring parish. Giles then rooted in the hedgerow in search of the weapon that he had seen half an hour before. Soon he drew out an old muzzle-loading shotgun. The stock of the weapon was broken in two at the lock. After shooting the clergyman, the murderer had delivered a series – perhaps two or three – of awful injuries to Parker's head with the stock of the weapon. It was a wild and merciless crime. The executioner would have stared down into his victim's eyes as he delivered the fatal blows. As if setting the scraps of evidence down in a hateful collage, Giles laid the broken, bent shotgun down beside Parker's corpse. Tustin picked up the gun bag and placed it over the clergyman's exposed groin.

At six o'clock Reverend Pyndar arrived in the glebe meadow to assume control of the investigation. With no police force people relied upon the scattered network of unpaid magistrates to marshal their communities and to act in emergencies. As a justice of the peace, 'the workhorse of everyday magistrate power', Pyndar held an ancient feudal title laced with imagery and prestige. A vast proportion of the JPs in England were well-to-do parsons and country squires (to be eligible an individual had to have an income in excess of £100 a year) like Pyndar. They were considered well suited to the role, which further raised their status and strengthened their influence over a community. Ever since the fourteenth century magistrates had been responsible for hearing minor offences, and they had the power to have petty offenders whipped or thrown into houses of correction and more serious criminals committed to gaol to await trial at the assize – or criminal – courts.

Pyndar looked down at Parker's corpse. He picked up the bag and asked Perkins what he thought. Perkins replied that he 'thought it came from Droitwich as it smelt salty'. Pyndar then ordered Parker's body to be removed to the rectory. But rather than carrying the corpse, a decision was made to send for a chair from the rectory on which the body could be transported more suitably. Several minutes later a pathetic cortège embarked for Church Lane. The corpse – slumped back in the chair – was carried by Tustin and some other farmhands towards the rectory as if it was the centrepiece of a bizarre religious procession. A train of parishioners, passers-by, children and curious onlookers walked behind.

What followed in the minutes afterwards would be disputed in the village for years to come. Susan Surman claimed that Pyndar, shocked at John Barnett's apathy, determined to seek him out for an explanation. Surman had told Pyndar that her master could be found at his farmhouse, but when he knocked at the door Old Mrs Barnett told him her son was out – 'that he had gone to the Captain's'. Pyndar then wheeled around to confront Surman, whom he accused of 'telling him a tale'. The dairymaid – in a dangerous breach of loyalty – protested, 'I have not at all, for Mr John Barnett is in the parlour [and] had just before stuck his head out of the window and told James Tustin to go to the stable [and her] to mind her milking.'

At this Pyndar returned to Pound Farm, forcing entry to the

farmhouse and dragging Barnett out into the yard. According to Surman, it was a dramatic scene. It was now early evening and knots of villagers were gathered outside Pound Farm watching the action unravel. They saw Pyndar interrogate Barnett, and as he did so the bearers of the chair carrying Parker's helpless corpse edged into view behind them. In full sight of the villagers Pyndar pressed Barnett asking 'if he knew anything of *that* job'. Barnett replied that he did not, and protested that he was 'very sorry that it had happened'.

There is something improbable in Surman's story. She seems to suggest that Tustin was at Pound Farm when several other sources have him transporting Parker's body to the rectory. More importantly, nobody who was present would ever corroborate her account of Pyndar fetching Barnett out of the parlour. There were, though, various reports of a confrontation between the magistrate and the farmer. John Perkins claimed that Pyndar met Barnett further along Church Lane as if, he reasoned, Barnett was returning from Captain Evans'. Perkins heard Pyndar call to the farmer, 'Barnett, you have had a very pretty job happen in your parish, are you not ashamed of it? When those two butchers came to your house to go in search of the murderer you refused to go?'

Barnett said nothing. The magistrate – seemingly overcome with fury or frustration: a friend and peer murdered, the suspect escaped and one of the parish's leading men apparently indifferent – then raged at the farmer. He shouted, 'You rascal! You villain! If you had a dog and had any love for him you would have saved him if you could! – I shall think of you as long as I live.' John Barnett dropped his head and 'never said a word'.

Parker's corpse arrived at the rectory at about 7 p.m., around two hours after he had set off up Church Lane for his cows. Gone in those few hours were the tranquillity of a summer afternoon and the fragile peace of the village, which so often in recent months and years had been threatened. The noises of labourers at work – the rattle of their handcarts, the swinging of scythes and the scrape of rakes – were replaced by the sound of horses' hooves as George Day, the Parkers' servant boy, left the rectory garden on Perkins' old nag for Worcester.

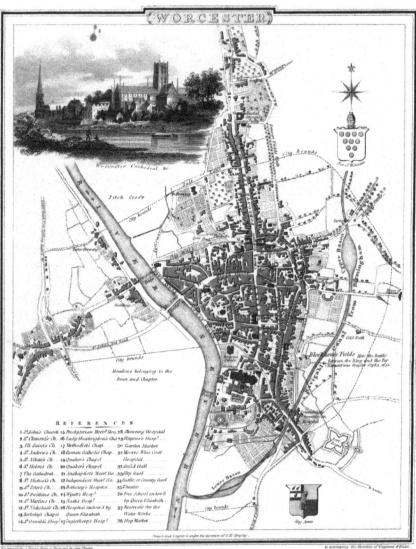

Worcester in the early nineteenth century,
printed by Roper & Cole, 1808

That all minds should now turn towards Worcester was logical. It was a fine city, built almost entirely of red brick with the exception of a handful of public buildings, its churches and exquisite medieval cathedral. Although its streets were capacious, newly paved and lighted, the city, with a population of 12,792, offered two sources of hope for the fleeing murderer. First, it would allow him to plunge into the crowds, where he might have friends or accomplices lying in wait. Second, it would give him access to a great number of routes of further escape. Worcester sat almost at the heart of England and was served by a rapidly developing network of turnpike roads heading off in all directions: towards Tewkesbury to the south, to Birmingham in the north and Evesham in the south-east. The city was popular with travellers and tradesmen, who came to view, purchase or collect orders of its famous porcelain or gloves, and at all hours of the day wagons, mail and stage coaches rolled sluggishly out of the yards of its major public houses into Foregate Street, Broad Street and the High Street. In his *Brief History of Worcester* (1806) J. Tymbs noted that Worcester 'is generally allowed by most travellers not to have an equal'. If the murderer could reach the city before the news of his crime, then he could easily secure passage onwards.

Worcester lay just six miles from Oddingley, but for a traveller on the winding lanes or wading through the long summer grass it was not a simple distance to cover. Without risking the turnpike – known locally as the Droitwich Road – there was little chance of him reaching Worcester in less than two hours. The Birmingham Light Coach had already left earlier that afternoon, and the next best opportunities to escape the county were the Bristol Mail, which occasionally took passengers and departed from the Star and Garter public house in Foregate Street at 8.30 p.m., and the London Stage Coach, which left Angel Street in the city centre at 10 p.m. each Tuesday. That coach, perhaps, was the most logical. It would arrive three days later at the Bull and Mouth coaching inn in the City of London.

The primary aim of George Day's gallop to the city that evening was to close these routes of escape. Then he would deliver Thomas

Giles and John Lench's description of the wanted man to the authorities. In contrast to the lightly policed community at Oddingley,
Worcester was tightly governed. It had five aldermen – senior
members of the local corporation – who also served as justices of
the peace, a sheriff, thirteen constables and four beadles. The centre
of Worcester was about forty minutes' ride away at the gallop. If
the murderer intended to take either the London or the Bristol
coaches that night, there was still enough time to catch him.

CHAPTER 7

Dead and Gone

Church Farm, Oddingley, Evening, 24 June 1806

Oddingley's lanes were far busier than usual on Midsummer evening. They were not only filled with the villagers who gathered at the top of Church Lane and beside the rectory gate, where they awaited orders from Pyndar or a dramatic appearance of the captured murderer, but with farmers, traders and artisans riding or walking home from Bromsgrove Fair. Among the travellers were Thomas Green, a tailor from Upton Snodsbury, a nearby village, and his son William. According to Green's later account, they had met John Perkins just north of Oddingley, near Newland Common at between half past five and six o'clock. Green was acquainted with several of the villagers, and Perkins told him that Parker had been shot. At this, Green and his son turned their horses towards the glebe, where they saw Parker's body lying where it had fallen. Shortly after, they formed part of the macabre procession to the rectory. Green recalled that he had 'staid [*sic*] some time' in the village before deciding, at between seven and eight o'clock, to visit Captain Evans at Church Farm.

Nothing had been heard of Captain Evans in the hours that immediately followed Parker's murder. He had not joined Thomas Clewes, Hardcourt, Marshall and William Barnett at Bromsgrove Fair, so it was natural for Green to suppose he might be found at Church Farm. It was just a few minutes' ride down Church Lane, which twisted sharply left around the borders of a pear orchard, from the rectory to the Captain's home. Green fastened his horse to the fold-yard gate and knocked at the farmhouse door. The tailor must have been well known to the household as he was instantly invited in by one of the servants. Green entered the parlour. There he saw Captain Evans and John Barnett sat at the table. 'They were drinking something out of a black bottle.'

Thomas Green, imagining the two men knew nothing of what had happened, told them of the murder, to which 'both seemed surprised as if they had never heard of it before'. The Captain, by way of an explanation, took up a scrap of paper from the table, telling Green that they had just been settling the income tax together. Barnett remained as silent as he had been for much of the past two hours.

Green's testimony was corroborated by Clement Churchill, a labourer who had worked at Church Farm several years earlier and had stood in for George Banks at the drawing of the militia. Churchill continued to be a frequent visitor to the property. He had spent the late afternoon at Church Farm and had heard two people who he supposed were the Captain and John Barnett talking in the parlour. He recalled that Green arrived later, and was admitted to the room. The door was then shut. At this point Churchill got up to begin his journey home. But as he left he heard Catherine Banks, the house-keeper, cry out, 'Lord have mercy upon me! He seems no more concerned than if a dog was shot.' Who *he* was, the Captain or John Barnett, remained ambiguous.

The news of Parker's murder arrived at Netherwood Farm at about seven o'clock. John Clewes recalled, 'Some men who were riding past my brother's house [along Netherwood Lane towards Crowle] shouted out the parson had been shot: I did not know who they were and I did not go in pursuit of the murderer as I did not think the report was true.'

Thomas Arden, one of the farmhands, was waiting for Thomas Clewes, who had been out all day. Arden saw him return to the fold-yard at about seven o'clock. He noticed that Clewes 'put the horse in the stable himself', that he was wearing his day clothes and 'the horse did not seem to have been ridden a great deal'. Clewes then disappeared, and Arden did not see him again until an hour or so later, between eight and nine o'clock, when they all gathered for supper. Not a word was said about the murder, Arden recalled, as they ate.

An explanation of Clewes' movements that evening was later provided by William Chance, a 27-year-old labourer who was employed at the time by Captain Evans at Church Farm. Chance had spent the afternoon mowing clover in the Church Field with his father. At around six o'clock they had seen George Banks coming down the meadows where they were working. Once Banks was within earshot he called down to them, 'By God boys! The parson is shot!' Chance noticed that, as he spoke, Banks 'laughed . . . and seemed glad it was done'. A little later William Chance set down his tools and made for the farmhouse 'for some drink'. At harvest time the workforce on any farm was nourished with a steady stream of weak local ale or – especially in the counties of Worcestershire, Herefordshire and in the West Country – an equivalent drawn in late summer direct from the cider presses or earlier in the year from cider casks or barrels. By half past seven Chance and his father would have been at the scythe for more than twelve hours, and with their supplies of drink exhausted he set off for the kitchen to fetch more.

The sunlight was waning but darkness would not fall for two hours yet. Chance arrived at the farmhouse and paused for a moment in the kitchen. He could hear men laughing from the parlour, voices that he instantly recognised. Leaving the farmhouse a second later carrying the drink, he passed the parlour window. He glanced inside. Captain Evans, John Barnett and Thomas Clewes were all sat around the table. There was drink of some kind and glasses on the table. Chance 'dared not wait long as he knew that if he had been loitering and the Captain had discovered it he would have sworn at him'. The vivid picture, though, impressed itself strongly upon Chance's mind. There was a distinct light in the faces of the men and a warmth and sparkle in their voices. Everything was caught in a snapshot imprinted upon his imagination: the oak table, the dark bottle filled with wine or cider, the glasses and men, all captured in the glow of the fading sun. It was 'as though they were rejoicing', William Chance would later say, 'as though something had happened'.

CHAPTER 8

The Man in the Long Blue Coat

24, 25 June 1806

Not a single villager had seen the man who had passed through Oddingley that afternoon, murdering the clergyman in his own meadows before vanishing almost as soon as he had arrived, for many of them as indistinct and silent as a soft summer breeze. The only description of him came from Thomas Giles and John Lench, who were strangers in Oddingley, unfamiliar with its lanes and most of its people. When questioned, they repeated the description that was soon to be circulated across Worcestershire and beyond: that the suspect stood about five foot five inches tall, that he had a round ruddy face and thick hanging lantern jaw; that he wore a round old-fashioned hat and – most strikingly of all – a dark blue greatcoat with white metal buttons.

This description was sufficient to supply most villagers with a theory. This theory went that Reverend Parker had not been killed by a stranger unknown to the parish, but by someone who visited it frequently and whose face and figure were a common feature of its lanes. At around seven o'clock the hypothesis that had been developing was all but confirmed with the appearance of Thomas Colwell, a carpenter from Tibberton. Colwell called at the rectory, where he found John Perkins comforting Mary Parker. Colwell told them both that he thought Richard Heming was Reverend Parker's murderer.

An hour before, the carpenter had been walking along a lane in the parish of Hindlip – just three miles west of Oddingley and a short distance from where Giles had given up his pursuit. He was passing the home of a farmer called Brookes when he had heard a thrashing noise, and Heming, whom he knew reasonably well, had come tumbling over the top of a high hedge 'although a gate was just by'. Colwell was taken by complete surprise. 'Heming looked very pale and confused, and he seemed as if fatigued.'

Richard Heming had not properly explained himself to Colwell, but did stop for a moment to beg him not to mention their meeting to a soul. 'Two men were after him,' he said. At this, Heming had turned on his heels. Colwell had not had the temerity to challenge him further. He had gone away 'at a good fast step, but was no way hurrysome', Colwell said. He was wearing 'a long blue greatcoat which appeared rather too long for him' and an old-fashioned hat with a low crown. As he disappeared along the lane in the direction of Tibberton, Heming had lifted the skirts of his coat up over his arms. Colwell knew Heming well. He was sure of his story.

This evidence, which was quickly relayed to Reverend Pyndar, marked an important milestone in his fledgling investigation. Until now the afternoon's events had comprised the fractured stories of various witnesses and had lacked a common thread to bind them together. But now, with a chief suspect identified, the case could begin to take shape and a narrative be formed. There were many implications of Colwell's evidence, but the first – and the most pressing – was that Heming had escaped the parish and was travelling in a south-westerly direction. It seemed plausible that he could have covered the three miles from Parker's glebe across country – wading through the long grass, vaulting fences and hedgerows – in approximately an hour. Once he reached Hindlip he could travel far more swiftly along the lanes that snaked down for two further miles to the outskirts of Worcester.

Unbeknown to those in Oddingley there were more sightings of Heming, which wouldn't be reported until later. Richard Page, the landlord of the Virgin Tavern, a public house in Newtown just outside Worcester, served Heming a pint of ale that evening, which he drank 'off as quick as he could' then 'went away directly'. Page noticed that Heming had 'a blue coat hanging on his arm' and that 'he seemed in a hurry and very much confused'. Some minutes later, outside the inn, Heming opened a gate for Thomas Hill, a farmer on his way home from Bromsgrove Fair. But by the time George Day called at the inn around 20 minutes later, Heming was gone.

Plotting the precise sequence of the sightings which marked Heming's flight from Oddingley is difficult. In 1806 few houses contained clocks, and most people, especially in rural areas, did not carry watches, therefore most times stated in later testimony were approximations which in themselves became even less accurate with the passing of time. Before the introduction of factory discipline those in rural areas for the most part worked and lived by the sun, listened for the chime of the church clock and estimated as best they could. Such processes worked tolerably well on a daily basis but were aggravating in criminal cases. For example, Page and Hill stated that Heming was at the Virgin Tavern at about six o'clock, whereas Thomas Colwell claimed to have seen him four miles to the north at precisely the same time. Richard Heming's exact whereabouts on Midsummer evening, then, is blurred by the contradictory voices. What can be assumed with some degree of certainty is that by around half past six or seven o'clock he was on the very edges of Worcester. He had evidently decided that his best mode of escape lay with one of the city's coaches. And the London Stage Coach would leave Angel Street in just three hours' time.

Richard Heming's identification as chief suspect would have surprised few in Oddingley. For around two months villagers had been growing increasingly conscious of the labourer's erratic behaviour. He would appear abruptly in certain lanes and fields – greeting labourers, posing questions and bothering dairymaids – before vanishing completely without either trace or explanation. Much of Heming's strange activity centred on the north of the village, about the coarse grass and thick furze bushes of Oddingley Common and Wash Pool Lane, and the hedgerows which ringed Pound Farm's meadows and Parker's glebe. Here he was a familiar sight in May and June, as the early-summer birds sang in the trees and dragonflies skimmed across the surface of Barnett's pool.

In mid-May John Perkins had noticed Heming pacing back and forth in Barnett's fields, where a faggot of thorns and a bolting of straw had been thrown down into the ditch adjoining the glebe meadows. Parker had also seen Heming nearby and had asked Perkins if he knew what the man was doing. The farmer had been unable to supply an answer.

Joseph Colley, a 55-year-old farmhand, had been more suspicious. During May and June he had been labouring near the Wash Pool Fields and had frequently seen Heming 'skulking' about the lanes and Parker's glebe. Colley was on friendly terms with his clergyman (according to his later account, he knew him 'as well as all who lived in the parish'), and one day Parker had told him that 'he could not think what Heming wanted' lurking in the lanes. Colley, who was evidently a straightforward man, had told the clergyman, 'Heming wanted to shoot him and knock him on the head'.

After Parker's murder Colley's pithy analysis of the situation appeared suspiciously prophetic, but the elderly labourer had reasons for making such a claim. Colley was a regular drinker at the Red Lion, a spacious brick hostelry just south of Droitwich on the Worcester road. On several occasions Colley had seen Heming and Thomas Clewes in the taproom. Each time 'Clewes was treating and urging Heming to drink.' One early June evening Clewes had proposed a toast in full view of the whole bar 'to the death of the Bonaparte of Oddingley'. Heming had said that 'he had a nasty job to do at Oddingley, but it was then too late to go as it was past five o'clock'.

Richard Heming was a curious slippery character. All sources agree that he came from Bredon's Norton, a beautiful village of handsome half-timbered cottages which sprawled languidly at the foot of Bredon Hill in the south-east corner of Worcestershire. But in the parish records he is as difficult to pin down as he would later prove to be in Oddingley. In the late eighteenth and early nineteenth centuries there was just one family in Bredon's Norton with the surname

Heming. It was headed by a Mrs Mary Heming, who had been supported by the parish for many years and was the mother of five children. She had been born Mary Barrow in 1751 and had become Mary Heming at the age of 22 when she married William Heming of Earl's Croome, a few parishes to the north-east. Over the next 15 years Mary Heming had busily applied herself to family life, producing a steady succession of children until her husband died in 1787 leaving her a widow at the age of 36. None of these children was called Richard.

But these records leave one child unaccounted for. When Mary married in 1773 she was already mother of a boy named Richard. This Richard was illegitimate, baptised on 23 April 1766 while Mary was just fifteen. Children born out of wedlock were usually glibly recorded as 'bastard' or 'base-born' in the local rolls, but Reverend William Davenport, Bredon's clergyman at the time, was an exceptionally careful chronicler. For this illegitimate child he entered the name Richard Jeynes into the register. It is one of just two sets of surviving evidence about the child. The other is a legal bond dated 22 April 1766 from Richard Joines, a yeoman from the parish of Beckford, who agreed to pay £30 towards the upkeep of a bastard child born to Mary Barrow of Bredon.

In all probability this was the Richard Heming who appeared to murderous effect in Parker's glebe field 40 years later. Whether he suffered in childhood from the stigma of being illegitimate it is hard to know. Perhaps it left his character scarred and unsettled? Perhaps Richard Heming never knew who his real father was. It does seem clear, however, that there was distance between the child and his supposed father. Young Richard adopted his stepfather's surname and most probably spent his youth under his mother's roof in Bredon's Norton with his half-brothers and -sisters.

Around the turn of the century Richard Heming left his family home and relocated to Droitwich at the opposite end of the county. This was an unusual move. Only rarely did villagers uproot in the middle years of their life, leaving behind their immediate family, contacts and the security that they offered. By 1800 Richard Heming was in his mid-thirties and his relocation probably reflected a change of circumstances. The most likely explanation is that Heming moved north to be with a woman, as around the turn of the century he had met Elizabeth Burton, the daughter of a successful carpenter. She was around ten years younger than Heming and, it seems, they fell for one another. Though they did not marry, in just a few years Elizabeth Heming – as she was now styling herself – had given birth to three daughters, whom she christened with unusual and romantic names: Mary-Agnes, July Ann and Harriet. Whether the couple's union was simply one of deep mutual affection, it is impossible to say. Perhaps Heming had been tempted north by love and the draw of family life. Or perhaps Elizabeth Burton had been – just like Richard's mother before – unlucky to fall pregnant with an illegitimate child. Or it may have been that Heming's swift departure from Bredon was forced: that he left the village of his birth because he was no longer welcome. Given his future conduct, this was a possibility.

In Droitwich Heming soon gained a reputation as the local rogue. He toured the nearby villages begging cider from farmhouse kitchens, fishing for part-time work and selling goods on the black market. Earlier in 1806 Heming had even knocked at the door of Oddingley rectory, desperate for a mug of cider. Mrs Parker remembered the little man who greeted her at the door much like a modern-day door-to-door salesman. He went on to tempt her husband with an offer on a quantity of malt at the rate of '6d. a strike under the regular price' and at the far more generous 'Tewkesbury measure'.

The profits Heming made from selling black market goods proved to be an important supplement to his more steady income as a skilled carpenter and wheelwright. One account of Heming had him, just a few months before Parker's murder, assisting Mr Smith, a brush maker from Worcester, to fell a good-sized coppice near Droitwich. However, before the job was satisfactorily completed Smith had received a letter informing him that Heming was selling a number of the harvested poles to Captain Evans, which he had no authority to do. Smith had instantly sought Richard Heming out at the Red Lion in Droitwich and threatened to have him sent to gaol. Only after Heming claimed that he had intended to settle for the poles separately did Mr Smith let the matter drop. And the evidence suggests that this was not an isolated incident. In Droitwich it was rumoured that Heming had begun a second career as a thief, with local gossip fixing his name to a number of unsolved robberies.

Heming had joined the ranks of the misty Georgian underworld, a concealed society of beggars, petty thieves, sharpers, rustlers, dossers and cheats; a class of entrenched criminals who festered in gloomy, unseen corners. His ability to source such a wide variety of products suggested that he may have had links with the smuggling gang at Trench Wood. Perhaps he was the resident of the robber's den discovered in 1805, less than a year before? No proof of this was ever presented to the authorities, but a report in *Berrow's Worcester Journal* as far back as March in 1801 records, 'Committed to our house of correction by the Rev. Arthur Onslow . . . of Worcester, Richard Heming, on suspicion of stealing out of the building of George Brooke at Kinlet, an iron mattock, a chisel, several boards and other things.' Whether this was our Richard Heming or not is once again uncertain as Kinlet lay almost 20 miles and a good day's walk to the north-east of Droitwich, but the details fit with the pattern in his behaviour.

Whatever scrapes with the law Heming had endured in the past six years, in the early months of 1806 he was at large in Oddingley, continuing his eccentric lifestyle: begging cider, bothering villagers, appearing from behind hedgerows one moment before vanishing into byways the next. Shades of Heming's character can be found in *Great Expectations*, in the wretched biography of the convict Abel Magwitch, who confesses to Pip shortly after his appearance that he spent many years in his youth 'Tramping, begging, thieving, working sometimes when I could, though that wasn't as often as you may think . . . bit of a poacher, bit of a labourer, bit of a wagoner, a bit of a haymaker, a bit of a hawker, a bit of most things that don't pay and lead to trouble'.

Heming's was a capricious existence that might have brought him

notoriety and certainly did not win him friends. When he approached
William Colley, one of Oddingley's most hardbitten labourers, in
the middle of May, asking whether he could borrow his horse for
a trip to Eckington – a riverside village in the south of the county
close to his mother's home at Bredon – Colley flatly refused. His
decision was reflective of local opinion: 'Heming was a bad one,'
Colley later said.

Throughout early June sightings of Heming intensified. He would
loiter in Barnett's meadows, engaging labourers in conversation when
they passed. Susan Surman saw him regularly when fetching the
cows down to Pound Farm for milking. 'For three week previous to
the murder,' she claimed 'night and morning he used to walk up
and down the meadow called the Middle Wash Pool. He came I
thought to court me; he had made quite a path in the mowing grass
and it leads to no place.'

Surman's suspicions were not based on mere vanity. There was
little obvious reason for him to be lurking in the lanes when he could
be working elsewhere. To her he was a perplexing stranger and his
attentions were unwelcome. At some point before the murder she
had complained to John Barnett that this odd man was 'detaining'
her in the fields. Perhaps this was too cryptic for Barnett, who rather
than investigate the matter further 'scoffed' at her. He used the
episode as an excuse to tease Surman, referring to this mysterious
man as her 'sweetheart'.

And Heming did not just cut a suspicious figure, but also a notable
one. 'Heming used to dress in a dark blue coat, red handkerchief
and corduroy breeches,' Surman recollected, a fact which in itself
was odd. During harvest most labourers donned smock frocks, airy
linen overgarments that were easily washed and mended – over
loose-fitting breeches – which combined to keep them cool as they
worked under the summer sun. But Heming's coat was reported
over and over again in eye-witness accounts. At once it seems clumsy,
heavy, uncomfortable and intriguing, its spacious pockets a possible
home for any number of hidden objects.

In the early nineteenth century Britons relied on greatcoats from

October to April, not just for warmth but also for their other func-
tion – as something like a portable suitcase. They were especially
popular with artisans, who had to haul their tools about from job
to job, but they weren't just limited to the lower classes; even the
great Dr Johnson preserved an air of his humble beginnings by
sporting a greatcoat long after he had become a national celebrity.
In Boswell's *Life of Dr Johnson* the author wrote, 'Upon his tour,
when journeying, he wore boots, and a very wide brown cloth
great coat, with pockets which might have almost held the two
volumes of his folio dictionary.'

Why should Heming have persisted with his coat in May and June?
It must have had a purpose. Was he making use of its deep pockets
to carry his carpentry tools – chisels, hammers and measuring rules
– about the county? Was the coat merely a faithful travelling
companion to protect him from sudden turns in the capricious
Worcestershire weather? Or did the long blue coat have a more
sinister purpose? Did Heming need a bulky overcoat to conceal a
weapon as he prowled the hedgerows and lanes? John Chellingworth,

A romanticised lithograph of an English gentleman out snipe hunting with a
flintlock shotgun from *Ackermann's Repository of Arts*, 1809

the labourer who had left Oddingley heading south before dawn on Midsummer morning, had recently seen Heming 'carrying a bag with something in it like a long stick' – 'It seemed long enough for a gun,' he mused later.

The need to conceal this gun perhaps explains why Heming persisted with the greatcoat in the late spring and early summer. The round hat that Lench and Giles observed on the day of the murder may also have had a sinister purpose – to shield his eyes as he lowered the shotgun and took aim. Brought together, these objects leave a powerful portrait of Heming the murderer. As John Lench explained to James Tustin as they raced towards Pound Farm earlier that evening: it was the man in the long blue coat.

On Midsummer evening Reverend Pyndar did not yet have evidence from Susan Surman, Joseph Colley or John Chellingworth. But Colwell's account was sufficiently detailed and certain for the magistrate to presume that Heming was the man they were after. It was time to cast his net. At around 8 p.m. he dispatched George Lloyd – the father of Sarah Lloyd – to the home of Richard Allen, a constable in Droitwich. Pyndar's instructions were simple. He was to search Heming's home, and if nothing was found, to keep a watch upon the property throughout the night.

Allen and Lloyd reached Heming's house at around 9 p.m., 'enquiring' tentatively of Elizabeth whether Richard was there. She replied that he was not and nor had she seen him since early that morning. The constable thanked her and slipped across the street and into the shadows.

Elizabeth Heming was many things that Richard was not. She was assiduous and level-headed, carefully recording his business accounts in a ledger and managing the family's income. She was not unduly concerned by the constable's first knock. Her husband's lifestyle was erratic and it was not unusual for him to be away from home at any hour. On Midsummer night she had her mother to keep her company and help watch her elder two daughters as she nursed Harriet, her two-month-old baby girl.

Half an hour later Allen knocked again, and Elizabeth repeated that she had not seen or heard from Richard. The constable returned for a third time at 10 p.m., and Elizabeth, growing uneasy, begged him to tell her what had happened.

Allen informed her that Reverend Parker of Oddingley had been murdered at five o'clock that afternoon, that Richard was the chief suspect in the case and that there were seven constables scouring the county for him. He requested permission to search the house, which she immediately granted. Finding nothing, he left.

Allen then widened his search. He called at several other proper-ties in and around Droitwich during the few hours of darkness that night. One was particularly notable. It belonged to Charles Burton, Elizabeth's younger brother. Burton and Heming had evidently been close, but his house was searched without success.

The hunt for Heming was gathering pace in other quarters too. At Oddingley Reverend Pyndar ordered the clerk John Pardoe and Edward Stephens, a labourer, to ride to Worcester and have a hand-bill printed with both the butchers' and Colwell's descriptions of the murderer.

One possibility was that Heming had bypassed Worcester alto-gether and headed towards Bredon, where he might find protection from his family and old friends. With this in mind, John Perkins and Thomas Colwell were ordered to take the road south, accompanied by George Day, Parker's servant, who had just returned from Worcester. Pyndar was making best use of the scant resources he had available to him, coordinating the community which had seemed so useless only hours before. Perkins lent Thomas Colwell a nag and George Day took Parker's horse, and as the sun set over Oddingley on Midsummer Day the three men headed out of the village. They passed the church and Netherwood Farm and then crossed the parish boundary towards Worcester, the same route that Pritchard and Chellingworth had taken much earlier that day.

The men arrived in Eckington, just north of their intended desti-nation, in the early hours of Wednesday morning. There was no sign of Heming. At 4 a.m., as the sun rose, they searched his parents'

home at Bredon's Norton but found nothing. On their way back to
Oddingley in the morning 'they made every enquiry on the Road,
but could get no intelligence of Heming, except that he had been
seen at Whittington [a small village on the outskirts of Worcester]
that night and had a Pint of Ale'.

Once again, Richard Heming had vanished.

CHAPTER 9

Droitwich

Droitwich Spa, Worcestershire, 1783–1806

Looking west from the edge of the escarpment that hung over Oddingley, and from the outer canopy of Trench Wood, villagers could watch over the variety of lanes and pathways that cleaved through the parish and out across the vista. Beyond Smite Hill, just out of view, was the bustling coach road, turnpiked in 1714, that ran between Droitwich and Worcester. Passing through the village were Oddingley Lane, Netherwood Lane, Church Lane, Pineapple Lane and Hull Lane. Then there were by-paths, bridal ways, drovers' roads and farmers' tracks, some of them well defined and worn bare, others overgrown and almost impassable for anyone but those with the lightest feet. Just to the north of the village the ancient saltways radiated out from Droitwich, jutting south towards the nearby villages of Sale Way and Sale Green.

This labyrinth of rural pathways was replicated right across the surrounding countryside, and confused Pyndar's hunt for Heming. Everyone knew their own favourite route, their own ingenious shortcut. And if he hadn't already vanished into Worcester's anonymous streets or the waiting door of a stage coach, then Heming's mastery of the roads and lanes would offer him his finest hope of eluding those who chased him.

Worcester had already been pinpointed as Heming's most likely destination, but Pyndar had been wise not to limit his attentions. Just seven miles to the north-east of the county city and little more

than two miles from Oddingley was Droitwich. Heming could easily
have doubled back and risked the trip homeward, which he would
have been able to complete, at a pace, in little more than an hour.

And for Pyndar there were already hints that whatever had taken
place in Oddingley that afternoon had its roots in Droitwich. Not
only did Heming live there but he had been seen with Clewes in
the Red Lion's taproom, damning Reverend Parker just weeks
before. Surely such an indiscretion would only occur in an environment where the men felt comfortable? A second reason to draw
suspicion towards Droitwich was that the gun bag had smelled
of salt.

Salt defined Droitwich. In his history of Worcestershire T. C.
Tuberville observed, 'Salt manufacture at Droitwich is one of the
most ancient businesses in the kingdom,' and the industry had left
its scars on the landscape: the sheds, workshops and tall smouldering
chimneys of the salt works, served by a steady stream of carts clattering to and fro between the pits (wiches) and packhorses lumbering
off to distant traders and their markets.

The market town itself was inconspicuous, set in a valley through
which the gentle River Salwarp flowed. To the untrained eye there
was little to set it apart from any other place of its sort, but 173 feet
beneath the marl-capped surface of the valley floor a subterranean
stream – just 22 inches deep – passed over a sheet of rock salt, trans-
forming the water into strong brine. 'The brine from all the pits is
perfectly limpid,' reported a paper for the *Philosophical Magazine* in
1812, '. . . and when in a large body had a pale greenish hue similar
to that of sea water. To the taste it is intensely saline, but without
any degree of bitterness.'

The process for converting this brine into Droitwich salt was
curious. The weekly Victorian magazine *Household Words* explained
the method to its readers in a lucid and colourful article in the 1850s.

Brine boiling and salt making is hot, steaming work. Go into any of
the works [at Droitwich] and you will see men naked to the waist,
employed in an atmosphere only just bearable by strangers. You will

see that the brine is pumped up from the pits into reservoirs; you will see ranges of large shallow quadrangular iron pans, placed over firecely heated furnaces; you will see the brine flow into the pans, and in due time bubble and boil and evaporate with great rapidity: you see that the salt evidently separates by degrees from the water and granulates at the bottom of the pan; you see men ladle up this granulated salt with flattish shovels and transfer it to draining vessels; and you finally see it put into oblong boxes, whence it is to be carried to the store room to be dried.

By the time this article was written Droitwich was producing around 60,000 tons of salt each year. This was a much smaller amount than came from Cheshire, where miners dug out salt with 'the pick, the shovel, the blast and the forge', but evaporation was a far more economical process. The effect of the industry on the neighbourhood was profound. It not only resulted in the 'saltways', which fanned out across the country, but also necessitated the building of Droitwich Canal – a masterpiece of enlightened engineering by James Brindley – for the enormous sum of £23,500 between 1767 and 1771. Furthermore, it was one of the chief factors in the near-total destruction of Feckenham Forest, with Hugh Miller, the Scottish geologist and writer, claiming that 'six thousand loads of young pole wood, easily cloven' were required to fuel the furnaces each year.

Long before 1806 the trees in Oddingley parish would have been among the first parts of Feckenham Forest lost to the salt works. Logging had continued until the completion of Droitwich Canal made coal a more efficient source of energy. Traffic along the saltways had also thinned, as packhorses had been replaced with barges. Nevertheless, at the beginning of the nineteenth century Droitwich's streets and the surrounding lanes were still a ferment of business and enterprise. *Household Words* contrasted the town with the more upmarket Malvern. It observed, 'If Worcester has a fashionable neighbour on the one side, Malvern, it has a sober industrious neighbour on the other, Droitwich. The one spends money; the other makes money. Worcester acts as a metropolis for both.'

To Hugh Miller, who arrived on a bleak autumnal day, Droitwich appeared a dull dispiriting place. The fields on either side of the valley had a 'dank blackened look' and the town's roads and streets 'were dark with mud'. He continued:

Most of the houses wore the dingy tints of a remote and somewhat neglected antiquity. Droitwich was altogether, as I saw it, a sombre looking place, with its grey old church looking down upon it from a scraggy wood covered hill; and what struck me as peculiarly picturesque was, that from this dark centre there should be passing continually outwards, by road or canal, waggons, carts, track-boats, barges all laden with pure white salt, that looked in their piled up heaps like wreaths of drifted snow. There could not be two things more unlike than the great staple of the town and the town itself. There hung too, over the blackened roofs, a white volume of vapour – the steam of numerous salt pans driven off in the course of evaporation by the heat – which also strikingly contrasted with the general blackness.

Droitwich was a prosperous place – the salt works yielded an enormous annual sum of £250,000. Such a steady flow of money meant it was more than a mere market town; it was also a destination for traders and a hive for the financially ambitious. For Oddingley it was a centre of trade, a place to meet friends, strike deals, purchase farming tools or seek new services. Most weeks farmers like Thomas Clewes and John Barnett would travel to the town for its Friday Market, stopping for a drink in the Barley Mow, the Black Boy or the Red Lion.

The town had also played a vital role in Captain Evans' life. In March 1783, when he retired from the 89th Foot, he had swapped a successful military career for an uncertain civilian future. Then aged about 50, Evans entered his retirement in strong financial shape. Several years of officer's pay would have been bolstered by any spoils he might have secured during the recruitment crisis or on his Atlantic tour, where captured enemy property and money would have been divided among the soldiers. But although he had money, Captain Evans decided against establishing his own household. Instead he took a room with the Banks family in Whitton, a village three miles from Ludlow. Why he preferred to do this is uncertain. His regiment had been stationed in the area the previous year, and Evans, being billeted with them and enjoying their company, might have simply decided to stay. Perhaps he enjoyed living in a traditional family unit, unaccustomed as he was to life outside his regiment. There is no sign that the Captain had any blood relations of his own.

The Banks family was headed by Mary and her husband William. They had a family of seven children, five daughters and two sons. The eldest son, George Banks, the future bailiff of Church Farm, was baptised in Whitton in 1782. This date coincides with Evans' retirement from the 89th Foot and when he first met the family. The later rumours that suggest he was George's natural father are questionable given William Banks was still alive at this point. It is clear, however, that whatever connection there was between Evans and George Banks stretched right back to his very beginning.

A certain mystery surrounds the Captain's movements over the next decade. It is evident, however, that throughout these years both his social status and financial means continued to improve. When he reappears in records in the mid-1790s it is as an older but more successful gentleman, financially secure and more powerful than ever. He may well have remained with the Banks family throughout these years, but it is clear that his attention had returned to his native Worcestershire. The town clerk of Droitwich made an entry in his books in 1794 marking Evans' formal return to county life: 'At a Chamber Meeting held for the Borough of Droitwich, on the 6th October, 1794, Samuel Evans, late of Kidderminster and now of the Parish of Burford in the County of Salop, Captain in His Majesty's late 89th Regiment of Foot, was elected and made a Free Burgess of the said Borough.' A second record was added, almost precisely a year later: 'At a Chamber Meeting held the 5th of October 1795,

Samuel Evans was elected and chosen one of the Bailiffs of the said Borough.'

The mid-1790s were years of conflict. Since 1793 Britain had been at war with the revolutionary government in France and Evans may have owed his new appointments to a growing sense of fear, as Britons strove to sublimate their anxieties by promoting experienced and decisive men to positions of authority. For Evans it was a personal triumph. He was now a burgess and a bailiff, part of the local magistracy, achievements to match and surpass any in his previous life.

Evans filled one of the two magisterial roles elected each year by the Droitwich Corporation. It was a powerful, prestigious and testing position, especially at such a time of civil unrest. To even be considered for the post, the Captain would have had to possess certain social and material qualities. As the historian Clive Emsley explains, 'He [the magistrate] had to be a man of some wealth and social standing to have his name entered on a county's commission of the peace in the first place; he then had to be of sufficient public spirit to take out his dedimus potestatem, which involved travelling to the county town, swearing an oath before the clerk of the peace, and paying the appropriate fees.'

As a magistrate the Captain was called on to impose summary justice in a wide range of cases, including felonies such as common assault, petty larceny and robbery, and other minor crimes such as selling unlicensed goods. Several records of the Captain's service have survived. On 3 October 1797 he took the testimony of a Richard Barber, who claimed to have been violently beaten by two men, Thomas Tagg and Joseph Taylor. Barber was a watchmaker, Tagg a cabinetmaker and Taylor a farrier, a specialist horseman. Perhaps it was no more than a drunken scuffle, or perhaps it was reflective of the resentment that festered in small towns between competing tradesmen. More significantly, though, the deposition is the first recorded mention of Joseph Taylor.

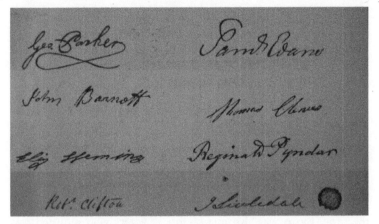

With physical images of almost all the key characters lost, these signatures
stand in their place

Two more records relating to Evans date from the following year. On 3 September 1798 he received an instruction to advance 30 weeks' pay to a Droitwich lady whose husband had been drafted into the Worcester Militia. Later that same month he took the deposition of a Miss Harrison who stated that she had been assaulted by two women. Harrison was illiterate and signed her evidence with a clumsy lopsided cross. Evans' signature also appears on all of the forms. As one of the few direct links we have with him, his writing is revealing. The S of Samuel is looped and florid, slanted at an almost jaunty angle slightly towards the right. The E of Evans is similarly formed. In both there are traces of a careless, slightly hurried hand, but if it is the hand of a pragmatist, it is also the hand of a student: someone who has studied a style without quite being able to effect it.

Such incidents were typical of a magistrate's workload, and Evans would have dealt with many similar cases. A further duty, and a far more prestigious one, involved overseeing elections in the borough. One of the earliest records of Captain Evans' service relates to the 1796 general election. The document states that the following 'oath was administered to Jacob Turner and Samuel Evans Esqs, bailiffs of the Borough of Droitwich on the 27th day of May 1796':

I do solemnly swear that I have not directly nor indirectly received
any sum or sums of money, office, place or employment, gratuity or
reward or any bond, bill, note or any promise of gratuity whatsoever
either myself or any other person to my use or benefit or advantage
for making my return at the present election, and that I will return
which person or persons as shall to the best of my judgement appear
to me to have the majority of legal votes.

This oath was read before a variety of local dignitaries, including
Edward Foley, the former Droitwich MP and the current member
for Worcestershire. It gives a rare glimpse of the Captain's connection with these men. In line with the exclusive electoral system of
the time, Evans was also one of just 14 voters who returned two
members to Parliament to represent the town nationally. It was an
uncommon privilege and another mark of his exceptional local
importance. He now had property; he most probably held shares in
the salt springs; he was connected – in different ways – to the highest
and lowest classes of Droitwich society. It is easy to see how he
secured the deeds to Church Farm from Foley in 1798, when the
property fell vacant. Here was a fine old manor house in a quiet
nearby parish. Church Farm was to become the Captain's country
residence, the final missing piece in a life built from nothing.

In the eight years up to 1806 he continued with his magisterial
duties. 'Captain Evans used to go up to Droitwich every Friday',
remembered Elizabeth Fowler, his dairymaid. This left him for the
remainder of the week at home in Oddingley, where once again the
Captain's irrepresible personality was to prevail. 'Captain Evans was
the leading man in the parish,' William Barnett would later declare,
which makes his quarrel with Parker doubly compelling, and shows
Perkins' verbal attack at the Plough – when he reminded Evans that
as a magistrate he should not be breaking the peace – to be even
more admirable.

Captain Evans' position in Droitwich and Oddingley was unques-
tionable. But what had not yet been established, as Pyndar set about
his hunt for Richard Heming on Midsummer night, were his

movements that day. Where had he spent the afternoon? Why had Heming been working at Church Farm that morning? Just how well did Evans know the man who had just murdered his clergyman?

There were no answers as the shadows of that summer evening stretched over Oddingley's fields. Clewes left the Captain at Church Farm and was now returning along the lane to Netherwood. '[He] seemed much confused and cut up, as if he had lost a friend,' remembered William Smith and John Collins, who saw him when he returned.

At Church Farm nothing had changed, despite the dramatic events of the day. Elizabeth Fowler, Thomas Langford and the other live-in servants prepared for bed. They slept soundly and did not hear anything at all.

CHAPTER 10

Seduced by the Devil

Oddingley, 25–27 June 1806

'There is a wound on the right side of the head, towards the back,' explained Pennell Cole, a surgeon from Worcester Infirmary. 'Here the skull has been fractured and the bone beaten in upon the brain. This in itself is sufficient cause of death.'

It was Wednesday 25 June, the day after Parker's murder. All interested parties had been called to Oddingley Rectory, where the coroner's inquest was being held, and Cole, the fourth witness of the day, was delivering his evidence. Already the 13-man jury had heard Thomas Giles' and John Lench's detailed accounts of what they had witnessed the previous afternoon, and they had just listened to James Tustin's tacit defence of his master, John Barnett, and his timorous assertion that 'to the best of his knowledge he had never seen the bag or the gun before'.

At 56 years old, Pennell Cole was an enormously experienced and respected local figure. He was one of six full-time surgeons and physicians employed at the Worcester Infirmary, an imposing example of enlightened architecture dubbed by one pamphlet one of the city's most 'ornamental structures'. Like Captain Evans, Cole was a military man and had served as a medical officer during the American war, but for the past 21 years he had been based in Worcester, tending to a daily professional staple of feverish, dyspeptic, rheumatic and gouty patients. But at the rectory he had been confronted with a quite different proposition as he performed a relatively simple yet highly unusual autopsy. Parker's wounds were severe and resembled those of a soldier killed at close quarters in a pistol battle or a dissident hacked down in a furious riot. They were not those commonly sustained by a country parson wandering in his glebe.

Cole had identified two major wounds to the corpse. The first was a broad bloodied hole in the right side of Parker's torso, a result of the shotgun blast. The skin around this area, between the bottom of the ribcage and the top of the pelvis, was charred black, and, peeling it back, Cole found a reasonable quantity of shot buried beneath. Some had perforated the main artery, he explained to the jurors – presumably meaning the descending aorta. The massive blood loss precipitated by the injury would have sent Parker into a lethal haemorrhagic shock.

The bludgeoned head constituted a second fatal injury. Parker had been struck three separate times: once on either temple and once on the right side of his head. Though the blows to the temples had laid his skin bare, the third impact had been the most devastating, leaving Parker with a horribly depressed fracture which had caused further haemorrhaging. The enormous quantity of blood lost from the first wound would have killed him in minutes; the second silenced him even more quickly. Cole's testimony was plain and pointed. He stood down.

The coroner's inquest was a necessary first step that followed any murder or, more commonly, any unexplained or accidental death. It was designed to expose all the evidence surrounding an incident, calling eye witnesses and medical men to testify before the coroner and his jury – who were usually respected men from the parish. When a hearing was concluded, the coroner would give his verdict on the case, indicating the most likely cause of death. Coroners worked closely with magistrates, who were responsible for pursuing cases on behalf of victim's families, locating and arresting suspects and having them committed for trial at the assize – grand court trials presided over by one of the King's judges touring the country.

It was traditional for proceedings to take place in full view of the deceased body and usually in the closest public house to the crime scene. Inns were a logical choice: they were familiar to everyone in a community and capable of catering for the swell of witnesses, family members and curious locals. In *The Maul and the Pear Tree* P. D. James and T. A. Critchley describe an inquest that took place at a London inn during the Ratcliffe Highway murders in 1811.

> The inquest was arranged for Tuesday, 10 December, at the Jolly Sailor public house in Ratcliffe Highway, nearly opposite to Marr's [the murdered man's] shop. While his wife bustled from tap-room to kitchen preparing for an unusual influx of customers, the landlord suitably arranged his largest room. An imposing table sat ready for the coroner, bearing candles to lighten the gloom of a December afternoon: two longer tables were placed together for the jury; a chair was set in place for witnesses. The fire was banked high. Outside could be heard the mutterings and movements of a vast crowd.

As there was no public house in Oddingley, the rectory had been selected as the most suitable alternative. The building was spacious, centrally located, close to the crime scene and also a place of authority – which, along with the need to keep the inquest within the parish boundaries, made it an obvious setting. Perhaps it was also considered a dignified choice, as rather than dispatching Parker's corpse on a further inglorious tour of the lanes, he could instead remain under his own roof. For Mary Parker, however, the influx of officials, witnesses and onlookers must have amounted to a horrible invasion of her shattered family home, the sight of her husband's dead body exposed on a table a frightful one to endure.

William Barnett, the parish constable, had summoned the coroner to Oddingley from Worcester that morning. At 29 years old, William was four years younger than his brother John, but he displayed many of the same family traits. He was hard-working, stoical and reticent. He had the community standing and spirit to be elected to one of the foremost parochial positions and he was a capable deputy to his brother at Pound Farm.

William Barnett, though, had been away from Oddingley on Midsummer Day, at Bromsgrove Fair, not arriving back in the village until dusk. Customarily he would be one of the first to be informed about a crime, but Oddingley's constable was among the last to learn of Parker's murder. Later Barnett's absence in the minutes and hours after the attack would be carefully examined. Had he been present he would have been expected to assume a leading role: sounding the hue and cry, encouraging villagers to pursue the suspect on horseback and sending for the nearest justice of the peace. He would have been a first point of contact for Surman, Tustin or the butchers, and as the attack happened minutes from Pound Farm Barnett should have been nearby and able to act swiftly. But at 8 p.m. he had still not returned, and Pyndar had been forced to appoint a number of deputised constables (John Lloyd, George Day, John Perkins, Edward Stephens and John Pardoe among them) to act in his place.

As important parochial officials, constables held real power. They could arrest and imprison felons without requiring warrants, and they could detain suspects until a justice arrived on the scene. If a constable had information that a felon was concealed within a house, he had the right to break open its doors if entrance was denied. And if a criminal resisted arrest or attempted to escape, then it was not considered murder if the constable killed him.

'It was very late when I got back [from Bromsgrove Fair],' William Barnett later told magistrates. 'It was nine o'clock. I did not wish otherwise than to go in search of him [Heming]. I heard other people were going in search.'

The following morning, though, Barnett assumed his duties with vigour and interest. He had risen early and ridden to the Worcester residence of Richard Barneby, the coroner, asking him to come to Oddingley at once. Following this he had called on Pennell Cole at the infirmary, briefing him and engaging him to perform the autopsy before the inquest began in the afternoon. Coroner's inquests were usually arranged some days following a fatality (the inquest into the Marr murders in Ratcliffe Highway in 1811 was held three days after they were killed), but Barnett was already acting with much more speed. By midday a 13-man jury had been assembled, which included three farmers (Marshall, Jones and Hardcourt), and the rectory had been prepared for the day's business. At five o'clock the day before, Reverend Parker had been alive and busy with his daily tasks. Less than a day later his dead body was laid out in front of a crowd, the subject of an official investigation. A contested report, years later, asserted that in his role as a magistrate Captain Evans sat as foreman of the jury.

Richard Barneby chaired the proceedings. Barneby was a young coroner who had been elected unopposed to his position in August 1801. Since then most of his cases had related to grim but common-place instances of accidental death, of men trampled by their horses, destitute or drunk city dwellers who had perished in the icy winters. On 9 January 1806 Barneby had conducted an inquest on the body of a female child found on the foot road from Powick to Stanbrook. The week after he had investigated the death of a man from expo-sure. Murder, though, was rare, and when it did happen the victim was usually a woman: as many as half of the recorded number being wives, mistresses or sweethearts, commonly members of the poor working classes. Parker's case was altogether different.

It was customary to view the crime scene before an inquest began, and presumably Barneby and the jury were taken to the glebe before returning to the rectory. Barneby opened the inquest with an initial address, and Thomas Giles and John Lench were called to deliver their evidence. For the next half-hour the butchers delivered detailed lucid accounts of their interrupted journey through the parish. Lench told the jury that after Giles disappeared after the murderer, he had seen John Barnett at Pound Farm and asked him directly 'if he would please go to the place to look at him [Parker]', to which Barnett had responded starkly, 'I will not go.'

This was an awkward moment for the farmer. Lench's evidence cast him as callous and indifferent, disinclined to offer the least help when it was desperately needed. His position was only somewhat improved by James Tustin's subsequent testimony, with the carter claiming that he had not heard the conversation between the two men.

After Pennell Cole's cogent analysis of Parker's corpse, the final witnesses were called. These were Thomas Colwell, who told the coroner that he had been startled by Richard Heming vaulting over the hedge in the lanes near Hindlip shortly after the murder, and George Lloyd, who informed the room that he had assisted Richard Allen, the Droitwich constable, to search Heming's home 'several times' without success. The witness testimonies concluded on this dispiriting note and Barneby prepared to sum up. The whole inquiry had amounted to little more than a fleeting tour through the facts of the previous day. Lench's and Giles' evidence aside, a breezy air had permeated the hearing, and none of the witnesses had been challenged on any points of detail or invited to speculate. It was a missed opportunity. Corner's inquests were not guided by the same stiff rules that existed in English courts of law, where suggestive comment was closely monitored and hearsay expressly prohibited. Had he lingered longer and studied the evidence more closely, Barneby may have elicited far more.

The corner and each of the jurors then read and signed every sheet of the clerk's account, which recorded in ornate and vivid prose their assessment of the facts. 'Some person to the jurors aforesaid at present unknown, not having the fear of God before his eyes, but moved and seduced by the instigation of the Devil' had ended the life of Reverend George Parker. The official verdict was 'wilful murder by some person or persons unknown'.

Barneby left Oddingley for Worcester, leaving behind him a sense of mounting frustration. A murder merited much more than the insipid investigation that had just taken place. In establishing the causes of death and movements of those involved, Barneby had performed his duty, but he had done no more. He had shown little inquisitive rigour, had failed to interview several crucial witnesses and had allowed an ambiguous verdict to be passed down by the

jury, who fixed the crime on an unknown rather than boldly declaring
Heming the chief suspect – a fact already generally held in the village.

A methodical inquest, however, was perhaps more than could have
been hoped for. Three members of the coroner's jury (Marshall,
Jones and Hardcourt) had good reason to resent Parker, and that the
Captain was involved after arguing publicly with the victim so
recently was highly unfortunate if not suspicious. Indeed, John
Perkins, Parker's closest ally among the farmers, was omitted
completely, as was Reverend Pyndar, who, as the responsible magistrate, must have expected to be called as a witness. Pyndar, watching
the inquest as a spectator, had been caught flat-footed; it had been
the constable, William Barnett, who had assumed control of proceedings. Had Pyndar fetched Barneby from Worcester himself, briefed
him and furnished him with a list of witnesses, the outcome may
have been quite different.

As it was, no mention was made before Barneby or the jury of
the feud. Countless villagers had first-hand experience of Captain
Evans, Thomas Clewes, John Barnett and George Banks damning
Parker, swearing drunken oaths and making chilling predictions of
his imminent death, but not one of these was called to testify. The
women in particular were excluded. Elizabeth Fowler, Sarah Lloyd
and Mary Parker all possessed vital pieces of evidence not brought
before the coroner. Fowler had discovered a shotgun which exactly
matched the murder weapon and which could easily have been
identified; Sarah Lloyd had heard the drunken jeers in the Pigeon
House; and Mary Parker could have testified that she and her husband
had been disturbed in the night by stones clattering against their
window, that Captain Evans had argued with George in the lanes
and that for years the parish had been characterised by resentment
and anger. Even Susan Surman, the last person to see Parker alive,
was somehow overlooked.

These gaping omissions could be attributed to prejudice. Women
were generally considered less reliable witnesses than men, and in
the countryside such beliefs were stronger. Historian Roy Porter
describes the extent of discrimination in English society at this time.

Public life on a grand scale was a men-only club (as were almost all clubs themselves). There were no female parliamentarians, explorers, lawyers, magistrates or factory entrepreneurs, and no women voters. For Dr Johnson, the idea of a woman preacher was 'like a dog walking on his hind legs' . . . Public opinion tight-laced women into constrictive roles: wives, mothers, housekeepers subordinate workers, domestic servants, maiden aunts. Few escaped. Such stereotyping created a kind of invisibility: women were to be men's shadows.

Such shadows loomed long in Oddingley Rectory on 25 June 1806. Perhaps the absence of women from the coroner's inquest is best explained by pure prejudice; perhaps it was considered indiscreet to have Surman, Lloyd, Fowler and Parker interrogated by men in public, or perhaps these women were marginalised and excluded from the hearing by William Barnett and the Captain, who were desperate to silence their voices. It left much of the story untold. No mention of the quarrel would be made in the newspaper reports over the following days and of all the deficiencies of the coroner's inquest, the failure to establish any context for the murder was Barneby's gravest. Thus far the crime was a one-sided story, told from a narrow perspective.

In 1806 murder was an alarming and unusual crime. In 1805, the first year for which there are official records, of the 350 death sentences passed in England and Wales, only ten were for murder. Occasionally, following an assize trial, felons would be hanged from the wooden scaffold at Red Hill on the eastern edge of Worcester, but these were rarely murderers. Of the nine people executed in the county since the turn of the century five had been convicted of burglary, two of sheep stealing, one of horse stealing and one of forgery. Parker's death, therefore, was guaranteed to attract considerable attention, and within days newspapers across the Midlands were carrying stories about the 'Barbarous and Inhumane Murder'. The news that a clergyman, a minor member of the gentry, had been attacked and killed in his own parish was sensational and disturbing, a story to stand out above even the weekly war reports. The social position of the victim and the familiarity of the setting lent the reports their most chilling edge: if a country parson could be attacked in his own glebe, then who could consider themselves really safe? Details of the murder would ripple across the county: the educated classes reading reports in the newspapers and workers swapping accounts in the inns and market squares, where news of a brutal murder so close to home was the most compelling of all.

There were similarities between Parker's killing and another case which had so recently horrified the country. On 5 April 1806 a man named Richard Patch had stood before a London jury charged with the murder of Isaac Blight, his master, a wealthy ship breaker.* The newspapers had devoted enormous amounts of coverage to the case, describing Patch as a man of uncertain character who had suddenly appeared outside Blight's home a number of years earlier under the pretext of visiting his sister. Patch, who was destitute and penniless, had soon won Blight's confidence, secured a job in his shipyard and been promoted to the point that, eighteen months later, he was considered the most trusted and important of Blight's servants.

But by 1805 Patch had devised a scheme to kill Blight, inherit his business and all its assets. On a crisp autumnal night he had lured Blight into a carefully arranged trap at his dockside home at Rotherhithe on the south bank of the Thames. As Blight lazed in his back parlour, drunk on grog in the evening gloom, Patch entered and fired a shot at him. The ball from Patch's pistol passed through Blight's abdomen and his chair and lodged in the wall. Blight, mortally wounded, had lingered through the night, but died in terrible pain the following day.

Patch very nearly eluded justice. Blight's assassination was ingeniously devised and almost perfectly executed. The murderer had provided himself with an alibi by feigning an upset stomach and making an ostentatious exit seconds before the fatal shot was discharged. Patch was only betrayed when magistrates searched his

* A ship breaker dismantled old vessels, salvaging what he could and selling it on, and disposing of the rest.

privy and instead of finding evidence it had been used by someone suffering from diarrhoea discovered the ramrod of a pistol jammed in the vault. A search of Patch's bedroom subsequently turned up a pair of white ribbed stockings that, although on first inspection seemed perfectly clean, were in fact soiled on their soles 'as if the wearer had crept about outside in his stockinged feet'.

In a 'very awful and important inquiry' these delicate strands of evidence linked Richard Patch inescapably to the crime. He was arrested and brought to court. In his long and eloquent assessment of the case Lord Chief Justice Baron MacDonald declared famously that 'the prisoner [Patch] had begun his career of guilt in a system of fraud towards his friend [Blight], he had continued it in ingratitude and he had terminated it in blood.' Patch was found guilty of murder and hanged at the New Prison in Southwark on Tuesday 8 April, the day after Elizabeth Fowler discovered the shotgun at Church Farm. *Berrow's Worcester Journal* joined other local newspapers in recording the event, describing in florid prose the 'awful moment when Patch was about to be launched into late eternity'.

Isaac Blight's murder shocked and enthralled all London. A long pamphlet detailing the particulars of the case sold in record numbers, and the trial itself was attended by the Dukes of Cumberland and Sussex, along with other members of the aristocracy, who sat in a specially designed box high in the courtroom. Outside, enormous crowds gathered in Horsemonger Lane to steal a glimpse of Patch as he was escorted into court, 'genteelly dressed in black'.

Blight's murder was similar to Parker's in certain ways. Like the clergyman, Blight had been a man of some importance and local standing, a fact which made him both a dangerous and seductive target. But most comment was reserved for Patch. He was described at great length in all the newspapers and pamphlets as their authors tried to get at the strange, terrible collision of personality traits that had created this monster. These writers highlighted his ambition, his unbridled courage, his ingenuity and natural ability, almost like an actor, to slip into different roles: the long-lost brother, the faithful business partner, the sickly patient and, ultimately, the horrified

witness. People were becoming more interested in the mechanics of
the criminal mind. Just what could drive a man to murder?

There were distinct similarities between Patch and Heming. Both
had histories of petty crime, both had abandoned their childhood
homes and both had gone on to commit murder. To some Patch
and Heming would have been examples of a criminal class: a tightly
defined breed of professional outlaws, burglars or smugglers, the
most courageous of which, Friedrich Engels would later argue,
became 'thieves and murderers'. But for others such individuals were
not products of society but human aberrations. Was there something
special in the anatomical make-up of these men that a trained eye
or a careful physician could detect? Could a murderer be betrayed
by an innocuous physical quirk or by something strange and distinct
in their manner?*

Although Patch and Heming shared similar personal histories,
their two cases were actually very different. While Patch had been
driven to kill Blight for financial gain, at Oddingley there was no
such clarity. No money had been stripped from Parker's body, nor
had he been assaulted at a time of day when he was likely to be
carrying any. Furthermore there was no known antipathy or even
connection between Heming and Parker. Their only encounters had
been brief meetings in the village lanes.

This left Heming without a clear motive for attacking Parker, a
fact that must have troubled the coroner. The severity of the assault
left little doubt that Heming wanted Parker dead. But why? Heming
knew his capture would be swiftly followed by a court case and then
almost certain execution. He would have known that Oddingley was
busy at five o'clock in the harvest months. He was fully aware it was
Bromsgrove Fair day, which meant that there would be more traffic
than usual along the lanes. And he would have known that Susan
Surman was close by, and that the sound of a shotgun was bound
to result in a chase. It was wholly unsurprising that Heming had

* Such questions fuelled the discipline of phrenology, which in 1806 was gaining popularity due to the work of Dr Joseph Gall (1757–1828). Phrenology focused on the size
and shape of a human skull, which were taken as indications of the mind contained.

been disturbed by the butchers while fleeing the scene. The case had none of the accuracy or finesse of Patch's murder of Blight, but in its own far more muddled myopic way, it was just as puzzling.

The first full printed report of the murder appeared in *Berrow's Worcester Journal* the following day. The piece must have been written on the Wednesday as it did not contain the verdict of the coroner's inquest, or designate Heming as the chief suspect. Instead the article referred to 'the murderer' throughout. After a long description of the assault, the report concluded,

> The unfortunate person who was murdered proves to be the Rev. Mr Parker of Oddingley, in this county. It appears that when the man shot him, he did not quite effect his horrid purpose and he beat him around the head with the butt end of the gun in so violent a manner that he broke it, and in his terror put only one of the pieces in his bag. He is described as wearing a blue coat and the forepart of his head rather bald.

In Oddingley the greatest hope for a quick conclusion to the case remained with Reverend Pyndar. Until this point circumstances had played wretchedly against him. There was still no news of Heming, who by now could well have escaped the county. Furthermore, Pyndar had inadvertently allowed William Barnett to outmanoeuvre him. The reverend had spent several hours on the morning of 25 June composing letters to magistrates in London and Bristol, informing them that a murder had been committed and warning them to be vigilant for any sign of Heming. The time Pyndar lost writing these letters had been put to good use by Barnett, three miles away in Oddingley.

Pyndar's investigation was also handicapped by his lack of experience or training. While country magistrates had wide-ranging and summary powers, they were not well-equipped to conduct murder enquiries – most rural cases involved drunken farm labourers, idlers, petty theft or poaching. Their counterparts in the cities would have had far more experience of violent assaults, but even they would often struggle to formulate a powerful response in the wake of a murder. It was still 26 years before the Metropolitan Police – the first police force in the country – would petition the Home Office to establish a unit for elite 'detectives', expertly trained, exceptional policemen schooled in the growing arts of scientific and logical detection. In the middle of the century these men would rise to fame and prominence for their ability to tease truths out of the most knotty situations. They would atomise a case, scrutinise its component parts, uncover clues, interview suspects, covertly gather evidence and arrive at indisputable conclusions.

Half a century before, Pyndar had none of the training of the men who were to follow him. He was a clergyman, educated in the classics, theology and the law. He had little insight into the criminal mind. Pyndar was part of the old police, a loosely knit organisation that the Victorians would look back upon as dreadfully inadequate. Charles Dickens lampooned the system in *Great Expectations*. Following the death of his stepmother, Pip complains:

> The Constables and the Bow Street men from London – for this happened in the days of the extinct red-waistcoated police – were about the house for a week or two, and did pretty much what I have heard and read of like authorities doing in other such cases. They took up several obviously wrong people, and they ran their heads very hard against the wrong ideas, and persisted in trying to fit the circumstances to the ideas, instead of trying to extract ideas from the circumstances.

Pyndar performed much better than this. While limited in experience and expertise, he was gifted with a natural sense of duty, a talent for organisation and an inquisitive streak. He was untrained but he had guile, and in the days following the murder he applied himself to the case with diligence. He sought out villagers, interviewing each one alone, and instead of committing facts to memory, he made records of everything on scraps of parchment which he stowed away for future reference.

One of his first moves was to engage John Perkins, who was proving a tractable ally, to lie in wait for Heming on the foot road between Droitwich and Oddingley. Perkins was instructed to seize the fugitive if he saw him. The letters to Bristol and London left Worcester in Wednesday's post and by now the handbill was in wide circulation. Pyndar knew that the chances of Heming still being in the neighbourhood were slim, but the possibility could not be completely discounted. In the first few days of the investigation he had received news of a number of potential sightings. Two came from nearby parishes: one in Tibberton, one in Warndon, just a mile to the west. Other reports arrived from Whittington and Pershore, villages further to the south. None, however, proved to be correct. As Pyndar waited in Oddingley for a lucky turn in events, his collection of notes began to mount. His pithy observations were often no longer than 50 or 60 words in length, but they showed that he was unearthing far more than Barneby had achieved before him.

Constructing a plausible narrative was chief among Pyndar's concerns. He was already convinced of Heming's guilt and from the start of his investigation set about discovering as much as he could about the labourer's movements. Working backwards he hoped to discover just where he had been on Midsummer Day, and to reveal the route that had wound from Heming's Droitwich home to Parker's glebe at five o'clock.

First he established that there was a working relationship between Heming and the Captain. Several labourers told Pyndar that Heming had laboured for Evans for some months as a carpenter and wheelwright, sawing wooden rails from local elms, mending buckled cartwheels and treating hurdles in the pool. Pyndar learnt that Heming had been at Church Farm on Midsummer Day, doing work for the Captain. He visited the property and found Evans. In his notes, he wrote, 'Cap. Evans says: That he paid Heming his wages of 6th of May & has not employed him since nor to the best of his recollection seen him till 24th June when he called at his house in the morning and pulled out some poles, that he had a mug of drink, but had no conversation with him.'

Evans' evidence seemed precise and emphasised how thin the ties between Heming and himself were. It did, however, include an admission that the suspect had visited his house on the morning of the murder, a fact that suggested to Pyndar the Captain's role was worth examining in more detail. He underlined the point in his notes with a bold, thick stroke of his quill.

Pyndar then questioned George Greenhill, a 15-year-old labourer rumoured to have been the last villager to see Heming before he vanished. Greenhill had been working for John Barnett in a meadow behind the rectory. At between nine and ten o'clock in the morning he had encountered Heming, who climbed over a stile into the field. Heming told the farmhand that he had been 'drinking a cup of ale' at the Captain's. He didn't seem to be carrying a weapon.

This scrap of evidence corroborated what the Captain had already said, but it also raised the question of what Evans had been doing the morning Heming had called. The Captain's claim that 'he had no conversation with him' seemed to settle one point, but it did not account for his movements. It seemed that, as he had not attended Bromsgrove Fair with Clewes and the other farmers, he must have spent the day at Church Farm. But then the Captain's story became more difficult to square. As a serving magistrate, he would have been expected to have been far more involved in the evening's events and yet he had played no part. It seemed perplexing that the Captain, so often the dominant parochial figure, would remain so detached from the action.

Pyndar's suspicions hardened when he talked to Thomas Green, the tailor from Upton Snodsbury. Green told Pyndar about his visit to Church Farm shortly after the murder, explaining how he had found Barnett and Evans in the parlour drinking. Green said that they both reacted with surprise when he told them about Parker's murder. Pyndar had already assembled enough facts to know that this was contrived. John Lench had testified at the inquest that he had informed Barnett of the murder only minutes after the attack, and according to Susan Surman's later evidence Pyndar had confronted Barnett an hour before Green saw him in the Captain's parlour. It seemed inconceivable that Barnett would not tell the Captain that the man they both despised had been shot dead. Pyndar returned to Church Farm and questioned Evans on this point.

'Barnett did not mention it,' the Captain declared flatly. He told Pyndar that the first he had heard about Parker's murder was from Thomas Green, who had burst into his parlour and exclaimed, 'Good God! Have you heard the news?' Evans had asked him what he meant. 'Mr Parker is shot!' the tailor had replied. Evans told Pyndar that he had then turned to Barnett, saying 'Surely it was not true?' 'It was too true,' Barnett had replied.

This account appears almost impossibly bizarre. Pyndar did not challenge him on the point, but the truth about the evening meeting at Church Farm was clouded further when he found John Barnett at Pound Farm. He asked Barnett whether he had spoken to the Captain about Parker's murder on Midsummer Day. Barnett replied that he had 'informed Captain Evans of the murder before Green came in', and also that Mary and Catherine Banks had joined the Captain and himself in the parlour, and had been 'talking over' the news 'before Green came in'.

It was a glaring contradiction. Pyndar may not have been trained in the art of deduction, but he was a long-serving magistrate with experience of distinguishing truthful evidence from false statements. It was clear to Pyndar that the Captain was lying, and in doing so was attempting to hide the details of his conversation with Barnett. It was a first slip and an early indication to Pyndar that his investigation was leading him into darker territory than he had encountered before. As the search for Richard Heming stretched out across the country, in Oddingley Church Farm and the role of the Captain were coming increasingly into focus.

CHAPTER II

A Dirty Job for Captain Evans

Oddingley and Worcester, June, July 1806

On Saturday 28 June an advertisement appeared in the *Worcester Herald*. Under the sensational title '*A most Barbarous and Inhumane MURDER!*' it read:

> Whereas on Tuesday Evening, the 24 instant, about five o'Clock the Rev. GEORGE PARKER, Rector of Oddingley, in the County of Worcester, was most cruelly MURDERED, in a Field within the Parish of Oddingley, and within a short distance of his own Dwelling-house, by receiving a shot from a Gun – which entered the right Side of his Body, near the short Ribs; his Skull fractured and his head otherwise very much beaten with the butt End thereof . . .
>
> And whereas RICHARD HEMING, late of the Borough of Droitwich, but heretofore of the Chapelry of Norton, near Bredon, in the same County, Carpenter and Wheelwright, stands suspected as being the Perpetrator of such cruel and inhuman Murder. The said Richard Heming is about five Feet four of five inches high, tight made, large Features, a large bald or high Forehead, dark brown Hair, inclined to curl, black Beard, round Face, rather a wide Mouth, sharp Nose, dark hazel Eyes, ruddy Complexion, but looked pale when pursued immediately after committing this most diabolical act; had on at the time such Murder was committed, a dark blue Coat, with white metal Buttons, which appeared too long for him, an old fashioned Hat with a low crown.

Four days had now passed since Parker's murder and three since Barneby's inquest. Heming was still at large and the authorities were changing their tone. This was an official announcement, not a piece penned by a journalist. It featured prominently in the middle pages of the newspaper, in the popular column on home news. The elusive 'man' who had appeared in *Berrow's Journal* was now being named as Heming. The tone of the piece was urgent and the detail it gave impressive. It marked a new phase in the investigation. Whereas Pyndar had seemed to be working alone for much of Tuesday evening and Wednesday, it was now clear that he had the support and attention of other powers.

'Whoever will apprehend the said Richard Heming, and lodge him in any of his Majesty's Gaols in the United Kingdoms, and thereof give Information to George Harris, attorney at Law, Edgar Street, Worcester,' the announcement concluded, 'will be handsomely rewarded for their trouble, and all reasonable expenses paid.'

On the same day, 50 miles to the east of Worcester, the initial report from *Berrow's Worcester Journal* was republished in *Jackson's Oxford Journal*. And at some point over the weekend the article must have caught the attention of a newspaper editor in London. On Monday morning, 30 June, a lightly edited version was reprinted once again, this time on the third page of *The Times* in London. News of Parker's murder was featured alongside reports of a gentleman who had tragically drowned in Hyde Park and the arrest of a surgeon's assistant accused of bodysnatching in Bermondsey.

But as the story drew glances from as far away as London, in Worcestershire there was still no trace of Heming. Many were beginning to treat the labourer's disappearance as almost as curious as the crime itself. There had been no confirmed sighting of him since the night of the murder, and it was assumed that he must be lying low in some woods or undergrowth, or being offered protection by a friend or confidant. The greater worry was that he had escaped either the county or the kingdom, evading the attention of the authorities in Bristol or London.

On 28 June Pyndar received responses to the two letters that he had written three days before. The first was a nimble note from Mr J. Read, chief magistrate of the Bow Street Office. He acknowledged receipt of Pyndar's letter, promising to 'take care that the description of Heming shall be circulated among the different Police Officers'. Read signed off optimistically, 'if he should make his appearance in London I dare say we shall get him and in that case you shall have immediate notice of it'. At the bottom of the letter, as an after-thought, he promised Pyndar he would have the description of Heming inserted in the next edition of *The Hue and Cry and Police Gazette*, a popular circular published each Saturday and sold for 3d. Heming's name would appear alongside those of wanted forgers, housebreakers, footpads, smugglers, rustlers and escaped convicts.

Read's response was prompt and had been written with a confidence that perhaps reflected his urban surroundings. In 1806 London was already a vast smouldering metropolis, developing with furious speed and on the verge of becoming the first British city to boast a million inhabitants. The tens of thousands of migrants drawn to the capital each year came both to find work and escape the countryside's hardships. Many of the poorest slipped invisibly into the labyrinth of London's slums or 'rookeries' like bees into a honeycomb. Such areas were stews of skinny alleys and gnarled tenements thronged that day and night with innumerable people, among them the poor and destitute, petty and career criminals, and it would have been the most obvious destination for a fugitive, a place where they could dive into the crowds and disappear without trace.

But Read's letter brought hope. Although there was no recognised police force in Britain, London was organised far better than the regional towns and cities. It was divided into seven administrative sections, each governed by police magistrates answerable directly to the home secretary. Within these areas a relatively high density of constables and watchmen was deployed, many with keener eyes than those of their counterparts in the countryside. Read's office at Bow Street had grown in stature and reputation over the past few years to become the most important among the embryonic policing units. Three different magistrates operated out of it; 60 Bow Street Runners patrolled the roads that fed into London, and there was even a special team of Bow Street Thief-Takers, who hunted down known criminals for the rewards offered privately or by the government. If Heming had decided to head to London, the authorities had been warned and lay in wait.

The news from Bristol was equally optimistic. Mr Richard Ward, the magistrate who had received Pyndar's letter, had immediately carried it to Richard Vaughan, the mayor, who had ordered his officials to use every means in their power to apprehend the murderer. Bristol was a busy port and only 50 miles to the south of Worcestershire. Here spry colliers and lumbering freight boats navigated the River Avon night and day, carrying cargoes of woollen cloth, tea, muslin, coal and spices along a stretch of water deep enough to allow ships of 1,000 tons to pass. Their destinations ranged from Dublin and the east shores of Ireland to the West Indies and the Americas. Almost 11,000 Bristolians were employed at the port, and if Heming could convince any of them to engage his services, or allow him a berth on a ship, then almost all chances of capture would be lost.

Pyndar's letter galvanised Ward. After visiting the mayor he called on the collector of customs, who in turn issued an order that all boats were to be searched before they were allowed to leave dock. 'If he is in the city or neighbourhood and should attempt to quit the kingdom by way of this port, I have every reason to believe that he will be taken,' Ward noted, adopting a similar tone to Read in London. He signed off his letter 'in great haste', promising Pyndar, 'Everything will be done, I hope, that can possibly be done.'

There were reasons for Pyndar to believe that Bristol was Heming's target. There had been a sighting of him south of Worcester, near Pershore, close to the Cheltenham and Gloucester road, and Pyndar had also heard that Heming was involved with a notorious smuggler who lived near his old home in the Tewkesbury area. This smuggler, Pyndar learnt in a note from a Worcester resident, had contacts in Gloucester and Bristol, where many of his goods passed through the port. 'That the course of his flight is towards that part of the country is highly probable,' the note concluded.

The letters from Bristol and London had been written on the same date, Friday 27 June, and the fact that they had been penned in such different quarters of the country was testament to Pyndar's swift action. But although he had dealt with the two most obvious destinations there were still many other routes of escape that remained open. Portsmouth and Liverpool both operated enormous ports, and just to the north of Oddingley and Droitwich industrial towns like Birmingham, Wolverhampton and Stourbridge offered anonymous urban havens.

On that same Friday Pyndar's thoughts were temporarily distracted from the investigation as he stepped beneath the thick oak porch into Oddingley Church for Parker's funeral. John Perkins and George Banks were among the mourners, but there were few other farmers and no representative from Worcester Cathedral. Parker was honoured, though, with a burial in the heart of the church, in the chancel, a little to the left of the pulpit and under the warm light of the tall stained-glass windows. His grave had been prepared that morning by Joseph Kendall, a stonemason from neighbouring Crowle. It bore a short inscription that made no reference to his murder: 'Sacred to the memory of the Rev. George Parker. Late rector of this parish, who departed this life, June 24, 1806, Aged 43 years.'

After the service finished Joseph Kendall witnessed a disquieting incident. Kendall was a respected tradesman from neighbouring Crowle. He occasionally took jobs in Oddingley parish and only a few months beforehand had replastered the church walls for Parker. Once the funeral had concluded and the congregation left, his final job was to close and seal the crypt, and the stonemason had waited patiently at the rear of the church as the mourners filed out. But before Kendall rose to complete his task, there was a fleeting moment when there was both an empty church and an open grave. Kendall explained what happened next, 'I saw George Banks there. As soon as the corpse was put in the grave, George Banks came and looked at it and laughed . . . He made a good deal of fun of it and seemed as though he was pleased that the parson was dead.'

Kendall was appalled by Banks' behaviour, and though he did not inform Pyndar about it directly may well have mentioned it to his workmen when he returned to Crowle that afternoon. Shortly afterwards the magistrate received a note from Kendall: 'This is to say that John Bridge an apprentice of mine heard Mr Evans abuse the Rev. Mr Parker a short time before his death and Thomas Perkins a workman of mine heard the same when they were repairing Oddingley Church. – Joseph Kendall, Crowle.'

This was an important moment. While everyone in Oddingley knew about Parker's quarrel with the farmers, there is little evidence to suggest Pyndar was aware of its extent. Buried within the parish were all the stories of drunken meetings, swearing and brazen threats. That a stonemason from a neighbouring parish was among the first to volunteer information is revealing. Oddingley, like any parish of its kind, was bound tightly together by ties of personal loyalty, decades-old friendships and blunt common sense. The farmhands knew that there was little alternative to working for the farmers, and villagers like Susan Surman, Sarah Lloyd and James Tustin would have been enormously reluctant to speak out against their employers, something which might well have cast their families into unemployment and distress. An employee who sided with the authorities against their employer also risked social stigma: being branded a snitch, turncoat, rascal or mischief-maker – a person better to be avoided.

Kendall, who lived outside Oddingley and had a wider pool of customers, clearly felt he could risk speaking out against Captain Evans – there is a hint of disrespect in his note when he refers to him as 'Mr' instead of 'Captain' – but his evidence was compromised by his failure to inform the magistrate about Banks' behaviour after the funeral. Pyndar's task, therefore, was a delicate one. He had to coax information from wary or unwilling subjects, record testimonies that were better not written, recall conversations that were better not had. Pyndar could offer to cleanse a person's conscience and he might appeal to their sense of moral right, but he could afford them very little protection from the consequences of their actions.

John Perkins, though, was willing to talk. 'Capt. Evans said there is no more harm in shooting Mr P. than a mad dog,' he told Pyndar on Thursday morning as the two men walked from St James' Church back up to Oddingley.

Perkins' evidence tallied with what Pyndar had learnt from Kendall, and it stirred him to further action. Over the next few days he sought out various villagers beginning with those who he knew or felt were most likely to reveal something. He carefully recorded interesting points from these meetings, dividing his scraps of parchment into halves and then quarters, underlining key points, jotting down supplementary questions, striking out factual inaccuracies and wondering out loud. Studying these documents at a distance of two centuries you can glean a sense of Pyndar's brain beginning to tick and a theory beginning to crystallise as his quill is applied with more or less pressure, as it stops for a second to be dipped into the ink or when a firm cross denotes a puzzling dead end.

Pyndar met Clement Churchill and Joseph Colley, two labourers who told him a little of what they knew, but not all. Churchill could have recalled the scene in Church Farm on Midsummer Day and Colley could have recounted the damning toasts in the Red Lion. Neither man did, but they both – in separate interviews – explained how they had heard John Barnett claim that 'he would give any man five guineas that would shoot Mr Parker'. The consistency between their accounts is striking. Colley's evidence matched Churchill's almost word for word.

'Last Saturday month I observed to Mr Parker that I was surprised that he was not afraid to go out at night for fear he should be knocked on the head,' John Pardoe, the parish clerk, informed Pyndar shortly after. Edward Stephens, a friend of Pardoe's who had travelled with him to Worcester on the night of the murder, corroborated this. Stephens also mentioned that Pardoe had told him that he'd heard Thomas Clewes say, 'he wished somebody would blow the parson's brains out'. It later transpired that Pardoe had been afraid to mention this as Clewes owed him £20 – a sum he was worried he might lose if the farmer was 'taken up and hanged'.

These six men's evidence suggested to Pyndar that the farmers who had quarrelled with Parker had finally determined to have him killed. All the evidence fitted. He already knew about the curious meeting between Barnett and Evans at Church Farm on Midsummer night, and he knew that the farmers had been unwilling to join the chase. This was reinforced when Betty Perkins volunteered further information on Sunday 29 June, telling Pyndar how Mrs Barnett had forbade Tustin from joining Mr Hemmus in pursuit of Heming. She included Tustin's claim that 'his mistress would not let him go, or he would have gone in a minute'. Underneath the account Pyndar noted, 'This all happened before I got there.'

Pyndar had held suspicions against Barnett and Evans from the very start, and by the weekend after the murder they were beginning to harden. There was a definite connection between Captain Evans and Heming; the tithe dispute offered a motive; the reported threats proved that at least three men – Evans, Clewes and Barnett – bore malice towards Parker; and there was also Barnett's failure to join the manhunt.

But there were reasons for the magistrate's initial reluctance to pursue the farmers. Heming was a well-known rogue and mischief-maker, and the possibility of him killing Parker for material gain could not instantly be dismissed. Equally, there is no evidence that Pyndar was aware of how bad relations in Oddingley had become. Tithe disputes were relatively common, and George Parker was an unusually proud man. It is possible that he shielded the embarrassing details of his arguments from his friend and peer in the neighbouring parish. So to immediately conclude that the farmers had plotted to have him killed would have been extraordinarily bold. And by committing himself to such a theory Reverend Pyndar was accusing several notable and respectable parishioners of being accessories to murder. That he shied away from this until he had the necessary evidence is wholly understandable.

Evans and Barnett were among the chief subjects of conversation when Pyndar met several other magistrates at an emergency meeting at the Crown Inn in Worcester, one of the city's largest coaching inns, over the weekend. Their aim was to devise a new strategy to ensure Heming's capture and they agreed to several new measures. They decided to advertise a reward of 50 guineas to anyone providing information leading to Heming's arrest. They also initiated a private fund, to which friends of Parker and other interested locals could subscribe. And finally Pyndar was urged to appeal directly to the home secretary, Earl Spencer. The magistrates hoped that a successful petition for a government reward might result in the great financial and moral might of Parliament swinging behind their investigation.

Rewards had formed a significant part of the state's strategy to apprehend criminals for more than a century. The payments were generous and widely advertised, intended to involve the wider public in the judicial system. They encouraged men to act as vigilantes who assisted magistrates and constables by performing tasks such as tracking down felons, following up on tip-offs and providing steady, lengthy surveillance of an area: tasks that overworked and geographically constrained parish officials simply did not have the means to do. Citizens performing these activities had been rewarded with monetary payments since the reign of Charles II.*

Rewards comprised the second key string of the justice system. They were offered when a suspect had outrun the hue and cry or vanished undisturbed from a crime scene. By the mid-1750s advertisements for criminal suspects – handbills and increasingly newspaper announcements – were so prevalent that the profession of thief taking or bounty hunting had sprung up in response. In 1748 and 1749 the British treasury paid out the vast sum of £206,000 in statutory and other rewards to such individuals, the two highest payments alone totalling £4,600 and £6,500, easily enough to support a person in a lavish lifestyle for the rest of their lives.

---

* During Charles II's reign a sum of £10 (an enormous amount for the time) was promised to any informant whose evidence led to the arrest of a robber or burglar. In 1692 the first statute to formalise the reward process was passed, designed to counter the growing threat of highway robbery. Men who apprehended highwaymen who were later convicted were offered rewards of £40 along with the offender's horse, arms and money.

More recently the offering of vast sums had been somewhat abandoned by the government, which was inching towards an independent police force on the Bow Street model. But such a paradigm shift would not be achieved for many decades yet, and in many criminal cases advertising a substantial reward was still seen as a natural step.

At Oddingley Pyndar had already enlisted the support of a professional thief taker, a man named Baker from Droitwich. Little is known about Baker's background or circumstances, only that John Perkins had been sent to fetch him by Pyndar on the Thursday morning. Once briefed the two men had headed to the narrow lane which ran between Oddingley and Droitwich. 'We went and watched at a new Barn belonging to a Mr John Nash of Newland, which was very near the foot-road,' Pyndar recalled.

The home secretary received Pyndar's letter on Monday 30 June. The magistrate had included a brief description of the attack and a copy of the handbill. Although the case's detail was unusual, it was a typical request. Spencer dealt with it astutely, perhaps considering Parker's killing an unnerving portent in a country battered by more than a decade of war and revolutionary unrest. He rebuffed the petition for an official reward, informing Pyndar that the government only stretched to such measures when the Crown's property had been damaged or stolen. In other ways, though, he offered his total support. Spencer promised to insert an extract of the handbill in *The Hue and Cry* (matching Read's offer from Bow Street several days earlier), and as a further incentive he made the Crown's usual offer of an official pardon to anyone involved in the crime, 'except for those who committed the principal deed'.

Earl Spencer was an able administrator and a man of some experience. As first lord of the Admiralty he had been heavily involved with wartime policy and had been in the thick of the successful efforts to defuse the naval mutiny of 1797, which marked one of the very lowest moments in Britain's struggle. Almost a decade on, Spencer was still in the political vanguard. His response to Pyndar was carefully worded and stuck tightly to protocol. If Parker's murder weighed heavily upon his mind, there is no surviving record of it.

Spencer's response would not arrive in Worcestershire for several days, but in Oddingley Pyndar was closing in on his suspects. Captain Evans and John Barnett, the two men with most questions to answer, had spent the last few days attempting to restore their standing in the parish by throwing their support behind the manhunt. Evans had called at the other farms, petitioning their masters to contribute to a local reward fund, while Barnett had ordered Tustin and Thomas Alsop, two of his most senior and physically fit farmhands, to comb Trench Wood for any sign of Heming. 'It was said that he was in the wood and some relations took food to him,' Alsop remembered. The hundreds of acres of woodland, carpeted with long grass, gorse and broom, and covered by a thick summer canopy, would have provided him with a perfect hiding place. Armed with Barnett's shotgun, they searched for three to four hours but did not find anything, and in either excitement or exasperation Tustin fired the gun at a tree as they headed home.

On Tuesday 1 July 1806, a week after Parker's murder, Pyndar finally had John Barnett and Captain Evans summoned before a meeting of seven magistrates at the Crown Inn in Worcester. The number of magistrates, all important men from prominent Worcester families, was a reflection of the seriousness of the crime. Barnett was the first of the two to be examined, being questioned alone while the Captain waited in a side room. He was not asked to take an oath. The case against Barnett rested on his failure to join the chase, his meeting with Captain Evans and his known hostility towards Parker, as shown by Clement Churchill's and Joseph Colley's evidence. For Pyndar this was an informal chance to scrutinise the farmer and record his evidence in writing.

Barnett spoke with freedom and at length, first describing his movements on Midsummer Day. He explained that when Lench had requested he go to Parker's body, he had replied, 'No, James [he meant Tustin] – you had better go.' He was then quizzed about his refusal to visit Mary Parker at the rectory. At first he denied this, stating 'to the best of my knowledge I was not desired to go', but then shifted his position subtly. 'I knew that if I had gone down, she would have shut the door against me,' he admitted.

Barnett's evidence was precise. He remembered that after seeing Lench and Tustin at a quarter past five he had gone into Pound Farmhouse and eaten his tea. About 5.45 p.m. he had set off down to Church Lane to find Captain Evans. The walk would have taken around 15 minutes, and Evans did not appear at Church Farm until Barnett had been there for around half an hour. At around half past six Barnett said that they settled down in the parlour to talk. There were four of them there, he recalled: the Captain, Mrs Banks, Miss Banks and himself, and they 'were talking over the murder before Green came in'. He stuck firmly to the story he had given Pyndar before. There was a conversation about the income tax, he said; Miss Banks brought a bottle of wine in and then Green had appeared.

'When Green came in to ask Captain Evans if he had heard of the unfortunate news', he recalled, 'to the best of my recollection Captain Evans said that I had just told him.'

Barnett's evidence was not delivered in a long monologue, as it might seem from the records, but in response to a series of leading questions from the magistrates. The scope of such enquiries was not tightly moderated, but magistrates were forbidden from posing direct questions which, if answered, would lead a suspect to accuse themselves of a crime. Set within these boundaries, the questioning dwelt on the content of the conversation between the Captain and Barnett after Green had left, and during the later part of his interview the magistrates elicited a steady narrative from Barnett regarding what had happened.

Barnett explained that after Green had departed he had been left alone in the parlour with Evans and the two Banks ladies. He had stayed for about fifteen minutes or a half-hour 'during which time much conversation passed between them respecting the murder'. Heming's name was not mentioned, he said, nor had he ever heard Captain Evans make any threats against Parker nor had he, himself, promised five guineas to any man who would shoot him. John Barnett made just one admisson, accepting that he had drunk to Parker with his left hand. A transcript of his evidence was then passed to him. He read it through and signed two copies. The farmer was excused from the room and Evans summoned.

In comparison with Barnett, the Captain's testimony was uptight, dismissive and opaque. Unlike the farmer, the Captain was asked to deliver his evidence under oath, swearing the truth on the Book of Common Prayer, which contained the Epistles and the Gospels. The case against him was based on his contact with Heming before the murder, his curses directed towards Parker and the fact that he was the master of Church Farm, a place Pyndar was increasingly viewing as a centre of operations for the farmers. The Captain recoiled into a stout defence in a setting which – as a sitting magistrate himself – must have been eerily familiar. The clerk recorded his statement.

Richard Heming has twice been employed by me to make Hurdles. I paid him the wages due to him on the 6th May last and I have not seen him from that time till the morning of the 24th June last, and I do not know of his having been employed by any persons since the 6th of May in the Parish of Oddingley. That in the morning of the 24th June, Heming called at my house between seven and eight in the morning and he pulled out of the Pool some of the Poles that were to make Hurdles and I thought that he had been coming to make Hurdles in a day or two. He had a Mug of Drink at my house but I had no conversation at all with him and that he afterwards went away and I did not think he staid [*sic*] half an hour.

Evans delivered each of these facts with firmness, producing exact dates and flat denials that he had anything more than the most fleeting contact with Heming. The Captain spoke throughout with cool precision. He all but dismissed his link to Richard Heming, treating him as one of any number of labourers, villagers and tradespersons who flitted in and out of his life. He was then pressed on his meeting with John Barnett. This too he dealt with as matter of fact: he had only learnt of Parker's murder when Green entered and 'mentioned it', he explained.

None of the magistrates was satisfied with his account, and before Evans could leave they requested that he testify in more detail. A further sheet of parchment was produced by the clerk and the Captain was asked to begin with an explanation of the income tax form to which Barnett had referred. What was its significance?

A paper about the Income Tax lay upon my table when Mr Green came in, but I do not recollect any conversation passing between myself and Mr Barnett about it. I knew nothing of the murder until Mr Green followed me into the room and said 'Good God, have you heard the news?' I said 'What news?' Mr Green said 'Mr Parker is shot.' I believe when Barnett and Green left me they went away together or very nearly so. Heming was mentioned as being the man who was suspected of being the murderer and that the Butchers were in pursuit of him and that they had no doubt but that he was taken. But I do not recollect whether it was Mr Barnett or Mr Green who mentioned it.

For a final time Captain Evans was asked who told him about the murder. He replied with certainty, 'Mr Barnett did not first mention the murder to me, and Green was the first person who mentioned it to me.' The seven magistrates – Pyndar, Anslow, Tuberville, Sayer, Hakeman, Bund and Gresley – all scribbled their signatures across the clerk's record of the day and allowed Captain Evans to leave. It had been a bold and forthright but jittery performance that left serious doubts about his innocence.

The inconsistencies between Barnett's and Evans' statements were obvious. The men had different versions of who had first mentioned the murder in the parlour, whether Heming's involvement was known and at what time Barnett and Green had left. It was difficult to find anything in common between what the men said, and yet there was no obvious reason for them to contradict each other. The only conclusion Pyndar could possibly arrive at was that the farmers were desperately trying to conceal what they had talked about that night. Most surprising was that after a week they had still not got their story straight.

Before Pyndar took further action he decided to call at Heming's house in Droitwich to interview his wife. The plight of the two women most affected by events had been lost amid the hunt for the killer and the terrible details of the attack. Mary Parker had been left widowed and penniless by her husband's murder, with her companion and financial security wrenched from her in an instant. Her rectory home would soon follow. Elizabeth Heming's situation was a sad echo of Mary Parker's. She too had been abandoned, caring for three infant daughters. Her partner had vanished and was featured in all the newspapers under suspicion of a horrific crime. If Heming was captured then he would surely be hanged, and if he was innocent then why had he disappeared?

'I saw him last on the morning of Midsummer Day,' she told Pyndar. 'He left home early on that day and was dressed in a dark long blue coat and leather corduroy breeches.' Heming had got out of bed and told Elizabeth that it was late, she remembered. He had then asked her for 'his old blue coat and said that he was going to do a dirty job for Captain Evans of Oddingley Church Farm'. It was around half past five in the morning when he left their house. She had neither heard nor seen anything more of him before Allen, the constable, came to the house enquiring whether or not he was at home.

It was now that Reverend Pyndar unearthed the most damaging piece of evidence yet against Evans. Elizabeth Heming was as careful and ordered as Richard was not, and she had kept a little accounts book on his behalf, listing in separate columns dates of payment, his billed hours and total amounts. For the past month Captain Evans' name dominated the pages.

As Evans had claimed, Heming had worked for him on 4 May, and that day he had billed him for four days' work at 6s. 8d., a bag of nails which had cost a shilling, and two further days at a rate of 5s. But what Evans had concealed in his conversation with Pyndar and his statement to the magistrates was that Heming had worked frequently for him since. On 20 May he had billed Evans for five days' work at 12s. 6d. On 7 June he had collected 7s. 6d. for three days' work, and on 13, 20 and 21 June respectively he had charged the Captain for 11 additional days for a total of £2 7s. 6d. All in all, according to Elizabeth Heming's account book, in the six weeks before Midsummer Day Evans had paid Heming on six occasions for work he claimed Heming had not done.

It was a breakthrough discovery: clear evidence that Captain Evans had concealed information from the magistrates, or worse, lied under oath, which added weight to the theory that Heming had been paid to stalk the lanes, waiting for a chance to strike at Parker. In any case Heming had been paid handsomely – the money he had collected from Evans in the previous month (almost £4) was around half the annual wage of a dairymaid. It was hard to believe that the Captain would have forgotten about such an amount.

Pyndar's investigation was gathering momentum, but he was about to run up against a problem. A statute passed more than a century before, during the reign of Queen Anne, in 1702, stated, 'no accessory can be convicted or suffer any punishment where the principal is not attained'. So although Pyndar had evidence suggesting that Captain Evans was guilty as an accessory before the fact ('one who being absent at the time the crime is committed, doth yet procure, counsel, or advise the commission of it') and had further reasons to believe he had paid Heming to kill Parker, no action could be taken against him until Heming – the principal offender – had been captured and tried.

This increased the importance of the manhunt further still. Having done as much as he could to alert those outside the parish and county, Pyndar now fixed his attention back on Oddingley. There was a final slim chance that Richard Heming had not left the village at all, but was concealed somewhere within it. If the farmers had promised Heming money to kill Parker, then it made sense that he would return to collect it or to meet them at a prear-ranged point. One possibility was that a rendezvous had taken place

at Pershore Fair one day after the murder as several farmers
including George Banks and Thomas Clewes were known to have
attended the event. A second possibility was that Heming had
returned to Church Farm, where he had been hidden in the spacious
farmhouse or one of the barns, sheds or workshops. Already some
villagers had suggested this was the case. Mary Chance, a servant,
had told Perkins that she had noticed 'a Knife and Fork and Plate
took upstairs . . . that the Captain and Miss Banks said was to cut
Bacon'.

William Chance, Mary's son, also had his suspicions. Before dawn
on 25 June, the day after the attack, he had arrived in Church Farm's
rick yard to find several men already hard at work – George Banks,
the carter and the carter's son. They had already got two loads of
clover onto a set of staddles much to Chance's surprise. 'It was a
very unusual hour to do so,' he remarked, also recalling how no
more clover was cut that day and every effort was put into building
the rick. Later, while Chance and his father were working with Banks,
the three men had fallen into a conversation about Parker's murder
and how Heming was responsible. Chance had exclaimed 'what a
cruel thing it was' – and Banks had responded, 'it was no matter if
Heming was not catched'.

The Chances were not the only people to think that something
was going on at Church Farm. Baker, the thief taker, was the first
to act on the growing feeling that something was concealed at the
farm – a telltale object perhaps, or even Heming himself. On 1 July,
shortly after the Captain's appearance at the Crown Inn, he secured
a warrant to search the property.

Elizabeth Fowler saw Baker arrive unannounced the next day,
accompanied by three others. They surrounded the farmhouse, two
at the back to cut off any escape, Baker and another man at the
front. When they were all in place, Baker knocked, demanded entry
and began a search for Heming. Their failure to find him did not
surprise Elizabeth Fowler. She later swore that he had never been in
the farmhouse after Midsummer Day. 'If he had,' she explained, 'she
must have known it [for] there was no room in the house but what

she went into.' Fowler made no mention of the clover rick, which remained untouched.

Pyndar's reaction to this latest disappointment is not recorded. It was generally considered, however, that he had spearheaded a competent investigation. The latest issue of *Berrow's Worcester Journal* was supportive in its tone, describing the inquest rather inaccurately as 'a minute observation of the business' and dwelling on Pyndar's 'strict search for Heming'. The *Worcester Herald* was much more profuse in its praise, declaring, 'For the detection of this flagitious [wicked] offender the magistrates have evinced determined and laudable zeal.' But despite what was written, the magistrates' efforts had added up to very little. The key point was that Heming had escaped and, until he was captured, there was little point in pursuing the case against the Captain or John Barnett. Pyndar was left with the option of charging the men with the lesser crimes of making threatening toasts and using abusive language in public, although these hardly seemed to fit the severity of the case. His best hope still lay with Heming's apprehension, and on 4 July he received news of a compelling sighting.

Mary Chance's evidence was hurriedly taken down by Pyndar under oath.

That on Wednesday the day after the murder of Mr Parker, about three o'clock in the morning I was making clover in a field in Oddingley belonging to Mr Perkins when I saw a man in a blue coat, whom I believe to be Richard Heming, come over a hedge (where there is no path) and run as fast as he could towards a wood in Crowle Parish, wrapping his coat over his left arm. In about ten minutes I went to my husband and son who were mowing in an adjoining field for Capt. Evans and told them I thought I had seen Heming. Capt. Evans was there and said: 'Damn your blood why had you not went after him, as all the Country need to be after him, but neither he nor either of the men moved a step.

Signed: Reginald Pyndar   The mark of Mary Chance   X

If she was telling the truth, then Heming had returned to Oddingley as Pyndar had speculated. Heming was known to the villagers, especially those like Mary Chance who spent time at Church Farm, and it seemed likely that she would be able to recognise him from a distance. The little detail of him wrapping his coat over his arm appeared to fit too, matching what Thomas Colwell had described before, and the wood in Crowle she mentioned was almost certainly Trench Wood.

But why had she not mentioned the incident sooner? More than a week had passed since the sighting, and throughout the early days of the investigation, the inquest, the newspaper reports and the search of Church Farm she had remained silent. The clear inference was that Mary, like her husband and son before her, had been intimidated into silence by Captain Evans, who had mentioned nothing about this. Mary's evidence raised a further issue too. At three o'clock in the morning it would have still been dark. Why should Evans have been in the clover field at such a time? Could he have been waiting for Heming himself?

It was another piece of evidence against the Captain, but it was ultimately useless. Reverend Pyndar had already played his hand. Trench Wood and Church Farm had been searched; letters had been dispatched to Bristol and London; testimony had been gathered from as many villagers as possible; rewards had been promised and announced. Pyndar had devised a motive, a probable scenario and even had evidence; the only part of the puzzle missing was the principal suspect. Until he was found the situation remained deadlocked.

Over the next few weeks reports of the suspect lingered in the newspapers. On 12 July the *Worcester Herald* noted there had been a sighting of Heming sheltering in a wood about five miles north of Evesham. The following week a man named Thomas Pritchett, who had been arrested on suspicion of stealing 70 rolls of flaxen cloth, was mistaken for Heming. Then at the end of July Pyndar received a message from the keeper of the gaol at Aylesbury. He informed Pyndar he had a man in custody whom he believed to be Heming.

The prisoner had been arrested after threatening to stab a woman, and although he had initially refused to give his name, he had at length admitted to being a Mr Humphrey Heming – a weaver from Worcester. '[He] appears to be a most desperate fellow,' the gaoler had written, and he had worn 'a blue coat which he tore to pieces, as also his hat – when taken'.

Among all the many sightings this seemed the most plausible. But after some initial excitement it too proved a false alarm. A month had now passed since the murder, and it was generally accepted that Heming had got clean away. As a result, Pyndar was forced to relax his investigations into Evans and Barnett, but he did manage to increase the county reward from 50 to 100 guineas and keep the notice in the newspapers for several weeks. In Oddingley the farmers returned to their harvests as the parish slipped back into its familiar summer rhythms of steady work and little rest. A further storm ripped across the county in the middle of July. *Berrow's Journal* described it as a 'tremendous storm of thunder and lightning, accompanied by a heavy torrent of rain'. Trees were uprooted, lanes submerged and horses killed when they stood. The tempest was felt as far away as London.

The harvest, though, was brought in reasonably well and prices remained stable at Worcester market. As August passed, the colours of Oddingley's meadows softened under the summer sun, blackberries appeared in the hedgerows and heather in the farm gardens. The lanes remained busy as ever with travellers and labourers walking from farm to field and one parish to another. One day John Perkins met George Banks, who was leaning on a gate by one of Captain Evans' meadows. Perkins asked, 'What do you think of those toasts at the Plough in Tibberton now Mr Parker is gone?'

'Who would have thought it?' Banks said.

'Those who performed it,' Perkins answered.

Banks' response to Perkins is not detailed, but it is clear the majority of the villagers were with Pyndar, reckoning that Captain Evans, the two Barnett brothers, Thomas Clewes and possibly Banks knew more than they were telling. This added layers of meaning to seemingly innocuous events, as if a hidden truth would at an unexpected moment suddenly reveal itself – in the sharp glance of a farmer's eye, the dramatic emergence of a new piece of evidence or the disturbing possibility that Heming would reappear in the lanes.

Such thoughts were never far from the minds of workers like William Chellingworth, who had been employed as a reaper by Captain Evans in 1806. A short time after the harvest had been brought in and stored Chellingworth was working in Church Farm's granary. At the foot of a bay the bottom of a bag caught his eye. There was no reason for it to be there. He pulled it out. It was far heavier than he had expected. Opening the bag he found a rusty saw and an adze, a tool resembling a hooked hammer used for smoothing rough-cut wood. For some reason he couldn't quite pinpoint, he instantly knew that they belonged to Heming. 'I gave them to the Captain and never saw them after,' Chellingworth later said.

CHAPTER 12

The Horrors

1806–1830

On Friday 23 June 1809, almost precisely three years to the day after Parker's murder, a little crowd of farmers, yeomen and artisans gathered in Church Farm's fold-yard. They had come to attend an auction which had been advertised in the last two editions of *Berrow's Worcester Journal*. 'The valuable FARMING STOCK and EFFECTS of CAPT. EVANS, at Church Farm', read the announcement, which gave a list of his livestock: two full-tailed geldings, mares, colts, sheep, pigs, cattle and a well bred Herefordshire bull. Also for sale were farm tools and various supplementary items, including wagon timber, old tarpaulins and several empty hogsheads. It was one of the major farm sales of the summer. Church Farm was to be gutted. Captain Evans had retired as a farmer and he had no intention of coming back.

This meant a sharp change in circumstance for Evans. He had spent 76 years seeking activity, stimulation and status, but now he was retreating from the spotlight. He may have decided that the uncertainty and stress that accompanied running a large farm was too much for a man of his age or he might have wanted to spend more time on his magisterial duties in Droitwich. But he had not retreated from the parish entirely. By the date of the auction he was already living in New House, a fine red-brick property in a secluded corner of Oddingley, surrounded by a little land, tangled holly hedges and a row of elms that arched darkly over his driveway. His old residence was acquired by William Barnett.

The Captain, though, had parted with more than Church Farm. Mrs Mary Banks, who had at the very least been a close and constant companion for more than two decades, chose not to accompany him to New House. Shortly before, George Banks had also left the Captain's household. There were rumours of a rift between the men, and later Banks would complain that he had been driven out of Church Farm 'by his [Evans'] cruel treatment of me'. For years to come the men, whose relationship had been so close it was speculated they were father and son, would remain estranged. For the first time George Banks was forced to fend for himself, but on his side he had youth, experience and skill. His time at Church Farm had given him the chance to learn much about farming and, still only in his mid-twenties, he had his best years before him. He soon found a new post in the nearby parish of Hanbury, where he worked as bailiff for a landowner named Mrs Parks, whose favour and friendship he soon won.

In the three years since Midsummer 1806 Oddingley had almost recovered its anonymity. In August 1806 *Berrow's Worcester Journal* had pulled the reward notice from its pages, tacit acceptance that Heming was unlikely to be captured anytime soon. At the end of the same month John Marten Butt was installed in Oddingley Rectory as Parker's replacement, bringing with him a fast-expanding family and a careful diplomatic style which helped rebuild links between Church and farmers. He stopped increases to the tithe at once and in 1807 conducted a special sabbath of contrition, intended to heal divisions still further. Butt slotted effortlessly into parish life in a way that George Parker never had. He was to stay for many years.

Reverend Parker's murder, though, was not forgotten. Rumours blew about the countryside and from time to time surfaced in snippets of evidence relayed to Reverend Pyndar, who continued to brood over the case at his home in Hadzor. One of the first accounts to reach him after the initial wave of investigations had ceased came from a Mrs Morris, of Droitwich. Her evidence diverted attention away from the Captain and John Barnett, refocusing it on Thomas Clewes. Morris told Pyndar that she had seen him at Heming's home shortly before Midsummer Day. She had been minding the infants when Clewes had knocked at the door. He was looking for Heming, who was out. On learning this he had told Morris he would wait nearby in the Red Lion. Clewes asked her to send Heming when he returned.

A far more significant development followed in July 1808. In the weeks after Parker's murder Pyndar had ordered many local properties to be searched in an effort to root out Heming. One man suspected of concealing him had been John Rowe, who lived in a house called Briar Mill in Ombersley parish, a few miles west of Droitwich. Rowe was a horse dealer, one of the slipperiest of nineteenth-century trades. Much like the modern-day used-car salesman, horse dealers had a reputation for mysterious bargains, hollow promises and opaque chains of supply. At worst they were seen as dangerous charlatans, at best they were useful business contacts. In both cases, they were almost always thickly embroiled in local affairs. As Pyndar's investigation stalled in late July 1806, one of his final acts was to order a search of Briar Mill. The warrant had been passed to John Perkins for execution, but Perkins – who by that point was being treated as a deputised constable – failed to uncover anything. Two years later, though, Rowe came forward on his own initiative. He gave Pyndar a tantalising account of a plot orchestrated, so he claimed, by the Oddingley farmers.

On Midsummer Day 1806 Rowe was riding through Droitwich on his way to Bromsgrove Fair. He told Pyndar that as he passed through the centre of town he was stopped in the street by James Taylor, a farrier. Taylor was well known in Droitwich, with one uncharitable pen sketch depicting him as 'a little dark short man, who usually rode a little brown horse'. Taylor called Rowe over and told him, 'if he would shoot Mr Parker he might get £50, which was collected and lay in Clewes' hands'. Rowe asked Taylor on whose behalf he spoke, and the farrier replied, 'Mr Evans, Mr Barnett and Mr Clewes.' He added that the job was easily enough done. All he had to do was creep up to a window behind the rectory and shoot Parker at eight o'clock as he was taking his supper.

Rowe warned Taylor that if he mentioned 'such a thing again to me, I will knock your brains out'. It was a truculent response but did little to stop the farrier from approaching him once more, later that afternoon. Rowe was returning from the fair when Taylor ran out of the White Hart Inn. 'Rowe! The money is ready for you!' he called. As before Rowe angrily reproached Taylor. When he arrived home that evening and learnt that Parker had been shot, he told his wife that all the farmers in Oddingley would be hanged. Ever since he had maintained that 'Had the murder been stirred into at the time, I'm sure it [the plot] would have been found out.'

Here Rowe was wrong. His suggestion that Pyndar had not investigated the crime properly rested on the fact that no formal proceedings had been brought and his belief that the magistrate had failed to uncover the farmers' intentions. This was not true. Pyndar had good evidence; he had a probable scenario and motive. His difficulty lay with the law, which required Heming to be convicted before the farmers could be charged as accessories. But Rowe's story could not be ignored. It added further evidence to the case against the Captain, Barnett and increasingly Clewes, and it also introduced a new participant in the plot, James Taylor.

James Taylor would already have been well known to Pyndar. As a farrier, he toured the local farms, tending to sick animals and providing a range of rudimentary services which included the creation and administering of various mercurial elixirs. Taylor was particularly known as an expert in the skilled art of bleeding horses, cattle or sheep, a practice which was believed to purge disease. It involved securing and blindfolding a feverish animal before opening its jugular vein and drawing off a portion of blood with the sharpened blade of a fleam, an instrument which resembled a physician's scalpel.*

---

* Farriers were often characterised by their hard-headedness, which made them suitable for tasks avoided by more squeamish members of a community. In 1776 Parson Woodforde had John Reeve, the local farrier, draw a tooth 'but shockingly bad indeed, he broke one of the fangs of the tooth and it gave me exquisite pain all the day after, and my face was swelled prodigiously . . . Gave the old man that drew it however 0–2–6. He is too old, I think, to draw teeth, can't see very well.'

Although Pyndar may have known Taylor for his skill as a farrier he would have more readily identified him as a man of murky repute. To William Barnett in Oddingley he 'bore a bad character' and for a chronicler in Worcester, who would set down a little biography of him several years later, 'he had the reputation for being the biggest rogue in the county'. In Rowe's testimony Taylor certainly emerges as a curiously loose individual. He had the temerity to approach an acquaintance in daylight with a proposal to commit murder and then, in spite of a sharp warning, to repeat the offer just a few hours later. Such actions bear the mark of a determined, amoral personality, seduced to collude in a capital crime. Some questions linger, though. If the money was to go to Rowe for committing the murder, then how would Taylor benefit? He neither lived in Oddingley nor had any known connection with Parker, so why should he want him dead? A further problem lay in the timing. Why would Taylor approach Rowe on Midsummer Day when Heming was already primed to commit the attack? It made little sense.

But James Taylor could not be discounted. He was already well known to local magistrates for a variety of petty offences and it seems possible that he might have somehow also entangled himself in the Oddingley affair. He was an opportunistic man who worked in a transient environment, visiting farm after farm, his course steered through the lanes by offers of work or rumours of trouble. And trouble is often what he found. Of all Taylor's little infamies throughout the years, one in particular had passed into local folklore. Around the year 1790 he had been arrested for sacrilege for stealing the communion plate from the parish church at Hampton Lovett, just north of Droitwich. The case had seemed clean cut, but a flaw in the indictments had led to him being unexpectedly acquitted. Having slipped so magically through the fingers of the law, Taylor was popularly remembered in the area as the 'Churchwarden of Hampton-Lovett'. And it was to dismay or amusement several years after that he managed to wed a pretty widow from Worcester, a triumph which only added to his cherished identity as the local rogue.

But Rowe's evidence suggested that Taylor might have had a

more sinister side. After receiving Rowe's testimony, Pyndar had the farrier arrested and committed to gaol, and the Captain and Barnett were once again called before magistrates to explain themselves. No records of these proceedings survive, but it is clear nothing more came of the matter and Taylor was released shortly afterwards. The incident, however, was significant. It added weight to Pyndar's theory that the farmers had plotted Parker's death and engaged Heming for the purpose. It also suggested that their operation had not been confined to Oddingley, but stretched into Droitwich and its adjoining parishes. That Rowe was approached indicates that he was considered of a sufficiently violent disposition to execute the task. There is a hint of this violence in his language and brisk treatment of Taylor. Was Rowe the man the farmers were looking for in 1806? Venal, ruthless, tractable, unfussy? Someone who could get the job done?

Yet John Rowe's evidence seems suspiciously elusive. He carefully shields himself from any accusation of wrongdoing by emphasising his reaction to Taylor's offer. But while he is defensive in this detail, in others ways he must have been astonishingly brave. Two years after Parker's murder Rowe became the first person to speak out against the farmers, and for this he risked being treated as a pariah by his peers in the Droitwich area. This appears to have been Rowe's fate. 'The boys used to call after me: "Who killed the Oddingley parson?"' he claimed years later, adding bitterly, 'They were set onto this by Captain Evans.'

Still the focus remained fixed on Richard Heming and his whereabouts. A popular theory maintained that he had escaped to a faraway corner of Britain, where he had blended into a new community under a different name. Various sightings supporting this argument were fed back to Pyndar, including a persuasive account from a servant girl who had grown up in Droitwich and claimed to have seen Heming begging in Portsmouth. Her story was relayed back to Pyndar by the son of a Worcester magistrate, but the speed of communication was such that no action was taken for a fortnight.

In the end nothing came of the report, which was filed away in Hadzor amid the growing piles of notes.

A more widely accepted explanation was that Heming had escaped overseas. For nearly a decade after his disappearance the Napoleonic Wars rumbled on, drawing men from British shores to battles on the continent. Around 300,000 of these were never to return, lost in campaigns and conflicts that stretched across Europe, from the Iberian Peninsula to the Netherlands, and it was imagined that Heming was among them. Another suggestion was that he had somehow slipped past Richard Ward's careful watch in Bristol in the days following the attack, and managed to steal himself away in a boat bound for the New World. A letter was circulated in Droitwich to this effect some years after 1806, 'stating that he had escaped to America, and giving a circumstantial account of the way in which he got out of the country'. This letter was supported by the evidence of a man named Creswell, a Droitwich resident, who told his friends he had seen Heming while travelling there. Although it appeared extraordinary to have chanced upon a figure as elusive as Heming in a continent as vast as North America, Creswell's account was accepted by many.

Mary Chance's claim that Heming had returned to Oddingley was generally not credited. Her sighting had been an isolated one, and the prospect of him dashing about the fields and lanes on Midsummer night while all eyes were watching for him seemed unlikely. Yet there were those who still suspected that Heming had met the Captain, Barnett or Clewes after his disappearance. Elizabeth Heming in particular was not placated by letters from America or by the farmers' dismissals and denials. In *The Bishop's Daughter*, a novel by the Reverend Erskine Neale, published decades later in 1842, Elizabeth Heming is portrayed. Neale had visited Oddingley after the murders. His plot drew heavily on the case and was strikingly accurate.

> She was assured by the Oddingley farmers that Heming was gone to America; and from time to time, names of persons were given who had seen him there; and more than once extracts of letters, said to

be written by him, were distributed in the neighbourhood. To none she gave credence. Her remark was, 'I know better. He would never abandon his wife, and his children, and his home, without a word. No; he is near me! I am sure of it; and it must be the business of my life to discover where. I know my mind is not so clear as it was; and that my troubles have nearly got the better of me; but still in my dreams he would not stand by me so often and warn me, if there was not an effort to be made and a secret to be discovered.

Elizabeth believed that Richard had been lured back to Church Farm by Captain Evans and John Barnett on Midsummer Day. What happened to him after this was unclear but she had heard about the clover rick that George Banks had built at Church Farm on 25 June, and she felt sure that something – perhaps Heming's body – was hidden inside. This theory drew on other evidence that placed him at Church Farm in the hours and days after the murder. William Chellingworth was one farmhand who said he had seen Heming slip out of the farmhouse as Baker searched it, boasting to a local man that 'he could hang all the head men in Oddingley'. William Rogers of Dodderhill, a neighbouring parish, quietly told friends that his son-in-law had seen Heming at Evans' on the night of the murder. None of these reports had ever been passed to Pyndar.

The clover rick stood at the heart of the mystery. For Elizabeth it was the key to discovering what had become of Heming. The years following his disappearance had been cruel. The suspicions against him had left her ostracised in the area, and in June 1807 Elizabeth and her three daughters had been issued with a removal order by their parish in Droitwich. Within a few years all three children were dead. These misfortunes preceded her marriage, to Edward Newbury, a labouring man, but shortly afterwards he died too. Battered by a sad series of circumstances, none of which were of her own making, Elizabeth Newbury – as she had now become – retained her conviction that the Oddingley farmers were hiding something about Heming's disappearance.

With little left to lose, in the spring of 1816 she finally testified against them. On 29 March she stood before a panel of seven magistrates in Droitwich and deposed that she believed that Richard's remains had been concealed in the clover rick. A warrant was granted for its search the following morning, and, almost a decade to the day after Elizabeth Fowler had discovered the shotgun under the staddles, a team of parish constables prepared to descend on Church Farm.

Elizabeth's theory was a plausible one. Why had a rick been built so hastily after the murder? Why had Banks not mentioned anything about it to William Chance before? Rick construction was an art and required careful planning. But this one had seemingly been built on a whim in the earliest hours of the morning before the clover harvest had even been completed. Since then it had stood for ten years and had been re-thatched twice by William Barnett.

A team of constables arrived at Church Farm the next morning to find that the clover rick was gone. Having stood undisturbed for a decade, the night before the warrant was due to be executed it had been dismantled and removed. The constables executed their orders as best they could, digging up the area around where the structure had been, but found nothing. The tension and anticipation created by Newbury's testimony and the issuing of the warrant had been replaced, once again, by frustration.

The vanishing clover rick was another riddle in a parish that seemed filled with secrets. Just as those who knew about Heming's escape kept silent in 1806, those who knew the truth about the rick did the same a decade later. Perhaps they were too scared to report what they knew; perhaps they were too loyal, too proud or too sensible to split. For all that John Rowe had told Pyndar about the plot to kill the parson, there were many others who must have known far more. But what these villagers did know was stowed away: like the harvest tools in deepest winter, fastened in their sheds, hidden out of sight. For those who lived nearby and others who occasionally visited, Oddingley was becoming known as an enigma and an ill-omened place. It was as if a hint of its shadowy, alluring character could be derived from its very name, with 'oddity' variously defined in the dictionary as 'a strange or peculiar person or thing / a strange attitude or habit / an eccentricity that is not explained'.

Mary Sherwood was drawn to Oddingley during these years. She was the sister of Reverend Butt, Parker's replacement, spent lengthy periods in the parish and later recorded a sadly vivid portrait of it full of pathos and lamentations. Oddingley was, she wrote, an unhappy place. Villagers crowded about their chimney corners in winter to discuss the murder again and again, turning the story over and over in their conversations, like a precious object – first to be examined and then understood. She visited Parker's glebe, that 'sanguinary field . . . where the assassin had affected his deadly purpose' and she complained of the parishioners, 'many of whom acquiesced or rejoiced in their bloody achievement so that land was defiled by blood, and filled with the images of death and horror'. With a heavy air of Gothic melancholy, she continued:

> And is it not astonishing that many who visited this place while its chief inhabitants lay under the dark suspicion, were filled with a sort of sadness, of which they could not divert themselves? In vain the sun shone on the fair fields of this unhappy parish. In vain an infinitude of beautiful wild flowers added perfume to every breeze, and every charm of rural life was scattered around, and a thousand interesting pictures presented themselves. For that alas! was wanting which could alone make these things delightful. Namely, a spirit of sincerity and harmony and benevolence, among its inhabitants, arising from the consciousness of being at peace with God.

To Sherwood, Oddingley was a community adrift. Only a parish blighted by vice and devilry could stoop so low as to murder its own clergyman. It was a view echoed by others in the years following the murder, as the idea that Oddingley was somehow cursed permeated the surrounding countryside. John Noake, a noted local antiquary, journalist and author of *Worcester in Olden Times*, detected a lingering sadness when he visited St James' Church. His piece chimed darkly with Sherwood's.

I don't usually encourage superstitious notions in others, nor harbour them myself, but somehow or other I felt a disagreeable, uneasy sensation during my stay here, and had any one of the two or three farmers who met together at the church invited me to dinner, I think I must have declined with a polite excuse. Indeed the village appeared as melancholy and deserted as though lying under the ban of some unatoned crime, and the few persons who formed the congregation hastened to and from the church, and avoided the stranger's gaze, as though it were painful to them. Some of the windows of the church, too, were broken, and the wind moaned through the shattered panes of the north transept like a sad spirit of the other world, raving round the walls of God's house in the sorrow of remorse and despair.

More worldly troubles awaited several of the farmers. The inflationary cycles that had swirled in the years before Parker's death continued to haunt them for years afterwards. A disastrous harvest in 1812 plunged Worcester to the brink of famine, leaving county-wide supplies of wheat and potatoes perilously low. At its worst, wheat was selling for the extraordinary price of £1 a bushel in the market, meaning that wheaten bread was almost impossible to obtain. Most villagers and townsfolk were forced to survive the winter on scanty rations of bran and root vegetables, and in Worcester the Bacon and Pease Charity was hurriedly established to feed the 8,000 helpless poor.

Worcestershire had barely recovered from the effects of famine by 1815, when the Napoleonic Wars concluded with Wellington's victory at Waterloo. The peace was greeted as an 'unnatural blessing', but the more prosperous age that was anticipated failed to materialise. Thousands of returning troops and the sudden influx of foreign imports combined to flood both the labour and commodity markets at a stroke, plunging the economy into a devastating recession. Its effects were felt right across the country, and in Oddingley it was enough to ruin several of the farmers. By 1815 John Perkins had fallen into debt and had been forced back into the labouring ranks. The next year Thomas Clewes suffered the same fate. Having pawned and mortgaged all of his land, he filed for bankruptcy and, leaving a large number of creditors unpaid, he left Netherwood Farm for good.

Clewes had never been skilled with money, but his profligacy at Netherwood had been compounded by a terrible run of bad fortune that had seen several of his most valuable animals die unexpectedly. 'As for Clewes,' recalled one of Erskine Neale's characters in *The Bishop's Daughter*, 'He warn't to thrive. A higher power was agen him!' Clewes had begun the decade as Netherwood's master; he ended it as a woodman struggling to survive with his wife in a little cottage on the outskirts of Trench Wood. He drank more, the locals noted, and struggled to sleep.

Not all the farmers suffered. William Barnett's move to Church Farm in 1809 reaffirmed the family's ascendancy in the parish. The younger brother soon established himself in the Captain's old property beside the church, where he was to remain for decades to come. Within a few years of his arrival the village was altered for ever with the appearance of the Birmingham and Worcester Canal. This enormous engineering project sliced right through Oddingley, from Dunhampstead to Tibberton, passing just 50 yards from Church Farm's door and dividing it from Netherwood, which was left more isolated than ever.

At Pound Farm John Barnett's position as the most powerful village farmer had been confirmed in 1814 when his mother died, enabling him to assume full control of the business which he had already stewarded for nearly two decades. Several years later Lord Foley decided to reward him for his contribution to parochial life and to recognise the family's long-standing loyalty to him as tenants by constructing him an expensive new property named Park Farm in the north of the village. Pound Farm, the Barnetts' former home, was rented out to the poor.

The 1820s was a decade at a pivot of British history, poised between the fading Georgian era and the modern Victorian age which would replace it. The Britain of these years was purposeful and pointed, spearheaded by revolutionary technological evolutions such as the telegraph, the steamship, macadamised roads and the railways. In north Wales Thomas Telford's Menai suspension bridge was one of the first of its kind in the world and was admired as a paragon of brilliant engineering. When the Liverpool and Manchester Railway was opened four years later, in September 1830, it meant that the 30 miles that lay between the two cities could be negotiated in little more than an hour.

The appearance of Worcester was also changing. In 1819 the city's new gasworks had opened, and for the first time its streets were illuminated at night. One resident described the 'splendid' spectacle of the city streets, 'the shops sparkling with vivid lustre'. He delighted at how the 'inflammable vapour winds its way into our domestic circles and surprises us with its sudden ignition'. Elsewhere, in 1821 Michael Faraday demonstrated the principles of the electric motor. The following year Charles Babbage delivered a paper to the Royal Astronomical Society describing his design for a 'difference engine' or mechanical calculator. In London and the growing industrial areas of the Midlands and the north-west a collective spirit of innovation, optimism and industry was converging to form a potent zeitgeist that swept scientists and engineers along with it. Canals, which had so recently been treated as wondrous advancements, had already lost their sheen and much of their practicality to the railways. Britons were on the brink of a new age: never had the old seemed so old and the new so new.

Parker's murder was now a fable lost in time, a crime that belonged to a different age. By the 1820s fewer than four out of ten living Britons had been born in the eighteenth century and very few remained wedded to the old customs that had governed society for so long. A new better-mannered society was emerging as a contrast to the uncouth, expressive and decadent England of King George III.

In 1803 Colonel Despard had been the last man condemned to be hanged, drawn and quartered. Over the following years Sir Samuel Romily had conducted an energetic campaign against the death penalty, and when the Cato Street Conspirators were tried for high treason in 1820, they became the last men to be hanged and publicly beheaded. The pillory, stocks, public whippings and all the other trappings of the old brutal methods of punishment would also soon be banned.

In 1822 the able young administrator Robert Peel was appointed home secretary and embarked upon a long policy of dismantling the Bloody Code and simplifying English law. The desire for such reform predated Peel, but it was his zeal that would be remembered. A total of 278 statutes were repealed or consolidated over the next eight years in a sustained attack on what Peel considered an obsolete chaotic jungle of legislation, altering for ever a system that had meant around 200 different offences were punishable by death. The statute of 1702 which had prevented the Captain and Barnett from being tried after Parker's murder was one superseded during this time. In May 1826 a new criminal justice act was passed, allowing accessories to be tried even if the principal was not present. The law was not made retroactive.

The decade also brought changes in Oddingley. In 1824 Reverend Charles Tookey arrived to replace John Marten Butt, and the following year the Foleys were succeeded as patrons and landowners after selling the entire estate to John Howard Galton. This man acquired a parish in gentle ascendancy. After the dip at the beginning of the century, the village population had slowly begun to rise. Farms lost in the 1810s were replaced by others in the 1820s, most controlled by a new generation of farmers. By now John and William Barnett were the only two surviving agriculturalists from 1806. Samuel Jones disappears from the parish records around 1815; John Marshall died in 1816; and Old Mr Hardcourt's long life in the parish came to an end in 1823.

The Oddingley story belonged to the past. Arguments about tithe payments had rumbled on across the country, but by now even the Church was accepting that reform was inevitable. Parker and his ratepayers were among the last to fight over the tax in such a way. And for the new generation reports of the swearing, expressions of hatred and malice and the left-handed toasts seemed scandalous. As the world's leading power, Britain was desperate to shake off the embarrassments of its past. Nostalgia was confined to the older generations, with the poet and novelist Horace Smith one of the few left to lament, 'We have no longer any genuine quizzes or odd fellows, society had shaken us together in its bag until all our original characters and impressions have been rubbed out, and we are left as smooth and polished as old shillings.'

Captain Evans, though, lived on at New House. Now among the very oldest of men, his existence was increasingly secluded and there is little sight of him in the records. On 22 September 1825, at the extraordinary age of 92, he performed his final duty as a magistrate at the George Inn in Droitwich. It was now around half a century since he had served in the American conflict, 42 years since he had retired from the army and 30 since he had been elected to the magistracy in Droitwich. During the Captain's three decades of unbroken service the British government had been led by six prime ministers and the United States by six different presidents. Such dazzling longevity was to become almost as notable as any of his many social achievements.*

  This last stretch of Captain Evans' life was touched by loss. Catherine Banks, who had remained with him after the departure of George and her mother, had served as his housekeeper for around 20 years when she died on 13 October 1822. She would have been aged about 50, and the Captain took her passing badly. In a life of bluster, adventure and many changes, Catherine Banks had remained with him longer than anyone else. She was buried in a fine vault he had prepared for her at St Peter's Church in Droitwich, and it seems her funeral stirred some religious feelings within him. Never a church-goer during his Oddingley days, the Captain is known to have

---

* In December 1829, six month after his death, Samuel Evans' name was added to the *Worcester Miscellany*'s 'Record of Remarkable Longevity from 1796'. The list also included 108-year-old Sarah Smith of Worcester, who had died in July 1811 and had spent her life as a 'mender of chair bottoms'.

attended St Andrew's in Droitwich shortly afterwards and received the sacrament.

These events heralded the beginning of the final phase in the Captain's life. The semi-retirement of his quiet existence at New House was now replaced by near-total withdrawal from local society. In 1826 he left Oddingley altogether and moved to a cottage on Friar Street near the centre of Droitwich, which he seldom left. He would remain here for three years until the early summer of 1829, when a strange and miserable illness brought a swift end to his long life. It was an unhappy death. Those who saw him in May 1829 encountered a troubled man. He swore and cursed from his bed, falling into desperate spells of quiet contemplation or murmured prayer. He seemed stricken by a shadowy terror against which he raged but could not escape. Early one spring morning he gripped his housekeeper's arm and begged her to turn 'these two Devils out of the room'.

A record of his last weeks was left behind by this housekeeper, a woman named Catherine Bowkett. Her account is both powerful and revealing, and there is little reason to question its veracity. She recalled that the first symptoms of his malady appeared at three o'clock on the morning of 12 May 1829. It was instantly clear that he was seriously unwell and she sent for assistance as soon as she could. In the afternoon the knocker on the cottage door fell once again and George Banks was shown upstairs.

Whatever ill feeling there had been between Banks and the Captain had by now dissipated, and on seeing his old bailiff, Evans confessed he was gravely ill. They asked Bowkett to leave them alone, and from the bottom of the stairs she listened as 35 guineas, heavy golden coins of more than half an inch in diameter, were counted out. She heard the Captain tell Banks 'he had had the money in his hand all day long'. When this was finished, Bowkett was called back and ordered to fetch a silver cup and a set of spoons that had been promised to Banks. The Captain instructed her to fill the cup with ale.

This was the first of Banks' visits to Evans' cottage during his final weeks. Bowkett did not know the farmer but later recalled that he would sit with the Captain in his bedroom, where they would hold long whispered conversations. Whenever she entered the room, they would fall silent.

Within days it became clear that the Captain's illness was not just attacking his elderly body, but also his mind. Bowkett saw Evans grow ever more tempestuous, veering between violent outbursts and periods of calm. At times these moods were interspersed by tortuous visions, and Bowkett later recalled his trembling appeals from his otherwise empty bedroom to 'take these two men away'.

The bleak scenes at the Captain's cottage were at odds with the mood outside in Droitwich, as the market town crept through late spring towards early summer. Horsedrawn carts hauling loads of freshly mined salt clattered between the pits and the canal, milling on the town streets with farmers' traps, drovers to and fro between nearby villages and the town market, wagoners calling at the harness makers and tradesmen heading south to the cathedral city of Worcester or north towards the smoking chimneys of the Black Country and Birmingham.

Amid the gossip was the testimony of a man named Doone, who had previously worked as a servant for the Captain and claimed to know his habits well. Doone told the *Worcester Herald* that Evans was an eccentric who had spent years brooding moodily in his cottage, drinking as much as a bottle of brandy each day. Visitors would always face some 'delay and difficulty in gaining admission' Doone said, a fact he attributed to Evans' fixation with security and his insistence that all of his doors remained closed and bolted.

Over the following weeks Evans continued to sink. Frightened and light-headed, he begged Bowkett to sit by his bedside at night, 'which she did till he swore at her'. One Sunday morning as Bowkett climbed the stairs she heard the Captain thrashing in a fit of delirium. He called out, 'Banks, Banks! Dick, Dick! Damn the parson!'

Bowkett sent for Banks, who arrived at the cottage shortly afterwards. She informed him that the Captain was haunted by visions and harrowed by madness. 'It was enough to break the heart of a stone to be with him,' she told Banks. 'He [Banks] changed colour very much,' she remembered. 'He seemed frightened, but did not say anything.'

The Captain lingered wretchedly for a week longer with, a local chronicler later recorded, 'a fearful apprehension and forebodings in his mind'. During the day he sat with his Bible opened before him, and visitors 'frequently heard him praying aloud'. But his mood was fragile and at the merest provocation he would scream 'the most horrid oaths and imprecations'. Captain Evans was a broken man, torn at his death between God and the Devil. In *The Bishop's Daughter*, Erskine Neale dwelt on those awful days.

> He became moody, restless, and reserved; abhorred being alone; and though at no period of his career discreet and guarded in his expressions, seemed, latterly, to lose all self-command, and indulged, when irritated, in a licence of thought and language mournfully inconsistent with his age and station.
>
> Illness came on. Death appeared imminent; and was most unwillingly contemplated. He was incessantly watched by certain individuals who were about him. For this vigilance various reasons were assigned. In his last hours he appeared extremely desirous to make some communication to a gentleman who visited him; but there were those who took care, by opportune interruptions, to frustrate his intentions. His death was anything but calm and peaceful – marked by little resignation to God's will, and no apparent realisation of his promises.

The Captain's death was recorded in a stark notice published in early June in the *Worcester Herald*: 'Died, lately, at Droitwich, in the 96th year of his age, Samuel Evans ESQ, for many years a magistrate in the borough of Droitwich.'*

In the months after he died the Captain's end was considered puzzling. Locals wrote to newspapers and exchanged views on street

---

* This report casts a slight doubt on Evans' age at the time of his death. Most sources agree that he was 96 years old, and the most likely explanation for the variation between these sources and the affirmation here that he was in his '96th year' is a simple reporting error.

corners. For Georgians the deathbed was a place of confession and remorse, where the condemned trembled before God, where the secrets of their souls were unlocked and exposed. While the wretched were doomed to suffer, the pious and the good were relieved mercifully.

Fascination with the deathbed was reflected in countless works of contemporary art and literature. In Charles Dickens' 'The Stroller's Tale', published in the second instalment of the *Pickwick Papers* (1836), Dickens vividly recounted the horried death of a pantomime actor, a wicked drunkard who had beaten his wife and starved his son. Helpless, wretched and frightened, the actor moaned and withered for two days, beset by violent visions from his tortured past.

> The walls and ceiling were alive with reptiles – the vault expanded to an enormous size – frightful figures flitted to and fro – and the faces of men he knew, rendered hideous by gibing and mouthing peered out from among them; they were searing him with heated irons, and binding his head with cord till the blood started; and he struggled madly for life.

Seven years previously, the Captain's death foreshadowed that of Dickens' clown, but between the two stories, one fictional, one real, there were crucial differences. Unlike the actor, Evans was neither young, helpless nor destitute, nor had he ever been convicted of any crime. Ostensibly, the Captain's life had been one of success and progress, marred only, perhaps, by his inability to settle and produce a family of his own. Yet his deathbed ravings hinted at something deeper: of an uneasy conscience or an unbalanced mind. It was a puzzle with a catch. For while the strange malady had loosened his tongue, it had not revealed his secret.

Perhaps Samuel Evans sensed that he was approaching the end even before his final illness struck. On 8 January 1829 he completed and signed a will which named Banks as executor. The farmer himself was one of the chief beneficiaries of the document, which stated that he was to inherit Evans' cottages at Droitwich and Oddingley and all other unspecified personal effects. Symbolic of the Captain's varied interests and many connections was his ownership of a 'Bullary of Salt' – a share in the profits of a local salt spring – which he left to Lord Foley. But his main legacy was reserved for a girl, Naomi R. Mary Cartwright Banks, who upon her eighteenth birthday was to receive a bond for £500 and all its accrued interest. He also bequeathed the infant girl his 'neat set of china, twelve silver tea spoons to match, and two other silver tea spoons, a tea caddy and also two books. One of which is the History of England and the other the History of Rome.'

His funeral was held on 6 June 1829 at St Peter's Church, which stood high in the grassy fields to the south-east of Droitwich town. Here his body was laid next to Catherine Banks' in the same stone vault that he had prepared seven years earlier, in the shade of an ancient yew tree. The Captain's life had spanned almost all of the Georgian era. He was born just 19 years after the accession of the first George and died almost precisely a year before the death of the last. He was one of the few survivors of a fading world: a military man, a magistrate and a gentleman. One of the chief mourners, George Banks, stood with his head bowed.

CHAPTER 13
The Old Barn

Netherwood Farm, Oddingley, 21–24 January 1830

The Christmas of 1829 passed and the new decade began with an exceptional spell of cold weather. Sharp frosts and swirling blizzards swept right across England, delaying mail coaches and rendering foot travel almost impossible. In London the *Morning Chronicle* informed its readers that 'coachmen and guards describe the cold to have been the most severe they have ever experienced', describing how 14 mail coaches had been buried in snowdrifts outside Marlborough. At Worthing on the south coast the local newspaper declared the cold had not been so intense for around 30 years. Further north the *Sheffield Courant* complained, 'This is the severest winter we have had for some years and since our last we have experienced it in its wildest characteristics.'

Worcestershire was similarly chilled by the cold. *Berrow's Worcester Journal* reported that the Birmingham and Worcester Canal had completely frozen over and that, in some stretches, sheets of ice extended right across the Severn. As the weeks passed, the temperatures showed little signs of change. On 20 January there was the heaviest snowfall yet. Roads leading into Worcester were blocked and London traffic was stopped indefinitely. The next day *Berrow's Journal* recorded, 'Yesterday morning Fahrenheit's thermometer stood, in an exposed situation, at eighteen degrees below freezing.' In the countryside the extreme weather made almost all farmwork impossible, and except for the carting of manure and the organisation of stables and barns all labouring jobs were abandoned in

Oddingley for the first three weeks of 1830. Across the valley, fields, lanes and hedgerows all lay swathed in ice and snow.

Far from the village crossroads, isolated from the bulk of the parish by the canal, Netherwood was the most vulnerably situated of all Oddingley's farms. The meadows and fields belonging to the property stretched out across the valley floor and were so deeply covered that no work could possibly be attempted. In Netherwood's fold-yard, however, Charles Burton and his son were continuing stoically through the worst of the weather. Burton was a well known and dependable local carpenter who took on short-term contracts around Droitwich. He had worked at Netherwood for Thomas Clewes years earlier, and had been engaged by Henry Waterson, the farm's current master, to pull down an old barn. It was a typical but time-consuming job for Burton, who had been forced to spend several frozen weeks in Oddingley, a place he was connected to through family as well as work: Elizabeth Newbury, whose first partner had been Richard Heming, was Burton's elder sister.

This link, though, was an almost-forgotten one. Thomas Clewes' tenure at Netherwood had finished in 1816, and since then the property had been leased by Waterson who had inherited a farm in disrepair.

A woodcut depicting Netherwood Farm in the early nineteenth century.
Trench Wood looms in the background

For years after his arrival he had strived to improve the condition of the barns and the outhouses, repeatedly petitioning his landlord, first Foley and later Galton, to replace a decaying barn that flanked one side of the yard. Each time he had been refused. Only at Christmas 1829 had Galton finally acquiesced and agreed that Waterson could engage Burton to dismantle the old structure and build a replacement. Burton had begun the job on 28 December 1829, and by 21 January he had spent three weeks at Netherwood, dismantling the barn roof and pulling down the supporting walls and wooden frame. All that remained was for Burton, now joined by his son, to dig out the shallow foundations, salvaging as many of the bricks as he could.

The twenty-first of January 1830 fell on a Thursday. It was late afternoon and almost all the light from the weak wintry sun had melted away in the clear Midland skies. It was a cold, lonely scene: father and son wrapped in thick frock coats and woollen scarves, gripping iron spades and hand forks in their gloved hands. They were two dimly lit figures at work on a bleak, white landscape. A woodcut depicting Charles Burton at the barn survives. It shows a tall man with a sharp nose, a thin mouth and breezy beard that flows to a point below his chin. Burton is wearing a tight pair of corduroy breeches, a loose-fitting greatcoat and a brimmed hat pulled down almost to his eyebrows from which unkempt hair escapes in little tufts at either side.

It was around four o'clock in the afternoon. Burton was digging at a foundation trench 'not quite two feet deep' a few yards from where the barn door had once stood, close to the edge of a frozen pool. Labourers dug trenches using iron spades or, when the ground proved too hard, the mattock – a pickaxe with a sharp blade, which was hacked into the earth to break it up. Burton lifted his spade and forced it down into the trench, scooping the clay away. He drove the spade down again, but this time it jarred against something blunt and hard.

It could have been a stray brick or the root of a dead, forgotten tree, but Charles Burton, so he later told a magistrate, instantly felt it was something more. He put down his spade and peered into the trench.

There was still enough light to reveal a smudge of a black object. Crouching down, Burton could see he had caught against the top of a leather shoe. Extending from the shoe were two thin flat bones that disappeared away into the earth. Burton clawed at the cold red clay. He found a second shoe and, stretching away at a steady depth, he began to uncover more and more bones as he dug further, and clusters of the frosty earth came away in his hands.

There were other objects too: hints of rotted fabric, something resembling a carpenter's rule and a coin. The terrible collection was scattered over a plot inside the boundary of the demolished barn, up against where the outer wall had previously stood. Here, under the barn floor, was a human skeleton, sprawled silent and undetected. A shallow grave in the red clay.

For a moment Burton recoiled from the scene, lost in thought. Seconds later he was working again, disguising the site and gathering up his tools. There was no chance to investigate further. The wintry daylight had almost gone, and by a quarter to five it would be dark. Forced into a decision, he chose not to alert the Watersons and instead told his son they were done for the day. Already Burton's mind was racing. Could these be the remains of Richard Heming, his brother-in-law?

Before he left Burton ensured his find was perfectly concealed. The trench was situated on the very edge of the fold-yard, beside a bridle path that branched off at a right angle from Netherwood Lane, wending away through several low thistly fields towards Trench Wood and Sale Green. To disguise the grave from passers-by or the attentions of the farm dog, Burton covered the trench with debris and heaved a stone over the plot.

Inside the farmhouse Mrs Waterson and her daughter saw Burton minutes afterwards. They noticed 'he looked pale and agitated'. He told them he had finished for the day and then set off.

Charles Burton's actions over the subsequent hours were striking. Having chosen not to speak to Henry Waterson he also decided against visiting a local magistrate. He simply went home. Burton had much to think about and for the moment remained silent as the questions burned. Were these Heming's remains? If so, then who had buried them under the barn floor? How long had they been hidden? Could anything be proved? If it wasn't Heming then who might it be?

That night Burton talked these riddles through with his wife, and the following morning acted decisively. On Friday 22 January he rose early and set off along the icy turnpike road to Droitwich. He soon arrived at the post office on Worcester Road, where he asked to speak to the postmaster. Richard Allen was well known locally; as postmaster he lay at the apex of local communications, managing the daily flow of letters and parcels across the county. Earlier in the century he had served as one of the town magistrates alongside Captain Evans and as such had been involved in the original hunt for Heming. On the night of Parker's murder Allen had executed the warrant to search Burton's home, so from that unhappy meeting, at the very least, the two men knew one another.

Richard Allen saw Burton at once. He listened to his story and then hurried him to the home of the nearest magistrate. From there, in a chain of whispered confidences, reports of the find began to circulate.

Burton was sent south, back to Worcester, carrying a carefully worded letter drafted by Allen and addressed to William Smith, a solicitor and the city coroner, who lived at Newport Street on the banks of the River Severn. Allen's letter to Smith was tentative. A skeleton had been found buried under a barn floor in Oddingley, he wrote. Burton *supposed* it to be Heming, the *supposed* murderer of Reverend George Parker. Perhaps Richard Allen had been unfavourably scarred by false rumours before; in any case he chose not to commit himself. He requested that Smith take charge of the incident and 'give what directions you thought necessary'. He implored Burton to deliver the letter with all possible haste.

From the very beginning of his involvement William Smith approached the Oddingley case in a wholly different manner to that adopted by Richard Barneby years earlier. When the coroner received Burton at his home later that afternoon he instantly took the matter seriously. Smith was earnest, well-intentioned, intelligent and dogged: traits that would combine spectacularly over the forthcoming days. He heard Burton's account then set about reacquainting himself with the facts of the case. He immediately composed a letter to Reverend Pyndar, by now an elderly man, who was living at Areley Kings near Stourport. 'If you have any depositions that can throw any light on the murder, perhaps you would be kind enough to send them to me?' Smith enquired.

Smith then asked Charles Burton – who must have been exhausted from his travels between Oddingley, his home at Smite Hill, Droitwich and Worcester – whether he would accompany a pair of constables to Netherwood so they 'could watch the bones' until officials could attend. Once the carpenter had left his office, the coroner penned his final letter of the day. It was addressed to Mr Matthew Pierpoint – a surgeon at Worcester Infirmary – and desired him to exhume a skeleton in Oddingley the following morning.

By remaining tight-lipped, Charles Burton had afforded William Smith a luxury that neither Pyndar nor any others investigating Parker's murder had previously enjoyed. He had generated some quiet hours in which official action could be taken before anyone with either the motivation or influence to distort the facts had the chance to do so.

Friday 22 January was a strange day at Netherwood. Henry Waterson still had no idea that a skeleton had been uncovered in his fold-yard, but the family were perplexed that, after leaving abruptly the night before, Charles Burton had not reappeared for work the following morning. In the afternoon rumours began to reach the farm that 'everyone in Droitwich was talking about the discovery of Heming's body'. The reports were dismissed by Mrs Waterson as gossip. Only when her son arrived home with the same news did she begin to think that they might be true. Minutes later Charles Burton had knocked at the front door accompanied by two constables.

It was already dark, and as the Watersons learnt about Burton's discovery, outside the constables settled into their disquieting vigil. That night temperatures dipped to their lowest levels since 1812. The men had been ordered to keep the site in the exact condition Burton had left it until Smith and Pierpoint arrived the following morning. But the cold was so intense they were forced to work in shifts, moving between the fold-yard and the farmhouse to warm their hands at the fire and beg a little beer. 'They didn't relish their employment at all,' Mrs Waterson recalled. 'They were cold and frightened; and as to ourselves we had none of us much rest that night. I shall never forget it as long as I live.'

Inside, the Watersons were left to absorb the implications of Burton's discovery. For years perhaps these bones had lain just yards from their door. The *Gentleman's Magazine*, years later, explored the horror of such a thought. In the 14 years since Clewes had left, their children had played in the old barn. Exhausted labourers had rested there, eating their wheaten bread and sipping perry or beer. Temporary harvest hands had been quartered there when the farm-house was full, and the dogs had scratched and rooted just above the site, as if they were looking for rats.

At nine o'clock on Saturday morning Charles Burton arrived back at the mound of marl and debris he had abandoned on Thursday evening. He was accompanied by a little party of officials including Smith, the coroner, and Pierpoint, the surgeon. A woodcut produced several weeks afterwards shows Burton standing beside the grave leaning languidly on a spade; Henry Waterson joins him wearing a flowing smock, along with his wife and two stout constables in tall hats and three-quarter-length coats. They are directing William Smith, a rotund man with lank thinning hair and a round inquiring face, to the bones. While Burton seems assured and still, all of the others wear expressions of horror and wonder as they point down into the trench. The woodcut shows that the stone had been removed, the marl brushed aside and the bones exposed for all to see. It was at this point that Matthew Pierpoint stepped forward to commence the exhumation.

Pierpoint began at the foot of the grave and then worked assiduously up, uncovering the fibula, the femur, the pelvic girdle, the vertebrae and ribcage, the bones of the arm and finally the skull. As each subsequent piece was revealed, it was carefully scrutinised for clues. It was immediately clear, Pierpoint noted, that the body had been thrown in on the left side with the subject's back to the wall of the foundations. When the full length of the skeleton had been exposed, he produced a rule and measured it to be 'as near as possible 5ft 3in in length'. The left arm had been resting under the skull, almost as a cushion; the right arm was doubled up across the ribs. The grave's dimensions, Pierpoint calculated, were about 4 feet in depth and 14 inches across.

Questions loomed over the exhumation of the skeleton. Was it Heming's? If not, then whose was it? Could it have been the ancient remains of a farmhand or destitute labourer, lost to memory generations before? How had the person died? Was there any evidence to suggest violence or was this simply a natural death? Pierpoint worked on under a weak sun that struggled through the wintry sky, the gloom and sharp cold air numbing his fingers and rendering the task ever more difficult. The surgeon noted that the body had almost certainly been deposited in the grave fully clothed. This was clear, Pierpoint said, as the many different bones of the feet were still contained within the shoes, indicating strongly that the body had been concealed while the flesh was still whole. All of the skeletal bones, he said, had subsequently fallen into positions consistent with the subsequent rotting away of the softer parts.

Pierpoint now drew each of the bones carefully out of the grave and placed them one by one in a deal box. As he lifted the skull from its resting place, he noticed that there were a series of severe irregularities which, he instantly pointed out, were most probably the cause of death.

On the forehead there was a blunt crack or 'fissure' which extended fully down the orbit. Despite the fact that the teeth were still in remarkably good condition, the surgeon noted that both the upper and lower jaw had been loosened from their sockets and beaten into many pieces. 'Great violence must have been used to fracture those parts of the head,' Pierpoint told Smith. The nature of these multiple fractures, he continued, was such that it seemed impossible for them to have been self-inflicted. Only heavy blows or a horrendous collision could have caused such severe damage, and interestingly, it did not appear that the force had been cushioned by a protecting hand. He concluded, in his professional opinion, 'that the injury must have been done to the skull before the body was put there – and that such an injury was committed whilst the person was alive or immediately after death'.

With the complete skeleton stowed away, Pierpoint explored the grave in greater detail. Aside from the leather shoes, almost all the fragments of accompanying clothing had wasted away. There were, however, a number of objects strewn about the skeleton. To the right side of where the femur had lain, Pierpoint found the wooden rule that Burton had glimpsed on Thursday night. Something that faintly resembled the waistband of a pair of breeches was pulled from the area around the pelvis, and from near the ribs came a portion of a waistcoat pocket. Other artefacts were salvaged too: a rusty knife, a whetstone used for sharpening knives, a sixpence marked 'F.W' and three half-pennies from the year 1799.

These clues, rescued from the frosty grave, suggested that Burton had discovered the body of a labouring man whose bones could not have been buried for longer than 30 years. His early conclusions were entirely consistent with the irresistible theory that Charles Burton had now entertained for almost two days: that these were Richard Heming's remains.

At Worcester that afternoon William Smith wrote directly to the home secretary, Robert Peel. The implications of Matthew Pierpoint's intial conclusions were of such gravity that Smith felt obliged to inform the government immediately. The coroner outlined the developing situation. He told Peel that a skeleton had been discovered in the parish of Oddingley within the bounds of a dismantled barn. He suspected these bones to be those of a labourer called Richard

Heming who had disappeared many years ago after supposedly murdering the parish parson. Smith added that the skull of the skeleton had been fractured by one or more blows, and that he could only conclude that a second murder had been committed by the same farmers who themselves were likely to have organised the first murder.

Smith was writing to Peel for advice, but also with the same request that Pyndar had made to Earl Spencer more than two decades before: he wanted to secure a royal pardon for anyone who could be tempted into providing information about the skeleton. His actions were driven by excitement and a genuine possibility of solving a case which had bewildered his predecessors. Smith had been thrown into a situation full of excitement and possibility. But any hope that he entertained of securing swift governmental backing would soon fade.

At 41 years old, Robert Peel was among the brightest lights in the Duke of Wellington's government. Two decades earlier he had come down from Oxford with a double first, and in the years since he had become a lynchpin at the centre of British politics. By 1830 Peel was an experienced home secretary, now occupying the post for a second time, and he was well placed to judge the merits of Smith's letter. He had served his political apprenticeship in Dublin as chief secretary for Ireland, a country consumed by religious divisions that tore across entire communities. Murders were far commoner in Ireland than mainland Britain and Peel had learnt to react to the violent cases he encountered with careful tenacity rather than a natural sense of outrage, an icy habit that led Daniel O'Connell, the Irish political campaigner, to compare Peel's smile to the silver plate on a coffin.

For Peel a murder case was to be treated and examined carefully before any speculative conclusions could be made. He had a tidy administrative mind. 'There is nothing like a fact,' he declared in 1814, a theme he returned to two years later, when he reaffirmed his belief that 'facts are ten times more valuable than declamations'. These views were entrenched in his political philosophy, and for William Smith they would be a stumbling block. Smith's letter had declared much but proved nothing. To Peel at the Home Office it appeared amateurish, hasty and speculative, traits that he instinctively shied away from and qualities that he was actively trying to dispel from England's policing system.

About four months earlier, on 29 September 1829, Peel's police force – the first of its kind in England – had been deployed in parishes within a 12-mile radius of Charing Cross in London. Four months on, Peel was still caught up in the introduction and workings of the new body, which had faced stiff opposition and contempt from the beginning. The policemen, dressed in blue, were derided as spies and snitches and – worst of all – a standing army released onto the streets of the capital. An unflattering crop of nicknames had arisen in the few months since Peel's police had been operational. Peel's Bloody Gang, the Plague of Blue Locusts, the Blue Devils and Raw Lobsters were all insults circulating in the streets and printed in the newspapers.*

But for Peel the introduction of such a body was a necessity in a rapidly developing society in which crime, so he argued, was rising sharply. He considered the old system of policing, which had its roots in the Middle Ages, unfit to deal with the challenges posed by innovative nineteenth-century felons. In a society where criminals could make use of swift modes of travel and fast transmission of information, there needed to be a trained, professional force that was equal to them. Peel's police were to be a disciplined and effective tool of the state in this new modern age. They were expected to react to crime intelligently, to protect and pursue.

This was the climate in which Smith's letter from Worcester was received. And for Peel in Whitehall it contained several flaws. First, although it appeared the skeleton belonged to Heming, there was no firm proof that this was the case. For a positive identification to be made a new inquest would have to be held, and after the passage of so many years it was uncertain that the bones could be shown to be Heming's. Second, Peel was more accustomed to corresponding

---

* Raw lobsters are generally blue, the colour of the police uniform. But when placed in boiling water they turn red, the colour of the army tunic.

with magistrates, whose role it was to investigate cases and apply to the Home Office for support. He was not just a man of detail but also a man of form, and to receive a request for the royal pardon from a coroner was irregular and an example of just the type of unregulated procedure that annoyed him.

In his reply the home secretary mingled inquisitiveness with non-commitment. He assured Smith that he understood both the gravity and significance of his letter, but he implored him to investigate the matter further. Peel ignored the coroner's request for a royal pardon entirely and instead asked Smith to keep him abreast of any further developments, pointedly asking for the name of the local magistrate at Oddingley. It was a typical, ponderous response.

While Peel remained sceptical, others took far less convincing. By 24 January reports of Burton's find were sweeping across Worcestershire. It was a news report like no other, as if a story had been plucked deliciously from the past to tantalise imaginations and set conversation alight. Those under the age of 25 would have only known the tale through local rumour or taproom gossip; for the older generation it would have been a misty memory, jumbled with other tales from the war years. Others who remembered Parker's murder well were now among the elderly and many of those directly involved in the manhunt were dead. Everyone, though, now returned to the story afresh and conjecture flared. Was this second killing the work of a single man or a band of murderers? How many of those implicated were still alive? Would they be finally brought to justice?

Following the exhumation, Pierpoint had spent Saturday evening at his home carefully reassembling the skeleton to complete a more detailed analysis. By Sunday morning he was able to present Smith with a list of further observations. Once again they matched Heming's profile. Without doubt, Pierpoint said, the bones were those of a man aged between 30 and 50 years of age. Having examined the fracture on the forehead more closely, he now declared the skull to have been shattered into twenty or more pieces. It was a fearsome injury, he said, 'quite sufficient to produce instantaneous death'.

Although Pierpoint was sure that the man had been bludgeoned, he had no idea what kind of weapon could have caused such fractures. He told Smith that it must have been something very blunt and heavy but was certainly not a pistol, as the coroner had initially speculated. He was also sure that it was not a self-inflicted wound, which ruled out suicide. To cause such an injury several blows would have been required. It was murder, of that he was certain.

As Matthew Pierpoint continued with his assessment of the skeleton, in the villages and towns that surrounded Worcester, Droitwich and Oddingley rumours started to circulate. It was well known that at the time of Heming's disappearance Thomas Clewes had been the master of Netherwood Farm. Clewes had cursed Parker with Evans and Barnett in the months before the murder. He had been seen at Heming's home in Droitwich, and his subsequent troubles with money and alcohol were well documented. That a grave could be concealed at Netherwood without Clewes' knowledge or approval seemed impossible.

Within days the newspapers were speculating, too. They focused their attentions on the barn, hoping that a careful description and analysis of the structure or the identification of an unusual feature might expose another of its secrets. *Berrow's Worcester Journal* dwelt on the geography of the fold-yard, 'the spot chosen for the grave being close to a pool which received the drainings of the fold-yard, appears to have been selected in the expectation that its contiguity to the pool would hasten the decomposition of the body'.

The use of 'selected' lent an eerie note of premeditation to the piece. To dispose of the body in the dampest corner of the barn demonstrated either a thorough knowledge of the farm, or sheer good luck. That Thomas Clewes must have been involved was also inferred by Charles Burton, who noted that access to the barn came from two strong double doors. The pair in the fold-yard were secured by a padlock, he said; the others opened out into the bridle path and were held shut with a strong wooden pole. Burton argued that nobody could have entered the barn without first acquiring the key, which, Henry Waterson explained, was always kept in the house.

On Sunday 24 January the number of curious locals who wandered into frozen Netherwood Lane to see the site for themselves rose from a steady trickle to a small crowd. The farm was surrounded by snowy meadows that behind the farmhouse sloped gently upwards towards Trench Wood, where Thomas Clewes now lived with his family. But Clewes was not yet the object of their attentions. Instead they looked at the small damp plot where the barn had so recently stood. The building had been rectangular, a little over 20 yards by four across, and split into three distinct sections: a single bay at the front, a threshing floor in the middle and at the rear a large double bay. It was in this part of the barn that the skeleton had been found, not ten seconds' walk from the farmhouse door.

Like Parker's glebe, Netherwood's barn had become a place of horror, its very ordinariness lending it a disturbing quality. But while the skeleton suggested much, it proved very little. In his office at Worcester this fact was troubling William Smith, who had thrown all his energies into arranging an inquest. For twenty-three-and-a half years secrets had festered beneath conversations just as the bones had been hidden beneath the ground. Almost all attempts to extract the truth had been met with blank denials and stony faces. Now, though, things felt different. Smith hoped the skeleton would prove more than a wondrous find, a cause of fantastical imaginings in the parishes and the newspapers, but rather a catalyst to loosen unwilling tongues.

Smith consulted Pyndar's notes and began to draw up a list of all of those involved, however slightly, in the events of 1806. Thomas Clewes, the previous master of Netherwood Farm, was his first name, but also on the list were John and William Barnett, both of whom were still farming in the parish. He also wrote to Elizabeth Newbury, John Rowe and John Perkins, and began a search for the two butchers – Thomas Giles and John Lench – who had disturbed Heming in

Parker's glebe over two decades before. Smith invited each of these individuals to Worcester the following Tuesday morning, where a second inquest would commence – this time on the Netherwood skeleton. Several men, though, would elude the coroner's summons. One of them, by just seven months, was Captain Samuel Evans.

CHAPTER 14

Extraordinary and Atrocious Circumstances

Worcester, 25–31 January 1830

At a quarter to eleven on the morning of Monday 25 January, a clear, frosty winter's morning with the remnants of a new moon fading in the sky above, William Smith prepared to open the inquest on the Netherwood skeleton at the Talbot Inn in Worcester. The Talbot lay near the end of a little row of pleasant Georgian houses which lined the Tithing, a long thoroughfare that snaked from the north into the city centre towards the cathedral. It was an impressive hostelry, an elegant assembly of gleaming red brick, ancient beams and pretty dormer windows. It stood three storeys tall and was lit from the outside by the glow of two gas lamps that arched imperiously over its oak entrance door.

Smith had considered Oddingley an unsuitable location for the inquest. Not only was it a small parish and therefore ill equipped for the anticipated influx of visitors, but it seemed improper to continue the investigation in a place which for so long had shielded the truth. As a statement of intent, Smith had taken the unusual step of drawing the inquiry out of the village and forbidding Oddingley parishioners from serving on the coroner's jury. Instead the evidence was to be laid before 23 men from the surrounding area: six from Crowle, six from Claines, four from Tibberton and the remaining seven from Himbleton. Like any parish, Oddingley was accustomed to administering its own business. Now it would be judged by its neighbours.

Long benches had been pulled across a large room to the rear of the building, which jutted back into the stable yard. The make-shift courtroom was filled with Oddingley men, many of them familiar to one another yet this time drawn together in an unusual

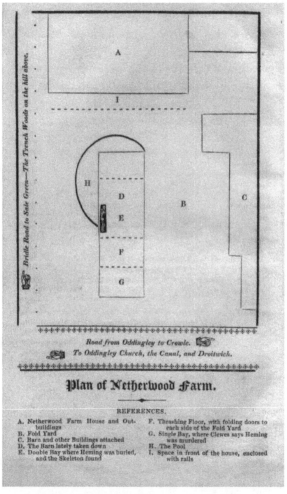

Bridle Road to Sale Green—The Trench Woods on the hill above.

A

I

H

D

E

F

G

B

C

Road from Oddingley to Crowle.

To Oddingley Church, the Canal, and Droitwich.

Plan of Netherwood Farm.

REFERENCES.

A. Netherwood Farm House and Out-
   buildings
B. Fold Yard
C. Barn and other Buildings attached
D. The Barn lately taken down
E. Double Bay where Heming was buried,
   and the Skeleton found

F. Threshing Floor, with folding doors to
   each side of the Fold Yard
G. Single Bay, where Clewes says Heming
   was murdered
H. The Pool
I. Space in front of the house, enclosed
   with rails

A plan of Netherwood Farm in January 1830.

Published by E. Lees, an innovative Worcester printer

environment. There was Thomas Clewes and the two Barnett brothers. Charles Burton was there along with other farmhands – James Tustin, William Chellingworth and George Day, Parker's old tithe boy. The occasion had the air of a reunion, nearly a quarter of a century having passed since the events they had been summoned to recall. There was also a hint of paradox. Smith was about to stir memories of a warm and lively June afternoon in Oddingley's airy fields in the cold bleak atmosphere of a city courtroom. The witnesses were not wearing smock frocks, but were wrapped tightly in thick greatcoats and over-cloaks, warm breeches and riding boots. At the head of the room the coroner and his jury huddled about a long rectangular table. The skeleton, now cleaned and glimmering brightly in the dim light, lay like a macabre trophy before them.

The jury was sworn in at 11 o'clock. Smith welcomed the men to the inquest and invited them to examine the bones. Then the first witness was called. Charles Burton narrated his movements over the past month and explained how he had discovered the skeleton 'on Thursday last'. He told the jury that Heming was his brother-in-law and he suspected the shoes found belonged to him. The shoes were exhibited, and Burton was asked whether he recognised them. 'These shoes now produced are as near as the size of Heming's as possible. I believe them to have been his,' Burton replied.

Burton's evidence was illuminating and precise, but at times it was also faintly speculative, as if he had already settled on his own theory. When a plan of the barn was produced and he was asked to indicate the location of the skeleton, he did so, pointing to the double bay while repeating several times that the barn was situated 'near to the house'.

This must have jarred for Thomas Clewes. In all, he would have heard his name mentioned three times during Burton's testimony – each time in connection with his spell as master at Netherwood. Both Smith and Burton seemed to dwell on the links between the skeleton, Netherwood Farm and Clewes. Much of the day's questioning would examine these connections, but the evidence against Clewes was far from conclusive. Burton told Smith that Heming had not worked for any farmer in the village but Captain Evans and that he had never once seen Clewes and Heming together. Burton remembered his brother-in-law well and retained a clear mental image of him: 'Heming had a full mouth; a most perfect set of teeth. I thought immediately on seeing the shoes and the rule that they were his.'

Matthew Pierpoint followed Burton to the stand. The surgeon represented a wholly different type of witness to the carpenter. He had no family ties to Heming and for the most part refrained from speculation. He was a man of science and logic: dispassionate, cool-headed and assiduous. The facts Peel desired were far more likely to flow from the erudite surgeon with 11 years of experience at Worcester Infirmary than from Burton, the theorising carpenter with a vested interest in the outcome.

Pierpoint replied to Smith's questions with brisk statements. He informed the jury of the dimensions of the grave and described the bones of the skull, 'which were beat into a great many pieces'. There was a crack or fissure in the frontal bone of the skull, Pierpoint said, 'which must have been occasioned by a very severe blow'. He explained that he was sure that what had been found were the remains of a male body.

Smith asked Pierpoint how long he felt the bones may have been buried.

'I should say the body, from its appearance, had laid there a good many years but this would much depend on the nature of the soil.'

'And do you have any observations about the nature of the soil?'

'The soil was damp, from its neighbourhood to the pool, and as such was calculated to hasten decay,' Pierpoint replied.

Smith then returned to the fractured skull. He asked Pierpoint if he could elaborate on the evidence he had already given.

'It [the injury] must have occasioned instantaneous death and must have been caused by many blows,' Pierpoint explained. 'The injuries were such as could not have been inflicted by the party himself and I should judge the remains to be those of a person between 30 and 50 years of age. I consider them to have remained there undisturbed, from the time of their being placed there.'

As the jury absorbed the implications of Pierpoint's testimony, the third witness was called. Elizabeth Newbury had long cut a tragic figure. For all of her qualities, her life had come to very little. She informed Smith that she was a widow and lived just to the south of Worcester in St Martin's Parish. As none of Heming's family from Bredon were present, Newbury was the only witness to have known him intimately and over a significant amount of time. Smith's chief motive for calling her was to achieve a positive identification of the skeleton and it was to be a further harrowing ordeal for Newbury. If she could identify Richard Heming, then she would confirm her fears that she was a widow not once, but twice.

Smith questioned Newbury gently. She remembered that Heming had risen at half past five in the morning on Midsummer Day 1806, saying he had a 'dirty job to do for Captain Evans, of Oddingley Church Farm.' 'What dirty job?' she had asked. 'To pull some poles out of the pool,' he had replied. Thereafter Heming had complained that he was late and had asked for his dark blue coat. Soon after that he left the house. She had never seen him since.

'Was he carrying a gun with him?' Smith asked.

'He had no gun at that time but some time before he had one, which he said he had sold.'

'Did he have any other tools with him?'

Newbury said he owned a rule, 'which he generally carried with him'. She remembered this distinctly as it did not close properly at the bottom and had a small crack by the rivet. The carpenter's rule which had been recovered from the grave was produced and given to Elizabeth to examine. It was cracked exactly as she had described.

'I firmly believe this to be the rule Richard took out on that day,' Newbury said.

So far Elizabeth Newbury's evidence had been lucid and cogent. This identification of the rule was important. Coupled with her brother's evidence regarding the shoes it was a second tangible link between Heming and the skeleton. A strand of circumstantial evidence quickly followed. Heming was five feet three inches tall, she recalled, precisely the length that Pierpoint had declared the skeleton to be. She was certain of this as Heming had been drawn to serve in the militia, only to be excused as he was an inch below five feet four, the minimum admissible height.

The coroner was satisfied with Newbury's answers so far; she appeared intelligent and in possession of a spotless memory. He now invited Pierpoint back to the table and asked him to hold together the jaws of the skeleton.

What followed was a hideous moment which silenced the room. For a second Elizabeth Newbury was confronted with the ghostly form of Heming's skull, clamped between Pierpoint's hands. All of the dark torments of the past two decades seemed to descend upon her in an instant. She rocked back on her heels. It was a 'peculiarly painful situation', the *Worcester Herald* observed; 'she was placed under considerable emotion and nearly fainted'.

'The mouth greatly resembles that of Richard Heming,' she stammered.

For Smith it was a distressing but necessary step. Newbury was allowed a short time to recover, while he turned and addressed the jury. 'Gentlemen, are you satisfied that these bones are those of Richard Heming?' The jury expressed themselves convinced; Smith had achieved the first of his aims. It was a rudimentary identification, but in 1830 forensic science remained a nascent discipline undergoing a difficult infancy. At a lecture on medical jurisprudence at the University of London in 1834 Professor A.T. Thomson noted, 'No part of testimony is more difficult or dangerous in its effects, if incorrect, than that which is intended to prove identity.' Once physical features and distinguishing marks – birthmarks, moles, burns, tattoos and so on – had wasted away, all that was left of the body was the peculiarities of its frame, and coroners were forced into blunt empirical reasoning. A careful coroner, such as Smith, would engage a surgeon to determine the height, age and gender of a body, but some inquiries barely did this. In 1834 a Dr Cummin, a lecturer on forensic medicine, wrote to the *London Medical Gazette* complaining, 'A "tale" of great mystery has been going the round of the newspapers during the last week. A skeleton, it seems, was found in a field near Oxford; and an inquest was held upon it. It does not appear that any professional investigation was made as to the sex, or age of the individual to whom the bones belong, nor as to the condition of those parts, whereby an opinion might be formed how long they had lain in the earth.'

In cases where murder was suspected, very little could be gleaned from a skeleton, which usually withheld most of its secrets. Whether the deceased had met with a natural death or had been poisoned, suffocated, strangled or had their throat slashed open, the bones would not say. 'Attempts have been made to identify persons who have been murdered from the skeleton,' Professor Thomson told his audience in 1834, 'but except as I have already pointed out to you in reference to age or unless some malformation affecting the bones or fractures, anchyloses or amputations have occurred, little confidence can be reposed on evidence from the osseous frame of the body.'

Smith had overcome all of these difficulties. There was little doubt in the room that the bones spread across the table belonged to Richard Heming. He was dead and had been for some time. The cracks which spread out across his skull like a spider's web stood testament to his murder. Only in very rare cases could such a certain identification take place. This was such an occasion. Charles Burton's suspicions had been converted into a fact no jury could dispute. Robert Peel would be satisfied.

Elizabeth Newbury had by now regained her composure. She told the court that Richard Allen had called at her house late on Midsummer Day, 'very reluctantly' informing her of his business on the third occasion. More episodes were recalled: the account book which detailed work done for Captain Evans, her suspicions about the clover rick and Heming's odd connection with Thomas Clewes, who 'was in the habit of coming to see Richard in the three months preceding the 24th of June'.

'When was the last time that Clewes came to your house?' Smith enquired.

'I think that he was there within a week before, but I cannot recollect properly the last day he came.'

'Did anybody else from Oddingley visit Heming during this time?'

'I do not recollect any other person besides Clewes coming from Oddingley,' she said.

Henry Waterson was interviewed next. Netherwood Farm's current master explained that he had succeeded Clewes in 1816 and had never met him before that date. He had inherited the barn in which the skeleton had been found, which had been in a state of disrepair for some years. Waterson had used the building to store grain and had noticed that one corner sloped down a little lower than the rest. This was where the grave was discovered. 'I do not think the body could be put there since I took the farm without my knowledge,' Waterson said. He added that he always locked the barn with a padlock.

Richard Barneby, the original coroner, then appeared, producing the broken gun that had been recovered from Parker's glebe as well as Heming's account book, which Elizabeth Newbury was asked to identify. Next John Lench, the butcher, recalled the minutes surrounding Parker's murder and how Thomas Giles (who had since died) had chased Heming across the fields. Though an interesting witness, Lench's memory appeared clouded by time and it was necessary for his original deposition to be read, which he then swore to be accurate. Following Lench was George Day – Parker's old tithe boy – who displayed similar forgetfulness, only very faintly recalling details from the years of village quarrelling. Day could not remember having ever seen Heming and Clewes together.

But if Clewes was cheered by Day's evidence, then his spirits were to be lowered once more by the appearance of Thomas Barber. Barber had lived around the Oddingley area for many years, keeping a store in Sale Green, just half a mile from Netherwood. He recalled the time Clewes and Parker had crossed each other in his shop, when Clewes had looked over his shoulder and muttered that he would give '£50 for any man who would shoot the parson'. The room quietened.

'Did you ever hear Clewes say anything else against Reverend Parker?' Smith asked.

'I have heard him damn the parson,' Barber replied. 'He never spoke in the praise of Mr Parker.'

Barber's evidence was significant. He was the first of those involved in 1806 to speak before a court against any of the farmers. His evidence seemed all the more important as he claimed not to have any ill feelings towards Clewes, who had visited him regularly and had been there 'as little as a week ago'. It was a propitious beginning for Smith, who knew that the success of the inquiry depended on the willingness of witnesses to speak openly.

Proceedings continued at an intense pace. The afternoon passed and the skies darkened as the farmhands Thomas Lloyd, William Nash and Richard Crockett were called. Their answers were more guarded. Crockett, who had worked for Clewes at Netherwood, said that there were holes in the side of the barn, but not of such a size that a man could crawl through. William Chellingworth, who spoke next, was evasive. His testimony ended with a stiff rebuke from Smith and was later described in an article in the week's *Worcester Herald* as given 'in a very unsatisfactory and contradictory manner'.

The gas lamps were lit and darkness had fallen by six o'clock, when Susan Surman, the final witness of the day, was called. While the four farmhands who had just testified had been reticent and opaque, Surman demonstrated herself far more eager to speak. She was a spinster, she told Smith, living in Swinesherd to the east of Worcester. This in itself was interesting. Having left Oddingley and constructed a life elsewhere, Surman was no longer constrained by ties of loyalty to the Barnett brothers. And this proved to be the case, as Surman instantly embarked on a testimony full of colour and suspense. She explained how she had met Heming regularly in the weeks before 24 June, how she had been the final person to speak to Parker before he was shot, and how on Midsummer morning she had seen Clewes on horseback near Mr Barnett's stable.

'Clewes said to some person with him: "He should be glad to find a dead parson when he came home from Bromsgrove Fair,"' Surman announced.

This statement was met by 'a general shrill of horror', noted a journalist from the *Worcester Herald*.

'Did anyone else hear this remark?' Smith rejoined.

'Mr Hardcourt's servant was along with me,' Surman said. 'She is since dead.'

'And did you mention this to anyone?'

'I told it to Mr John Barnett that night after Mr Parker was shot. He did not seem alarmed. I have [also] thrown it in the teeth of the parish officials when they have refused me parish relief,' she said.

A streak of malice could be detected in these answers. The parish records reveal an untold story. In 1808, shortly after Parker's murder, Surman had given birth to a bastard son. The child had lived just long enough to be baptised, and it is likely that her application for parochial relief stemmed from this time. None of this was told to Smith or the jury, but Surman had established herself as a dangerous witness – perhaps with an old score to settle.

The final half-hour of the day saw Surman trace her fire on John Barnett. She told the courtroom that he had hidden from Pyndar when he arrived in the parish. She recalled Pyndar dragging him out into the lane and admonishing him, and how Old Mrs Barnett had stopped James Tustin from joining Mr Hemmus in the pursuit. All told, her evidence was so damaging to John Barnett and his family that it seemed vengeful. It was to be the closing act of an extraordinary day.

At seven o'clock William Smith adjourned the inquest until nine o'clock on Friday morning, binding all in the jury and list of witnesses to return to the inn. It had been as auspicious a start as he could have wanted. Smith knew that a successful and rigorous coroner's inquest was crucial to the outcome of a case. Often such occasions were indolent, scarcely worth more than the three-sentence summary that followed, after a pause of a week, in local newspapers. In his letter to the *London Medical Gazette* in 1834 Dr Cummin had complained bitterly about the ineffectiveness of inquests and had vented his anger on coroners, whom he considered overworked men of little capacity.

The officer who presides is held in no very great public estimation; he is frequently a man of very limited acquirements – a mere lawyer; his field of labour is generally extensive, and he has, of course, much labour on his hands. He gathers a jury, as chance throws them in his way, of personages commonly more superficial than himself, and who being pressed into the service, and acting reluctantly, are easily satisfied and find whatever verdict is suggested to them. If medical evidence be called at all, it is such as gives least trouble to procure, for the coroner has no means of remunerating competent witnesses whose testimony might be desired; so the evidence which is obtained is generally volunteered and obtruded by persons who have no valuable information to give, nor object perhaps, except to acquire a little petty notoriety.

Cummin's complaints were valid. Many coroners were not the enlightened referees that Peel and the English justice system desired, but bureaucratic relics who relied more on antique prejudice than common sense. Inquiries were often rushed, sophisticated medical opnions were seldom sought, small numbers of witnesses were generally allowed to grandstand and juries all too frequently arrived at the most obvious conclusion. The problem, though, was not with the system but with the fact that it relied too heavily on the calibre of the official in charge. Where a disinclined or lazy coroner might fail, his competent and energetic peer might fare better. With the right man at the tiller, coroner's inquiries remained potent judicial devices. This was mainly because they were not governed by the stiff rules of court cases, which forbade various types and lines of questioning. Coroner's inquests were much more flexible, more spontaneous, more likely to thrill, shock or surprise.

Richard Barneby and William Smith represented two different classes of coroner. Barneby had been languid, timorous and tractable when William Barnett had called for him in 1806. Two decades on, Smith was his antithesis: zealous, inquisitive and determined. He had succeeded in creating an environment of contained excitement at the Talbot, intelligently utilising Pierpoint's expertise and assembling a jury that, ostensibly at least, was fit for its task. In this distinctly public arena, not much more than a mile from the centre of Worcester, he had demonstrated beyond doubt that the skeleton belonged to Heming. Thomas Barber and Susan Surman had supplemented this achievement by becoming the first two parishioners to testify against Clewes and Barnett in public – more would surely follow on the Friday. On his side Smith had intrigue and he had momentum. As he stepped out of the Talbot onto the cobbles and into the cool wind that blew along The Tithing the truth felt tantalisingly close.

News of the discovery of Heming's skeleton was now spreading past the county bounds. *The Herefordshire Journal* published reports of Burton's find as Smith's inquiry was beginning in Worcester. Within a few days an article in *Berrow's Worcester Journal*, the first of the city's papers to print after the discovery, was being syndicated in columns across the country. The public mood was captured in a letter composed by a resident of Worcester on 25 January.

> The inhabitants of this city and of the towns for many miles around it are at this moment in a state of great excitement, in consequence of the discovery of a skeleton of a man found buried in the bay of a barn at Oddingley, near this city, which has been recognised as that of a carpenter named Heming who disappeared in a miraculous manner immediately after a murder had been committed in that village, in June 1806. Notwithstanding a period of upwards of twenty-three years has elapsed since this horrible transaction took place, Providence had ordered that the extraordinary and atrocious circumstances attending the two-fold murder should now be disclosed.

The author of the letter dwelt at great length on Burton's discovery, before turning his focus on Thomas Clewes.

> The occupier of the barn at the time of the murder, and in which the skeleton has been found is still in existence. Ever since the death

of the first victim, the neighbourhood fixed their suspicions on one
man, who has never prospered from that period: – 'His cattle died
and blighted was his corn' – he afterwards became a bankrupt.

The letter was published in the Chelmsford Chronicle and other
newspapers in the east of England a few days later. It reflected the
generally held belief that Clewes had guilty knowledge of the crime.
This appeared plain enough. As Burton and Waterson had explained,
the old barn could only be opened with the master's key. And even
if the key had been stolen – and Clewes had never said that it had
– Clewes must have noticed that a corner of his barn had been dug
up. But he had said nothing. The growing feeling was that Clewes
knew all along about the grave because he had put the body there.
Having paid Heming to commit Parker's murder (Thomas Barber
and Susan Surman had testified in support of this theory), Clewes
had lured him to Netherwood, where he had dispatched him in
turn. The case seemed simple. If one man could stoop so low as
to arrange the murder of another then surely he would have little
trouble carrying the horrible affair to its miserable conclusion.

Clewes now lived quietly in Trench Wood with his family, but he
had recently appeared in the local newspapers for an entirely different
reason. Just before Christmas 1829, six weeks before the beginning
of the inquest, he had spent an evening drinking heavily at the Virgin
Tavern on the outskirts of Worcester. It was late when Clewes stag-
gered out of the taproom to begin his journey home, and as his path
included a stretch along the towpath of the Birmingham and
Worcester Canal the landlord had persuaded another drinker to see
him safely home.

This man, named Footman, had hurried after Clewes and had
caught up with him by Tibberton Lock, 'where by accident or design'
Clewes had stumbled into the canal. Intoxicated, unable to swim
and with no light to illuminate the scene, Clewes may well have
drowned had Footman not dived in and dragged him to the bank.
To show his appreciation, Clewes had testified to the secretary of
the Worcester Humane Society, which, the newspapers reported,

had conferred a reward on Footman on 2 January, acknowledging his bravery.

A month later this incident was being seen in a sinister light. It was held up as an example of Clewes' torrid state of mind: senseless with alcohol, swaying on the banks of the canal, a lost soul indifferent to his fate. In Oddingley other rumours began to surface. One of Henry Waterson's daughters remembered seeing him outside the barn at Christmas, just after Burton had begun dismantling it. She said that 'he had stopped for a while [in the lane] and gazed as if apprehensively'.

Another labourer recalled drinking with Clewes in the taproom of the White Horse in Worcester. It was shortly before Wellington's victory at Waterloo, and the subject of conversation was the return of Bonaparte from Elba. One of the drinkers had suggested that once again there would be a terrible slaughter of the army. Clewes – with his tongue loosened by drink – had rejoined that 'there would not be half so much fuss about that as there had been over the death of a parson'. The conversation had then shifted to Parker's murder, and there was a discussion about where Richard Heming might be. One of the party said, 'Wherever Heming is, he will come to the gallows in time,' to which Clewes had replied wistfully, 'I know better than that. Heming is safe enough.'

A similar story was told by Thomas Bunn, another local farmhand. In 1826 Bunn had found Clewes drinking alone in the taproom of the Barley Mow in Droitwich. The men had shared a drink and then set off back towards Oddingley. As they strolled along the country lane, they complained about the local farmers' hard treatment of the poorer parishioners. 'They had better not be too hard with me, or I'll tell them something,' Clewes had said. Bunn instantly supposed that Clewes was referring to Parker's murder, but when pressed on the subject he was silent, and they parted shortly after at a fork in the road.

It seemed, in these unguarded moments when alcohol had weakened his senses, that a confession was about to come. It never did, but few believed that the worst crimes could be completely hidden.

Although a guilty conscience could be disguised, a damned soul had other ways of revealing itself. Signs that Clewes was being punished for his sins were found in his dead animals at Netherwood, his heavy drinking, his debts and bankruptcy. Taken independently any of these could be dismissed, but they added up to something more. It was something intangible but definite. It was a pattern. A theme. Something bad.

But as speculation mounted, Clewes made no public comment, and the increased certainty that he was involved was beginning to be a problem for William Smith. He was aware of the rumours but had no firm evidence against Clewes. Furthermore, he had no idea about the circumstances which had surrounded Heming's death: what the murder weapon had been, when it had happened and how it had come about. If he was to arrest Clewes on suspicion of murder he needed answers to at least one of these puzzles. Somebody had to testify against him.

In a community as small and tightly knit as Oddingley Smith felt that someone had to be able to implicate him: a farmhand, a jobbing trader, a taproom confidant? In more than two decades, Clewes *must* have muttered something indiscreet to a labourer in the fields or between the walls of a barn or stable. Two labourers in particular had attracted his attention. John Collins and William Smith had worked for Clewes at Netherwood during the summer of 1806. They were both still alive and recalled events at the time of the murder. Their evidence might prove vital.

All the while letters flew to and fro. On 26 January Smith wrote again to Peel in London informing him the matter was being investigated and 'the identity of the skeleton has been proved beyond the profitability of doubt'. Smith had learnt his lesson, and in approaching Peel a second time he delved into such detail to suggest that he had an impressive and firm hold upon events. He told Peel that in both 1806 and afterwards a great many depositions had been taken by Reverend Pyndar, who was set to attend the second day of the inquest on Friday. Smith then listed the names of the magistrates in Worcester in reply to Peel's direct question and signed off, enquiring whether the home secretary would like a copy of the depositions.

Peel received Smith's letter on 27 January and responded the following morning. By now reports of the discovery were sweeping the country, verifying Smith's initial communication and reinforcing his request for a royal pardon. By now Peel had considered the case for a week and his reply was suggestive. He asked for a copy of all the depositions proving Heming had been murdered 'before I recommend the promise of a pardon'. As was his habit Peel refused to commit himself fully. But the news that Smith had captured the home secretary's attention came as a boost to the investigations when it became known in Worcester.

Smith reconvened the inquest at 9 a.m. sharp on Friday 29 January. Those travelling to the city from Oddingley would have woken in cold darkness and been well on their way by the time the first traces of gloomy sunlight had hit the Malvern Hills at a quarter to eight. Arriving in Worcester they would have heard the 'gladdening peals' of the cathedral's bells ringing out in celebration of the tenth anniversary of King George IV's accession. A mile to the north an eager crowd jostled for seats at the Talbot, with those who missed out left standing one against the other, prompting the *Worcester Herald* to complain that the courtroom 'was crowded to excess'.

The first parishioner to speak was Joseph Colley. Reverend Parker's friend was now 77 years old, an elderly man with a wizened frame, grizzled hair and an unshaven face. He told Smith about his suspicions of Heming and his warning to Parker: 'Why sir, he wants to shoot you.' At length Smith asked Colley whether he had seen Heming and Clewes together.

'I've seen Heming and Clewes drinking together at the Red Lion, Droitwich, two or three times before the murder of Mr Parker,' Colley said.

'How long before Midsummer Day was this?'

'It might be a fortnight or three weeks before.'

'And what did you see the men doing?'

'Clewes was treating and urging Heming to drink. He said: "Here's to the death of the Bonaparte of Oddingley!" This was the last time I saw Clewes and Heming together.'

'Did they say anything else?'

'Heming was a bad one. Heming said he had a nasty job to do at Oddingley but it was then too late to go as it was half past five,' Colley replied.

Smith then asked Colley why he had not volunteered this evidence before. Colley replied that he did not know why the previous coroner had not examined him, for he frequently told people what he had just said to the courtroom. 'I have no spite against Clewes and have worked for him since the murder,' the labourer concluded.

The next witness, William Rogers, was the father-in-law of a labourer called Henry Halbert who had worked for Captain Evans in 1806 and had claimed to have seen Heming at Church Farm on the night of the murder. Halbert was dead and Rogers was little troubled by the coroner's questions. The courtroom was already anticipating the next witness, William Smith, who had laboured for Clewes in 1806. Smith had been at Netherwood on Midsummer Day, and his evidence was expected to provide the first account of Clewes' movements at the time of Parker's murder.

From the start there was something suspicious about Smith's testimony. Rather than responding to the coroner's questions with clear statements, he shuffled nervously between forgetfulness and ambiguity. Only when asked whether Clewes had attended Bromsgrove Fair did he deliver a straight answer, swearing that his master had *not* gone to the fair on Midsummer Day. But if Clewes had not been to Bromsgrove Fair on 24 June then Susan Surman could not have encountered him waiting for Hardcourt by his gate, thus casting doubt upon the dairymaid's claim that Clewes had wished to find a dead parson on his return to the parish. The coroner lingered on the point.

'What was Thomas Clewes wearing on Midsummer Day?'

'He was dressed as usual,' Smith said.

'Could he have attended Bromsgrove Fair without you knowing it?'

'He was not absent from me long enough to go to Bromsgrove that day.'

'Did your master often attend Bromsgrove Fair?'

'I cannot tell whether my master was in the habit of going to Bromsgrove Fair or market.'

Here the coroner paused. Clearly intrigued by the labourer's capricious memory, which had wavered on so many matters yet was so clear on this point, he departed from his line of questioning and asked Smith bluntly whether he had spoken to Clewes in the last few days. His enquiry elicited an unconvincing reply. Yes, he had seen Clewes this morning in the Talbot. No, nothing had passed between them. Yes, Clewes' brother and his son were also there.

'Would you swear before the court that Thomas Clewes did not ask you to declare that he had not attended Bromsgrove Fair?' the coroner asked.

'No, I will not swear,' the labourer replied.

It was a jumbled account that made little sense, and for some moments it threw the courtroom into disorder. At length the labourer admitted that Clewes had spoken to him before proceedings began that morning and had reminded him that he had not been at Bromsgrove Fair. It was a brazen case of witness interference and for Clewes an ill-considered move. The coroner ordered that Clewes be kept apart from witnesses henceforth, under the care of a constable. William Smith the labourer was ordered to leave the court with another constable so he could properly and carefully rearrange his thoughts.

For those journalists encountering the case and its characters for the first time, the labourer's reluctance provided an insight into why the initial inquest had gone so badly wrong. Proceedings were still dogged by sly whispers in the ear; facts were still being bent, stretched or distorted and vital questions avoided by malleable witnesses. Many years had slipped by since William Smith had worked for Clewes, but it was noticeable that he still insisted on referring to him as 'master' throughout his testimony. Was this reflective of an old allegiance or a sign of respect, or fear?

Smith having left the courtroom, Thomas Colwell, who along

with Lench was the only surviving witness from Barneby's original inquest in 1806, was called. He told the court how he had seen Heming on Midsummer Day, fleeing from the murder scene. His evidence was delivered quickly. The emphasis had now shifted away from Parker's murder and towards Heming's.

John Collins was called with an air of expectation. Like Smith he had worked at Netherwood during the summer of 1806 and had been employed there on 24 June. Having seen his old workmate admonished by the court just moments before, Collins began his testimony by revealing that Clewes had also approached him that morning. Their meeting had been brief, Collins said, and the content of their conversation inconsequential. The labourer then began his evidence. He said that he had left Netherwood Farm at Michaelmas in 1806 and had not seen Thomas Clewes since. It was clear any emotional ties to his old master had long since faded, and his evidence appeared carefully recalled and objective.

Collins told the court that he had been out working in the fields on Midsummer Day and had arrived back at Netherwood at 9 p.m., finding the barns and the brewhouse shut up and the curtains drawn as usual. He had his supper and retired for the night.

'Did you know Richard Heming and have you ever seen him with Thomas Clewes?' the coroner enquired, changing the subject.

'I know Heming,' Collins replied. 'I have seen him at Clewes'. He was there on the Sunday morning before the murder.'

'What was Heming doing?'

'It was between breakfast time and church time. I saw Heming and Thomas Clewes on a footpath leading into the inside of Trench Wood.'

Collins explained that they had not seemed surprised to see him, but when he approached they had walked away. It was the first time he had ever seen them by the wood. It was about midday when Clewes returned home, he added.

'When else have you seen Heming?'

'Heming had been at Clewes' backwards and forwards, a fortnight or three weeks before.'

'Did Heming ever work for Clewes?'

'No. To the best of my remembrance he did not.'

The importance of Collins' testimony and his willingness to speak was lost on nobody. It was becoming increasingly clear that Clewes had been central to arranging Parker's murder. Whether doing so on Captain Evans' orders or of his own accord was unclear, but the evidence that had been growing since Burton's spade had hit Heming's shoe was now looking almost conclusive. Collins had now been questioned for around half an hour, and with his efforts still being rewarded, Smith continued, turning his focus to the barn.

This part of Collins' evidence turned out to be the most revealing. He remembered the barn being almost empty on 24 June 1806, but for 'some rough straw'. A few weeks later Clewes had asked the labourer to dig some marl from the field nearest the house, which was carted away and put into the barn. 'I went to work between six and seven in the morning, we drawed [sic] six cartloads,' Collins said. He could not remember who put the marl into the barn, but reasoned that 'Clewes would have had time to shoot the marl and level it, as well as cart it whilst I was away at the pit.'

'Did you ever hear any odd noises coming from the barn, Mr Collins?' Smith asked.

'I never heard any moaning or cry of murder,' Collins concluded.

The day had progressed as badly as it possibly could for Clewes. A clear narrative had emerged from the evidence. It began with Clewes' visits to Heming's Droitwich home, continued with the drinking session at the Red Lion and the surreptitious meeting in Trench Wood on the Sunday before Parker's murder. Finally, on Midsummer morning Clewes had wished to find a dead parson on his return, and that is exactly what he got.

By Collins' estimation it was a week before harvest when the marl was tipped into the barn, giving Clewes about a month to commit the second murder. Around this same time, Collins then remembered, a field of vetches – tall climbing plants – were also 'put in the bay next to the pool'. Each incident flowed neatly, like a series of tributaries into a widening river, into the main thrust of the theory – that Clewes had arranged Parker's death and then murdered Heming.

The remainder of the afternoon passed amid such conjectures. Clewes had also attempted to interfere with the next witness, William Crockett, needlessly as it transpired, as he had little to say. Then a further witness remembered riding to Worcester on Midsummer night with the parish clerk, John Pardoe, who was now dead. He recalled Pardoe saying that he had heard Clewes making many threats against Parker.

John Perkins, so long a thorn in the other farmers' sides, then delivered a typically scathing account of life in Oddingley in 1806. It included an account of the quarrel at the Plough in Tibberton, Captain Evans' vicious oaths and curses directed at Parker, and his memory of Clewes and Heming drinking together at Droitwich. He finished darkly, 'Clewes paid for Heming'. The coroner had heard enough. At five o'clock in the afternoon, as the jury broke for refreshments, Smith called Mr Bass, the foreman of the jury, and Reverend Clifton, a city magistrate, into a private room and stated his conviction that 'such evidence had been adduced . . . to believe that Thomas Clewes had guilty knowledge of Richard Heming's murder'. Under common law this was sufficient for an arrest, and Smith recommended that he be taken into custody until the inquest had concluded. Clifton and Bass agreed. Clewes was summoned into the room and informed of their decision.

'He betrayed not the slightest agitation; he protested himself entirely innocent of having been in the slightest degree privy to Heming's death, and when told that he was about to be sent to prison, said he should go there without any fear as to the result,' one journalist later recorded. Clewes was led from the Talbot by two constables who escorted him the short distance to Worcester County Gaol.

All evidence now seemed to strengthen the case. It even seemed oddly distracting when others rose to speak later that evening. Thomas Green testified about the perplexing meeting between

Captain Evans and John Barnett that had so preoccupied Reverend Pyndar; Thomas Langford reminded the jury that Heming had been at Church Farm on Midsummer morning; and Betty Perkins delivered a stinging attack on John Barnett for not joining the chase.

Such matters seemed of secondary importance. Captain Evans was dead, and Barnett had not been inconvenienced by the sudden appearance of a skeleton in one of his barns. More interesting was the evidence of Thomas Arden, another labourer who had worked at Netherwood in 1806. He remembered Heming visiting before the murder. Even the appearance of George Banks, now a respectable bailiff in his mid-40s, did little to capture the attention of the room, which had been distracted by Clewes' arrest.

The day had been a spectacular success, even eclipsing the thrill of identifying Heming's skeleton three days before. It was to end, however, on a poignant note. The final witness was Mary Parker, who along with Elizabeth Newbury was perhaps the individual who had been most touched by the case. She was now approaching her seventieth birthday and had travelled to Worcester accompanied by her daughter from their home in Lichfield, Staffordshire. As a mark of respect, in a gesture of sympathy not extended to any other witness, she was excused from testifying before the court. Instead the evidence she gave in 1806 was read aloud in her presence. She listened to it carefully: to the reports of the stones against the window, to Captain Evans' curses and, finally, her dead husband's tragic epitaph: 'I know not what they want, unless it is my life!' She indicated that it was accurate and then stood down.

It was half past nine at night when Smith adjourned the inquest for the second time. Exhaustion mixed with exhilaration as those present tramped out into the street in the knowledge that on Tuesday the inquest would reconvene yet again. As the courtroom candles were extinguished and the skeleton gathered up for safekeeping, a quarter of a mile away Thomas Clewes was in a cell at the gaol on Castle Street, left to endure the memory of a ruinous day.

'This is an altogether strange case,' mused a journalist from the *Morning Chronicle*, setting down his thoughts that night for his readership in London. A double murder, 'the second arising out of the first, is a singular event'. Stories of tithe disputes and parish quarrels were familiar enough, 'though they seldom reach the height of inducing the parishioners to offer a purse for the assassination of the parson'. In this respect, he concluded, the affair at Oddingley was unique. In this unhappy parish a quarrel had culminated in two successive flashes of violence. The case was a terrible one, and over the past few days it had been gaining notoriety in the British newspapers, which were now publishing their reports under the stark headline: 'The Case of the Murdered Murderer'.

CHAPTER 15

In the Words of Thomas Clewes

*The City Gaol, Castle Street, Worcester, 29 January–
2 February 1830*

The Worcester County Gaol was a formidable structure, a tangible symbol of power and punishment that stood on Castle Street, north of the city centre. Opened in 1809, this building had replaced the previous prison, which had been derided in the press as unfit for purpose. It had cost the county a total of £19,000 and catered for all types of inmate from thieves and debtors to murderers. Its cells, walls and yards were concealed behind a 20-foot wall of palisaded Bath stone, which radiated all the menace of a fortress. The entrance to the gaol – through which Clewes was escorted at half past five on Friday 30 January in the careful company of two constables and Reverend Robert Clifton, the arresting magistrate – was through a neat arch flanked by two battlemented turrets. Clewes was apprised of his rights by the governor, Mr Lavender – he was still only a suspect and would therefore enjoy more privileges than most of the other inmates. He was then conveyed to his cell.

Life inside the gaol was hard and unpleasant, locals regarding it as a place of punishment and correction rather than moral reform and tuition. The unheated cells were cold and damp in winter, and a sour, fetid stench escaped from the latrines. Apart from the officials' quarters, no part of the building was lit, meaning that after dark prisoners saw little more than the occasional swing of a warder's lantern till dawn. There was minimal flexibility in the treatment of inmates. Daily life was simple but exhausting. It was considered best to keep prisoners busy with the maximum amount of work. 'Labour is severe,' the author of a report into working standards at the prison reported in the 1820s. Prisoners worked all day beating hemp, cranking handmills or feeding looms. In 1824 the authorities had controversially voted to erect a treadmill, a vast frame of slatted steps that projected from a revolving cylinder, in the yard. Teams of inmates silently turned the treadmill in endless shifts, the exhausting machine serving two functions: grinding the corn used to make the prison bread, and satisfying the prevailing belief that dangerous criminals should be occupied with continuous activity so their minds would be diverted from schemes or subversive thoughts.

Those who broke the rules were punished in several ways. They could have their ration of tobacco or snuff taken away, or in more serious cases they could be thrown into one of the seven solitary cells, two of which were completely dark. One visitor in 1823 found four prisoners in this state, two of whom had been in confinement for three days. 'The door of one of these dark cells being opened,' it was declared, 'the poor fellow immediately fell on his knees, most earnestly entreating that some alteration might be made in his situation.'

By six o'clock it was long since dark and Clewes was left alone in his cell, a sparsely furnished room with an iron bedstead, straw bed, pillow, two blankets and a rug. He was left with painful memories of Collins' evidence and his foolish attempts to interfere with the other witnesses. Worse still, he had no idea of what was now being said at the Talbot. Smith would continue to question witnesses for three and a half hours yet, and if any villager was to testify to screaming or shouting at Netherwood in the summer of 1806, however vague their recollection might be, then his fate might well be sealed. Clewes had no one to advise or console him. His wife and family were in Oddingley, and no lawyer or clergyman came to counsel him. He could only dwell on a situation that had worsened by the day, the combined agonies of fear, conjecture and detachment closing in on him.

Just a few weeks before, the year had started brightly. Clewes had been appointed temporary bailiff at a nearby farm, signalling a welcome change of status and better wages. After many years toiling in Trench Wood with his axe, it was an opportunity that Clewes seemed determined to seize. Within a few days he had taken lodgings at the farm and applied himself to his new position, drawing up lists of fold-yard tasks and planning for a thaw in the snow.

This was Clewes' situation on 21 January, the date of Burton's find. His first reaction to the news – like his later reaction to his arrest – had been of cool reticence. Marta Davis, the housekeeper at the farm, had not noticed any perceptible change in his manner or attitude, only observing that he arrived back from the first day of the inquest 'hungry and tired'. Davis had asked him whether the business was over and he had replied that it was not, and that he was going again on Friday.

On Thursday evening Clewes told Davis that he needed to visit his home at Trench Wood. Perhaps he wished to spend the evening with his family or to have some uninterrupted time to think. He called in the following morning, though, in a frantic rush. Davis saw him hurry into a room and change his clothes. He explained that he was 'rather late . . . had a cup of cider and left'. On his way to the Talbot Clewes would talk to William Smith and John Collins, his old farmhands. It was an imprudent move. He would not return that night.

After his committal locals discussed Clewes' position. While it certainly seemed as if he had had some hand in Heming's murder, there was still no hard evidence against him. Just as the smuggler waited for a dark lonely field and a burglar for an empty house, Clewes might have found a quiet moment in his barn to dispose of Heming. If this was so, then how would it be possible to mount a successful prosecution? If nobody had seen and nobody had heard, what could be proved?

*

That Friday night there was no sign of an improvement in the freezing weather, which had coated the streets in ice, and *Berrow's Worcester Journal* had begun to urge 'the sprinkling of salt on the pavements'. In the city residents could huddle around their hearths to shelter from the cold, but at the gaol there was no adequate means of keeping the inmates warm. It was a brutal initiation for Clewes. Even in fine weather the prison was a nest of disease, a hundred or so coughing and wheezing bodies thrust into a tiny area and given insufficient protection from the elements. The weakest of the inmates succumbed to fevers and jaundices or went down with other, putrid infections: abscesses in the ears or ulcers on the legs and hips – some within days of their arrival. For Clewes, who was now in his sixtieth year, the prospect of prolonged exposure to this environment must have been terrifying. And his age did not just make him physically vulnerable; it also singled him out from the transient and mainly young prison population. The days ahead would be a test of both mind and body.

Worcester glowed white in the snow that night, beneath a clear starry sky. Clewes lay hunched on his iron bed, wrapped in blankets, glassy-eyed, lost in thought. This picture of the prisoner on his first night in gaol comes from the surviving sources and knowledge of subsequent events. It is one of the enduring images of the Oddingley story. In 1818 Mary Shelley wrote, 'Nothing is as painful to the human mind as a great and sudden change.' Clewes had begun January 1830 as a fallen farmer, he had glimpsed financial and social redemption for a few fleeting weeks, but then it had gone, and he had ended the month a murder suspect, his disgrace and downfall played out in public. William Smith's inquest had narrowed the beam on him alone. He had come to represent both murders: his name was becoming synonymous with both crimes. The scrutiny of others – Captain Evans, John and William Barnett and George Banks – was fading into nothing.

At dawn on Saturday the turnkeys noticed a change in Clewes' manner. He was no longer the confident and protesting man he had been the evening before. He applied for a Bible and prayer book and at midday asked to see a clergyman. The request was relayed to the governor, who in turn sent a note to Reverend Robert Clifton.

The request reached Clifton's home in the early afternoon. He lived a quarter of an hour's walk away from the gaol at St Nicholas' Rectory in the city centre. William Smith had asked Clifton to escort the farmer to gaol the previous evening in his capacity as a magistrate, and it was under his authority that Clewes had been detained. Many clergymen enjoyed a dual identity as spiritual leader and law enforcer, but it was rare for them to be employed in both positions in the same case. This may have struck Clifton but it did not prevent him setting out for the gaol. Clifton was a man of form and duty. He supplemented his chief role as rector of St Nicholas Church with a lengthy list of additional responsibilities. As well as being a city magistrate, he was the official county chaplain and secretary of the Society for Promoting Christian Knowledge. He had a master's degree, was erudite and evidently pious, but when it came to magisterial matters of law and form, he was horribly inexperienced.

Clifton spent Saturday afternoon locked in private conversation with Clewes. It was dark when he returned to his rectory. Bewildered by what the farmer had revealed to him, he decided to write to the home secretary for advice. He began his letter to Peel the following morning.

> In the course of yesterday I visited Clewes in the Gaol, and after a very long interview, in which I drew from him certain expressions which confirmed me in the opinion that he had guilty knowledge of the affair, I told him that <u>probably</u> I could obtain the promise of his majesty's pardon for any person (but the actual striker of the fatal blow) who might give information which might lead to the conviction of any person present at, or accessory to, the murder of Heming. He then made <u>some</u> declarations but not sufficient in my judgement to secure the conviction of any living participant in the crime.

Clifton believed that Clewes was teetering on the brink of a confession. If Peel could offer the farmer a royal pardon – therefore allowing him to turn King's witness – then the balance would be tipped and the facts, which had been concealed for so long, would be exposed for the first time. It was a reasoned conclusion, but Clifton was advancing blindly into a mire of legal quicksand. Lawyers understood that when a case developed at speed it was liable to be ruined by inexperienced or unskilled hands. Robert Clifton was primarily a clergyman, and his duties as a magistrate – like Pyndar before him – ran to little more than adjudicating on instances of petty crime or delinquent behaviour. He was now embroiling himself in a complex and uncertain case. With only threadbare legal knowledge, he had grasped the reins from William Smith at a vital juncture, and rather than conferring with his peers in Worcester had opted to communicate directly with Peel in London.

On Sunday morning Clewes attended divine service in the prison chapel. He then sent for Clifton again. When the clergyman arrived, Clewes told him that if Clifton promised to obtain a royal pardon, 'he would disclose all the circumstances of *both* murders, as far as he knew them'.

Clifton's letter to Peel lay half-finished on his desk at home. He had still not spoken to William Smith, but here was Clewes, prepared to confess. Clifton informed the farmer he would do his utmost to secure a pardon from Peel if he revealed all he knew about the murders. He then cautioned him, reminding Clewes that if he was guilty of striking the fatal blow, there was nothing that could be done to save him. Clewes paused for a second then replied that he understood. During the next few hours the magistrate sat in silent horror as Clewes, in his words, 'presented a narrative unparalleled in the annals of crime'.

At around two o'clock that afternoon Clifton hurried along the frozen Foregate Street to his rectory. His involvement in the case had spanned no more than a week – from the opening day of the inquest – but within the space of a few hours he had learnt more about what had happened in Oddingley than any other investigating official before him. The result of the inquest and several men's lives rested on his actions over the next few hours, and his first thought was his letter to Peel. With the inquest due to resume on Tuesday morning, it was crucial for the home secretary to be informed as swiftly as possible. The London mail left Worcester Post Office at half past four in the afternoon, and Clifton was determined to catch it.

'I write with unsteady nerves and with great haste for the post,' Clifton resumed his letter. 'My persuasion is, that enough had not, nor will, come out before the jury to *convict* anyone & it was under this persuasion that I ventured to make the promise of applying for his majesty's pardon, without which I could not get the slightest information from Clewes.' He signed off breathlessly, that he most 'respectfully and anxiously, awaited Peel's response'.

A biting easterly wind swept up the Thames, over the port and Old London Bridge – a structure that would be demolished the following year – towards Whitehall. Like much of the country, London was frozen to the bone and buried in snow. The rigging, masts and timbers of craft moored in the waters outside the Houses of Parliament were iced white. Growing sheets of ice slid over the black waters, leaving the *Morning Herald* to remark that the view between Westminster and Vauxhall Bridges now formed 'as characteristic and complete a winter scene as could well be imagined . . . it could be only superseded by the Thames being completely (and it is now very nearly) frozen over'.

At the Home Office, a short distance from the river, Robert Peel received Clifton's letter on Monday 1 February. Reports of the Oddingley affair were now a daily fixture in the national newspapers, and the coroner himself had sent the home secretary the latest issue of the *Worcester Herald*, which was replete with transcripts of everything that had been said at the Talbot. To Peel, Clewes' guilt seemed assured, so he was confused to learn that a confession had suddenly been made and a royal pardon was required. More perplexing for the home secretary was the fact that the letter had come from Reverend Clifton – a man he had never heard of before. Until now all Peel's information had stemmed from William Smith. Clifton, then, was an unknown quantity, who appeared to be acting arbitrarily, outside the realms of Smith's inquiry.

Peel decided it was unwise to discard all the evidence at a stroke and to offer a royal pardon before the facts had been established. His reply was assured and forthright. He told Clifton that the promise of clemency had been 'most indiscreet'. He pointed out that the inquest was still ongoing and that subsequent discoveries 'may prove that Clewes had a greater share in the murder of Heming than any other person now living'.

Peel's decision was relayed to his clerk, Mr Phillips, who was left to acquaint Clifton with the crushing news. 'Mr Peel directs me to say, he cannot offer the promise which had been held to Clewes. He thinks it precipitate under the peculiar circumstances of this case and cannot be party to such a procedure,' Phillips wrote. The letter closed with a word of advice. 'Mr Peel desires me to add that he thinks it would be improper to hold out any promises of any kind to Clewes as an inducement to him to give any information.'

The speed of communication meant there was no chance of Clifton knowing Peel's decision until the following day. This left the clergyman dangerously out of step with instructions from Whitehall. In these disjointed hours, Clifton made several errors. He revealed to some peers that Clewes had confessed, letting slip some details of the narrative. More seriously, he signed a warrant for the arrest of George Banks, who 'in a matter of notoriety' was double-handcuffed by two constables at his home in Hanbury and swept off to Worcester in a chaise. When Banks was told he was being charged in connection with Richard Heming's murder, he remained silent. Only when he realised he was being taken to gaol did he speak: 'If you do that, then I don't care afterwards what becomes of me.'

Peel's letter to Reverend Clifton arrived at Worcester Post Office at 9.08 a.m. on Tuesday 2 February. Within an hour it had been sorted and delivered to St Nicholas' Rectory. By half past ten Clifton had read the contents and was rushing towards the gaol.

It was another frozen day. The three red-brick chimneys that rose high over the Talbot's steep roof smoked steadily in the feeble light as William Smith reconvened the inquest in the inn below. There was already a feeling that the coroner had generated enough momentum to bring the case before the assize court. The news that George Banks had joined Thomas Clewes in the cells of the county gaol had also seeped out, generating further excitement. Each new witness was now called by the coroner with the atmosphere loaded with expectation.

Fifty-six-year-old Joseph Taylor, son of the farrier James Taylor who had been imprisoned on suspicion of involvement in 1808, was called to testify at around ten o'clock. Taylor had followed his father into the trade and taken over the business after his death. He refuted the suggestion that his father had played any part in either murder. He told the coroner that John Rowe, who had supplied Pyndar with his account of the farmers' plot, had been 'put up' to do so by a bitter man named 'Lawyer Milner', who had plotted against James Taylor 'out of spite'.

Taylor was questioned for almost an hour, giving meandering answers, resorting to speculation and making stark denials. He concluded his evidence with a plain declaration to the court: 'I have never heard of any secret meetings in Oddingley about the tythes and no oath has been administered to me to keep secret what I know about the affair.'

Susannah Taylor, Joseph's wife, was next, and was also questioned for some time. She was asked to list the instruments James Taylor would have carried with him on a working day. 'A fleam, a blood stick and a piece of cord to bleed cattle', she remembered. A blood stick was a foot-long truncheon made from hard wood used for striking the fleam into the horse's vein.

Meanwhile, Clifton had arrived at the gaol. It was less than an hour since he had received the home secretary's letter, but he had instantly absorbed Peel's message and realised the gravity of his mistakes, which now threatened the whole legal process. He should not have held out to Clewes any inducement to confess, least of all a royal pardon. He should not have shared any details of the confession with anyone else, as each could now bring it forward as evidence in their own right. And he should not have ordered George Banks' arrest. Clifton had set in motion a series of interconnected events that were now beyond his control. His only hope was to return to the gaol and retract everything he had previously promised. In Clewes' cell, Clifton told him, 'I have utterly failed in my endeavour to obtain any promise or hope of mercy from the Government.' He explained that 'he felt himself duty bound . . . not to make use of his knowledge to your hurt' and that he would 'rather be committed to prison for contempt of the coroner, than disclose what had passed between us'. Clifton promised that his transcript of the confession and the letters between him and Peel would be destroyed immediately. Most importantly, he reassured the prisoner that nobody but the two of them was 'cognizant of its many particulars'.

But Clewes' reaction was not to recoil into silence or introspection, but to state his determination to produce his evidence before the inquest. Three days had passed since he had first confided in Clifton, two since he had revealed all that he knew. The intervening hours had brought about a deep change inside Clewes. Before, he had seemed a mournful, distracted and self-contained man who relied on drink to get by; now his defences appeared to have dropped. Perhaps Clewes craved the cathartic release of unlocking years of caged memories? Perhaps he felt there was no going back? In any case, his resolve was gone, deliquesced in the shivering gloom of the gaol. Clifton warned Clewes afresh that he could not offer a royal pardon. Clewes repeated that he understood. The governor was then called and apprised of the situation. He wrote a note to Smith, which arrived at the Talbot as Susannah Taylor was concluding her evidence. It stated that 'Clewes had expressed himself desirous of making some communication to the jury'. Smith adjourned the session until the afternoon, informed those present that he was required at the prison and left.

Within half an hour Smith was seated in the magistrates' office at the gaol. He was joined by the magistrates Lords Deerhurst and Coventry, the governor Mr Lavender and Reverend Clifton. A handcuffed Clewes stood before them all. Smith told Clewes it was his duty to warn him that any statement he made 'would be produced against him on his trial at the assizes'. Smith added that neither he nor anyone else would hold out any hope for him if his confession or disclosure, of 'whatsoever nature it might be', implicated him in 'the crime of which he stood charged'.

Clewes hesitated a moment. He then told Smith that he was anxious to reveal all that he knew of the murder of Richard Heming. Before he began his testimony, he added earnestly, 'I did not do it.'

The following is a transcript of Clewes' evidence.

That on the morrow morning after the Rev. Mr Parker was shot, I recollect it took place on Bromsgrove fair day but cannot state exactly the year, in the morning about 7 o'clock George Banks came down to me and said we have got Heming at our house who shot the parson and do not know what to do with him. Will you let him come down here? I said – 'I won't have him here nor have nothing to do with him.' Banks went off at that. Banks said he is lurking down in the meadows. Then I went up to Oddingley about 11 o'clock in the day to Mr Jones's (who is since dead) Mr Nash lives in the farmhouse now. As I went up by the road side, I suppose Captain Evans could keep sight of me all the way. Captain Evans called to me. He was in his garden by the road side, and he followed me out of the garden into the field and said he wanted to speak with me. And Captain Evans said I have had Heming at our house this morning, and something must be done by him. He is lurking down towards your house now. I ordered him to get in your buildings by day-time, if possible, or at the edge of night that you or your family might not see him. The Captain said 'something must be done by him. I shall come down to your house at night, and bring somebody with me and we must give the poor devil some money or do something with him to send him off. Will you get up and come to the barn? It won't detain you a minute.' I refused coming and said I did not like to come. He [Captain Evans] said it can make no odds to you. You need not be afraid to come at 11 o'clock. Captain said just come out. It will make no difference to you at all, for if you don't come I am afraid of your dogs.

I went out at the back door and went down to the barn door at eleven o'clock, and there was the Captain Evans and James Taylor and I thought it to be George Banks, I believed it to be him. The Captain, Taylor and George Banks went into the barn and I with them. As soon as the Captain came into the barn, he called 'halloo, Heming where be'st?' Heming says 'yes sir' but not very loud. The Captain and Taylor then stept on the mow, which was not higher than my knee. Captain then pulled a lantern out of his pocket or under his coat. I saw him on the threshing floor with George Banks. Captain said 'Get up Heming I have got something for thee.' Heming was at the time covered up with straw. He was rising up on end as if he had been lying on his back and as he rose up Taylor up with a blood stick and hit him two or three blows on the head. I said this is bad work. If I had known you should not have had me here. The Captain said he's got enough. Taylor and the Captain come down off the mow directly and Taylor said what's to be done with him now? Captain said damn his body, we must not take him out of doors. Somebody will see us may happen. It is not very dark. Taylor went out of doors and brought a spade from somewhere, it was no spade of mine. We'll soon put him safe says the Captain to Taylor. Taylor then searched round the bay of the barn and found a place where dogs and rats had scratched holes. Taylor threw out a spade full or two of soil and cleaned it from the side of the wall. Taylor then said to the Captain this will do for him. Captain Evans stood by and lighted him. Banks and I were present on the floor of the barn. Captain and Taylor then got up on the mow and pulled Richard Heming down to the front of the mow and Captain said to Taylor catch hold of him, and dragged him across the floor and into the hole made in the opposite bay which Taylor had dug for him and Taylor soon covered it up. I can't tell how he was put in. I never stepped off the floor into the bay. I thought I should have died where I was. The Captain said to Taylor, well done boy, I'll give you another glass or two of brandy. Captain said to me, 'I'll give you anything. Damn your body, don't you never split.' They were all four present – we all parted at that and went off. He darkened his lantern. The

Captain, Taylor and Banks went towards Oddingley and I went to bed. The whole was not half an hour about. Heming's clothes were all on. Heming did not say anything. There was no blood, not a spot on the floor. Nothing more was done that night.

On the morrow [26 June] I was at Pershore Fair. George Banks came to me in the afternoon at the Plough at Pershore about four or five o'clock and called me up an entry towards the privy, and said here's some money for you that Heming was to have. Mr John Barnett was with Banks, and Banks and Barnett each of them gave me some money which I did not count till I got home, both saying to me when they gave it, 'be sure you don't split.' There was no more said about it that night. It was in two parcels, it was between £26 and £27 in all. I put it all in one pocket. This was to have taken Heming off as Banks and Barnett informed me.

I was at Captain Evans' a few days afterward. The Captain Evans sent for me, by my son John, a boy then about 7 years old. When I got there I found the Captain alone. He said to me, if you will but keep your peace you shall never want for £5. There's £5 for you any time if you will but keep your peace. But I never received any money from him afterwards.

On the same day Catherine Banks came to me while in the parlour in the Captain's house, and went down on her knees and begged and prayed of me, not to say anything as she feared the Captain Evans had been doing a bad job and she was afraid if I spoke some of them would come to be hanged. I promised not to say anything.

Captain Evans had a sale some years afterward and he said to me at the sale if you want anything at the sale I shall make you a present of a trifle. I purchased a mare at the sale for £22 or there abouts. In the evening of the sale Mr Handy the auctioneer asked me to settle for the mare and the Captain Evans said to Mr Handy there is a settlement between Clewes and me and he can settle with me for the mare. But I was never asked for the money.

In about nine or ten days, more or less, after Heming was knocked on the head the Captain Evans asked me to put some soil in the barn, where Heming was buried at Netherwood Farm. I hauled a good many loads to the barn doors to rise it as I might draw it into the barn better and some was put into both the bays and another barn as well, many loads to each of the doors. After it was done the Captain asked me if it was done. I told him it was, and the Captain said he was very glad of it. Mr John Barnett some time after that, and before I left Netherwood Farm, lent me £100, part of which is owing to him at this time. I gave a bond or note of hand for it and he might have been paid out of my effects when I assigned them over to Mr Waterson, if he had seen after it. The money was lent to me after the murder of Heming. But I borrowed some before that.

Some time after the parson was shot, Taylor was put to gaol from what a man by the name of Rowe said, about the murder of Mr Parker. Captain Evans and John Barnett were had up, and examined but George Banks never was. Captain Evans asked me to bind myself with an oath which he would administer, he being a magistrate.

The magistrates' office was silent as Clewes spoke. For around an hour his narrative progressed with eerie confidence, transporting those present away from their bleak surroundings to Oddingley on 25 June 1806, from Netherwood to Church Farm and then back to the old brick barn where the murder had been committed. Each of Clewes' words was selected carefully. He delivered the 'horrible detail with perfect firmness and in an unfaltering tone throughout', it was later declared. For William Smith and the other officials crammed into the magistrates' room it was a staggering account – unequalled in length, depth and colour by anything they had heard before.

All that Clewes said was copied down by the duty clerk, James Hooper. And once finished, Smith asked Clewes to read through the document, which he did, making only a few clarifications. He then signed across the foot of every page, before he was escorted from the room by a turnkey.

The story had at last been rounded off. The conspiracy to kill Parker had been followed by Heming's murder the next day. Clewes, if he were to be believed, was not a lone wolf but a man entangled in a community-wide conspiracy headed by Captain Evans and executed by James Taylor. Before Smith left to resume the inquest at the Talbot, he performed one last task, signing a warrant for the arrest of the man who seemingly had bankrolled the enterprise: Mr John Barnett.

CHAPTER 16

Marvel-Hunters and Wonder-Lovers

February, March 1830

On Thursday 4 February *Berrow's Worcester Journal* published a full-length transcript of Clewes' dramatic confession. Just three days had passed since the farmer had first divulged details of Heming's murder to Reverend Clifton in private, but now his involvement in the night-time execution was known by all. The newspaper sold quickly. In London *The Times* noted, 'The avidity with which the paper is bought is a proof of the intense interest excited in the neighbourhood.'

The confession was beyond compelling. At almost 1,500 words, it captivated readers with its its lucidity, colour and Clewes' remarkable recollection of dialogue. Clewes had not merely explained how Heming's skeleton had appeared in his barn, but had also – were he to be believed – vividly evoked the crime scene. The Devil lurked in his little observations. There was the dull glow of the Captain's lantern in the barn, Banks standing silently by in his smock frock, James Taylor's bloodstick, the limp body being dragged across the floor and then the Captain's impassioned threat: 'I'll give you anything. Damn your body! Don't you never split!'

It was a lurid tale of calculated murder, rendered more powerful by Clewes' telling. Nothing appeared invented. Clewes' recollections were not muddled or ambiguous but detailed, linear and coherent. Yet again Captain Evans plays the part of the village Rottweiler: first ordering Heming to the barn and then later coercing Clewes to join them. He sends George Banks on errands, pours Taylor brandies and afterwards binds them all to silence with threats and oaths. In the background is John Barnett, supplying money and lending the scheme his tacit support. There is a hint of authentic panic too, as Clewes sees the dreadful situation develop before his eyes. Throughout, Clewes remains desperate to detach himself from blame, peppering his narrative with pleading interjections. 'It was no spade of mine,' he says. 'I never stepped off the floor into the bay. I thought I should have died where I was.'

The truth of Clewes' confession was soon being judged by a wide audience. Over the next three days the *Berrow's* report was syndicated to publications across the country. The paper, now in the thick of a sensational news story, mused

In the early part of this inquiry, the evidence was of a nature to attach violent suspicion to certain individuals; but the impression upon the public mind was, that unless facts of a more decisive character were disclosed, it was scarcely probable that anyone could be convicted of the murder of Heming. Since that time, however, circumstances have occurred which lead us to the expectation that . . . the arm of justice may overtake one or more who were implicated in the murder of Heming. That wretched being appears to have been made away with within a few hours after the death of Mr Parker – thus speedily becoming the victim of those who had tempted him to take away the life of a fellow-creature! This case, when considered in all its circumstances, is one of the most extraordinary that has become the subject of judicial inquiry. Not only is the public attention in the neighbourhood riveted to it, but in distant parts of the kingdom the inquiry has caused a deep interest.

Such levels of interest spurred editors in London and Birmingham to dispatch reporters of their own in pursuit of fresh material, and the final two days at the Talbot were attended by a growing number of journalists. In the public house the mood had changed. Previously the emphasis had been on locating witnesses in the hope that – joined together – their testimonies would provide a likely explanation for

Heming's murder. But Clewes' confession had changed everything. He had admitted to being present at the scene, and if enough evidence could be gathered to demonstrate he had played a more active role than he claimed, he might be convicted as the principal offender. And if Clewes could be prosecuted, then Banks' and Barnett's prospects seemed equally gloomy. All three might hang together.

At the Talbot new evidence continued to surface. Gilbert Jones, the surveyor who had spent almost a month in Oddingley in May 1806, remembered how he had worked in an atmosphere of resentment and anger. George Harris from Droitwich claimed that he too had been approached by Captain Evans, about half a year before Parker's murder, with an offer of £50 to shoot the clergyman. He remembered Evans saying there 'would be no more harm in shooting him [Parker] than a crow that fled in the air'. Shortly after, Clement Churchill, the farmhand who had stayed quiet for so long, told the coroner that he had been at Church Farm on Midsummer Day and that there had been 'laughing and joking'. And Elizabeth Fowler, the Captain's old dairymaid, testified about the shotgun she had found hidden beneath the staddles on Easter Monday 1806.

The evidence against John Barnett also began to mount. One labourer told the coroner how Barnett had assaulted Parker at Pound Farm years before his murder. Thomas Reed then remembered the drinking session at the Raven two weeks before Midsummer Day. 'They all seemed in liquor,' he said, 'and talked a great deal about how they plagued the parson. John Barnett said he would give £50 for a dead parson. They all, except me, then stood up at once, took their hats off, and drank damnation to the parson.'

There were indications that John Barnett knew about Heming's murder too. One of his farmhands explained that Barnett had been annoyed by Henry Waterson's decision to have the old barn pulled down. Barnett had complained that it was foolish to begin such a job in the middle of winter, leaving all the animals outside to freeze. On the day Burton demolished the roof, Barnett had seemed unduly riled. He told the labourer that he was tempted to fetch his gun and shoot at him.

John Barnett's plight was made worse still when his younger brother was called to testify. William Barnett, now in his mid-fifties and a successful farm master in his own right, quickly managed to aggravate the coroner with a string of blank denials. He said that John had not mentioned Parker's murder when he had returned from Bromsgrove Fair on Midsummer Day. He did not know whether or not his brother had visited Church Farm that evening. He could not recall who had said Heming might be involved. Furthermore he could not remember being at the vestry meeting in 1806, nor could he recollect his brother or George Banks ever speaking angrily about Parker. 'I never in my life heard my brother say what became of Heming,' William Barnett told the coroner. 'I do not believe he knew any more of what had become of him than you.'

As constable in 1806 and the current master of Church Farm, Barnett was a pivotal figure, and before long his forgetfulness began to jar. After a stern lecture from Smith it transpired that he had been warned by the family solicitor not to commit himself to any firm statement. Smith, intolerant of any new attempt to interfere with the proceedings, dismissed him. Barnett left the Talbot embarrassed and discredited.

One of the final witnesses was Matthew Pierpoint, returning with fresh evidence. The surgeon had 'heard that the murder was supposed to have been committed with a blood stick'. Pierpoint told the jury that he had a little knowledge of blood sticks and since Tuesday he had examined one. Some 'had a round knob at one end', he informed them, and others 'had a covering of lead around the knob'.

Pierpoint told Smith that if Heming had been in the position described by Clewes (rising from the floor, his head about three feet high) the leaden knob of a blood stick would have been quite sufficient to produce the fractures to the skull. One strike would not have been enough to cause death, but two or three heavy blows would have. 'At that moment,' the *Morning Chronicle* reporter recorded, '[Pierpoint] could think of no instrument more calculated to produce the fractures he had seen than a blood stick, being round and not over-heavy.' It would have been perfect, he explained, for fracturing the bones of the skull without breaking the skin so as to 'cause an effusion of blood'. 'A heavier sharp-angled instrument would most likely have broken the skin as well. In the situation in which Heming was said to have been, he [Pierpoint] thought one blow would have been sufficient to have stunned him, so as to have deprived him of the power of speaking.'

At four o'clock on Friday 5 February Smith signalled an end to the long and exhausting process of interviewing witnesses. After a break of two hours the jury accompanied William Smith to Worcester County Gaol, where he was required to read through the depositions before the prisoners. Thomas Clewes and George Banks were led, handcuffed, into the magistrates' room. John Barnett, who had been in the gaol since his arrest on Tuesday, forwarded a message to Smith stating that he did not wish to attend.

It was the first time Clewes and Banks had come into contact that week. They glowered at each other from across the room, and an exchange of words was only averted by the intervention of the chief gaoler.

It took four hours for William Smith to read out the depositions. At times Banks seemed agitated 'and made several remarks', and when Smith read Clewes' confession he shouted out that 'he would suffer himself to be torn limb from limb if he was ever in that barn'. Clewes, who remained reserved and detached, simply commented that 'it was true'. As the reading ended, Banks turned and locked his eyes on Clewes. He warned him 'to be careful how he took the life of a fellow creature'. 'I was never in the barn when Heming was murdered,' Banks shouted, 'and nor did I know anything of him being murdered or butchered!'

'Do you remember coming down to me that morning?' Clewes replied. But as Banks started to speak he was silenced by Smith, who told him to 'reserve his protestations of innocence for his lawyer and the jury at the assize'. The two men were escorted back to their cells, and the jury left for the Talbot, where they were invited to consider their verdict. After a few minutes of deliberation, they returned to the courtroom.

The Jurors summoned to enquire for our Sovereign Lord the King, when, how, and by what means, RICHARD HEMING, late of the Parish of Oddingley, in the county of Worcester, Carpenter and Wheelwright, came to his death, do find a verdict of WILFUL MURDER against THOMAS CLEWES and GEORGE BANKS, and that such Murder was committed on the night of the Twenty-Fifth of June, One Thousand Eight Hundred and Six. And do further find, that John Barnett, of the Parish of Oddingley, in the said County, Farmer, was AN ACCESSORY TO SUCH MURDER BEFORE THE FACT.

It was a climactic and significant procedural moment. When an inquest jury accused a named person of either murder or manslaughter, the coroner had the power to have the suspect detained – an act usually performed by magistrates – and all the witnesses bound over to appear at the next assize sessions. The verdicts were now equivalent to official indictments and the case would move to the assize court where the accused would be tried by one of the King's judges. Assize courts were part of a tradition that could be traced back to the twelfth century, when judges were sent out into the provinces to deal with breaches of the peace and other matters which touched royal interest. In 1830 the King's judges still travelled the ancient assize route, each of which comprised several counties. Worcestershire lay on the Oxford circuit, and the next sessions in the county were planned for early March. Until then the case would rest.

There was still, though, much to digest from the last fortnight. Smith had gone far beyond the limits of an ordinary coroner's inquest. He had sat for five days and a total of around 60 hours. He had encouraged witnesses who had remained silent for upwards of two decades to speak out for the first time, and he had concluded with three suspects under arrest and with substantial evidence against each of them. The newspapers were quick to acknowledge these successes, and Smith was hailed again and again in reports. 'Throughout the enquiry he has evinced an anxious desire to conduct it in such a manner as should promote the great end of justice, and to his zeal and intelligence the public is much indebted for the thorough investigation which this horrible and extraordinary affair has undergone,' a typical piece recorded.

The days passed and the weather improved. 'The frost has at length broken up, after having continued with more or less severity for upwards of forty days,' *Berrow's Worcester Journal* reported on 11 February. The paper expressed its hope that the canal would be navigable within days, and that the Severn, which had been covered

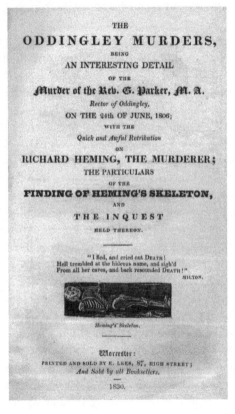

Frontispiece of *The Oddingley Murders*, one of a number of commercial pamphlets to appear in the wake of William Smith's inquest and Clewes' confession

by vast plates of ice and had flooded in the thaw, would settle back into its normal character.

Clewes, Banks and Barnett had been incarcerated for a week. Now the verdict had been given, and they had been formally charged, their status changed. They were compelled to don regulation prison dress – yellow velveteen frocks and matching caps – and to undergo the full rigour of the gaol's regime. This meant rising at a quarter to six, labouring until nine o'clock, and then from ten until one and two to six. The three men were kept apart on different wards.

Although the inquest had ended, the clamour for information persisted. Journalists sought out talkative locals, listened to taproom tales and inferred as much as they could from the suspects' personal appearances. They penned potted histories of Clewes, Banks, Barnett, Heming, Captain Evans, Reverend Parker and James Taylor, revealing little vignettes as they unearthed them. Their reports were then swapped and syndicated across the country. Captain Evans was the acerbic military man, George Banks a respectable local, John Barnett a wealthy farmer (one newspaper speculated he was worth £20,000), Richard Heming and James Taylor both cast as opportunistic villains, and Thomas Clewes a pitiful character, a prisoner of his past.

They also raked over details of George Parker's life and stories from the tithe dispute. Some claimed that Parker was the son of the Duke of Norfolk. The *Morning Chronicle*, which had historically opposed the tithing system, published a mischievous article about the Oddingley dispute: 'In what is anything but unusual [Parker] quarrelled with his parishioners respecting tithes,' they wrote. 'Being a Cumberland man, and therefore, probably, like all mountaineers, obstinate and determined, he resolutely fought the good fight till 1806, caring equally little for the love or the enmity of the parishioners, and disregarding all warnings to take care of himself, when one afternoon he was shot at from behind a hedge and afterwards despatched.'

It was unsurprising that the *Morning Chronicle* adopted the case for campaigning purposes, but for other papers the Oddingley affair was most notable for its similarities to a more recent sensation. One newspaper, the *Leicester Chronicle*, was typical of many when it published its account of the inquest under the sub-heading 'Parallel to the Polstead Murder'. Polstead was a small village in the south of Suffolk which had been thrust into national focus just two years earlier when the remains of Maria Marten, daughter of the village mole catcher, were discovered in a barn. Twenty-five-year-old Marten had disappeared 11 months previously, and had last been seen on her way to meet her companion William Corder at his barn, where her body was later found.

The story had fascinated the country. Corder, who had a bad reputation, had left Polstead soon after Maria's disappearance. He had told her family they had married and settled on the Isle of Wight. The lie had held for a year, but in April 1828 Maria Marten's mother began to have strange dreams suggesting that her daughter had been murdered and buried in Corder's red barn. On 19 April 1828 she persuaded her husband to search the building. '[I] put a mole spike down into the floor . . . and brought up something black, which I smelt and I thought it smelt like decayed flesh,' Mr Marten told a court several weeks later. It was the decaying remains of his daughter's body.

The public interest that followed Marten's discovery had been immense. Corder was traced to London and amid a circus of press coverage was brought back to Suffolk, where he was convicted of murder. Much of the country was caught up in the frenzy. A preacher travelled from London to Suffolk to deliver a sermon to around 2,000 people outside the barn, which now was referred to as *the* Red Barn; Staffordshire pottery figures were produced, and everyone clamoured for a memento. The Red Barn was pulled down and sold as 'tooth picks, tobacco-stoppers, and snuff boxes', and after 7,000 people gathered at Bury St Edmunds to watch Corder's execution the hangman sold sections of the rope at a guinea an inch.

The similarities between the murders were obvious. Both victims had been lured to quiet barns in rural England to be killed by men they knew and trusted. Thereafter their graves were concealed and fictions invented and peddled to those who would miss them. It also seemed odd that both Heming and Marten had been discovered by family members. Was this chance, or providence? But while Maria

Marten had been buried for just under a year, Heming had been missing for nearly 24. This fact troubled journalists as much as it excited them. How could those responsible live for so long with such a wicked truth? How could Clewes have continued to live at Netherwood with the skeleton of a murdered man buried just outside his farmhouse? How could Captain Evans have continued to reside in the parish after organising not one but two murders?

It was not unusual for newspapers to speculate on criminal cases. Although the law stated that any publisher could be committed for contempt for distributing articles that prejudiced a trial, in reality few titles took heed of this. The *Worcester Herald* did little to cloak its opinions. It reported all Clewes' statements with gentle cautionary asides, taking every opportunity to remind its readers what type of man he was. Conversely their descriptions of Banks were supportive. The paper judged Banks 'a fine man of most respectable appearance and of rather pleasing manner'. His reputation was, it confirmed, 'much esteemed' in the locality, and it rubbished the suggestion that he was the Captain's son. One broadsheet, published on Valentine's Day, went further, brazenly declaring, 'We trust [Banks] will be able to clear himself from the serious charge brought against him.' This pamphlet, which ran to more than 30 pages and consisted of newspaper accounts of the depositions, ended with a strangely contradictory paragraph.

> In concluding our account of this tragical event, we wish to caution our readers not to prejudge the case against the prisoners, more especially Banks and Barnett; though two atrocious murders have been committed; they may be innocent of participation in them; they still have to be tried by God and their County; may the Jury calmly weigh every fact that has a favourable bearing towards them – and, if innocent – God grant them a true deliverance. Let justice be done at all events.

Press involvement had long tainted the objectivity of legal procedures. In 1828 Justice Gaslee at the Old Bailey had complained,

'It was much to be lamented that . . . no case now occurred . . . which was not forestalled by [accounts in the newspapers] which created a prejudice against accused persons from which it was very difficult, if not impossible, to divest themselves.' The trial for the Elstree murder in 1823 was notoriously marred by press intrusion. The chief suspect John Thurtell, a frivolous libertine who had killed a fellow gambler after an argument, was falsely accused by *The Times* of having murdered before, and the *Morning Chronicle* managed to refer to all three suspects in the case as 'the murderers' before any verdict was reached. The Elstree murder ended up generating so much public attention that two plays telling the story were scheduled for the weeks before the trial. Eventually Thurtell managed to have his trial postponed for a month to allow the excitement to subside, but this did little to improve his chances, and it was said that a crowd of 40,000 watched his execution.

Although the reports of the Oddingley murders did not plunge to such depths, even outside the county the case remained a distracting sensation. Long accounts of the crimes were published in London, Canterbury, Newcastle and Edinburgh, and across the sea in Belfast and Dublin. Each retelling of the story adopted a different slant, attributing the murders variously to the evils of the tithing system, the wickedness of the farmers or the obstinacy of Parker.

In particular, attention was turning to Captain Evans. If Clewes was to be believed, then the Captain was the most culpable of them all. He had organised the opposition to the tithe. He had cursed Parker more violently than anyone else. On Midsummer night Heming had turned to him for protection, and it was on Evans' orders that he had hidden at Netherwood. On 25 June events had been driven by the Captain, who had improvised, summoning one of his wolfish contacts – James Taylor – to remove Heming for good. How could this behaviour have gone unpunished? How could the Captain have expired peacefully in his own bed, rather than swing from the gallows before the eyes of a pitying crowd?

This puzzle was solved by the growing number of accounts of the Captain's miserable death. Papers dwelt on the report of sleepless nights, tormented visions and wild furies that characterised Evans' last days. *Berrow's* soared to new heights of imagery, evoking the 'scorpion stings of conscience' and on Saturday 20 February the *Ipswich Journal* added,

Captain Evans, who in May last, passed to 'that bourne from whence no traveller returns,' and whose name has been mixed up with the diabolical murders at Oddingley, appears to have been singularly visited with compunctious feelings of conscience, after those acts had been committed. An aged man named Doone, engaged with the monster, after his participation in the crimes, as servant; but such was his turbulent character, such his dread of persons approaching the house, lest apprehension should follow their entry, that ingress was rendered sometimes troublesome, in consequence of the doors and window shutters being kept in a state of closure and bolted; but this fear seems to have somewhat subsided as the case became involved in perpetuity and mystery. These agitated movements, however, plainly betokened that there was something within that harrowed the soul, and held him a felon in his own mind until the day that death 'marked him as his own'.

More unsettling accounts seeped out into the newspapers. There were reports of neurotic swearing and fervent prayers. At times both Heming and Parker would loom horribly over his bedside as Evans quivered in their shadows below. While Clewes' suffering had been portrayed through subtle stories of barroom slips, heavy drinking and insomnia, the Captain's torments were presented in a more dramatic and unnerving way to a readership familiar with the concepts of punishment and atonement. These were not just themes preached from the pulpit but ones that featured heavily in contemporary literature. Mary Shelley's Victor Frankenstein, a towering literary figure of the day, lamented in a passage which seemed eerily relevant to the Captain's plight, 'Memory brought madness with it, and when I thought of what had passed, a real insanity possessed me; sometimes low and despondent, I neither spoke nor looked at anyone, but sat motionless, bewildered by the multitude of miseries that overcame me.'

There are more parallels with Thomas Hood's ballad *The Dream of Eugene Aram*, which was composed in 1828, just two years before Heming's bones were discovered. This enormously popular work revisited the story of Eugene Aram, an eighteenth-century school-master and philologist executed in 1759 for the murder of Daniel Clark. Aram had killed Clark 14 years earlier and concealed his body in a shallow grave near Knaresborough in Yorkshire. Aram then left the area and started a new life in King's Lynn in Norfolk, where he worked at a school as an usher. These are the years in which Hood's ballad is set, depicting Aram as a kindly, able man with a blackened soul and a terrible secret.

Hood's Aram is a 'melancholy man' detached from the happy society and beautiful countryside that surrounds him. One day Aram comes across a schoolboy reading the story of Cain and Abel. He sits with the boy and begins to talk of Cain 'And, long since then, of bloody men / Whose deeds tradition saves / Of lonely folks cut off unseen / And hid in sudden graves.' Aram continues, explaining to the schoolboy,

> He told how murderes walk the earth
> Beneath the curse of Cain, –
> With crimson clouds before their eyes,
> And flames about their brain:
> For blood has left upon their souls
> Its everlasting stain

Did the Captain suffer like Aram? Did he retain the same clear picture of the murder scene? Had Heming's or even Parker's blood stained his soul as Daniel Clark's had stained Aram's? These misfor-tunes were all suggested in the newspaper accounts of his death and supported by the testimony of his housekeeper, Catherine Bowkett. But could it be that these accounts were exaggerations? That the Captain suffered no more than any elderly invalid with an iron will and a thirst for life? The stories of frenzied fits might have been influenced by the social and cultural mores of the time. As the Georgian era drew to a close and the Victorian age beckoned, people were becoming more concerned with questions of personal morality, guilt and repentance. Felons like Aram and Evans were expected to

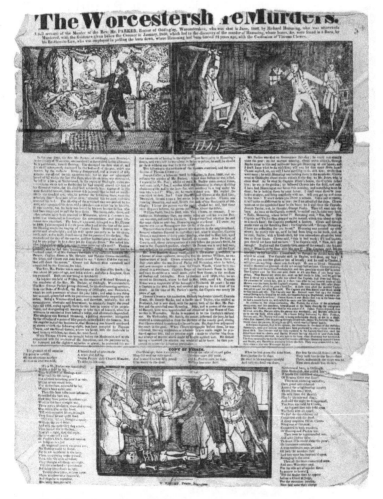

Ballads and woodcuts combined in *The Worcestershire Murders*, a broadsheet printed by W. Wright in February 1830 and sold in Birmingham

suffer, and just as Aram had been mythologised by Thomas Hood, the Captain may have received the same fate at the hands of his housekeeper and the newspapers.

Meanwhile relatively little attention was given to James Taylor, who according to Clewes had dealt Heming the fatal blows. The *Morning Chronicle* published the story about the communion plate at Hampton Lovett and how Taylor had escaped due to a 'legal quibble', but the *Liverpool Mercury* was typical of many regional newspapers, doing little more than observing, 'James Taylor was a farrier at Droitwich, he is dead.'

The newspapers were not the only medium to spread the story. By mid-February three woodcuts published by a W. Wright of Birmingham charting the Oddingley case were circulating. The first shows Heming's head peeping malevolently out from a hedgerow as he levels his gun at Parker. The second depicts Heming's murder the following day: Taylor with his blood stick held high in the midnight gloom, the scene lit only by the lazy light of the Captain's lantern. The third of the set shows two men (presumably Pierpoint and Smith) wearing tall hats and greatcoats pointing in astonishment at the exposed bones. Four other figures are shown: one must be Charles Burton, who is leaning on his shovel with a satisfied expression on his face, while the others (perhaps members of the Waterson family) look on, aghast.

These woodcuts were published on a single broadsheet which also featured the transcript of a street ballad inspired by Burton's discovery. With access to newspapers still limited and literacy largely confined to small areas, the street ballad was an essential link in the dissemination of any sensational story – murder, divorce, affair or fraud. They were sung to a familiar rhythm by balladeers outside shops, public houses or markets. Many ballads have been lost, but this one survives. It begins:

> The greatest of all miracles
> Is going to unfold
> Of two atrocious murders
> As true as ever told

> A horrid band of miscreants
> A cruel plot did lay
> Against Parker their Church Minister
> To take his life away
>
> One Heming there a carpenter
> They did send for with speed
> And promise to him fifty pounds
> If he would do the deed
>
> And for the sake of cursed games
> Until their voice did yield
> And Mr Parker soon he shot
> Within a lonesome field

This ballad is likely to have appeared very early in February, shortly after Clewes' confession, as it includes information that could only have been drawn from that document. It pins the blame squarely on Clewes: 'A strong suspicion fell on Clewes / being one of the crew/ connected in both murders / of Heming and Parker too'. No other farmers are mentioned at all – not Captain Evans, John Barnett or George Banks. It is an example of how street ballads could distil a story in a simple linear narrative to render it comprehensible, but it demonstrates how Clewes was continuing to receive little sympathy from the general public.

A second ballad survives. It is different in tone, more didactic and literary, and it sees the Oddingley murders through a disapproving Christian eye, as evil drifts imperceptibly into the parish, subverting its inhabitants and poisoning the air. Instead of explaining Heming's disappearance, it dwells on the farmers' fate, particularly that of the Captain ('Ill thoughts to drown, he deeply quaff'd / Th' intoxicating bowl; / But madness curs'd the frequent draught, / And horror fill'd his soul') and Clewes ('He droop'd, an alter'd, broken, man, / Cowering 'neath human eyes. / Like one guilt-stain'd – so gossip ran – / But who on such relies?').

Whereas the first ballad is populist, the second is a morality tale, its imagery and frequent references to the scriptures designed to shock and provoke. Oddingley's sunny lanes and fertile fields form a blithe and bucolic scene, but even here there is evil. Heming is depicted as a personification of sin, creeping invisibly through the parish with terrible intent. The Captain and Thomas Clewes, who are responsible for Heming's appearance, will suffer divine vengeance. All of them are damned.

As the ballads and engravings circulated, other publications continued to emerge. Three chapbooks were printed and distributed in both Worcester and London, where the *Morning Chronicle* continued its steady coverage of the case: 'Publications, taking all shapes and bearing many names are daily issuing from the Press upon the above theme [the Oddingley Murders]. A Mrs Sherwood, the authoress of *Stories for Infant Minds*, has unfolded a tale, and a Rev. Gentleman, in a pamphlet replete with quotations from *Macbeth* & the Scriptures, has, in the sublimest language, enlarged upon the Providence that never fails to discover the murderer,' one report concluded.

As news of the crimes continued to swirl across the country, Clewes, Banks and Barnett remained in gaol. Of the three, Banks took his confinement most harshly, the *Worcester Herald* noticing 'the alteration which had taken place in his person since his apprehension'. Initially Banks refused to see anyone, and only at the end of February did he talk to Mrs Parks, his landlady. Others were refused altogether. 'It pains me to see them,' Banks told one of the turnkeys.

Clewes seemed in brighter spirits. For most of February he remained 'cheerful and composed' and was visited by his wife and children. Only at the end of the month, as the trial drew near, did he succumb to a bout of depression. In another ward John Barnett remained stoical, stoutly protesting his innocence and his confidence that he would soon be acquitted. His chief concern, it was said by his visiting family, was the danger the gaol posed to his delicate health.

The incarcerated farmers had been far from idle. Despite Banks' protestations in the Talbot Inn that he wanted no legal adviser, he had quickly changed his mind once the gravity of his situation had become apparent. In early February he engaged Spurrier and Ingleby of Birmingham to conduct his defence. Shortly after, perhaps in an attempt to present a united front against Clewes, Barnett had also signed with the firm.

Clewes did not have the resources of the other men. His years as an aspiring young farmer at Netherwood were well behind him, and at 59 years old his finances were as worn as his body. He judged himself too poor to afford the counsel of attorneys or solicitors and stated that he would have to rely on the presiding judge to ask questions on his behalf. However, in early March Clewes' relatives hired Stephen Godson, a local attorney. Godson was not of the rank or education of Banks' or Barnett's representatives, but he did give Clewes access to a degree of legal expertise.

The brief for the prosecution was passed to William Smith, the coroner, and his firm, Smith and Parker. Smith was at the height of his reputation following his successful inquest, and knowing the facts of the case far better than any other lawyer, it made perfect sense for him to take the role of state prosecutor. Over the next few weeks, sergeants, King's councils and barristers were added to the growing number of legal representatives. They would each play a role when the assize judges had concluded their business in Oxfordshire and completed the 50-mile journey to Worcester.

The legal tussle ahead would be decided by the finest of subtleties. While English law remained highly technical and afforded prisoners various routes of escape, the system favoured the prosecution. None of the defendants would be given notice of the specific case to be answered until the day of their trial, and the prosecution was not compelled to disclose the material it was planning to use, raising the unnerving possibility of surprise witnesses. Furthermore, there was no court of appeal, meaning that judgements were usually final.

William Smith spent much of February preparing his case, faced with the troubling question of whether to bring additional charges against the men. The 1826 statute repealing the need for the principal perpetrator to be first convicted raised the possibility of a prosecution for Parker's murder, but this, as Smith conceded in his notes, was unlikely to succeed. There was a much stronger chance of convicting the men for Heming's killing. But should additional charges be laid in addition to those brought by the inquest? Was Clewes merely an accessory to the murder or was it possible that he had landed the fatal blow himself?

In his city office William Smith had his clerks draw up a detailed document entitled *The Case for the Prosecution*. This survives today and much of what is known about the Oddingley case comes from it. On the first page Smith outlined his intention to prosecute all three of the prisoners as accessories before the fact in Parker's murder as well as for their involvement in Heming's. He collected together proofs of the coroner's inquest in 1806, minutes from Captain Evans' and John Barnett's interrogations at the Crown Inn in 1806, all the depositions taken informally by Reverend Pyndar and copies of the voluminous evidence given at the coroner's inquest over the past few weeks.

On 7 March, little more than a month after the inquest had concluded, the assizes arrived for the Lent session in Worcester. At least ten different journalists from newspapers across the country were waiting in the city, where for weeks the *Worcester Herald* had been promising readers a special edition containing 'a full and accurate Report of the Trials of the above Assizes and more particularly of that of THOMAS CLEWS AND OTHERS for the murder of Heming'. Its rival, *Berrow's Worcester Journal*, reassured its readers, 'we shall use every exertions to furnish a full report in our journal published that evening [11 March]. If the trial is not concluded when we go to press, we shall on the following day continue the report in A SECOND EDITION.'

The entry of an assize judge into a town was intended to be an impressive affair, a vivid and lasting symbol of the Crown's power before its subjects in the provinces. Late on Sunday 7 March Justice Joseph Littledale was met at the county boundary and escorted into the city by the high sheriff to the ringing of the cathedral bells. Spring was advancing and only the cold breeze lingered as a reminder of the frosty winter weather. The Star and Garter, Unicorn and Rein Deer hostelries were already busier than usual, the *Morning Chronicle* noting that the 'innkeepers are in eager expectation of a plentiful result, and look proportionally smiling and jolly'.

The article continued,

> With respect to Oddingley itself, the excitement to visit it is in a great measure passed away, for the barn where the body of Heming for so long lay undiscovered is razed to the ground – the hole that served for his grave is filled up, and the bones of the murderer are long since removed. With all of these drawbacks to the scene of action, the curiosity of the public mind naturally turns to those it presumes to be the living monuments of the transaction; and, therefore, instead of Oddingley being the great attraction for the marvel-hunters and wonder-lovers, the run is all in favour of Worcester, with an anxious expectation for the result of the trial.

CHAPTER 17

The Assize

The Guildhall, Worcester, 8–11 March 1830

Early on the morning of Monday 8 March the Lent assize opened at the Guildhall on Worcester's High Street. The Guildhall was the most elegant building in the city and one of the finest examples of early Georgian architecture in England. Built of red brick and dressed with stone, it had been designed by Thomas White, one of Sir Christopher Wren's pupils, and it was believed that the architect had

An ornate symbol of power: Worcester Guildhall in
the early nineteenth century

personally carved the bust of Queen Anne which loomed over its arched doorway. The Guildhall was a permanent symbolic and administrative hub in the heart of the city. It had hosted assize sessions since its opening in 1723, and it was a suitably imposing and solemn setting for an orderly dispersal of the King's law.

As part of the preliminary steps, Judge Joseph Littledale convened with members of the grand jury to introduce himself and to offer guidance on the more complicated of the cases that awaited them. A grand jury was a body of between 12 and 23 important local men, whose role was to filter out cases unworthy of Littledale's court. They met in private, interviewing witnesses and analysing indictments – formal written statements detailing the charges against a defendant. Once a majority was persuaded that a suspect *probably* had committed a crime, the grand jury endorsed the bill of indictment – proclaiming it a true bill – and the case was forwarded to the courtroom for trial.

This process was usually straightforward. The Oddingley case, however, promised to be quite different as it was unclear just which charges Clewes, Banks and Barnett would face. Smith's coroner's inquest had already ruled that all three had played a role in Heming's murder. As this verdict had been reached by a jury of more than 12 people, there was no need for the charges to be ratified and theoretically they could proceed directly to the courtroom. But matters were about to be confused. Over the past few weeks William Smith, as solicitor in charge of the prosecution case, had decided to lay additional charges in connection not just with Heming's murder but also Parker's. If these were put, they would have to be written into fresh indictments and then fed through the grand jury filter like any other case. What would happen next, therefore, was uncertain, and Judge Littledale, acknowledging this, chose to issue the grand jurymen some cautionary words.

GENTLEMEN, there is a very important case in the kalender [sic], which had occupied a great deal of public attention – I need not say you must not pay any attention to what you have heard out of doors upon the subject, but confine yourselves to the witnesses who shall

appear before you – that is, the three persons charged with the murder
of Richard Heming, at Oddingley, in this county, of the names of
Clewes, Banks and Barnett, who are charged in different degrees upon
the finding of the Coroner's Jury; but you Gentlemen are to look at
the evidence yourselves. Gentlemen, the murder of Heming appears
to have been committed very nearly twenty-four years ago: at that
distance of time, it may be extremely difficult to get at the truth of
the case. In the first place, several persons who might give information upon the subject, either for the prisoners or against them,
perhaps, are dead; with regard to others who are alive to be examined,
from the length of time it cannot be supposed their recollection will
be so perfect as it otherwise might have been. At the same time, you
will see whether there is sufficient before you to find any bill against
these persons, from what the witnesses shall say. They appear, at
present, Gentlemen, only to have been committed for being concerned
in the murder of Heming; but from what I have seen of it, it appears
to me to deserve consideration (and you will see if it is the case)
whether there is not ground to charge all or some of them as accessories before the fact, or after the fact, or as principals in the murder
of Mr Parker himself, as well as of Heming. They do not appear to
have been committed upon that charge, but still it may be material
for you to enquire whether there is any evidence to affect any of
them with regard to Mr Parker.

Worcester was lucky to have been allotted Littledale. While assize
judges were generally able, not all of them shared his pedigree. Some
were little more than retired politicians passing from one courtroom
to another, drawing the generous salary that accompanied the position and enjoying the prestige in the cosy years of their lives. As
there was no fixed retirement age, many judges clung on to their
wigs long after their mental abilities had started to wane. An alarming
three quarters of the judiciary died in harness between 1790 and 1875.

Littledale was a tall man with calm brown eyes and an air of
gentle conviction. At 63, he remained intellectually active and devoted
to his work. A portrait by William Beechey shows him in court,

dressed in a flowing wig and long scarlet robes, an official document in his right hand. In 1830 he was approaching the peak of a long and brilliant career, his reputation in the country only eclipsed by that of the lord chancellor, Lord Eldon. Littledale was cautious, steadfast, erudite and patient. It was said that he had read all five volumes of *Comyn's Digest* of English law from cover to cover and retained every detail. As one of only 12 full-time judges he received an annual salary of £5,500, and just three and a half months after presiding over the Oddingley trial he would walk alongside the grandest nobles in the kingdom as part of King George IV's funeral cortège.

Littledale was also notoriously conscientious. He was late for the Worcester assize as he had sat in an Oxford courthouse debating until one o'clock on the previous Saturday morning, and in his initial address to the grand jury had delivered something of a surprise. He had hinted that they might yet find charges in connection with Reverend Parker's murder, a cause that had seemed lost ever since Heming had disappeared on Midsummer Day.

It was an opportunity that the prosecution, headed by coroner William Smith, was determined to grasp. As Littledale set to work on the 48 prisoners who awaited trial (42 men and six women, of whom six faced capital charges), Smith and his team worked industriously on the case, drawing up a number of new charges. Two days later they were ready, and on the morning of Wednesday 10 March Smith presented the grand jury with three fresh indictments. The first two related to Parker's murder and charged all three defendants with being accessories, both before and after the fact. The third bill, however, was perhaps the most important. It concerned Heming's murder and was intended to clarify and enlarge on the words of the coroner's verdict. It comprised two counts: one asserted that Clewes, Banks, Taylor and Evans had gathered at Netherwood Farm on 25 June 1806, where Taylor had killed Heming: the second was identical except it had Clewes striking the fatal blow. The bill was written in the weaving and repetitive language of legal documents and was an aggressive move from Smith, who had decided there was enough evidence to convict Clewes outright as the principal in Heming's murder.

The indictments were left with the grand jury, who spent the whole of Wednesday examining them behind closed doors. The day passed slowly amid mounting anticipation. It was seven in the evening before its business was complete and they emerged. It was announced to the court that from Smith's indictments they had found a total of three true bills. One was against all three farmers for being accessories before the fact in Parker's murder. The second and third had been found true for Clewes alone, accusing him of being an accessory after the fact to Parker's murder and the principal killer of Richard Heming. They had thrown out two of the charges against Banks and Barnett and absolved them completely of having any hand in Heming's murder. This was, on the face of it, encouraging news for Banks and Barnett, but they knew that – like Clewes – they still faced the possibility of being tried on the findings of the coroner's inquisition. None of them could feel safe.

As the day's business was concluded, officials, journalists and members of the public were left to digest this tangle of different charges: four against Clewes and two each against George Banks and John Barnett. It was the outcome of weeks of legal manoeuvring. Ever since Charles Burton had dug his spade into Heming's grave on 21 January a series of escalating dramas had been being played out: the identification of Heming's skeleton, Clewes' arrest, his confession, Banks and Barnett joining him in gaol, the coroner's verdict and now the decision of the grand jury. Almost 24 years after the crimes had been committed, the path to justice was finally clear. The following morning Thomas Clewes, George Banks and John Barnett would be tried for the Oddingley murders.

For many, the day began long before sunrise on Thursday 11 March. At six o'clock the first keen onlookers were already beginning to mill in the High Street outside the Guildhall's tall iron palisading. Although the city centre remained cloaked in the chilly gloom of a spring morning, those who hoped to catch a glimpse of the suspects or gain entry to the courtroom knew they would have to be patient and lucky. The city was 'crowded with strangers desirous of hearing this extraordinary investigation', the *Birmingham Journal* wrote, adding, 'several persons at the trial having come expressly from Norfolk and other distant parts of the kingdom'. This was echoed by the Morning *Chronicle*'s reporter, who had roamed the inns the night before and encountered several gentlemen who had decided to sit up all night in anticipation of the trial and planned to arrive early to do 'justice to their curiosity'.

By about eight o'clock the knots of visitors and curious locals had grown into a large and excitable crowd, blocking the path of the dogcarts and trade wagons that usually dashed through the city centre. Just after eight a cry went up. A prison van carrying Thomas Clewes had pulled to a stop in the street. It was followed closely by a hackney carriage containing Banks and Barnett. The authorities had, seemingly, decided to keep the two others separate from Clewes. In any case, the farmers could be thankful for the closed coaches and a degree of anonymity. These were new luxuries for prisoners. Traditionally criminal suspects were conveyed to the courthouse in open carts, and in the West Riding of Yorkshire prisoners had still been marched between the gaol and shire halls in chains as recently as the 1820s.

As the vehicles' doors swung open, the crowd heaved in excitement, and for the next few minutes constables pushed and shouted as they strove to clear a path through which the men could be escorted into the building. The Crown Court was hidden away at the back of the Guildhall, behind the central staircase, which swept up to a banqueting hall on the floor above. Like the rest of the Guildhall, the courtroom was panelled in gleaming oak, its atmosphere a mix of quiet authority and proud tradition. Portraits of sheriffs, lord lieutenants and mayors hung from the walls, gazing over a room which had been specially prepared to receive the large audience that was expected.

The sheriff had planned to keep the courtroom closed until Littledale had assumed his seat, but the crowd made this impossible. 'So intense was the throng and the pressure against the door that bolts and bars gave way and a general rush into the interior took place,' a journalist for the *Worcester Herald* wrote. Another reporter, safely installed in the press gallery, watched as 'the court and hall in front became momentarily filled to an overflow', 'the eye', he wrote, 'in every direction met with a sturdy contention not only for seats, but for the occupation of the smallest nook affording even standing room and a glimpse of the bench'.

At a little after eight o'clock Littledale entered the court and Clewes, Banks and Barnett were called before the bench. It was the first chance for many to examine the characters they had read so much about. Banks 'appeared to excite the greatest interest in court', the *Birmingham Journal* reported. Now in his mid-forties, he was a powerful-looking man dressed in a new suit of black. On 'entering the dock he at first appeared stultified by the awful situation in which he was placed', it

Judge Joseph Littledale in his ermine robes at the height of his career, painted by William Beechey

observed. Next to Banks was John Barnett, standing motionless, gazing forward, not displaying the slightest emotion, and then a short distance away was Thomas Clewes. Clewes seemed 'heavy-looking' with 'the appearance of a humble labourer, of anything but a sanguinary disposition'. In contrast to Banks he was dressed in a shabby black suit, or – as one paper drily put it – 'a rusty suit of mourning'.

Before the trial commenced Littledale called the court to order. He announced that he had reconsidered his position on the charges that related to Parker's murder. Having initially suggested that a prosecution might be mounted, he said that he had since changed his mind. He told the court he thought it was doubtful that the prisoners could be tried, as the principal had not been convicted and the statute removing the need for a prior conviction had not been made retroactive. He explained that the three defendants could therefore object to being tried on any of the charges concerning Parker's murder. However, he added, according to a precedent, 'if the prisoners choose to be put on their trial, my objection will be waived'.

It was a strange proposition, as it seemed plain that any defendant would object to being tried on a capital charge and John Curwood, chief counsel for the prosecution, was the first to rise in response. Curwood was an enormously experienced and eloquent barrister with upwards of 30 years' service in England's courtrooms. All hopes for a conviction rested on his ability to navigate a path through the complexities of the case and fend off any legal objections that the defence raised. Curwood began by acknowledging Littledale's point but argued that the defendants should still be arraigned – formally charged before the court – with the indictment as a matter of form. This suggestion was roundly attacked by each of the defence counsels, who argued that as there were no grounds on which the charge could be put, arraigning their clients was a waste of time. Their objections were short and pointed, but they gave the crowd a first glimpse of the defence barristers. Banks and Barnett had spared no expense. William Taunton, chief counsel for Barnett, was 57 years old, an experienced and fierce performer with a reputation as a heavyweight on the trial circuit. John Campbell, defending Banks,

was a precocious talent with political ambitions: three decades later
he would become Queen Victoria's lord chancellor. Clewes, without
the means of his fellow defendants, had not been able to select from
the glittering stars of England's courtrooms. His counsel, Ebenezer
Ludlow, was a veteran sergeant-at-law with 25 years' experience.
Ludlow did not have the education, class or reputation of Campbell
or Taunton, and representing Clewes, by far the most vulnerable of
the three prisoners, was going to be an enormous test of his skill.

Ludlow argued that charging Clewes with a crime he could not
be tried for was distracting. 'Clewes is indicted for a murder,' he said.
'On that murder he ought to have a fair and unprejudiced trial, which
will not be the case if he is borne down by the extraneous circumstances which belonged to the other indictments.'

'But at all lengths it would be proper to arraign the three prisoners,'
Curwood countered. Littledale agreed, and they were asked to stand
as the indictment charging them with Parker's murder was read. It
was a moment of procedural farce, perhaps a little bewildering to
those packed into the Guildhall, dressed in greatcoats, holding tall
hats in their laps and decoding as much as they could.

'How say you, Thomas Clewes, George Banks and John Barnett?
Are you guilty or not guilty?' asked the clerk of the arraigns.

They said nothing, and one by one Taunton, Campbell and Ludlow
interjected, objecting on behalf of their clients. Littledale acknowledged their right to do so, and the first of Oddingley's two murders
thus went unpunished. There might yet be justice for Richard
Heming, but for Parker, by far the more innocent of the two victims,
there would be no vengeance under English law.

For the audience it may have seemed a disappointment, but in
reality it was the outcome that those familiar with the esoteric details
of the case had long anticipated. 'It is believed that the prisoners
will, as regards this indictment, endeavour to escape by the death of
the principal,' William Smith had written in his notes before the trial.
Having realised this, the prosecution had adopted the tactic of pres-
surising the court into arraigning the men. Thereafter, 'if they do
not consent the Bills will hang over them and very properly so',

Smith had added. It was a good point. A lingering sense of thwarted justice would pervade the remainder of the case. Smith knew that Clewes, Banks and Barnett were within their rights to avoid the charge, but he was keen to display their good fortune to the court. The men had escaped a capital charge not through their innocence, but via a technicality so obscure that it had even confused Littledale and members of the grand jury. Hereafter the momentum would shift. More charges awaited, and on these there were no legal loopholes to slip through.

The clerk was called forward again to read the remainder of the charges. These included the findings of the coroner's inquistion and the true bill passed by the grand jury accusing Clewes of murdering Heming. The defendants were asked to stand.

'How say you, Thomas Clewes, George Banks and John Barnett? Are you guilty or not guilty?' asked the clerk.

'Not guilty,' said Clewes.

'Not guilty,' said Banks.

'Not guilty,' said Barnett.

As they spoke, each prisoner was compelled to raise his right hand beside his head. Clewes' 'grey hairs lay straight upon his forehead', noted one reporter; Barnett paused momentarily before responding firmly; Banks, who had been drawing the most attention from the press gallery, seemed shaken. Throughout his time at the bar his lips quivered and moved 'as if [he was] engaged in subdued and silent conversation', one journalist noted.

The charges read, the 12-man jury was empanelled, all of them men between the ages of 21 and 60 holding the requisite property qualifications. They included an innkeeper, an ironmonger, a tailor, a mercer, a weaver, two farmers and a scythe manufacturer, and were headed by the foreman, James Allport, a cabinet maker from Stourport.

Before the case proceeded any further, Clewes' counsel Ludlow enquired for a second time which of the indictments was to be tried first. He pointed out that Clewes had been charged twice, the other defendants only once. Littledale answered that it was customary to try the most serious case first, therefore it made sense to begin with the murder charge against Clewes. Curwood seconded this suggestion and Ludlow acquiesced. Banks and Barnett were then removed from the bar, leaving Clewes to hear the indictment a second time.

As with any criminal case, the prosecution was invited to lay its evidence before the jury first, and Curwood made his way to the front of the court. His opening speech had doubtless been carefully rehearsed. The aim was to set the scene and stroll through the facts of the case, introducing his argument as he went. Curwood's effort was commendable, an equal mixture of flattery, persuasive rhetoric and lucidity that at times glowed with a mellifluous, rhythmic quality. He began by declaring the case 'almost unparalleled in the legal annals and totally unparalleled in my recollection'.

'On 24 June Mr Parker was murdered in one of his own fields, and I believe it will be proved without question that the murderer was Richard Heming, between whom and Mr Parker there was no enmity,' Curwood observed. It was a strange crime, he went on. Heming and Parker belonged to different parishes; there was no quarrel between them. Only after a time, he explained, did it turn out that he 'was hired by other persons to do the deed of horror'. Gaining a little momentum, Curwood shifted his attention to subsequent events and Heming's disappearance.

> Years, however, rolled away, and nothing was heard of him, until his remains were found in the barn; those were recognised; his shoes were remarkable; and the bones were identified by his wife. It appeared clear that Heming was the murderer of Mr Parker, and therefore, the inference was that Heming had been murdered by those who employed him, because it having been known that search was made for this man, it became of vital importance to those who instigated him to do the deed that he should be removed. With respect to the others, I will abstain from saying anything; I shall merely observe that Clewes, the prisoner, had a motive, and I shall prove that he used expressions of the most deadly hate to Mr Parker. He said he would give £50 to have him shot. In 1815 he had said he knew Heming would never appear

again; and on Bromsgrove fair day, the very day of Mr Parker's murder, he stated, he hoped he would find a dead parson before him at home. Gentlemen, he did find a dead parson before him at home, and I will produce a witness to show you he knew what became of Heming, and Heming was heard of no more.

Curwood now turned to the subject of Clewes' confession. He picked up a copy of the document in his right hand, but before he could begin to read it, Ludlow sprang to his feet, objecting that it was unusual to mention a confession in an opening speech. Littledale submitted to the point: 'Perhaps it would be as well to abstain as much as you can from referring to it, unless you consider it necessary,' he advised.

But this was more a gentle warning than a stiff rebuke and did little to deter Curwood from his course. The confession was the most incriminating piece of evidence the prosecution possessed and its validity lay at the core of the case. The earlier Curwood could introduce it to the jury the better, but already the barrister was entering choppy legal waters. Ever since the eighteenth century involuntary confessions (those 'got by promises or threats') had been deemed inadmissible in court, and there was every danger Clewes' confession would be regarded as such by Littledale. The judge would have to consider how Clewes had come to confess: whether he had been offered any inducements to do so, or had been pressured into making his statement. Being probed by a figure of authority (however gently) was considered unacceptable as a suspect might feel compelled to confess out of fear or duty. Some inducements, such as an offer to remove a pair of handcuffs or the promise of a meeting with a family member, were considered acceptable. But the line was thin. In 1833 a female prisoner's confession would be declared inadmissible because an officer had stated that she had better speak, 'otherwise the matter would lie on her and the guilty would go free'.

The first confession – made orally to Clifton at the gaol – failed both of the legal tests. The defence was sure to argue that Clewes had been seduced by Clifton's promise of a royal pardon, about as strong an inducement as could exist. They could also point out that Clifton was a figure of authority: he was not just the prison chaplain but also the magistrate who had committed Clewes to gaol just hours before. Clewes had genuine reason to respect or even fear what Clifton said, giving Ludlow a strong argument for having the confession dismissed as evidence. The only hope for the prosecution was to demonstrate clearly that Clewes had made two independent confessions: a first, to Clifton at the gaol, which had been rescinded and destroyed, and a second to the coroner's inquest two days later, which was legally admissible. Such arguments would come later, but for now Curwood stuck to the matter in hand. He warned the jury to expect the defence to use the confession 'as a means of escape'. He continued,

> The whole of this confession must be given to you: but you are not bound to believe the whole of it. You may believe the prisoner when he says he was present, but you are not compelled to credit his statement when he attempts to explain away his presence. And gentlemen, I may here remark to you, that in the whole course of my practice, I never knew an accessory who did not, according to his statement, fill a very insignificant part in the transaction. He never confesses to being the person who struck the blow or gave the poison.

Unlike the relative informality of the coroner's court, rule and form permeated grand jury cases. Questions had to be concise and relevant. The tone was formal, and almost every address was accompanied by flattering asides to the judge and the jury. Bad manners, uncouth language or any other solecism were not tolerated, and the judges and barristers – who often knew each other from other stops on the circuit – occasionally betrayed traces of familiarity, though they did their best not to show it. Describing a London courtroom in *Sketches By Boz*, Charles Dickens recorded, 'Nothing is so likely to strike the person who enters them [criminal courts] for the first time, as the calm indifference with which the proceedings are conducted; every trial seems a mere matter of business. There is a good deal of form, but no compassion; considerable interest but no sympathy.'

Charles Burton, fresh from his month as a local celebrity, was the first witness called by the prosecution. He repeated his evidence, stating how he had come across the bones at Netherwood a month and a half earlier and describing how he had cooperated with Smith and Pierpoint in the exhumation of the skeleton and accompanying artefacts. Burton was subject to a light cross-examination from Ebenezer Ludlow, but no more. He admitted that two-foot rules such as the one found in the grave were also carried by masons and other workers as well as carpenters.

Surgeon Matthew Pierpoint also breezed through his evidence without trouble from Ludlow. He was a respected man, and questioning his evidence was unlikely to impress either the court or the judge. Like Burton, Pierpoint narrated his movements throughout January with careful precision; as did the next witness, Elizabeth Newbury. She told the jury about Richard's disappearance, then proceeded to identify, as they were produced, his shoes (nailed on the heels, low and tied with string), his rule ('witness examined the

An early photograph of Netherwood Farm and its fenced fold-yard, from about 1910. The replacement barn can be seen on the left-hand side

rule and put her finger on a mark near the rivet which did not quite close') and the teeth of the skull. When confronted with the sight of Heming's skull for a second time, Newbury was ready and composed. 'He had very good teeth, sound, very strong and tolerably white,' she said. 'I will swear they are his teeth.'

'Do you know Thomas Clewes?' asked Curwood.

'I know Thomas Clewes. He came to the house three times on pretence of work, before Mr Parker's death,' she replied.

The first of the prosecution's points had been proved: the bones discovered in the barn at Netherwood were Heming's. Curwood could now proceed to his second task – to demonstrate that Heming was a hired gun tempted into the parish to dispose of Parker. Shopkeeper Thomas Barber was the first to support this. He repeated his evidence from the coroner's inquest, recalling that Clewes had promised '£50 for any man who would shoot the parson' after brushing past Parker in his store. 'Did he offer you any money?' Ludlow enquired. 'The £50 was not offered to me, it was only said in the way of conversation,' he replied.

As one witness followed another, Ludlow's attempts to cast doubt on their testimony increased. When Joseph Colley recalled Heming talking about 'a dirty job at Oddingley' in the Red Lion, Ludlow suggested he might have been referring to getting the poles out of Evans' muddy pond. During his cross-examination of Sarah Lloyd (now Sarah Rogers) he discovered there were no living witnesses to corroborate her account of the left-handed toasts and curses in the Pigeon House. 'I told my father and sister of this the same night, but gave them no particulars,' she said. 'Both are now dead.' Susan Surman was also challenged. Valentine Lee was Ludlow's deputy and initially more combative. He attacked Surman's claim that Clewes had said, 'I shall be glad to find a dead parson in Oddingley when I come back [from Bromsgrove Fair]' – an important part of the prosecution's case and the key element of her testimony.

'You say that two people, a servant of Mr Hardcourt and a friend of yours, heard Clewes make this statement. Could you tell me where these people are?'

'The girl is dead, and, I believe, the man in whose presence Clewes made use of this expression.'

A break was timetabled for early afternoon, but before it arrived a string of further witnesses stood to verify – beyond all of the efforts of Valentine Lee and Ebenezer Ludlow – that Parker was killed by Heming. The Captain's old dairymaid Elizabeth Fowler informed the court about finding the shotgun 'which Heming called for a week after'; a man called Gore explained that he had repaired a gun of the very same description for Heming in May 1806; and John Lench remembered disturbing him in the glebe with Parker's smouldering body just a few feet away.

As Lench concluded his evidence, the court was suddenly distracted by a curiously comic moment. A mysterious letter had been rushed into the room addressed to one of the jurors. Confused by the unexpected arrival Littledale supposed it must relate to a domestic emergency and ordered the juror to read the communication at once. The judge's fears were allayed when the man admitted the message was nothing more than a love letter full of 'tender enquiries' from his wife, who hoped he was coping with the stresses of his responsibility. The incident amused the court and mortified the juror.

By early afternoon journalists from *The Times* and *Morning Chronicle* had already dispatched their copy on the midday express from Worcester to London. Those in the capital would have to wait a further day and a half before the first tidings of the result came. In court, however, the prosecution's pace was quickening. Thomas Colwell, Richard Page, landlord of the Virgin Tavern, Reverend Pyndar and Richard Allen of Droitwich were all asked to recall events on Midsummer Day 1806. Pyndar, now in his mid-seventies, appeared to be suffering from that ailment that renders memory more colourful with age. 'I found Parker seated on the grass in a field, and I heard him draw his last sigh. He was supported on a chair by poor persons,' the old clergyman said. It was clearly a muddled account, a sign either that Pyndar was losing his faculties or that the occasion had got the better of him – in any case it did not much matter.

Next the prosecution introduced a new sighting of Richard Heming on Midsummer Day. Thomas Hill was a farmer from Newtown, and he had run into Heming at the Virgin Tavern shortly after Richard Page served him a drink. Hill said that Heming did not rush away from the hostelry or head off on the Worcester road; he simply stood for some time, almost inanimate, at a gate. Could this have been the moment Heming chose to return to Oddingley? 'He was standing there with his coat on his left hand,' Hill remembered. 'He was drinking, it was a blue coat.' Hill was followed by John Perkins, a clear target for the defence. Perkins had reason to dislike his peers and Ludlow was keen to expose this. After revealing all he remembered about the Easter meeting and the left-handed toasts at the Plough, he was cross-examined viciously by the sergeant.

'How long before Mr Parker's death did you say that Clewes was paying for Heming's drinks in the Red Lion at Droitwich?'

'This was about five or six weeks before Mr Parker's death. It is about 23 years ago, but I recall that it was five or six weeks,' Perkins replied.

'Are you sure of this? You stated to the coroner that it was five or six months,' Ludlow rejoined.

'I will not swear I did not say five or six months before the coroner. If the coroner did put down six months, it was a mistake.'

Ludlow continued to press the point, and Perkins, unnerved, managed to contradict himself several times. Finally, Ludlow demanded a straight answer. 'I meant five or six weeks,' Perkins stammered, displaying the first palpable emotion of the day. 'Ah! Put your hat down and don't be in a passion,' Ludlow said, 'for you won't put me in one!' Perkins was dismissed from the stand, still protesting.

The last witness connected to the first murder was Pennell Cole. Now almost 80 years old, the surgeon who had performed Parker's autopsy had retired from Worcester Infirmary in 1815 and instantly re-enlisted in the army for the Waterloo campaign. Cole was a man of the old school, skilled and impressive. When his retirement eventually came he had settled in France on half-pay until in 1821 he had been appointed deputy inspector of British hospitals. Cole had travelled to Worcester that day from his house in Manchester. He provided a cogent and empirical description of Parker's bloodied body and suggested that 'a blunt instrument must have given the wound [on the head]'. There was no cross-examination – there seemed little point.

It was late afternoon. The court had heard about Burton's discovery of the skeleton, the identification of the bones as Heming's, the tithe dispute, the threats and the circumstances surrounding the first murder. Now the most important question lay before them. How had Heming been murdered and concealed in the barn at Netherwood? There was little evidence relating to this, and it was clear that Clewes' confession would have to be raised soon. John Curwood relieved his deputies and took to the front of the court-room. He called to the witness box a clerk from the firm of Parker and Smith in Worcester. Curwood asked the man to state his name.

'I am James Hooper, a clerk to Messrs Parker and Smith. Mr Smith is the coroner.'

'Were you present when Thomas Clewes made a confession?' Curwood asked.

'I was.'

'And how was this confession made?'

'Clewes was not brought before the coroner. He sent a request to Mr Smith and the jury to attend [at the gaol].'

Mr Lavender, governor of the gaol, was now called. He explained that he had written a note to Smith at Clewes' instigation. The letter was produced and he testified that it was his hand. The note was read to the court.

Dear sir, – I have seen Thomas Clewes; he expresses a wish to see the Coroner and the Jury at the prison.

Respectfully yours,
J. N. Lavender.

Thereafter Lavender was cross-examined by Ludlow. He asked Lavender why the interview had taken place at the prison and not at the Talbot where the coroner's inquest was on-going. As governor, he had no contact with the prisoners, so who had passed the message between Clewes and himself? What was Reverend Clifton doing in the gaol? Had he interviewed Clewes before this note was written?

As befitting the governor of a gaol, Lavender's answers were stark and to the point. He told Ludlow the note had been written at the express wish of Clewes. Reverend Clifton was at the gaol as a visiting magistrate, he explained, 'coming with an understanding that if I wanted anything particular I was to apply to him'. And had there been any interviews? 'I knew that previous to my writing that note to the coroner, an interview had taken place between Mr Clifton and Clewes,' Lavender revealed. 'I cannot tell exactly, but I think that it was more than one.'

Lavender had avoided explaining why the confession was taken at the prison instead of the Talbot, and Curwood, re-examining, offered him the opportunity to explain this decision. 'The reason why the words *at the prison* are underlined is because I begged the coroner and jury to adjourn to the gaol. Mr Smith said he did not know that they could adjourn unless by the desire of Clewes. I went to Clewes and communicated this to him. He said it was all the same to him where he saw them.'

Curwood now sought to further underline why the confession was admissible. He had James Hooper recalled and asked him to explain the context in which Clewes' statement was received.

Before the prisoner made any confession, Mr Smith addressed him in these words: 'Thomas Clewes, it has been intimated to me that you wished to see myself and the Jury, and that you have something to communicate to us.' Mr Clewes said 'yes Sir.' Mr Smith said, 'it is my duty to inform you as one of His Majesty's Coroners for this county that any confession, admission or deposition you make will be produced in evidence against you at the next Assizes, on a charge of the murder of Richard Heming, and that no hope or promise of pardon can be held out to you either by His Majesty's Government

or by any other person.' Having been told this more than once by
the coroner, he said, 'well Sir, I shall state all I know about it,' and
then he made a confession which I took down in writing.

The case had arrived at a crucial juncture. If the confession was
deemed admissible then all details of the murder in the barn could
be brought before the jury: evidence against the Captain, James
Taylor, George Banks, John Barnett and Clewes himself. If it were
not, it would be omitted from the proceedings, the case against
Clewes would crumble and in all likelihood he would be acquitted.
Ludlow, persevering doggedly with his line of attack, appealed to
Littledale to exclude the confession altogether or else compel the
prosecution to call Reverend Clifton.

'The court should be satisfied that the confession is voluntary,'
Ludlow said. If it had been obtained by any threat or persuasion
then it could not be admitted. He had several concerns relating to
the document.

> If this confession had followed an interview with a private friend
> or unauthorised person, I would not have asked his Lordship to
> require the appearance of that person [Reverend Clifton] in the
> witness box. But when the party stood in the situation of a visiting
> magistrate – when in that capacity he had gone to the gaol and had
> been locked up alone with the prisoner, I would ask his Lordship
> whether it was not the duty of the prosecution to put Mr Clifton
> in the box?

There was more to Ludlow's argument. It was imperative, he
suggested, that everyone in the court understood what had passed
between Clewes and Clifton in the cell. The first confession 'must
naturally have been operating on his mind, and he [Clewes] was not
in the fair exercise of his judgement.' A day may have passed since
Clewes had spoken to Clifton for the first time, encouraged by the
false promise of a royal pardon, but 'the mark of torture had not
yet been removed from his mind'. It was a strong performance from

Ludlow. He concluded his speech by imploring the prosecution to put Clifton on the stand.

Littledale was swayed by Ludlow's arguments but stopped short of assisting him outright. 'I do not see how I can insist upon the prosecution calling any particular witness,' he said. 'I think at the same time it would be candid and fair of them to do so.'

There was a pause in the court. But with no sign that Curwood was about to act, Ludlow seized on the ambiguity of the judge's remark. 'In that case I will call the Reverend Mr Clifton,' he announced.

This was an unusual step but it passed unopposed. Clifton left his seat at the front of the room and entered the witness box. From the start he seemed downcast and contrite. He admitted signing a warrant for Clewes' arrest, and that subsequently the men had spent hours together over the next days.

'How many times did you see the prisoner in the gaol,' asked Ludlow, 'before he made the statement now in discussion?'

'Several times,' Clifton said. 'Three, I think, or four.'

'Four, perhaps?'

'Possibly four, three I have distinct recollections of.'

'Did you communicate to Clewes that you would write to the Secretary of State?'

'I think I did,' Clifton replied. 'I said to Clewes I would use all my interest with His Majesty's Government to prevent any ill conse-quences falling upon him, if he would dispose to me all he knew of the Oddingley murders.'

'Now, Mr Clifton,' said Ludlow. 'Was it at your desire that Clewes was left alone with you?'

'Yes. It was at my express desire.'

'And you are a clergyman, Mr Clifton, and you felt great desire to have the mystery developed?'

'Yes,' said Clifton.

Perhaps Clifton's kindness, the empathy that stemmed from his Christian upbringing and his life as a minister, had been his undoing. The private interviews, the cautionary words and the nudging advice are all reminiscent of a pastor schooled to listen, to counsel and to steer the souls of men to God. These impulses might have been natural for Clifton, but they flew in the face of his legal responsibilities, which required him to remain objective and dispassionate. Clifton's bungled role in Clewes' confession exposed an integral weakness in the legal system, which encouraged members of the clergy to fill their spare hours in the dual role of a magistrate. The two positions, clergyman and magistrate, may be united by their need for educated and respected men, but in essence they required very different minds, skills and training. Clifton had muddled the two roles disastrously, and this had thrown the case – already complex enough – into further confusion.

It was vital for Curwood to distance the two confessions from one another, and he now asked Clifton to explain what had happened in his third interview with the prisoner. 'I told Clewes that I had utterly failed in obtaining any promise or hope of mercy, and read to him a particular part of the letter to that effect,' he explained. 'I said he might consider the circumstances as locked up in my breast, for I considered myself in the double capacity of magistrate and clergyman, and should state nothing against him.' He went on, 'I would rather be committed by the coroner for contempt, than disclose what had passed.'

'But had not George Banks been committed to gaol under your warrant between the meetings?' Ludlow asked, recommencing his cross-examination.

'Certainly he had,' Clifton replied.

'And was it a matter of some notoriety that Banks had been brought to gaol?'

'Certainly it was.'

'And did you inform anyone that Clewes had made a confession?'

'I had mentioned to several persons the general fact that a confession had been made. Assuredly, the coroner knew of the general nature of Clewes' statement,' Clifton admitted.

'And do you recollect having mentioned to the prisoner that if he did not tell there were others that would?'

'At the second conversation I said it appeared to me that there were so many living persons who had knowledge of the transaction that some or other of them would tell.'

'I strongly consider that I have a case to make out against the confession,' Ludlow announced, turning away from Clifton. 'The alternate effusions of hope and fear held out by a magistrate and a clergyman must, in Clewes' case, have had great influence with him.' There were three parts to Ludlow's argument. Firstly Clifton had promised to apply to the home secretary 'to prevent any evil consequences'. Secondly he had given him hope of being pardoned – though Ludlow conceded that this had subsequently been removed. Thirdly Clifton had suggested that it was in Clewes' interests to speak out. Two of these inducements had not been withdrawn and must have played upon his conscience, Ludlow claimed. 'And let me remind your Lordship that in the interval of Mr Clifton receiving the letter from Secretary of State, Banks had been taken into custody. Who can tell how this might operate on the mind of the prisoner?'

A prosecution counter-attack ensued. Curwood reminded Littledale that there had been two confessions not one, and that much of what Ludlow had said referred to the former, rather than the latter. He was supported by both his junior counsels. William Whateley argued that 'Mr Smith, in his caution to the prisoner at the inquest, had warned him that no hope of mercy could be held out. Surely this last phrase was quite sufficient to eradicate any hope he might entertain from the personal influence of Mr Clifton?' Richard Godson contended that 'If these words were not strong enough, [then] there were no words in the English language that could remove the impression from Clewes' mind.'

The arguments had been made. Littledale would have the final word and the court quietened in anticipation. The judge had one more question to ask and he recalled Clifton to the stand to establish what time he had informed Clewes there was no hope of a pardon. 'Ten o'clock in the morning of 2 February,' Clifton replied. Hooper was then summoned to testify to the time Clewes had delivered his confession. 'It was five o'clock in the afternoon of the same day,' he said.

'It seems to me that this confession is admissible,' declared Littledale. 'I entirely concur that if he acted under the influence of any promise or threat, such a statement ought not to be received in evidence; but Clewes having been told that there was an end to all hope from the Secretary of State, the influence on his mind from that time ceased.' A crucial point, Littledale noted, was that Clewes was not summoned before the coroner; instead he wrote a note of his own free will. 'Therefore under all the circumstances I consider the confession is good evidence and it is to be admitted at this trial.'

It was an enormously significant moment. Had Clewes' confession been omitted, then the evidence that he played any part in Heming's murder would have vanished in an instant. Littledale's ruling was a grave blow for him, but the individual most obviously affected was Reverend Clifton, whose legs buckled as the judge spoke. He fell back into his seat. His inexperience had come within an inch of costing the prosecution its case. 'Restoratives' were sent for to allow him to speedily 'regain his faculties'.

The judge, lawyers, journalists and the public now listened in silence as Thomas Clewes' statement was read aloud. This was their one chance to hear what they had all read in the newspapers, the details repeated once again: Banks visiting Clewes at Netherwood, the panicked meeting between Clewes and the Captain, the dark barn, Taylor's blood stick, Heming's bloodless murder and hasty burial. It took 45 minutes for the confession to be read in full. By now the court had been in session for approaching ten hours and for the barristers this was a chance to relax and refresh themselves in preparation for the closing witnesses.

These came soon enough. William Smith had found three men to corroborate what Clewes had admitted. John Collins, Clewes' farmhand, remembered heaving the marl into the barn on his orders; a man named William Perkins recalled seeing Clewes at Pershore Fair; and William Low – another to have come forward since the inquest – told the court that Clewes had alluded to Heming at the White Horse in 1815. Low said that Clewes had told him, 'Heming would never come to be hanged, for he was safe enough.'

'That is the case for the prosecution, my Lord,' said Curwood.

*

Ebenezer Ludlow had said little since Littledale had decided to admit the confession, allowing the three final prosecution witnesses to slip by without serious trouble. Earlier in the day Ludlow had seemed effervescent, sparring with Curwood and conjuring arguments in spite of all the evidence. The early evening, however, saw him a quiet and thoughtful figure. At last he rose to begin his defence. He told Littledale that, taking every word of the evidence to be true, 'Clewes was entitled to his acquittal.'

Ludlow's argument was beautifully simple and a compelling application of logic. He explained to the court that nothing the prosecution had achieved had contradicted Clewes' confession; indeed they had actually confirmed some of the details. In points of law, Ludlow reasoned, 'before a man can be made one of the principals in a charge of murder, it must be proved that he was present, aiding and abetting others to do the deed. All that Clewes had done, according to the confession, did not constitute him as an aider or abetter; and if he was not that, then neither could he be a principal.' 'What single tittle of evidence was there to show that was the fact?' he enquired.

He now turned to the confession itself.

If they chose to take the case exclusive of Clewes' confession there was nothing from which the inference could be raised that he was even present at the scene. The most that the remainder of the evidence went to show was that there had been some vague expressions made use of by Clewes, which might throw some slight sort of suspicion on him. Then, if his confession was to be received at all, it must be received whole and entire, for the low knew no such harsh proceedings as to take that one part of a man's confession which was calculated to tell against him, and to leave out the other that was in his favour; either it was a confession or it was not a confession.

'What then did this confession go to show?' Ludlow asked rhetorically. It was true that he was present when the murder of Heming took place, 'but so far from being an aider and an abetter, he had actually been inveighed by Captain Evans into being present at all;

and certainly when he had resolved to comply with that wish, he had not in the least contemplated the catastrophe forced upon him'.

It was now nearing eight o'clock in the evening and the morning's frantic scramble for seats seemed a distant memory. Both the prosecution and defence had outlined their cases, and now, as was customary in complicated trials, Littledale summed up for the jury. 'The discovery of this murder, so long concealed, and now so strangely brought to light, is one of those extraordinary incidents which now and then occur in human affairs,' he began. While most of the evidence applied to the murder of Mr Reverend Parker – 'a very wicked act' – this was not the crime for which Clewes was being tried. Instead he was suspected of Heming's murder, and the jury must remember that.

Now, that Clewes was desirous that some mischief should be done to Mr Parker is certain, and that he entertained this feeling in common with Captain Evans is, I think, equally clear; but even though I should own that Clewes was an accessory before the fact in the murder of Mr Parker, it does not follow that because Captain Evans wished to murder Heming I should allow that Clewes participated in this desire. You will observe that, in the evidence before you, the confession of Clewes forms the leading feature. In this he confesses himself a criminal amenable to the law – he confesses himself an accessory after the fact; but it does not seem that he knew anything of the intention of murdering Heming until the fatal blow was struck, and Gentlemen, the rule of law is, that when you take a criminal's confession, you must take the whole of it as it stands, unless you have evidence to contradict any part of it, or evidence to supply its deficiencies. But what here have you to supply?

Gentlemen of the Jury, I must say that I think the evidence is hardly sufficient to convict the prisoner as principal. You must decide. The whole question rests on the confession. There are not, in my opinion, sufficient grounds for thinking that Clewes has made false statements. There is no reason to conclude that, because Clewes consented to the murder of Parker, and because it would have been

an advantage to him to get Heming out of the way, he should, therefore, have consented to the death of Heming. It remains for you
Gentlemen, however, to consider if the evidence be sufficiently strong
to induce you to bring in a verdict of guilty.

The jury retired for several minutes, then reappeared. Littledale
asked if they had reached a verdict. They replied that they had. After
a moment's silence they announced to a confused courtroom that
they had found Thomas Clewes guilty as an accessory after the fact.

Littledale instantly interjected, silencing the gasps of the crowd.
'Gentlemen, you must have misunderstood me,' he said. 'The prisoner is not indicted as an accessory after the fact, but as having aided
and abetted in the murder – and it appears to me, although it is for
you to determine, that there is hardly sufficient evidence to justify
you in finding him guilty.' The jury then retired again, emerging
after a brief absence with a verdict of not guilty.

The Guildhall was overcome. For the past 12 hours it had been a
place of emotional restraint, with the crowd's allegiances, emotions
and anxieties concealed beneath a veneer of stony faces and glassy
eyes. But as the jury announced its verdict the little courtroom filled
with spontaneous applause. The clapping was accompanied by
audible sighs, the murmur of voices and shuffling bodies animated
in a release of long-suppressed energy. The tension, which had been
mounting ever since Littledale had approved the confession as
evidence, snapped. In response, Mr Gillam, the under sheriff, was
forced to intervene, quietening those whose 'indecorous conduct'
was distracting the court from its business.

With Clewes' acquittal, the prosecution's case had run its course. All
hopes of a conviction had hung on convicting Clewes for murder.
Clewes had faced the strongest case, but now the charges against him
had been dismissed it was clear there was insufficient evidence to convict
either Banks or Barnett. John Campbell, Banks' counsel, who had spent
the day in quiet observation, rose and asked Littledale whether the
prosecution wished to proceed on the coroner's charges. Littledale
forwarded this question to Curwood, who replied that 'after the

decision of the jury, I feel it would be very wrong in me to detain your Lordship by going through the whole of this case again'. For the coroner's charges to be dismissed, Clewes, Banks and Barnett were called to the bar and asked to plead against this remaining indictment. As no evidence was to be offered against them, the jury were able to return a second verdict of not guilty – and the last of the charges was disposed.

One further legal technicality stood before the prisoners and their liberty. As they had refused to enter a plea on the charge of the first indictment – which accused them all of being accessories before the fact in Parker's murder – it had already been established that they could not be tried for this. However, neither could they be discharged with the bill hanging over them. A discussion ensued between the defence lawyers and Littledale, who shortly declared that the men would be released by a special law of court that he would draft himself.

As this judgement would not come into force until the following morning, the three men were told that they would be returned to the gaol for a final night. Throughout everything they had remained passively attentive, listening carefully as the trial had unravelled before them. Only Banks was stirred from this state by Littledale's final decision. 'As an instance of the strange way in which the human feelings will be sometimes affected by the slightest ills, after sustaining the most terrible, Banks, who had borne himself all day with an air of entire firmness, when he learnt that his liberation was to be delayed for a few days [sic], burst into tears', recorded the Examiner.

As the public filtered out of the Guildhall and into the High Street it was approaching nine o'clock and darkness had long since fallen. Jubilation characterised the mood of those present, and news of the verdict hurtled from mouth to mouth, from the city centre into the suburbs and from there on into the countryside beyond. Five miles away in Oddingley a little knot of parishioners convened at St James' Church to toll the bells, to drink and smoke in celebration. Two men had been murdered, almost every detail of both crimes had been exposed and understood, yet none of those brought to court would be punished. How strange it seemed.

CHAPTER 18

Damned

The doors of Worcester County Gaol were opened for Clewes, Banks and Barnett at eleven o'clock the next morning. Lavender advised the men to leave the city as quickly and anonymously as they could. Banks was the first to go. A group of friends had acquired a brace of horses from the Hop Pole Inn, and they immediately set off for his home at the Pump House in Hanbury. Barnett slipped away quickly too, leaving Clewes alone in the gaol. Clewes had applied to stay on for a few additional hours. Michael Toll, an Irishman from Newry, was to be hanged outside the prison gates that evening for murdering his wife, whom – it had been decided – he had thrown head first into a lime pit. Only after dark, when the gallows had been dismantled and the last footsteps had died away, did Clewes pass beneath the gaol's broad stone archway in the comfort of his own clothes. His wife met him, and together they set off on foot on the hour-long journey to Oddingley.

Clewes was returning to a community which remained divided on the outcome of the case. This split was epitomised by the celebrations at Oddingley church the previous night, where initial joy at the verdict had soon descended into a violent quarrel. The confrontation was only broken up when Reverend Charles Tookey, Oddingley's current clergyman, arrived back in the parish to find the church's bells still clanging. Tookey had acted swiftly – suspending the clerk on the spot and threatening others with prosecution in the ecclesiastical court – but he could not prevent the incident being picked up by the press. Over the following days the newspapers concluded their reports of the trial with breezy anecdotes of the disorderly scenes at the church. Most adopted a lofty moral standpoint, declaring 'feelings of remorse and shame' at the behaviour of the parishioners. The scene was considered an undignified end to a shameful case, but if nothing else it did lend a degree of symmetry to the story, which had begun and ended with a quarrel under the church roof: the first at the vestry meeting in 1806, the second almost exactly 24 years later. The incident also stood in noisy testimony to the depth of feeling which still festered in Oddingley.

The parochial split over the outcome of the trial was replicated in wider society. Surprisingly, in some quarters the farmers had gained support during the past few weeks. One journalist who had been at the Guildhall estimated, 'Every second man in the court seemed to be a friend of the accused,' something explained, perhaps, by the fact that a tithe dispute had prompted the first murder. By 1830 the issue, so long unaddressed, was coming to a head but the problem would not be entirely resolved until 1836, and the abolition of the tax by the Tithe Commutation Act.

Others who agreed with the verdict had a more rational take. They believed the sheer number of years that had elapsed since the murders meant there was no real chance of exposing the truth. The very worst of the villains, Captain Evans, James Taylor and Richard Heming, were already dead or had met with arbitrary punishment for their roles in the crime. What sense did it make now to single out a handful of members of a community when so many could be accused of having had some involvement in the crime? Why should Clewes, Barnett and Banks stand trial at the assize when others like James Tustin and William Barnett did not?

This view, however logical, was not widely held. The *Observer* was more reflective of popular opinion, openly regretting the verdict, which it branded a terrible aberration 'wrung from an unwilling jury' which left potentially dangerous felons loose in society. This opinion was echoed by the editors of several other publications including the *Carlisle Patriot*, which displayed the shortest temper in its response to the judgement. The paper complained that the laws of England had been shown to be deficient before a wide audience. 'That a man who confessed to have been present at the perpetration of a crime should escape punishment is another instance of the wretched state of our law,' it lamented.

In *Sequel to the Oddingley Murders*, the second of her pamphlets on the subject, Mary Sherwood also expressed indignation that the farmers had been released. 'I should not hesitate to say that the result of this trial has been by no means acceptable in my immediate neighbourhood,' she declared, adding that her friends were 'alarmed rather than gratified at the idea that such villainy could escape its due and proper punishment'. She did concede, however, that English law 'could not be framed as to suit every case and to meet every form and variety of crime'. Sherwood rounded off her highly individualistic coverage of the case with a series of biblical quotes addressed directly to Clewes, Banks and Barnett, encouraging them to repent and atone: 'Though your sins be as scarlet, they shall be as snow; though they be red like crimson, they shall be as wool.'

It seemed Littledale's warning to the grand jury at the beginning of the assize – 'at this distance of time it might be very difficult to get at the truth of the case' – had been proved accurate. And, reasoned many of the newspapers, there was a distinct difference between a legal and a moral acquittal. In a long meditation *Berrow's Worcester Journal* pondered:

> The acquittal of Clewes, after he had confessed he was present at the murder and that he received money to conceal the murder, has occasioned much remark, and those who are least capable of forming an opinion on the subject refer his acquittal to causes which had no influence whatever on the decision. He was acquitted in strict accordance with a known rule of law, and though the application of a general principle may, in some peculiar instances, enable a great criminal to escape, it is far more consistent with the due application of justice that general and known rules exist. Were it otherwise the criminal code would be a code of uncertainties. Such then has been

the issue of a trial which was expected to produce a very different result.

It is now highly probable that none of those who were engaged in the bloody conspiracy will ever be reached by the arm of human justice, but

THE WAYS OF HEAVEN, THOUGH DARK ARE JUST.

In this dispensation of Providence, there is much that our finite minds cannot comprehend, but the day of Retribution will 'vindicate the ways of God to man' – will bring to light 'the hidden things of darkness' and make manifest the justice of HIM who has said 'Vengeance is mine; I will repay.'

As these sentiments poured from the presses, Judge Joseph Littledale and his sergeants, barristers and sheriffs were far from Worcester, already distracted by details of a new slew of cases.* But the precedents established at the Guildhall in the case of Rex vs Clewes would endure for many decades. These reflected the uniqueness of the case but also stood as testimony to the skill, eloquence and persistence of the defence barrister Ebenezer Ludlow who had helped establish them. Many of England's finest legal minds had gathered at the Guildhall that day – Curwood, Taunton, Littledale and Campbell – but Ludlow had managed to eclipse them all. It had required a nimble, shrewd performance from the sergeant, who had used all his mental resources to outfox the masses of prosecution testimony, but he had succeeded. Had the prosecution not been so bold as to press for an outright conviction of Clewes as principal and instead charged him as an accessory after the fact – something he had admitted in his confession – then the outcome might have been different. As it was, a cocktail of Ludlow's clever counsel and an overly aggressive prosecution had set the men free.

For some weeks articles continued to appear in the newspapers, and George Banks for one was not ready to let matters rest. He had

* John Curwood and Judge Littledale would be reunited in 1831 in the trial of Bishop, May and Williams, bodysnatchers accused of killing a street boy. The case was a sensation and is the subject of *The Italian Boy*, by Sarah Wise.

not had the chance to counter Clewes' claims publicly and, fearing
that his character had been unjustly tarnished, he opted to use the
Worcester Herald as a mouthpiece. On 20 March the paper published
a full account of the defence he had intended to present at the assize.
It was a fiercely worded and powerful document which branded
Clewes a 'wicked and wretched man' and bemoaned the fact that
Banks had not had the opportunity to defend himself against the
slanderous 'idle rumours or fallacious reports' that had circled freely
in the marketplaces and squares of English cities. If he were guilty,
Banks contended, how was it that the coroner had sat for five days,
interviewed 50 witnesses and still not found any significant evidence
against him apart from that given by Clewes? And how could they
believe what Clewes said? If he was 'wicked enough to participate,
as he admits he did, in this foul and cold-blooded deed, and afterwards
conceal it, and bear the burden of it on his conscience without
remorse for more than 20 years, [he] would not hesitate to sacrifice
100 lives to save his own'. Banks continued,

> Who, Gentlemen, has heard of four men meeting to rob a hen roost,
> to steal a horse or a sheep, to rob upon the highway, to break open
> a house or commit any other crime without previous consent? Would
> they not, I ask you, in all probability, have had frequent meetings
> beforehand to discuss and arrange their plan, the time of executing
> it, the part that each was to take in it and how they should afterwards
> repel and escape suspicion?
>
> And yet, Gentlemen, if the story of this wretched man Clewes
> were true, four men met, as it were by accident, and that Taylor,
> instantly and without ascertaining who his associates were, and
> without one word being said, proceeded to murder Heming.

According to Banks, Clewes' confession was all a ludicrous story
riddled with unsubstantiated and erroneous claims. 'Is it within the
scope of possibility,' Banks asked, 'that a grave of five feet six inches
deep and fourteen inches in width could have been dug by the throwing
out of two or three spadesful of earth?' Could Taylor have completed

the job, without any assistance, in as little as half an hour? Why had nobody else helped? How could Taylor have even dug the grave with a spade, the ground in Oddingley being so hard? At the very least, Taylor would have needed to use a mattock, about the only implement fit for the task. And Banks had more to say about the spade.

> Gentlemen, observe the artful but futile attempt and caution which Clewes uses to make it to be supposed that not even the spade was his, 'the spade' he says, 'was none of mine'. Then whose was it? He has not said that Taylor or any of the others had a spade with them when he met them at the barn; neither has he said that they took it away with them. Whence, then, did the spade come? Whither did it go?

There were more anomalies. Banks claimed that the Captain had never owned the type of lantern he was supposed to have been carrying. And who held this lantern, lighting the path, as the Captain and Taylor dragged Heming's corpse to the grave? Banks then cast doubt on Taylor being involved at all, reiterating that the farrier had no motive for murdering Heming and reminding readers that he had an alibi. Even more absurd, Banks pointed out, was the suggestion that Taylor had committed the murder. Banks had located witnesses to prove that by 1806 Taylor was 'an emaciated, drunken, feeble old man, between 70 and 80 years of age, utterly incapable of fracturing Heming's skull with a blood stick, or to have dug Heming's grave in half an hour – or half a day'.

Most dubious of all was Clewes' allusion to a mysterious fourth man in the barn. If he was to be believed, then this fourth man had remained impassive throughout – just like Clewes himself. Clewes had supposed this fourth man to be Banks, though he had not stated so explicitly. It was a glaring weakness, and Banks seized upon it, deriding it as the one artful lie that exposed Clewes' words for what they were. His whole statement, Banks countered, was a long string of lies, cobbled together by a desperate amoral man in a frantic bid to claw himself out of a perilous situation. The only sliver of truth in the whole sulphurous invention, Banks asserted, related to the moment that he had given Clewes some money at Pershore Fair. But he knew nothing about what this money was for.

It certainly seemed bizarre that Clewes had remained meek and impassive for half an hour while Heming, a man he knew well, was beaten to death and buried in his barn. And the accuracy of his confession was called into further question with the revelation that Clewes himself had admitted it contained a flaw. According to the *Worcester Herald*, just before he was released from gaol Clewes had declared his evidence to be true 'except in one point'. The *Herald*, exhibiting a talent for melodrama, did not enlarge on this statement, which served only to strengthen the long-held suspicion that Clewes was untrustworthy. And several days later Clewes was to suffer another stinging attack. John Barnett, breaking his silence at long last, joined Banks in ridiculing the entire confession as a 'false and wicked invention'. He stated that he had never met Clewes at Pershore Fair or given him any money. Ever since their arrests in February, Banks and Barnett had maintained a united front, and now they were closing ranks.

This was how matters came to rest in the spring of 1830, as life in Worcester and Oddingley reverted to its normal rhythms and the public's attention settled elsewhere. And while the trial had not resulted in convictions, it had at least exposed enough to leave people with an almost complete picture of what had happened during those two days in June 1806. Nobody seriously doubted the main facts of the case: that the farmers had conspired to have Parker murdered, had hired Heming to complete the task and then killed him to keep him quiet. But there were still unanswered questions relating to the accuracy of Clewes' confession, and 200 years later these puzzles still linger, as perplexing now as they were in the spring of 1830.

Clewes' confession is a fascinating document. The eerie, panicked tone is evocative of both the long June day in Oddingley which it described and the chilly magistrates' office at Worcester County Gaol where it was taken down years later. Today when scouring the document for the truth we have some advantages over the trial jury at

Worcester in 1830. Unlike them we are not compelled to see the confession in absolute terms – as a true account or a complete fabrication. Instead we are free to navigate a middle course, accepting some of Clewes' claims and rejecting others. Banks had planned to appeal to the assize jury: 'You cannot, I am persuaded, place any confidence in the contradictory and improbable statements which have been made, especially by Clewes.' But this was going too far, because, for all the logic, power and venom of both Banks' and Barnett's attacks in the press, there is good reason to believe that the bulk of what Clewes said was true. Above all, the confession has two driving qualities: it is cogent and comprehensive. Each assertion Clewes makes, however much disputed, does at least fit the known circumstances, and the sheer length of his statement (nearing 1,500 words) means he gives answers to almost all the hanging questions. He tells us how Richard Heming died, when he died, how his body ended up in the grave, who was in the barn, how the money was distributed afterwards and why he kept quiet. Also implicit is information about Parker's murder. The description of the Captain and Banks at the beginning of his statement is revealing. They are frantic, pestering, distracted and improvising. Why should this be so if they had not conspired to have Parker killed and hired Heming for the task? Why had Captain Evans been so eager to give Heming money to get rid of him? Why had Clewes been desperate to wash his hands of everything ('I won't have him here, nor have anything to do with him')? And why did they not alert Reverend Pyndar? The whole confession is a tacit acknowledgement that the farmers were implicated in Parker's murder. This is the engine that propels the action that follows, and therefore Clewes does not just explain the circumstances of one murder but two. And to think a depressed isolated man with no legal knowledge had invented such a piece of fiction to explain all the facts yet still allow himself to escape goes beyond credibility.

There is also a great deal of evidence to support what he said. At the assize witnesses testified that Clewes had been at Pershore Fair on 25 June 1806 and that he had ordered marl to be brought up to the barn. James Taylor's connection with the murders was backed up by John Rowe's two statements (one to Pyndar in 1808 and the other to Smith in 1830) and by the surgeon Pierpoint, who was convinced Heming's injuries had been caused by a blood stick. In addition, Henry Halbert could have testified that Heming returned to Church Farm on Midsummer night, and Mary Chance could have confirmed that he had fled through the meadows towards Trench Wood and Netherwood early on 25 June. By March 1830 both Halbert and Chance were dead. Had they lived, more of Clewes' story may have been confirmed.

Less obvious but equally persuasive are the little details – derided as 'artful' by Banks. Clewes recalled the precise spot in the barn where each of the men had stood as the blow was struck. He remembered how the dogs and rats had scratched holes in the wall where the grave was dug, and he asserted that Banks gave him the money in two parcels. None of these splashes of colour were vital to his narrative, but he provided them nonetheless, as if they were seared in his memory. If Clewes' statement was a complete invention, then it would have concealed as many details as possible, knowing one slip would expose him. As it was, Clewes had the confidence to litter his testimony with vivid asides and even snippets of dialogue. The Captain's demand is also darkly familiar: 'Damn your body. Don't you never split!' It's a vicious curse, strikingly reminiscent of the language Evans is known to have used elsewhere throughout the summer.

And the roles Clewes allots to the farmers seem to tally with what we know about their characters. Taylor plays the incorrigible villain, Banks the Captain's able deputy, John Barnett the aloof financier, and Heming the slinking rogue. Meanwhile, the Captain remains the dominant personality throughout, his actions fully in line with his military background and instincts. He bullies Clewes into meeting them at the barn, orders Heming about, bides his time and plots his trap. This version of events is more plausible than the alternative scenario: that Clewes killed Heming alone. The improvisation and resolution that would have been required to remove Heming in the wake of his return to Oddingley on Midsummer night was most likely to have come from Captain Evans. It was a dangerous and fluid situation, one that must have reminded the Captain of the fraught campaigns of his military days.

Here there is no real reason to doubt Clewes' statement. Heming's ambush was devised on 25 June, a plot which emerged as the hours passed. Indeed, at seven in the morning, when Banks was dispatched to Netherwood, it seems that the Captain had little idea of what to do with Heming. The decision to have him killed must have come at some point during the day. It was a nimble and ruthless move. Heming had a brittle character: if he could be persuaded to kill a man, it seems likely that he could also be convinced to confess. In such a desperate situation it was logical for the Captain to turn to James Taylor, a man with such a foul reputation he was considered 'the biggest rogue in the county'. And once Evans had brought Taylor into the scheme, he would only have to ensure that Clewes was not kept informed. If Clewes had foreknowledge of the plan to kill Heming he might refuse them entry to his barn or warn the fugitive and allow him to escape. Time was crucially important. The job had to be done – and concealed – that night.

Thereafter, Heming's murder bears the marks of an intellect far closer to that of the Captain than Clewes. The blood stick was a suitable murder weapon because it was silent. A shotgun or pistol would have roused all Netherwood and caused the same problems that Heming had faced the day before. Its second quality was that it allowed for a clean execution. Several forceful blows would shatter Heming's skull in an instant, but no blood would be spilled on the floor or splashed against the bricks. There would be no telltale signs. 'There was no blood, not a spot on the floor,' Clewes said in his confession – a slight detail but one that rang true.

Heming was attacked seconds after they entered the barn. Once again the scene fits together. The barn door creaks as it swings open. Heming flinches beneath the straw as he hears the boots of four men softly enter from the fold-yard. Who are they? Could it be Evans, who has promised to come with his money? Or might it be Clewes or one of his servants? Why are there *four* people? There is a pause.

Heming can see the dull glow of a lantern through the straw. A second later, through the thick summer air, comes the sound of the Captain's voice. Heming answers timorously. He puts his hands down to push himself up towards the light. There is the gentle tread of feet, the smooth rustle of wood against fabric, the smell of burning oil, and then there is only darkness.

Clewes did not have an opportunity to intervene, and once Heming was dead, he was hopelessly implicated. Just as the Captain had hired someone to remove Parker, he had subsequently engaged Taylor to dispose of Heming. This is a pattern: a delegation of tasks or a gift for putting others in harm's way before himself, demonstrated once again perhaps by the fact that the murder took place at Netherwood and not Church Farm. Once the body was buried, Clewes would have been ill advised to have dug it up and carted it about the parish. And how could he have explained the presence of a corpse in his barn if it was found?

As for George Banks' attacks, all presented eloquently and persuasively, several of them can be unpicked. His main argument, that Taylor was an elderly man physically incapable of murder,

A popular reconstruction of Richard Heming's murder that shows his lantern jaw and high forehead. It also gives us our only glimpse of Captain Evans

contradicted what he described elsewhere. Banks asserted that Taylor could not possibly have killed Heming as he was travelling at the time of the two murders. 'I shall show you that on the day the Rev. Mr Parker was shot, in the morning of that day he [Taylor] went to Cotheridge about 11 miles from Droitwich, and thence on to the Hyde Farm near Bromyard in Herefordshire, a distance of about 23 miles from Droitwich, to attend to some cows of a Mr Gardiner's, which were ill of the black water.'

These claims served only to undermine his argument. If the farrier could complete 40-mile round trips in less than two days, stopping to drive fleams into the arteries of diseased cows, then murdering Heming wouldn't have been difficult. Taylor's alibis for these journeys were his son and daughter in-law, both of them compromised witnesses, and if the farrier is removed from the barn then so is the blood stick, the weapon that Pierpoint was certain had caused the injuries. Unlike scythes, pitchforks, spades and harrows, blood sticks were not typical agricultural instruments, and there was never any suggestion that Clewes owned one himself. No alternative murder weapon was ever proposed at either the coroner's inquest or the trial, so if a blood stick was present then it is almost certain a farrier was too.

Banks also declared erroneously that Taylor had no motive to attack Heming, but John Rowe's evidence shows that before Parker's murder on Midsummer Day Taylor was already involved in the scheme. He had approached Rowe on behalf of Captain Evans with the offer of £50 so would have had a vested interest in the crime being executed cleanly. When he learnt that Heming had been seen and pursued, he knew he was as exposed as Barnett, Clewes, Banks and the Captain, and if Rowe or anyone else spoke out, equally likely to be arrested as an accessory before the fact. In addition, Clewes asserted that he was only given between £26 and £27 by Banks and Barnett at Pershore Fair on 26 June. If a total of £50 had been originally raised for Heming, what became of the rest? It's highly likely that the Captain split the blood money between Clewes and Taylor. One paid to keep quiet, the other rewarded for his work.

A third strand of Banks' defence that can be debunked relates to his allusion to a feud between the Captain and himself. 'I was driven from Captain Evans' house by his cruel treatment of me,' he declared. But this occurred after June 1806 – by Banks' own admission as much as a year or two later. All other evidence suggests that during the summer of 1806 he remained firmly in the Captain's favour. And although the rift between the men was certainly deep, by the time of the Captain's death in June 1829 they had settled their differences. Banks inherited much of the Captain's estate and had visited him during his last weeks.

There are however elements of Clewes' confession that are questionable. Clewes' desperation to absolve himself from any connection to Heming's murder leaves him looking like that most familiar of judicial paradoxes, the unwilling criminal. John Curwood, the prosecution barrister, had quipped, 'I never knew an accessory who did not, according to his statement, fill a very insignificant part in the transaction.' Surely Clewes played a greater role than he admitted? If Clewes had not unlocked the barn, how could Heming had gained entry to the building in the first place? As Charles Burton's evidence showed, one of the two pairs of double doors was barred by a thick rail and the other secured with a padlock. Also, how did Heming get into the barn without rousing Clewes' hounds? Then there was the spade – rightly cited by Banks as mysterious. It was possible that it had been brought along by Captain Evans, but Clewes' outburst, 'It was no spade of mine,' seemingly shoehorned into his confession, has an almost exaggerated element of protest about it. Almost as if Clewes was trying too hard to conceal something.

Most peculiar of all was Clewes' failure to identify the fourth man in the barn. He supposed that it was George Banks, although he would not swear to it. This is difficult to square. With all the details and dialogue of the night so strongly retained in his mind, he must have known who this individual was, but all he would assert in the confession was 'I thought it be George Banks – I believe it be him.'

To Banks this was a scurrilous falsehood. But why should Clewes place him in the barn if he was not there? Clewes had nothing to gain by doing so and would only incur Banks' wrath as a result. The only plausible explanation is that Clewes suggested Banks was in the barn because he was. There is evidence that supports this theory very strongly.

This clue is contained in Reverend Clifton's first letter, written to Robert Peel at the Home Office after Thomas Clewes' oral confession on Sunday 31 January. Clifton subsequently tried to destroy all traces of this confession, but he had no access to this letter – copied by a clerk in Peel's Whitehall office – which was released on the declassification of the information decades later. In his letter to Peel, Clifton wrote that Clewes had admitted to being present at Heming's murder. In addition to him, there were 'three other persons, two of whom are since dead'. Clifton told Peel that he had already issued a warrant for the arrest of the third person, and he expressed his hope that they should 'doubtless have him in gaol tonight'. 'The person whom I have sent to apprehend is the nephew of the man who planned the whole affair, & who assisted to drag the body to the hole in which it was immediately buried in the barn where the murder was committed. The great principal, & the man who struck the blow, by which Heming was killed, are both dead.'

If this small scrap of evidence had been destroyed or lost, then the case against Clewes would be far stronger. As in Clewes' second confession, the Captain is accused of planning Heming's murder and Taylor lands the fatal blow. But it is the reference to the 'nephew of the man who planned the whole affair' which is interesting. This must be Banks: he was arrested the night that this confession was given amid swirling rumours about his links with Evans, and Clifton must have mistakenly recorded him as the Captain's son or nephew. The crucial point is that in his first confession Clewes asserted that Banks was present at the murder and taking an active role – dragging the body into the grave.

Therefore, rather than incriminating Banks, the likelihood is that Clewes was actually covering for him. There was little need to shield either Evans or Taylor as they were both dead, but to be vague about both his own and Banks' roles might just have saved their lives. In this version of events Clewes is not the sly tactician that Peel had him down for; he is a scared and depressed farmer, locked away in a miserable gaol with evidence quickly mounting against him. For years he had been tormented by the events of 25 June 1806, and when Clifton visited him in his cell he told him everything. It is revealing that Clifton, who as a clergyman and magistrate would have conducted many interviews of various types during his life, believed Clewes to be telling the truth. A reasoned guess would also have Clewes, as well as Banks, in a more active role: perhaps unlocking the barn for Heming earlier in the day, providing the lantern and a mattock to break the earth, pointing Evans to the dampest corner and helping George Banks to haul the body across the ground. Such things, however, can never be known.

Captain Evans' role in the murder, though, is beyond dispute, and this was plain to all of those who attended the inquest and trial in the opening months of 1830. Having spent almost a century building his reputation, within nine months of his death the Captain was being vilified in all the local newspapers. In mid-March *Jackson's Oxford Journal* printed a scathing piece.

> Capt. Evans (and we cannot refer to that man's name without horror) was evidently the prime mover in the diabolical conspiracy, which gave rise to two murders. He passed to his last great account a few months before the discovery which led to this investigation. We have heard many and dreadful details of the horrors which agitated his spirit when about to pass before the dread tribunal of HIM 'unto whom all hearts be open, and from whom no secrets are hid'; and though all that is related of his last hours may not be true, it is vain to imagine that the soul of a man whose conscience stung him with the recollection of a double murder, could anticipate death without these horrors which some of the most callous of mankind have exhibited in the prospect of eternity.

The newspapers had passed their verdict. Evans may have avoided justice in life, but he was already being punished in death. He had damned all those who had stood in his path, but those curses that he had thrown so liberally at others seemed to have come true for himself. It was too late for him to be saved. It was too late to repent. As a victorious Sherlock Holmes would exclaim to Dr Watson, later in the century, 'Violence does, in truth, recoil upon the violent, and the schemer falls into the pit which he digs for another.'

It was a judgement that might equally be applied to Heming, who met with a far brisker punishment. *Berrow's Worcester Journal* wrote:

> The fate of Heming is replete with instruction: here was a man who, probably for some paltry gain, was seduced to murder a fellow-creature against whom he does not appear to have entertained the slightest enmity; but how long did he enjoy the wages of inquiry? In a few hours after the perpetration of the deadly-deed, the avenger of blood overtook the murderer and those who tempted him to the deed of darkness were made the instruments for hurrying him before his offended MAKER with all his sins upon his head.

Just a few weeks after the conclusion of the trial the newspapers announced that Mary Parker, widow of Oddingley's murdered clergyman, had died at her home in Lichfield. Perhaps the ordeal had been too much for her, although she had lived long enough to discover that Heming had not escaped unpunished. Another piece informed readers that Charles Burton had attempted to claim the substantial rewards offered back in 1806 for the apprehension of Heming, arguing that he had delivered the fugitive to the authorities. It was a spirited effort but was batted swiftly away by unimpressed officials.

Over the next two years Reverend Pyndar and Pennell Cole died, and in March 1834 John Barnett was laid to rest at the age of 60. 'We have not heard whether the deceased, as his end approached, made any reference to the heavy imputation under which he rested, of having been concerned in this double deed of blood, or divulged any thought tending in any degree to remove the mystery in which those horried transactions have hitherto been shrouded,' remarked the local paper, its appetite for new information as strong as ever. John's death left William Barnett head of the family, and he carried on for 24 years more, dying in 1858 at the age of 81. But even he was outlived by Thomas Clewes, who like Captain Evans before him lived to a remarkable age. Rather than fading from view after his acquittal, Clewes seemed rejuvenated. He took the lease of a public house on the fringes of Oddingley parish in the little hamlet of Dunhampstead and supplemented his income by setting up as a coal merchant on the little quay that flanked his home. George Banks, meanwhile, lived out the rest of his days in Hanbury, never again appearing in the local or parish news.

Taken alone, Thomas Clewes, George Banks and John Barnett were not notable individuals. A traveller in rural England would expect to find men like them in any small village: managing the fields, bullying their workers, drinking in the local inns and monopolising the official positions that existed in each parish. Had they lived at a different time or in another place their stories may have been quite different and completely anonymous, for what happened over the few ill-tempered months and two dramatic days in Oddingley in 1806 was an aberration. The man responsible was Captain Samuel Evans.

One can only imagine the first meeting between Parker and Evans. It is 1798, the year of Nelson's glorious victory at the Battle of the Nile, and *Lyrical Ballads*, with which Coleridge and Wordsworth gave a fresh voice to the new Romantic age. But detached from such events and hidden among the rolling hills and fruit orchards north of Worcester, the village of Oddingley lies apart. Here, outside St James' Church, the clergyman – a haughty man, some say, yet fair and able – is talking to his newest parishioner across a little stone wall. The new master of Church Farm, Samuel Evans, is an old military man, stoical, swollen with success and equipped with a cool heart and a quick mind. As the men shake hands they stare into each other's eyes. They cannot know it yet, but this meeting will be fatal.

For Reverend George Parker it will culminate with his murder in the tall clover of a summer meadow, and for Captain Samuel Evans it will end many years later, tortured by an uncontrollable mania. Damned, some said.

Epilogue

Netherwood Farm, Oddingley, April 2011

A skinny tarmac road, Netherwood Lane, sweeps down from
Oddingley towards Crowle to the spot where Netherwood Farm lies
low and lonely in the south of Oddingley parish. It's a damp April
day, and I have come to Oddingley to see where Heming was
murdered for myself. A stretch of white metal fencing flanks the
five-bar entrance gate, which stands open, leading into a muddy
fold-yard that is criss-crossed with the prints of tractor tyres. A restless collie scampers in and out of the sheds and barns on some
determined quest. I meet the farmer who is young and friendly, and
talks with a gentle Birmingham lilt. He tells me about a legend they
have at Netherwood. They say that when it rains, and the rushing
water runs over the stiff red clay, the ruby pools that collect in the
nearby ditches contain the blood of Richard Heming, the murdered
murderer. He points to a spot behind the barn where a little section
of an old hawthorn hedge is interrupted several times by sudden
gaps, wide enough to allow workers to pass into the meadow beyond.
These gaps are supposed to mark the route along which Richard
Heming's corpse was dragged on 25 June 1806.

He tells me these stories with half a smile and then disappears
into the farm, leaving me alone by the barn. It's a tall red-brick
structure, riddled with ventilation holes in its outer walls, standing
to the left of the yard on the site of the original pulled down by
Charles Burton in early 1830. Today there is no element of mystery

to the place that once drew officials, curious locals, journalists and artists from across England, desperate to capture the scene. The only clue that the barn was ever at the centre of a sensational news story is a worn plaque nestled into its brickwork. This is the final tangible trace of the artful life and violent death of Richard Heming. The plaque comprises two slabs of local limestone. Each carries a bleak inscription: the top one '1806 RH 1830'; the second – deeply set, in a Roman typeface – 'RH'. The stones seem deliberately cryptic: just dates and initials, almost as if they dare not spell out Richard Heming's name.

Perhaps even this stark, dismal memorial will not last much longer. The barn has come to the end of its long working life and is shortly to be demolished. Its blue-tiled roof is half-consumed with wispy moss and at one point bulges inwards in semi-collapse. Its walls are chipped and crumbling, and the edge of the bridle path, which runs behind the building, is strewn with mounds of bricks, offcuts of timber and bundles of rope. It feels apt to have found the barn in this condition – about to be replaced, just as it was in 1830. I'm left with a sense of history turning. Just a few feet from where I stand the earth dips into a damp hollow. One hundred and eighty-one years ago Charles Burton was labouring here on a winter day, digging and clawing at the foundations beside the waters of a frozen pool. Just one yard beyond this and one yard below, he would find Heming's skeleton, and the story of the Oddingley Murders would erupt.

People still visit this spot, some from as far away as America, to see the barn, which stands like an almost forgotten outpost of English history that nonetheless retains a flicker of its old pull. And for those who do make the journey to the mid-Worcestershire countryside, Oddingley remains very much as it was back in 1806. Its grassy meadows and tangled hedges still flank the narrow lanes that weave and dive through the valley. Pound Farm is still here, as are Pineapple Farm, Park Farm and Old Mr Hardcourt's former home near the crossroads. Church Farm and St James' Church both survive intact too, lasting symbols of the struggle between the farmers and Reverend George Parker. They gaze out across a sedate, picturesque landscape – the Birmingham and Worcester Canal in the foreground, the railway just behind and Trench Wood lying darkly in the distance.

Other buildings connected with the murders have vanished. The Barnetts' Pigeon House has been converted into a modern home; the rectory is gone, as are the farms that were leased by Samuel Jones and John Perkins. Lost too is Parker's glebe and the site of the first murder. In the early twentieth century Captain Hubert Berkeley of nearby Clink Gate Farm developed a special interest in the murders. To commemorate the events, he erected a stone in the old glebe meadows on the spot where he estimated Parker had been shot. It was another plain memorial: an irregularly shaped stone no more than two feet in height several yards from a sparse hedge and a shallow ditch. The stone was adorned, presumably by Captain Berkeley himself, with the pithy inscription 'G.P.' and, below, '24 JN. 1806'.

Rex Jackson who still farms in the parish today remembers Parker's memorial stone from his youth. Born in 1926, Jackson grew up with stories of the murders. His grandfather had, for a short spell during the First World War, taken the lease of Netherwood Farm, only to recall it years later as a haunted place of swinging doors and crashing plates. In time Jackson would have his own connection with the story. During the many desperate months of 1940, with the British economy increasingly strained, he worked as an agricultural contractor in Oddingley converting inefficient pastures into valuable crops as part of the government's Dig for Victory drive. Parker's stone stood in one field marked for cultivation and being considered a hazard for tractors or threshing machines Jackson and another farmer decided to move it. They coiled a chain around its base and wrenched it out of the ground, pulling it fifteen yards away to a nearby hedgerow.

Presumably the stone remained here until the 1960s, when Oddingley gained yet another transport artery. In 1962-3 the opening stretch of the new M5 motorway sliced unsentimentally through the parish, passing Captain Berkeley's old home at Clink Gate, continuing through the glebe meadows and off towards Worcester. At some point during construction the stone vanished forever. Some say it was thrown into a nearby pool; others maintain that after being rescued by an interested villager it was declared unlucky and discarded. Whatever the truth, Reverend Parker must be accustomed to such discourtesies by now, the scene of his death being – and perhaps uniquely so – now crossed by many thousands of travellers every day.

A handful of miles away, at St Peter's Church in Droitwich, I find Evans' grave similarly disturbed. 'Pitifully behold the sorrows of our hearts,' reads an inscription carved into the oak of a pointed lychgate at the entrance to the churchyard. I walk along a tunnel of neatly clipped conifers which opens out into a sombre mass of stones and crosses. The Captain lies in a far corner, to the left of an old yew tree. There was room for an epitaph on the face of his stone, but

The story as remembered today at the Fir Tree Inn in Dunhampstead, on the edge of Oddingley parish, where Thomas Clewes was once the landlord

the job was never completed as Evans intended. After Heming's skeleton was discovered at Netherwood and the coroner's inquest and trial exposed the role he had played in the conspiracy, it was decided to utilise the space for a different purpose. The alternative inscription carried not an air of malice or vindictiveness, but one of calculated rectitude; so much so that the words could almost have come from Judge Littledale himself. Under the name of Catherine Banks, with whom the Captain shares the grave, it reads, 'Here also lies Captain Samuel Evans whose name is connected with the double murder at Oddingley in the year 1806.'

The monument the Captain had intended to serve as testament to his power and importance in Droitwich had been turned forever for another use, standing for more than a century and a half as a reminder of what he did. I cannot read the inscription today, and perhaps nobody has been able to decipher the words clearly for a generation. Two centuries of English rain, wind and frost have worn down the lettering and eaten into the stone, which is now half-consumed by moss. The grave was in this state in the early 1990s, when vandals broke into the churchyard. The attack was indiscriminate. They hit the Captain's stone with something like a sledge-hammer and left it very nearly cracked in two, as it remains today.

Artefacts from the Oddingley case have dispersed, some of them into public libraries and others into private collections. The Fir Tree Inn in nearby Dunhampstead, where Thomas Clewes once served as landlord, displays a shrine to events. There is a 'Murderers' Bar' replete with a flintlock shotgun hanging malevolently from a beam, a copy of one of the ballads, a parochial map and a black and white photograph, supposedly of the tithe barn. Outside a sign stands in the car park: 'Every old inn has a story to tell but none as gruesome as the Oddingley murderers.' The history has been harnessed well here, yet the shotgun is not the murder weapon. That has long since disappeared, last sighted in the hands of Richard Barneby in 1830. Also vanished without trace are Richard Heming's bones and James Taylor's blood stick, both of which were last displayed publicly at the Guildhall in 1830.

For more than a century local researchers have returned to the story, drawing out details and lingering on the finer points of the case. One of these was Reverend Sterry-Cooper, who lived and worked in Droitwich in the first half of the twentieth century. On 14 July 1939 Sterry-Cooper received a letter from Captain Berkeley. 'I am 75¼, I am probably near the end, but must show you the site of the robber's cave (now a hole) in the Trench Wood,' he urged. Ten years had passed since Berkeley had ventured into the wood, and when Sterry-Cooper joined him to search the following week it was without success. The den *Berrow's Journal* had described so eagerly in 1805 had gone, either overgrown or filled in, and over the next decade it would be followed by much of Trench Wood, which was clear-felled during the 1940s, with many oak, elm and ash trees being replaced by other species designed to yield quick timber for paintbrush and broom handles.

Sterry-Cooper's interest, though, extended beyond Trench Wood:

Pound Farm in the 1930s, taken by Reverend Sterry-Cooper. The farm is almost unchanged from how it was a century earlier when Barnett and Parker clashed in the fold-yard

he delved into details of the tithe dispute and explored the finer points of law. The clergyman hoped to prove that the Oddingley case was a catalyst for the Tithe Commutation Act of 1836. This was a grand thesis and difficult to justify, but it brought Sterry-Cooper back to Oddingley again and again. On these visits he befriended locals, scribbled notes and, intriguingly, produced a set of atmospheric, grizzled black and white photographs which now provide something of a window into the village's past.

In one picture there stands the ghostly figure of a matriarch, hands on hips, outside Park Farm. She glares into the lens suspiciously from a distance of 15 yards. The brick farmhouse, several barns and a little slatted wooden fence stand behind her, but the picture still feels sparse and lonely. Another is taken on a dry winter's day at the village crossroads. A girl stands pencil-straight on the verge outside Pound Farm; a spry terrier dances at her feet. In the background the hedgerow is neatly trimmed and the half-timbered farmhouse stands proudly, its three great chimney stacks rising high into the sky. It was a century since the Barnetts had given their orders in the fold-yard, and in that time the property had shifted from farmhouse to poor house then back into private ownership. At one point the building also served as the village inn, being known as the Bricklayer's Arms. During this time a cryptic warning hung from its sign: 'Blazing fire, here lies danger. A friend must pay as well as a stranger.'

Sterry-Cooper's photographs give one of the earliest glimpses of Oddingley, an empty place of wizened oaks, overgrown gardens, abandoned buildings and outhouses. There are only fleeting traces of the farmhands, dairymaids, shepherds and drovers and there is little sense of action, movement or purpose. There's an elusive quality that seems to befit the Oddingley story, where the complete picture is always obscured. In the years after the trial, the nineteenth century would come into sharper focus with a new-found thirst for statistical data and record-keeping, and the invention of photography. From 1841 onwards, increasingly detailed censuses recorded more facts than ever before about the lives of British subjects. The landscape was captured, too, by a wave of tithe commissions that trawled the country in the 1840s, noting down the names of buildings, fields, woods, hills, roads and streams. The Oddingley Murders languish in the shadows of nineteenth-century history, just before this new modern age. Only the single untrustworthy woodcut of Parker and Heming remains, and there are no pictures of Clewes, Barnett or Banks. When he died in 1850, Robert Peel would be the last prime minister not to be photographed. Like Sterry-Cooper's black and white images of Oddingley in the 1930s, the surviving documents suggest much but they don't reveal all.

In the nineteenth century the Oddingley case had a long afterlife. Nine months after the assize trial finished *The Age* magazine included the story in its annual round-up, alongside the accession of William IV and the eruption of Mount Etna. A decade on, in 1842, Erskine Neale's *The Bishop's Daughter* was published, and later in the century Theodore Galton wrote *Madeline of St Pol*. Both fictionalised retellings of the story which drew on the authors' local connections and knowledge. Thomas Hardy, a habitual note-taker, included a nimble description of the Oddingley affair among his research papers: 'Murder of clergyman planned by several villagers, because he was obnoxious to them by rigid manner in wh. he exacted his tithes &c. Murder carried out by one named Heming. Heming soon after disappears – It is found years after that a reward being offered the planners feared H wd. not stand it & murdered him in barn – Skeleton found there, a 2ft rule beside it. He was a carpenter.'

But as the century wore on, Britons busied themselves with a fresh set of horrible yet fascinating crimes. George Orwell would later describe the second half of the nineteenth century and the first quarter of the twentieth as an 'Elizabethan Period' in English murder, citing the cases of Dr Palmer the Rugeley Poisoner, Jack the Ripper, Dr Neill Cream and Dr Crippen as examples. And as each new case emerged, its details were reported in increasingly intense and complex ways by a more professional press, whose coverage had evolved to include photographs of suspects, victims, crime scenes and crowds – jeering, hissing or sobbing – outside the courtroom.

These fresh scandals and sensations overtook the Oddingley affair, which dwindled into shy obscurity in the early years of the twentieth century, a position it has retained ever since. And even when set beside contemporary stories like the Ratcliffe Highway Murders, John Thurtell, the Red Barn Murder and, at a stretch, Eugene Aram, it feels somehow lost, often absent from period articles or anthologies of nineteenth-century crime. Perhaps because no one was ever successfully prosecuted for either murder – most sensational criminal investigations concluded with an execution, a climactic moment in the arc of the story. The Oddingley case did not.

Long into the nineteenth century thousands of spectators of all classes gathered to witness the execution of a murderer. An estimated 7,000 turned up to see William Corder hanged in Suffolk in 1828 and an enormous assembly of between 30,000 and 50,000 watched the final moments of the notorious Frederick and Maria Manning at Horsemonger Lane in Southwark in 1847. On these occasions a diverse and fantastic array of memorabilia was offered for sale, including scraps of the hangman's rope, pieces of the condemned felons' clothes, transcripts of their last confessions and even, on special occasions, limited-edition medallions struck by enterprising local mints. In high-profile cases a second wave of mementos would follow the first: engravings of the scene, public waxworks and death masks and other macabre relics from the anatomised bodies.

However narrowly, Thomas Clewes, George Banks and John Barnett avoided such a fate. The law had declared them innocent, and they were free to merge back into society, thus robbing the press of a dramatic conclusion and the public of an awful spectacle. Perhaps this goes some way to explaining why the Oddingley case was later overshadowed by others. Had Clewes, Banks and Barnett been executed, the sheer density of tangible objects recording their fate – the chapbooks, the pottery figures, the artistic recreations would have been far greater. All of these objects would have served as tactile little hooks, catching over and over again in people's minds and dragging their memories and imaginations back to the case anew.

In Worcestershire, however, the story has always been remembered with strength and feeling. When Mary Pyndar, the youngest daughter of the Reverend, died in 1894 at the great age of 98, she left a bequest of 'letters, papers, memoranda, notes of evidence, and copies of the local newspaper' to the county records office, all of them concerning her father's role in the original investigation. It was an extraordinary collection, and its receipt was announced in an article that reminded readers of the importance of the case. The piece began darkly, 'Perhaps no event in the catalogue of crime ever occasioned more horror and excitement in this part of the country than the double murder at Oddingley.' Its author enthused, the 'circumstances of this frightful occurrence have so often been narrated that it was by no means expected that anything hitherto untold with regard to it would turn up, especially after a lapse of nearly a century'. It was a matter of profound interest, then, that these papers had come to light, all of them 'relating to the awful tragedy which has made the little village of Oddingley unenviably conspicuous ever since'.

And at intervals, like a periodic comet, the Oddingley story has returned to delight new audiences. In 1901 E. Perronet Thompson wrote a long essay for the *Gentleman's Magazine* documenting the peculiarities and legal implications of the case. In 1960 David Scott Daniel published *Fifty Pounds for a Dead Parson*, a novel loosely based on the events, and in 1975 Angela Lanyon composed a play entitled *The Oddingley Affair*. The first faithful recreation of the murders would be published in America in 1991 by a American historian named Carlos Flick. His book *The Oddingley Murders* carried the tale across the Atlantic to a new readership, 185 years after Heming had supposedly made the journey himself.

It is Easter time in Oddingley now, and the verges are dotted with daffodils and dandelion. A gentle spring breeze blows from the Malvern Hills to the south-west. There is blackbird song, and lambs play in the pastures. Half a mile away Trench Wood looms on the escarpment above Netherwood Farm, where primroses, bluebells and pink campion are rising in the glades. In the sky a solitary buzzard circles over the young crops, its eyes fixed on the ground below.

Acknowledgements

This book has developed over a three year period in which I have accumulated many debts of gratitude. Firstly to two other students of the story, Gael Turnbull and Carlos Flick, who led new research during the 1980s and 90s. Credit must go to Carlos Flick for outlining the evidence against George Banks; and I am enormously grateful to Gael Turnbull – whose eclectic biography remembers him as a poet, doctor, performer and morris dancer – for his methodical, unpublished notes on the case, now kept at Worcester Records Office, which proved a valuable source on the shadowy lives of Captain Evans and Richard Heming.

For the permission to consult archives and republish images I would like to thank Worcester Records Office, the British Library, the National Portrait Gallery, the National Maritime Museum, the National Archives, the Honourable Society of Gray's Inn, the Estate of Miss B.M. Beer, Reverend Canon J.H. Green of Tibberton and the Estate of Reverend Sterry Cooper. I am indebted to Dr Lisa Snook at Worcester Records Office for her help finding copyright holders and Andrew Mussell, archivist at the Honourable Society of Gray's Inn, whose diligence produced not one but two portraits of Judge Joseph Littledale just at the point when I'd resigned myself to writing a faceless book. At IALS I am grateful to Laura Griffith who helped locate legal sources and, far away in Melbourne, I also want to thank Leanne McCredden who scanned and sent me a copy of Mary Sherwood's long-lost pamphlet *Sequel to the Oddingley Murders*.

Damn His Blood began as part of an MA programme at City University and had it not been for that course this book would not have been written. For early words of wisdom and for guiding an unruly child along the mountain path I would like to thank Julie Wheelwright, Kate Summerscale, Sarah Bakewell and my fellow students. I was then lucky enough to meet Tom Williams, now of the Williams Agency, who saw the potential of this book and my warmest thanks go to him as well as the industrious team at Peters, Fraser and Dunlop: Juliet Mushens, Rowan Lawton, Laura Williams, Tim Binding and, most of all, my agent Annabel Merullo who has been an intelligent and intrepid counsel throughout.

At Chatto and Windus and Vintage I've had the good fortune to work with so kind and talented editors as Juliet Brooke and Clara Womersley, and my thanks also to Becky Hardie, Clara Farmer, Fiona Murphy and the designers who have made the book so striking. Along the way I have received excellent advice on legal complexities from Professor Steve Uglow of the University of Kent. Dr Christopher Burke of St Thomas' Hospital kindly (and swiftly) completed a modern-day analysis of Parker's injuries and I reserve special thanks for my old friend Dr Christopher Prior of University College Dublin who read the manuscript and made several valuable suggestions on the historical background. Needless to say, any remaining mistakes are my own.

In Oddingley local sages Alan and Christine Hawker have consistently been generous with both their time and hospitality and I'm indebted to them for their discovery of Benjamin Sanders' connection with George Parker. I am also very grateful to Andrew and Sally Jones and, particularly, Rex Jackson who shared his story about George Parker's memorial stone. My thanks go to them and to Paul Jones in Droitwich whose knowledge of the story and eagerness to assist with photographs has been greatly appreciated. To Claire, my friends and family who've all assumed the role of literary midwives at various times, thank you. And to my father last of all, for all he has done, this book is for you.

Illustrations

4   Map of Worcestershire, Charles Smith, 1804

14   Map of Oddingley village, c.1806

18   Woodcut of the shooting of Reverend George Parker, W. Wright, *A Broadsheet on the Oddingley Murders*, 1830

23   Reverend Parker's handwriting, the Marriage Register of Oddingley. Reproduced by kind permission of Reverend Canon J. H. Green

36   St James' Church and Church Farm, Oddingley, 2011

41   Etching of St James' Church, E. Lees, *The Oddingley Murders*, 1830

58   'A Birmingham Toast as given on the 14th July by the Revolution Society', James Gillray, 1791 © NPG Images, London

72   'The Friend of the People & his Petty-New-Tax-Gatherer, paying John Bull a visit,' James Gillray, 1806 © NPG Images, London

81   'Manning the Navy', a press gang in action, S. Collings, 1790, © National Maritime Museum, Greenwich, London

106   Map of Worcester, Roper and Cole, 1808

121   'Snipe Shooting', *Ackermann's Repository of Arts*, 1810

131   Signatures of Reverend George Parker, Captain Samuel Evans, John Barnett, Thomas Clewes, Elizabeth Heming, Reginald Pyndar, Reverend Clifton and Judge Joseph Littledale. Reproduced by kind permission of the Estate of Dr Gael Turnbull

192   Etching of Netherwood Farm, E. Lees, *The Oddingley Murders*, 1830

207   The layout of Netherwood Farm, E. Lees, *The Oddingley Murders*, 1830

250   Title page of E. Lees, *The Oddingley Murders*, 1830

257   'The Worcestershire Murders', W. Wright, *A Broadsheet on the Oddingley Murders*, 1830

264   Etching of Worcester Guildhall in the early nineteenth century, J. Noake, *Worcestershire Relics*, 1877

270   Judge Joseph Littledale, William Beechey, c.1830. Reproduced by kind permission of the Masters of the Bench of the Honourable Society of Gray's Inn

277   Netherwood Farm, H.R. Hemsworth, c.1910. Reproduced by kind permission of the Estate of Miss B.M. Beer

302   'James Taylor strikes the blow', from W. Wright, *A Broadsheet on the Oddingley Murders*, 1830

309   Woodcut of a devil at the left shoulder, E. Lees, *The Oddingley Murders*

313   Fir Tree Inn, Oddingley, 2011

315   Pound Farm, Oddingley, Sterry-Cooper, 1930s. Reproduced by kind permission of the Estate of Reverend Sterry-Cooper

Notes

Abbreviations

The following commonly cited publications have been abbreviated:

CFP – Case for the Prosecution
TWM – E. Lees, *The Worcestershire Miscellany*
TOM – E. Lees, *The Oddingley Murders*
TTC – T. Eaton, *The Trial of Thomas Clewes*
PP – Papers Formerly in the Possession of the Reverend Reginald Pyndar
Inq – Inquisition on the Body of the Reverend George Parker at the Parish of Oddingley,
    25 June 1806
WNC – T.C. Tuberville, *Worcestershire in the Nineteenth Century*

Archives:

WRO – Worcester Records' Office
BCA – Birmingham City Archives
NA – National Archives
BRO – Berkshire Records' Office
HO – Home Office files at the National Archives

EPIGRAPHS

'Tis a sad thing to die . . .', *Letter from Arian Elwood to Bishop Compton*, 28 October
    1697, DRO, Chanter 757.

'I fled, and cried out DEATH! . . .' John Milton, *Paradise Lost*.

INTRODUCTION

1   'Expect the French every dark night', William Pitt the Younger, quoted from a letter to Josiah Wedgwood on 10 October 1803 by his son. From R.C. Litchfield, *Tom Wedgwood: The First Photographer*.

2   'Mysterious conspiracy', *Caledonian Mercury*, 6 February 1830 'Strange case', *Morning Chronicle*, 2 February 1830, *Examiner*, 7 February 1830.

3   'If ever there was a secluded, humble, quiet-looking village . . .', Mary Sherwood, *The Oddingley Murders: An Account of the two Murders in Oddingley, Worcestershire*.

PROLOGUE

This account of events in Oddingley on 24 June 1806 and the movements of characters is chiefly drawn from E. Lees, *The Worcestershire Miscellany*, E. Lees, *The Oddingley Murders*, T. Eaton, *The Inquest Held Upon the Remains of Richard Heming* and the unpublished brief for the prosecution held at WRO ref. 899.749, BA/10106. The primary source of information about Parker's murder comes from *Inquisition on the Body of the Reverend George Parker at the Parish of Oddingley*, 25 June 1806, kept at the NA, ASSI 5/126/23.

6   'The most vivid flashes of lightning', *Berrow's Worcester Journal*, 19 June 1806.

6   Solar eclipse in Worcestershire, mentioned in *Worcester Herald*, 14 June 1806.

7   Day by which rents were due to Lord Foley, Galton papers, BCA MS3101/A/B/5/4.

7   'peep-shows, toy-stands, waxworks . . .' Thomas Hardy, *The Mayor of Casterbridge* and 'a school-boy let loose from school . . .', G. Hazlitt, *New Monthly Magazine and Literary Journal* Vol. X.

7   Information about Worcestershire's fairs from W. Pitt, *General View of the Agriculture of the County of Worcester with Observations on its Means of Improvement*.

CHAPTER I

15–16   Descriptions of Worcester. Its 'forty or fifty master glovers' T.C. Tuberville, *Worcestershire in the Nineteenth Century* and 'a fine and flourishing city', from Robert Southey, *Letters from England by Don Manuel Alvarez Espriella*.

16   Pen sketch of Oddingley, 'most beautiful... one combination of noble hills . . .', from W. Pitt, *General View of the Agriculture of the County of Worcester*, while the name of fields across the parish come from the tithe survey, *Agreement for the Commutation of Tithes in Oddingley*, 16 January 1838, WRO.

17   Statistics regarding the fluctuations in the price of wheat in 1805 come from
        T.C. Tuberville, *WNC*.

17   Wasps in London parks, *Morning Chronicle*, 21 September 1805.

17   Gunfire on the northern French coast, *Worcester Herald*, 17 August 1805.

17   The woodcut of Parker features in *Broadsheet on the Oddingley Murders* by
        W. Wright of Birmingham, WRO ref. X705.627, BA/5312/1.

18   '. . . tossing up a penny piece', Thomas Alsop, *CFP*.

19   Biographical details about Parker's childhood from T. Eaton, *The Trial of
        Thomas Clewes*, and about Charles Howard from Gordon Goodwin,
        Dictionary of National Biography.

22   '. . . an occasional visitor can pick up but few' and Worcestershire's provin-
        cialisms, W. Pitt, *General View of the Agriculture of the County of Worcester*.
        The Worcestershire accent is perhaps best displayed in the writing of local
        author Fred Archer whose many works on rural life in the nearby Vale of
        Evesham beautifully capture local dialogue.

22   '. . . to pass through the artificial boundaries of a parish . . .', Adam Smith
        quoted in Asa Briggs *How They Lived*.

23–5   Details of Parker's first years in the parish come from the Oddingley parish
        records, WRO ref. b850, BA/4038.

25   'At Worcester I became acquainted with a clergyman . . .', A. Richards, *The
        Extraordinary Adventures of Benjamin Sanders, Button Maker of Bromsgrove*.

26–7   Anecdotes of Parker's popularity among the labouring classes in Oddingley,
        from John Chellingworth in E. Lees, *TWM*, William Chance and William
        Colley, *CFP*.

28   Details of the nationwide split between the Church and King enthusiasts,
        and Painites or Jacobins comes from Roger Wells, *Insurrection: The British
        Experience 1795–1803*.

29   'I believe that revolution inevitably must come', Robert Southey, quoted in
        Mike Jay, *The Unfortunate Colonel Despard*.

29   England's last view of Nelson as he disappears into the sea fog by the
        Needles, taken from Tom Pocock, *Horatio Nelson*.

29   '. . . a genteel-dressed man', Highwayman's attack on John Hilcox, *Worcester
        Herald*, 2 April 1805.

30   An account of the 'extraordinary and interesting discovery' of the robber's
        den in Trench Wood comes from *Berrow's Worcester Journal*, 3 October 1805.

30   '. . . inherited all the romantic terrors of the ancient chase', Theodore
        Galton, *Madeleine de S. Pol*.

31   'We trust we shall shortly have to publish their apprehension', *Berrow's
        Worcester Journal*, 3 October 1805.

CHAPTER 2

32   Details of Elizabeth Fowler's daily routine are drawn from Elizabeth Jones, *CFP*.

32–3   Details of the storm on 9 January and the spring-time weather from *Berrow's Worcester Journal*, 16 & 23 January 1806, *Hampshire Telegraph* and *Sussex Chronicle*, 7 April 1806 & *Morning Chronicle*, 1 May 1806.

33–4   Physical observations of Captain Evans taken from Mary Sherwood, *Sequel to the Oddingley Murders*; Mary Sherwood, *The Oddingley Murders*; E. Lees, *TWM* & Theodore Galton, *Madeleine de S. Pol*.

35–6   A good brief account of the history of Oddingley parish and its connections with the Foley family is to be had in the Victoria County History, *A History of the County of Worcester*. The legend about Odd and Dingley appears in 'Oh! Dingley, Dingley, spare my breath', E. Lees, *TWM* and names of local woods – Bow Wood, Thrul Wood, Oakley Wood and Goose Hill Wood – all come from the tithe survey, *Agreement for the Commutation of Tithes in Oddingley*, 16 January 1838, WRO.

37   Physical description of Thomas Clewes comes from the *Observer*, 14 March 1830. Other supplementary details appear in E. Lees, *TWM*. His move to Netherwood Farm is charted in the Oddingley tax records, WRO ref. 206.2091, BA/4609.

37–8   On the etymology of Netherwood, John Noake, *The Rambler in Worcestershire*.

38   'a very cross one', 'Testimony of John Clewes', *Information and Examinations of Witnesses*, ASSI 6/1/2.

38   'one who regarded the cottagers', Theodore Galton, *Madeleine de S. Pol*.

38   '[I] was hung up half an hour or more', E. Lees, *TOM*.

38   Physical descriptions of John Barnett come from *Berrow's Worcester Journal*, 18 March 1830 and the *Observer*, 14 March 1830.

39   'The tenant farm system was well established . . .', the voluminous records regarding tenants' contracts for farms in Oddingley have survived and they chart the changing fortunes of farmers like Barnett, Clewes and Evans. All details are housed at BCA in the Galton Papers, MS3101/A/B/5/4.

39   Oliver Goldsmith quoted in Asa Briggs, *How They Lived*.

40   Account of the footpads' attack on John Williams is from T.C. Tuberville, *WNC* & *Worcester Herald*, 12 April 1806.

40–1   Account of Elizabeth Fowler's discovery of the shotgun, Elizabeth Jones, *CFP*.

42   Description of St James' Church, John Noake, *The Rambler in Worcestershire*.

43   'Every parish officer thinks he has a right to make a round bill', Francis Grose, quoted in Roy Porter, *English Society in the Eighteenth Century*.

44–6   Details about tithe law, examples of moduses, compounding the tax and William Wilberforce's claim that one clergyman had been forced to supplement his income with a job as a weaver are all taken from Eric Evans, *A Contentious Tithe*.

44 'The poor, in general, exclaim loudly against the dearness of provisions', T.C. Tuberville, *WNC*.

45 '. . . corn, hay and all other things growing', *Glebe Terrier*, WRO ref. 721.091, BA/2358.

46 Cost of wages data taken from the diary of Richard Miles, cited in W. Pitt, *General View of the Agriculture of the County of Worcester with Observations on its Means of Improvement*.

47–8 'Suckling Pig', a ballad, taken from Malcolmson & Mastoris, *The English Pig*.

48–9 The tithe dispute, incidents in Oddingley, 'Damn your blood!', 'Testimony of Thomas Lloyd'. *CFP*; George Parker's legal expenses, Mary Parker, *CFP*; '. . . would give any man five Guineas who would shoot the parson', William Colley, *CFP* & '. . . it was no harm to shoot such a fellow as that', William Chance, *CFP*.

50 'No war, no Pitt, cheap bread', Mike Jay, *The Unfortunate Colonel Despard*.

51 'Baby, baby, naughty baby', ballad taken from Robert Harvey, *War of Wars*. A French version of this popular ballad is mentioned in *Wellington Anecdotes: A collection of sayings or doings of the great Duke* (1852), whereby Napoleon's name was substituted for Wellington's – 'Hush your squalling, or it may be, Wellington will come this way'. If accurate, it's a good example of how different factions could hijack ballads and use them for their own ends.

52 'All common men were thrilled by the sight . . .', Eric Hobsbawm, *The Age of Revolution 1789–1848*.

53 'None of the family or servants ever frequented Oddingley Church . . .', John Collins, *CFP*; 'Barnett, Banks and Captain Evans always abused Mr. Parker . . .', James White, *CFP*; 'Take that or you shall not have any one!', and account of the argument between John Barnett and Parker, Thomas Griffin, *CFP*.

54 'There is no more harm in shooting him than a mad dog!', John Perkins, *CFP*.

CHAPTER 3

This chapter, documenting the quarrel at the Plough in Tibberton, is predominantly drawn from the testimony of John Perkins as recorded in *CFP*, *TWM* and *TTC*.

56 'Perry is the liquor of this country', Robert Southey, *Letters from England by Don Manuel Alvarez Espriella*. Other evidence in literature that Worcestershire perry was commonly sold as champagne to unwitting customers in London comes in chapter three of Henry Fielding's *The History of Tom Jones*.

57   Details of the Birmingham Toast from R. Dent, *Old and New Birmingham*.
57   '. . . a time when every newspaper poet', *The Gentleman's Magazine*, 1901.
59   'Thou hast some left-handed business . . .', Walter Savage Landor, *The Works of Walter Savage Landor*, Vol. II.
59   '. . . with a kist [chest] or shelf full of Radical books . . .', E.P. Thompson, *The Making of the English Working Class*.
60   'I dare say the person that left it will call for it', Elizabeth Jones, *CFP*.
60   Physical description of Richard Heming comes from E. Lees, *TWM* and *Worcester Herald*, 28 June 1806.

CHAPTER 4

62   'The grasses, both natural and artificial . . .', *Morning Chronicle*, 1 May 1806.
63   '. . . hideous, whitewashed, brick structure . . .', Theodore Galton, *Madeleine de S. Pol*.
63–4 'Neither of us spoke' and the account of the night-time disturbances at Oddingley Rectory, Mary Parker, *CFP*. Details about Mary Parker's background come from Dr Gael Turnbull's notes on the Oddingley murders, held at WRO ref. 899.1327, BA/12.133.
65   'the grand toy-shop of Europe', *Monthly Review*, Vol. 40. Burke's famous description of Birmingham is somewhat misleading. The 'toys' referred not to children's toys but the infinitude of small items – buttons, buckles, brass candle sticks and so on – that were manufactured in the town. For a good account of Birmingham's thriving toy industry and the great variety of different items that it produced, see Jenny Uglow, *The Lunar Men*.
65   Account of Sadler's voyage from *European Magazine and London review* Vol. VIII/*New Annual Register*, 1785, *New London Magazine* Vol. IV 1785.
66–7 'Time was when these commons . . .', Reverend Richard Warner, quoted in Roy Porter, *English Society in the Eighteenth Century*.
67   '. . . tempest of war and confusion' and '. . . in ire and chagrin . . .', T.C. Tuberville, *WNC*.
69   'They were all highly pleased . . .', diary entry for 30 November 1784, James Woodforde, *The Diary of a Country Parson*.
70–1 Account of Reverend Skinner's battles with the residents of Camerton comes from John Skinner, *The Journal of a Somerset Rector*. News of his suicide – 'On Friday morning, in a state of derangement . . .' – is from the *Bath Chronicle*, 17 October 1839.
71   'Irritable, nervous, apprehensive . . .', Virginia Woolf, *The Common Reader*. Virginia Woolf made the comparison between Woodforde and Skinner in *Two Parsons* – a beautiful meditation upon the act of diary-keeping and the waxing and waning of their respective fortunes.

71   '[it] leaves no man anything in this world . . .', *Cobbett's Political Register* Vol. IX, 5 April 1806.

71–2   James Gillray, 'The Friend of the People & his Petty-New-Tax-Gatherer, Paying John Bull a visit'.

CHAPTER 5

74–5   The account of the farmer's meeting at the Pigeon House and the subsequent chase through the meadows is taken from the testimony of Sarah Lloyd, *CFP*.

76   'Banks was the most violent . . .', Gilbert Jones, *CFP*.

77–8   Examples of the mounting tensions in Oddingley throughout May and June come from the testimonies of Elizabeth Jones, Thomas Reed and Thomas Green, *CFP*.

79   'I will swear my life against them all . . .' and the clashes between the Captain and Reverend Parker in Church Lane come from the testimony of Mary Parker, *CFP*, with some supplementary details from *Papers Formerly in the Possession of the Reverend Reginald Pyndar*, WRO ref. 899.38, BA/866.

80–3   Information about the formation of the Worcestershire Volunteers comes from *The First Regular Worcestershire Regiment, Firm and Forester* Vol. 5 no.1, and details concerning the British recruitment crisis in 1779 are from Edward Curtis, *Organization of the British Army in the American Revolution*.

83–4   Samuel Evans being gazetted an officer, reported in the *London Gazette*, 30 October 1779. His subsequent promotion to lieutenant was announced in the *London Gazette*, 3 May 1780.

83   There is a good account of the 'torrid zone' and the physical perils of travel to the West Indies during the late eighteenth century in Mike Jay, *The Unfortunate Colonel Despard*.

84   'Whatever his parentage . . .', Mary Sherwood, *Sequel to the Oddingley Murders*.

85   'He attends every vestry meeting . . .', Charles Dickens, *Sketches By Boz*.

86   'Damn Priestley', detail of the Priestley Riots from R. Dent, *Old and New Birmingham, a History of the Town and Its People*.

87   Examples of the word 'damn' in use: 'I am afraid that I . . .', James Boswell, *The Life of Samuel Johnson*; 'Damn his eyes', Lord Byron *Don Juan*, Canto the Seventh, XLVI; 'Damned lawyers and judges', Jonathan Swift, *The Works of Jonathan Swift*; 'Damn you!' Charles Dickens, *Oliver Twist*. There is an excellent overview of the cultural power of bad language throughout history, and also a good section on oaths, in Geoffrey Hughes, *An Encyclopaedia of Swearing*.

89   '. . . a brisk gay widow', Clifford Morsley, *News from the English Countryside 1750–1850*.

90 'Hence he reached the church without observation . . .', Thomas Hardy, *The Mayor of Casterbridge*.

90–1 'Constitution: The Independence of Great Britain', Mike Jay, *The Unfortunate Colonel Despard*.

91 'Take it in your right hand!', Charles Dickens, *Great Expectations*.

CHAPTER 6

93 An overview of farming methods in the English countryside at the beginning of the nineteenth century can be found in J. Main, *The Young Farmer's Manuel*. The account of Perkins on 24 June 1806 draws on this. The list of implements in his workshop derives from an inventory in W. Pitt, *General View of the Agriculture of the County of Worcester with Observations on its Means of Improvement*.

94 'Oh, he had got his dying dress on' and information about Parker's final service at St James' Church, E. Lees, *TWM*.

95–100 Scenes from the aftermath of Parker's murder are drawn from James Tustin, John Barnett, Thomas Langford, John Perkins, Elizabeth Perkins and Susan Surman and Thomas Alsop *CFP*; Thomas Giles and John Lench, *Inq.*, with supplementary details from E. Lees, *TOM*.

100 'Six gentlemen upon the road . . .', William Cowper, 'The Diverting History of John Gilpin', *Poems of William Cowper*.

101 '"Stop thief! Stop thief!"' Charles Dickens, *Oliver Twist*.

101 'The town being alarmed', J.M. Beattie, *Crime and the Courts in England, 1660–1800*.

104 '. . . the workhorse of everyday magistrate power . . .', Roy Porter, *English Society in the Eighteenth Century*.

107 Coaching timetables are from T. Eaton, *A Concise History of Worcester* and J. Tymbs, *A Brief History of Worcester*.

CHAPTER 7

109–12 An account of Thomas Green's journey through Oddingley on 24 June and his visit to Church Farm, testimony of Thomas Green, *CFP* along with some supplementary facts from Anon., *The Murdered Murderer or the Worcester Tragedy*. Events at Netherwood Farm are described by Thomas Arden, *TWM* and William Chance *CFP*.

CHAPTER 8

113 Physical description of Heming – 'round, ruddy face and thick hanging lantern jaw' – from *Worcester Herald*, 2 August 1806.

114 'Heming looked very pale and confused', Thomas Colwell, *CFP*. Other details of Colwell arriving at the rectory appear in E. Lees, *TOM* and John Perkins, *CFP*.

115 '. . . he seemed in a hurry and very much confused', Richard Page, *CFP*. Additional information about Heming's flight across Worcestershire that evening can be found in T. Eaton, *TTC* and the twenty minute claim comes from Anon., *The Murdered Murderer or the Worcester Tragedy*.

115–116 Information about Heming's movements in May and June 1806 are from E. Lees, *TWM*, John Perkins, Susan Surman and Joseph Colley, *CFP*.

116–7 The biographical sketch of Richard Heming has greatly benefitted from the work of Dr Gael Turnbull who researched Heming in detail during the 1970s and 1980s. Dr Turnbull's notes and his typescript on the Oddingley Murders are kept at WRO ref. 899.1327, BA/12.133.

118 '. . . 6d a strike under the regular price . . .', Mary Parker, *CFP*.

118–9 Anecdote of Heming illegally selling the poles comes from E. Lees, *TTC* and rumours about his second life as a thief are reported in E. Lees, *TWM*.

119 'Committed to our house of correction . . .', *Berrow's Worcester Journal*, 11 March 1801, and there are further signs of a deviant Richard Heming in other archives. On 8 March 1806 a Richard Heming appeared at the Lent Assize in Worcester charged with the theft of a copper pot, a cast iron saucepan, a pair of leggings, two towels, one duck and one drake. It's difficult to resist the temptation that these may be the same men, but in reality it is unlikely that they are as no mention of this other incident was made in the wake of Heming's disappearance.

119 'Tramping, begging, thieving . . .', Charles Dickens, *Great Expectations*.

121 'Upon his tour', Boswell's description of Dr Johnson's greatcoat, James Boswell, *The Life of Samuel Johnson*.

122 An account of the constables calling at Heming's Droitwich home on Midsummer night comes from Elizabeth Newbury, *CFP*.

124 'they made every enquiry. . .', John Perkins, *CFP*.

CHAPTER 9

126 'Salt manufacture at Droitwich . . .', T.C. Tuberville, *WNC*.

126 'and when in a large body', *Philosophical Magazine* 1812.

126 'Brine boiling and salt making', *Household Words*, 14 July 1855.

127 Information about Droitwich Canal comes from Joseph Priestley, *Historical Account of the Navigable Rivers, Canals and Railways of Great Britain*.

127–8 'six thousand loads of young pole wood . . .' and the later Hugh Miller quote from Hugh Miller, *First impressions of England and its People*.

128   'If Worcester has a fashionable neighbour', *Household Words*, 14 July 1855.

130   'At a Chamber Meeting' and other information about Captain Evans' time
       in Droitwich is drawn from the Droitwich magistrates' records kept at *WRO*
       ref. XXX, BA/1006/485. There is also much relating to the Captain's period
       of service in Droitwich in T. Eaton, *TTC*.

130   'He [the magistrate] had to be a man . . .', Clive Emsley, *Crime and Society
       in England, 1750–1900*.

132   'Captain Evans used to go up to Droitwich', Elizabeth Jones in Anon., *The
       Murdered Murderer or the Worcester Tragedy*.

132   'Captain Evans was the leading man in the parish', William Barnett, *CFP*.

133   '[He] seemed much confused and cut up . . .', testimony of John Collins,
       in Anon., *The Murdered Murderer or the Worcester Tragedy*.

CHAPTER 10

134–5 'Here the skull has been fractured', Pennell Cole, *CFP*. Other biographical
       facts about Pennell Cole come from T.C. Tuberville, *WNC* and Ackroyd et
       al. *Advancing with the Army* – which includes an interesting glimpse into
       Pennell Cole's early life. The modern-day interpretation of Parker's injuries
       and his likely cause of death come from Dr Christopher Burke of St Thomas'
       Hospital, London.

134   '. . . to the best of his knowledge . . .', James Tustin, *Inq*.

134   '. . . ornamental structures . . .', T. Eaton, *A Concise History of Worcester*.

136   'The inquest was arranged for Tuesday . . .', P.D. James and T.A. Critchley,
       The Maul and the Pear Tree.

137   'It was very late when I got back', William Barnett, *CFP*. Additional infor-
       mation about a parish constable's responsibilities comes from W. Toone,
       The Magistrate's Manual.

138   The question of Captain Evans being foreman of the jury during Parker's
       inquest was raised and subsequently questioned in T. Eaton, *TTC*. A lengthy
       note on the publication's final page dealt with the matter, and it concludes
       with uncertainty, 'We cannot, however, fully affirm the fact'.

138   'I will not go', John Lench, *CFP* and the search of Heming's house in
       Droitwich is from John Lloyd, *Inq*.

141   'Public life on a grand scale . . .', Roy Porter, *English Society in the Eighteenth
       Century*.

141   '. . . of the 350 death sentences passed in England and Wales . . .', this
       information comes from *The Report and Evidence of the Select Committee into
       the State of the Police of the Metropolis in 1828* and statistics about executions
       in Worcestershire is taken from T.C. Tuberville, *WNC*.

142–3   Account of Isaac Blight's murder comes from *The Gentleman's Magazine for 1805*, with several additional details from P.D. James and T.A. Critchley, *The Maul and the Pear Tree*. Remarks on Patch's trial ('the prisoner [Patch] had begun his career of guilt) are from Gurney and Gurney, *Trial of Richard Patch for the Wilful Murder of Isaac Blight* and the 'awful moment when Patch' is taken from *Berrow's Worcester Journal*, 17 April 1806.

144   'thieves and murderers', Friedrich Engels, *The Condition of the Working Class in England in 1844*.

145   'The unfortunate person . . .', *Berrow's Worcester Journal*, 26 June 1806.

146   'The Constables and the Bow Street men . . .', Charles Dickens, *Great Expectations*.

147–9   'Cap. Evans says . . .', the beginning of Reverend Pyndar's investigations and the conflicting accounts of what happened at Church Farm on 24 June 1806 are reconstructed from *PP*, WRO ref. 899.38, BA/866.

CHAPTER 11

The bulk of this chapter, documenting the early stages of the investigation and including the letters from magistrates and interviews of suspects in Oddingley, comes from Reverend *PP*, WRO ref. 899.38, BA/866.

150   'Whereas on Tuesday Evening', *Worcester Herald*, 28 June 1806; subsequent reports as the story spreads are from *Jackson's Oxford Journal*, 28 June 1806 & *The Times*, 30 June 1806.

153   'carrying cargoes of woollen cloth, tea, muslin . . .', and other details about Bristol's trade and port are from T. Mortimer, *General Dictionary of Trade, Commerce and Manufacturers*.

154   'I saw George Banks . . .', account of George Banks after Parker's funeral, testimony of Joseph Kendall, *CFP*.

156   '. . . taken up and hanged', E. Lees, *TWM*.

158   Statistics for governmental rewards from J.M. Beattie, *Crime and the Courts in England, 1660–1800*.

159   'We went and watched at a new Barn . . .', John Perkins, *CFP*.

160   'I knew that if I had gone down . . .' and the remainder of Barnett's questioning at the Crown Inn, Worcester, John Barnett, *CFP*.

162   'Richard Heming has twice been employed by me . . .', Captain Evans, *CFP*.

164   'He left home early on that day', Elizabeth Newbury, *CFP*.

165   'no accessory can be convicted . . .' and full wording of the statute demanding that the principal first be convicted before accessories are put on trial, in Pickering, *The Statutes at Large*. The definition of an accessory to murder is taken from W. Toone, *The Magistrate's Manual*.

166   '. . . a Knife and Fork and Plate took upstairs', testimony of Mary Chance, *CFP*.

166   '. . . it was no matter if Heming . . .', testimony of William Chance, *CFP*.

167   '. . . she must have known it . . .', testimony of Elizabeth Jones, *CFP*.

167   'For the detection of this flagitious offender . . .', *Worcester Herald*, 5 July 1806.

167–8 'That on Wednesday the day after . . .', Mary Chance, *CFP*.

168–9 Potential sightings of Heming are reported in *Worcester Herald*, 12 July 1806 & *Worcester Herald*, 19 July 1806 and the summer storm is reported in *Berrow's Worcester Journal*, 17 July 1806.

169   'What do you think of those toasts . . .', John Perkins, *CFP*.

170   'I gave them to the Captain and never saw them after', E. Lees, *TWM*, the adze is mentioned in Anon., *The Murdered Murderer or the Worcester Tragedy*.

CHAPTER 12

171   'The valuable FARMING STOCK . . .', *Berrow's Worcester Journal*, 13 June 1809.

172   Biographical details of Reverend Butt can be found in Mary Sherwood, *The Oddingley Murders* and also in the Butt Family Papers, housed in BRO D/EZ/106. Butt was likeable, intelligent but also unstable and susceptible to bouts of severe depression. The first of these periods of madness descended in 1818 following the death of his first wife, Mary Ann, but he recovered sufficiently to take a new parish away from Oddingley at East Garston in Berkshire with his second wife, Jemima Hubbard, in 1821. Here he was once again welcomed into the community where he became known for his 'eccentricity of character'. In the 1830s Butt's depression returned and he was ultimately declared insane and was placed in an asylum in Staffordshire, where he died in 1846.

173–4 John Rowe's account of the farmer's conspiracy is revealed in *PP* with additional details from Lees, *TWM* and John Rowe, *CFP*. 'a little dark short man' and biographical sketch of James Taylor is from *TWM* and William Barnett, *CFP*.

177–8 'She was assured by the Oddingley farmers . . .', Rev. Erskine Neale, *The Bishop's Daughter*.

178   '. . . he could hang all the head men in Oddingley . . .'. E. Lees, *TOM*.

180   'And is it not astonishing . . .', Mary Sherwood, *The Oddingley Murders*.

181   'I don't usually encourage superstitious . . .', John Noake, *The Rambler in Worcestershire*.

181   Descriptions of the Worcestershire storms come from T.C. Tuberville, *Worcestershire in the Nineteenth Century*.

182　'As for Clewes . . .', Rev. Erskine Neale, *The Bishop's Daughter.*

183　'the shops sparkling with vivid lustre', Ambrose Florence, *The Stranger's Guide to the City and Cathedral of Worcester.*

184　A good overview of Robert Peel's overhaul of the criminal justice system can be found in Douglas Hurd, *Robert Peel.* The statute relating to the requirement for a principal is 7 Geo IV c 64 s 9.

185　Information about the inhabitants of Oddingley during the 1810s and 1820s is taken from the parish tax records, WRO ref. 206.2091, BA/4609, and S. Lewis, *Worcestershire general and commercial directory.*

185　'We have no longer any genuine quizzes', Horace Smith, *New Monthly Magazine.*

186–9　'. . . these two Devils out of the room' and other details of Captain Evans' final illness and last weeks is from taken from the evidence of Catherine Bowkett, *CFP.*

188　'. . . delay and difficulty in gaining admission', *Morning Chronicle*, 10 February 1830.

188–9　'He became moody, restless . . .', Rev. Erskine Neale, *The Bishop's Daughter.*

189　'Died, lately, at Droitwich', *Worcester Herald*, 20 June 1829.

189–90　'The walls and ceiling were alive', Charles Dickens, *The Pickwick Papers.*

190　'neat set of china', *The Last Will and Testament of Samuel Evans.*

CHAPTER 13

191　'Yesterday morning Fahrenheit's thermometer . . .', *Berrow's Worcester Journal*, 21 January 1830, 18F converted gives a reading of –27.8C.

191–3　Accounts of the severe winter are taken from a report in *Morning Chronicle*, 25 January 1830, which in itself listed reports from around the country.

194　'. . . a day which the guilty might well regard as unlucky', *The Gentleman's Magazine.*

193–7　An account of Charles Burton at Netherwood farm and his actions over the next days comes principally from Charles Burton, *CFP*, but supplementary facts are in *TWM*, *Worcester Herald*, 30 January 1830 and *Birmingham Post*, 6 February 1830. The woodcuts of Charles Burton finding the skeleton and William Smith at the site are from *Broadsheet on the Oddingley Murders*, WRO ref. X705.627, BA/5312/1.

196　'. . . give what directions you thought necessary', from letter to William Smith from Richard Allen, *PP.*

198　'They were cold and frightened . . .', Rev. Erskine Neale, *The Bishop's Daughter.*

199　'as near as possible 5ft 3in in length', and account of Pierpoint's exhumation of the skeleton comes from the *Worcester Herald*, 30 January 1830.

201   'like the silver plate on a coffin', and a sketch of Peel's personality from Douglas Hurd, *Robert Peel*.

202   There is a good section on the introduction of Peel's police in Judith Flanders, *The Invention of Murder* and also Sarah Wise, *The Italian Boy*.

203   Copy of Peel's letter to Smith, HO/43/38/157–158.

204   'quite sufficient to produce instantaneous death', Matthew Pierpoint, *CFP*.

204   'the spot chosen for the grave', *Berrow's Worcester Journal*, 28 January 1830.

CHAPTER 14

The bulk of this account of the first day of William Smith's inquest at the Talbot is taken from two detailed articles: *Worcester Herald*, 30 January 1830 and *Berrow's Worcester Journal*, 28 January 1830. Between them, the two rival papers preserved a vivid record of proceedings at the inn. The inquest's second day continues to draw on these article, as well as second from the *Worcester Herald* on 6 February 1830. Other sources used in this chapter are noted below.

212   'No part of testimony . . .', *London Medical Journal* Vol. VI.

212   'A 'tale' of great mystery . . .' and also Dr Cumin's later complaint about the effectiveness of coroners, *The London Medical Gazette* Vol. XIII.

218   'The inhabitants of this city', *Ipswich Journal*, 30 January 1830.

219   The account of Clewes' fall into the canal and his rescue is from *Morning Chronicle*, 8 February 1830 and E. Lees, *TWM*.

219–220 '. . . he had stopped for a while . . .' and Clewes' claim Heming 'is safe enough', *The Gentleman's Magazine*.

220   'They had better not be too hard with me . . .', Thomas Bunn, *CFP*.

221   '. . . the identity of the skeleton . . .', Smith to Peel 27 January 1830 and Peel's reply the following day, HO 43/38.

228   'The Case of the Murdered Murderer', *Morning Chronicle*, 2 February 1830.

CHAPTER 15

229   A description of Worcester County Gaol comes from *Sessional Papers Printed by Order of the House of Lords*, Vol. XLIV; *The Fifth Report of the Committee of the Society for the Improvement of Prisons* and T. Eaton, *CHW*.

230   '. . . an iron bedstead, straw bed, pillow, two blankets . . .', *Berrow's Worcester Journal*, 21 January 1830.

231   Clewes' brief stint as the bailiff of a local farm is chronicled by Marta Davis, *CFP*.

232   'the sprinkling of salt', *Berrow's Worcester Journal*, 21 January 1830.

232 'Nothing is as painful to the human mind . . .', Mary Shelley, *Frankenstein*.

233–6 Reverend Robert Clifton's correspondence with Robert Peel and his interviews with Clewes at the gaol are described in HO 52/11/529–30. Peel's subsequent response is from HO 43/38.

235 '. . . as characteristic and complete a winter scene . . .', *Morning Herald*, 3 February 1830.

236 'If you do that, then I don't care afterwards . . .', *Worcester Herald*, 5 February 1830.

238 '. . . cognizant of its many particulars . . .', Reverend Clifton in E. Lees, *TTC*.

238 'Clewes had expressed himself desirous . . .', E. Lees, *TMW*.

239–42 Confession of Thomas Clewes. Such a long and compelling document as this was bound to spawn various versions, which duly appeared with their slight differences in the wide range of media that reported the story. To get as close as possible to Clewes' words I have used the text recorded in the unpublished prosecution brief (*CFP*) as this would have been made directly from the copy taken down at the gaol by James Hooper, William Smith's clerk.

242 '. . . horrible detail with perfect firmness . . .', *Worcester Herald*, 5 February 1830.

CHAPTER 16

244 '. . . the avidity with which the paper is bought . . .', *The Times*, 5 February 1830.

245 'In the early part of this inquiry . . .', *Jackson's Oxford Journal*, 6 February 1830.

246 'They all seemed in liquor . . .', E. Lees, *TOM*.

246–49 An account of the final days of the inquest comes from *Worcester Herald*, 6 February 1830; E. Lees, *TOM* and *Morning Chronicle*, 8 February 1830.

249–250 'Throughout the enquiry . . .', *Berrow's Worcester Journal*, 11 February 1830.

251 'Being a Cumberland man . . .', *Morning Chronicle*, 2 February 1830.

252 Details of the Red Barn Murder are drawn from Judith Flanders, *The Invention of Murder*.

253 'In concluding our account . . .', E. Lees, *TWM*.

254 Details of the Elstree Murder and Thertell's execution come from David Bentley, *English Criminal Justice in the Nineteenth Century* and Judith Flanders, *The Invention of Murder*.

255 'scorpion stings of conscience', *Berrow's Worcester Journal*, 11 February 1830.

255 'Captain Evans, who in May last . . .', *Ipswich Journal*. 20 February 1830.

255–6   'Memory brought madness with it . . .', Mary Shelley, *Frankenstein*.

256–60 Thomas Hood's *Dream of Eugene Aram* is taken from *The Poetry and Varieties of Berrow's Worcester Journal for the Year 1828*; 'The Greatest of Miracles', on the Oddingley Murders is from *Broadsheet on the Oddingley Murders*, WRO ref. X705.627, BA/5312/1, and the second, more literary ballad, is printed in J. Waldron, *Metrical Tales and Other Pieces*.

258   'James Taylor was a farrier at Droitwich', *Liverpool Mercury*, 12 February 1830 & *Berrow's Worcester Journal*, 11 February 1830.

260   'Publications, taking all shapes', *Morning Chronicle*, 11 March 1830.

260   'the alteration which had taken place', *Worcester Herald*, 6 February 1830.

262   Newspaper reports charting the build-up to the Assize trial are *Worcester Journal*, 4 March 1830 and *Morning Chronicle*, 10 March 1830.

CHAPTER 17

264–5   Description of Worcester Guildhall comes from J. Tymbs, *A Brief History of Worcester* and V. Green, *The History and Antiquities of the City and Suburbs of Worcester*.

265   The presence of the Grand Jury was required by a tradition that stretched back into the medieval age when a jury of important local people would be summoned in the days before a trial to see if there was a prima facie case to answer. A trial could not proceed until this presentment – either from an inquest or, more commonly, through the grand jury – had taken place. In either case twelve men had to agree that a crime 'probably' had been committed. The Oddingley case is confusing and somewhat unusual as the prisoners were indicted by both the coroner's inquest and the Grand Jury, rather than one or the other. The practice of using a Grand Jury was abandoned in the UK in 1933 and now committal proceedings are conducted before a magistrate. There is a good chapter on this part of the legal process by James Baker in J.S. Cockburn, (ed.) *Crime in England 1500–1800*.

265   'Gentlemen, there is a very important case in the kalender', T. Eaton, *TTC*.

266   Three quarters of the judiciary dying in harness and other useful facts about the nineteenth century criminal justice system are to be had from David Bentley, *English Criminal Justice in the Nineteenth Century*.

266–7   Biographical sketch of Judge Joseph Littledale is from *The Gentleman's Magazine* Vol. XVIII; *The Annual Biography and Obituary 1831* Vol. X and *House of Commons Papers* Vol. 35. There are two surviving portraits of Littledale, one by Sir William Beechey and another by Thomas Phillips. Both are now owned by Gray's Inn.

267   A list of the indictments is taken from NA ASSI 5/150/19.

268–91 Description of the scenes outside the Guildhall on the morning of the trial are from *Morning Chronicle*, 12 March 1830; *Birmingham Journal*, 13 March 1830 and J. Pigot, *Pigot and Co's National Commercial Directory*. Thereafter an account of the trial is taken from the detailed accounts that appeared in the Worcester papers in the following days: *Berrow's Worcester Journal*, 18 March 1830 and *Worcester Herald*, 13 March 1830. A few interesting supplementary details are to be had from *Birmingham Journal*, 13 March 1830; E. Lees, *TOM* and T. Eaton, *TTC*. Probably the most accurate record of the trial is W. Wills, *Report of the Trial of Thomas Clewes*. Wills attended the trial and hoped to record proceedings as a legal peculiarity for the future. He was the only person to produce a verbatim transcript and most of the direct quotations come from his work.

275   'otherwise the matter would lie on her . . .', David Bentley, *English Criminal Justice in the Nineteenth Century*.

276   'Nothing is so likely to strike the person', Charles Dickens, *Sketches by Boz*.

291   'As an instance of the strange way', *Examiner*, 14 March 1830.

CHAPTER 18

292   Account of the prisoners leaving the County Gaol comes from *Worcester Herald*, 20 March 1830 and *Birmingham Journal*, 13 March 1830. Initial reaction to the verdicts, the *Observer*, 14 March 1830 and *Carlisle Patriot*, 20 March 1830. Mary Sherwood's individualistic take on events from Mary Sherwood, *Sequel to the Oddingley Murders*.

294   'The acquittal of Clewes . . .', *Berrow's Worcester Journal*, 18 March 1830.

295   Distinct precedents set by the Oddingley case, as taken from Carlos Flick, *The Oddingley Murders*:

1. That while the prosecution was not bound to call as a witness a person in office who may have exerted undue influence to get a confession from a suspect, it was fair for the defence to do so before the confession was introduced as evidence.

2. That if a promise of clemency was extended to a subject to get a confession and afterwards the promise was withdrawn and the suspect carefully warned that no mercy could be expected in return for a confession, then the suspect proceeded to confess, his statement was admissible as evidence.

3. That when a confession was read into the record during a trial it must be read in its entirety, including the names of people who might be thus incriminated; and,

4. That a confession must be taken as evidence in its entirety, including statements that were favourable to the accused, and that while a jury might not believe all the confession, it must have outside evidence to convict the accused of more than what was in the confession.

5. There is also an entry on REX vs. CLEWES in F.A. Carrington & J. Payne, *Reports of Cases Argued and Ruled at Nisi Prius, in the Courts of King's Bench and Common Pleas, and on the Circuit; from the Sittings after Trinity Term 1829, to the Sittings in Trinity Term, 1831*.

296–8 Banks and Barnett's defence, E. Lees, *TOM* and also W. Wills, *Report of the Trial of Thomas Clewes*.

304 'I thought it be George Banks', *Worcester Herald*, 20 March 1830.

305 Reverend Clifton's first letter to Robert Peel, Worcester 31 January 1830, HO 52/11/529–30.

306 'Capt. Evans (and we cannot refer to that man's name without horror)', *Jackson's Oxford Journal*, 20 March 1830.

307 'Violence does, in truth, recoil upon the violent', Sir Arthur Conan Doyle, *The Best of Sherlock Holmes*.

307 'The fate of Heming is replete with instruction', *Berrow's Worcester Journal*, 18 March 1830.

EPILOGUE

314 'I am 75¼, I am probably near the end . . .', WRO ref. 899.290, BA/3221, *A Collection of documents formerly belonging to Rev. Sterry-Cooper*.

315 A wonderful pictorial history of the Oddingley Murders has been produced by Paul Jones and features many of Reverend Sterry-Cooper's black and white images alongside a number of contemporary photographs of scenes from the story, Paul Jones, *The Oddingley Murders*.

317 'Murder of clergyman planned by several villagers . . .', W. Greenslade, *Thomas Hardy's 'Facts' Notebook*.

317 'Elizabethan Period', *Decline of the English Murder*, George Orwell, *Essays*.

318 'Perhaps no event in the catalogue of crime . . .', *PP*.

Select Bibliography

Details of most primary sources, including archives, newspapers and commercial pamphlets, are dealt with in the notes section.

Primary Sources

Amphlett, John & Carlton Rea, *The Botany of Worcestershire* (Birmingham, Cornish Brothers Ltd, 1909)

Carrington, F.A. & J. Payne, *Reports of Cases Argued and Ruled at Nisi Prius, in the Courts of King's Bench and Common Pleas, and on the Circuit; from the Sittings after Trinity Term 1829, to the Sittings in Trinity Term, 1831* (London, 1831)

Dent, R.K., *Old and New Birmingham, a History of the Town and its People* (Birmingham, Houghton & Hammond, 1880)

Eaton, Thomas, *A Concise History of Worcester,* 3rd edition (Worcester, Eaton, 1829)

Florence, Ambrose, *The Stranger's Guide to the City and Cathedral of Worcester* (Worcester, Lees, 1828)

Galton, Theodore Howard, *Madeleine de S. Pol: A Glimpse of Worcestershire at the Dawn of the Nineteenth Century* (Oxford, Burns & Oakes, 1881)

Green, V., *The History and Antiquities of the City and Suburbs of Worcester* (Worcester, Bulmer, 1796)

Gurney, J.B. & W., *Trial of Richard Patch for the Wilful Murder of Isaac Blight at Rotherhithe on 23 September 1805* (London, Gurney, 1806)

Holden, Edith, *The Country Diary of an Edwardian Lady* (London, Michael Joseph, 1906)

Lees, E., *The Worcestershire Miscellany* (Worcester, Lees, 1830)

Lees, E., *The Worcestershire Miscellany*, Supplement (Worcester, Lees, 1831)

Lewis, S., *Worcestershire General and Commercial Directory, for 1820* (Worcester, J. Heming, 1820)

Main, J., *The Young Farmer's Manuel Showing the Practice and Principles of Agriculture as Applicable to Turnip Land-Farms in the South of England* (London, Ridgeway, 1839)

Miller, Hugh, *First Impressions of England and its People* (New York, Boston, Gould & Lincoln, 1865)

Miller, Rev. George, *The Parishes of the Diocese of Worcester* (Oxford, Griffith, Farran, Okeden & Welsh, 1890)

Neale, Rev. Erskine, *The Bishop's Daughter* (London, W.H. Dalton, 1842)

Noake, John, *The Rambler in Worcestershire, or stray notes on churches and congregations* (London, Longman & Co., 1851)

Perronet Thompson, E., 'The Oddingley Murders', *The Gentleman's Magazine*, 1901

Pitt, W., *General View of the Agriculture of the County of Worcester with Observations on its Means of Improvement* (London, Sherwood, Neely & Jones, 1813)

Robinson, W.M., *The Magistrates' Pocket Book – Or an epitome of the duties and practices of a Justice of the Peace* (London, Hunter, 1825)

Skinner, John, *The Journal of a Somerset Rector* (Oxford, The Chaucer Press, 1971)

Southey, Robert, *Letters from England by Don Manuel Alvarez Espriella* (London, George Dearborn, 1836)

Stanton, G.K., *Rambles and Researches among Worcestershire Churches* (London, Simpkin, Marshall & Co., 1884)

Stephens, Henry, *The Book of the Farm: Detailing the labours of the farmer, farm-steward, ploughman, shepherd, hedger, farm-labourer, field-worker, and cattle-man* (Edinburgh, William Blackwood, 1854)

Toone, W., *The Magistrate's Manual: Or a summary of the duties and powers of a justice of the peace* (London, Butterworth & Son, 1818)

Tuberville, T.C., *Worcestershire in the Nineteenth Century: A complete digest of facts occurring in the county since the commencement of the year 1800* (London, Longman, Brown, Green & Longmans, 1852)

Tymbs, J., *A Brief History of Worcester or 'A Worcestershire Guide Improved' with a description of the neighbouring towns, villages and seats that are most worthy of notice* (Worcester, Tymbs, 1806)

Waldron, J., *Metrical Tales and Other Pieces* (London, Smith, Elder & Co., 1839)

Woodforde, James, *The Diary of a Country Parson: The Reverend James Woodforde* (London, Milford, 1926)

The Poetry and Varieties of Berrow's Worcester Journal for the Year 1828 (Worcester, Tymbs, 1828)

Secondary Material

Ackroyd, M. et al., *Advancing with the Army: Medicines, the Profession and Social Mobility in the British Isles 1790–1850* (Oxford, Oxford University Press, 2006)

Archer, Fred, *The Distant Scene* (London, Coronet, 1967)

Barsley, Michael, *The Left-Handed Book: An investigation into the Sinister History of Left Handedness* (London, Souvenir P, 1966)

Beattie, J.M., *Crime and the Courts in England, 1660–1800* (New Jersey, Princeton University Press, 1986)

Bentley, David, *English Criminal Justice in the Nineteenth Century* (London, The Hambledon Press, 1998)

Briggs, Asa, *How They Lived: An Anthology of Original Documents written between 1700 and 1815* (Blackwell, Oxford, 1969)

Clark, Peter, *The English Alehouse 1200–1850* (London, Longman, 1983)

Curtis, Edward, *Organization of the British Army in the American Revolution* (New Haven, Yale Historical Publication, 1926)

Emsley, Clive, *Crime and Society in England 1750–1900* (London, Longman, 1987)

Evans, Eric, *A Contentious Tithe: The Tithe Problem and English Agriculture 1750–1850* (London, RKP, 1976)

Flanders, Judith, *The Invention of Murder: How the Victorians revelled in Death and Detection and invented Modern Crime* (London, HarperPress, 2011)

Flick, Carlos, *The Oddingley Murders* (Newark, University of Delaware Press, 1991)

Godfrey, Richard, *James Gillray: The Art of Caricature* (London, Tate Publishing, 2001)

Greenslade, W., *Thomas Hardy's 'Facts' Notebook: A Critical Edition* (Aldershot, Ashgate, 2004)

Hammond, J.L. & Barbara, *The Village Labourer* (London, Longman, 1978)

Harvey, Robert, *War of Wars: The Epic Struggle between Britain and France 1789–1815* (London, Constable, 2006)

Hughes, Geoffrey, *Swearing: A Social History of Foul Language, Oaths and Profanity in English* (London, Penguin, 1998)

Hughes, Geoffrey, *An Encyclopaedia of Swearing: The Social History of Oaths, Profanity, Foul Language and Ethnic Slurs in the English-Speaking World* (London, Barnes & Noble, 2006)

Hurd, Douglas, *Robert Peel* (London, Weidenfeld & Nicolson, 2007)

Hobsbawm, Eric, *The Age of Revolution 1789–1848* (London, Weidenfeld & Nicholson, 1962)

James, P.D. & T.A. Critchley, *The Maul and the Pear Tree: The Ratcliffe Highway Murders, 1811* (London, Faber, 1971)

Jay, Mike, *The Atmosphere of Heaven: The unnatural experiments of Dr. Beddoes and his sons of genius* (London, Yale University Press, 2009)

Jay, Mike, *The Unfortunate Colonel Despard: The tragic true story of the last man condemned to be hung, drawn and quartered* (London, Bantam Books, 2004)

Jones, Paul, *The Oddingley Murders* (London, Blurb, 2009)

Malcolmson, R. & S. Mastoris, *The English Pig: A History* (London, The Hambledon Press, 1998)

Morsley, Clifford, *News from the English Countryside 1750–1850* (London, Harrap, 1979)

Pocock, Tom, *Horatio Nelson* (London, Bodley Head, 1987)

Porter, Roy, *English Society in the Eighteenth Century* (London, Penguin, 1991)

Richards, A., *The Extraordinary Adventures of Benjamin Sanders, Button Maker of Bromsgrove* (Bromsgrove, Bromsgrove Society, 1984)

Scott Daniel, David, *Fifty Pounds for a Dead Parson* (London, Jonathan Cape, 1961)

Smith, Michael, (ed. Peter Smith) *The Church Courts: From Canon to Ecclesiastical Law 1680–1840* (Oxford, Edwin Mellen Press, 2006)

Stiff, Neville, *The Church in Dorking and District* (London, McCorquodale, 1912)

Summerscale, Kate, *The Suspicions of Mr. Whicher or the Murder at Road Hill House* (London, Bloomsbury, 2008)

Thompson, E. P., *The Making of the English Working Class* (London, Gollancz, 1980)

Uglow, Jenny, *The Lunar Men: The friends that made the future* (London, Faber & Faber, 2003)

Wells, Roger, *Insurrection: The British Experience 1795–1803* (Gloucester, Allan Sutton, 1983)

Williamson, Tom, *The Transformation of Rural England* (Exeter, University of Exeter Press, 2002)

Wilson, Ben, *Decency and Disorder: The Age of Cant 1789–1837* (London, Faber & Faber, 2007)

Wise, Sarah, *The Italian Boy: Murder and Grave Robbery in 1830s London* (London, Jonathan Cape, 2004)

Index

Entries in *italics* indicate photographs or illustrations.

Allen, Richard 122, 123, 139, 164, 195, 212, 279
Alsop, Thomas 18, 98–9, 160
Aram, Eugene 2, 256, 257–8, 317
Arden, Thomas 38, 110–11, 227

bailiffs 34, 35, 64, 76, 129, 130, 131, 172, 186, 227, 231
ballads 258–60, 314
Banks, Catherine 35, 40, 41, 60, 110, 149, 185, 190, 241, 313
Banks, George 34, 35, 50, 85–6, 110, 129, 169; appearance 34; arrest of 236, 237, 238, 246, 285, 286; character 34; charged with Heming murder 251; Clewes confessions and 239, 240, 241, 242, 245, 287, 295–306; clover rick at Church Farm and 178, 179; damns Parker 53, 76, 87, 140; day of Parker murder 94, 111; death 308; Easter meeting and 55–6, 59, 60; Evans and 34, 35, 77, 85–6, 129, 172, 186–8, 189–90, 245, 304; family 34–5 *see also under individual family member name;* Heming inquest and 227, 232, 247, 248, 249; jail 260–1, 285, 286; Jones and 76; murder weapon, Parker's and 60; Parker's funeral, attends 154–5; Perkins and 59, 169; Pershore Fair, at 166; Pigeon House meeting 74, 75, 87, 94; press depictions of 253; released from jail 292; Sarah Lloyd and 74, 75, 87, 94; stands trial for Heming murder 265, 268, 269, 270–2, 273, 274, 285, 290–1; vestry meeting and 41

Banks, Henry 35, 55–6, 59, 60

Banks, Mary 34, 35, 40, 77, 126, 149, 172

Banks, Naomi R. Mary Cartwright 190

Barber, Thomas 77–8, 213–14, 216, 218, 278

Barneby, Richard 137–8, 139–40, 141, 147, 151, 196, 213, 216, 223, 314

Barnett, Mrs 103, 215

Barnett, John 3, 10, 39, 50, 64, 96, 116, 126, 134, 148, 172, 184; appearance 38; background 38–9; charged with Heming murder 251; Clewes confession and 241, 242, 243, 245, 246, 298, 299, 300; court cases and violent incidents involving Parker 19, 48, 49, 53, 246; damns Parker in Raven 77, 87, 140, 246; day of Parker's murder 8, 97, 98, 99, 102, 104, 105, 110, 111, 137–9, 148–9, 247; death 307–8; Easter meeting and 55, 56; Heming inquest and 207, 216, 227, 247, 248, 249; indifference to Parker's murder 98, 134–5, 138, 148, 160; jail 260; magistrates, summoned before meetings of 160–2, 163, 176; offers £50 for 'a dead parson' 77, 156, 246; overseer, election as 42; Park Farm and 182; Pigeon House meeting 74; Pyndar's investigation into Parker murder and 160–2, 163, 167, 226; released from jail 292; Smith investigation and 204; stands trial for Heming murder 268, 269, 271, 272, 273, 274, 290, 291; throws weight behind search for Heming 160; tithe and 28, 53, 76; vestry meeting and 42, 43; 'would give any man five Guineas who would shoot the parson' 49, 156

Barnett, Thomas 39, 55, 56, 77

Barnett, William 42, 64, 184; Bromsgrove Fair 109, 137; character 136–7; Church Farm, acquires 171, 182; clover rick at Church Farm and 179; day of Parker's murder 136–7; death 308; Evans and 132; Heming murder trial and 293; inquest into Heming death 247; parish constable 136, 137; Parker inquest and 136–7, 138, 140, 141, 145, 216; Smith investigation and 204, 207; Taylor and 175

Bath Chronicle 70

Berkeley, Captain Hubert 312, 314

Berrow's Worcester Journal 44,

169, 171, 191, 232, 250; Clewes confession and 244, 245; depictions of Evans 255; discovery of Heming skeleton and 203, 217; Heming and 119, 151, 172; Heming murder trial and 262, 294–5, 307, 314; Parker inquest and 167; Parker murder and 119, 145, 151, 172; Richard Patch and 143; reports subterranean den in Trench Wood 30, 31

Birmingham 16, 26, 57, 86, 107, 187; industry in 65, 66, 69, 154; interest in Oddingley murders within 245, 257, 258; migration from Oddingley to 1, 66; reformist and dissenting movements in 69

Birmingham and Worcester Canal 36, 182, 191, 218, 312

Birmingham Journal 268–9, 270–1

Bishop's Daughter, The (Neale) 177–8, 182, 188, 316–17

Black Country 1, 187

Blight, Isaac 2, 142–4

Bonaparte, Napoleon 28, 31, 50–1, 52, 219

Bow Street: Office 152; Runners 153; Thief–Takers 153

Bowkett, Catherine 186–8, 256

Bridge, John 79, 155

Bromsgrove Fair 7, 9, 93, 98, 102, 109, 115, 137, 144, 148, 173, 214, 222, 223, 239, 247, 275, 278

Bunn, Thomas 219

Burton, Charles: Allen and 123, 195; background 192; discovers Heming skeleton 193–5, 196, 197, 199, 202, 203–4, 207, 208, 209, 212, 217, 218, 219, 225, 231, 246, 258, 268, 277, 281, 304, 307, 310, 311; dismantles barn at Netherwood 193–5, 310; Heming and 123, 192, 208; Heming murder trial and 277, 281, 304, 307, 310, 311; home searched 123; infers Clewes involvement in Heming murder 203–4, 208, 218; inquest into Heming death and 196, 197, 199, 202, 203–4, 207, 208, 209, 212, 217, 218, 219, 225, 231, 246, 258, 268,; Waterson and 192–3, 194, 197, 204

Butt, Reverend John Marten 172, 180, 184

Campbell, John 271–2, 290, 295

Case for the Prosecution, The (Smith) 262

Cato Street Conspiracy, 1820 2, 184

Chance, Mary 166, 167, 168, 177, 300

Chance, William 27, 49, 111–12, 166, 179

Chellingworth, John 5, 121–2, 123, 170, 178, 207, 214

Church Farm, Oddingley: appearance of 33, 36; Banks at 76, 129; Barnett at 157, 161, 178; clover rick 178–9; day of Parker's murder 5, 8, 94, 109–12, 133, 147, 148, 149, 156, 157, 161, 178, 222, 226, 246, 247, 300; Evans and 19, 28, 33–5, 77, 85, 111, 132, 148, 149, 156, 157, 161, 162, 172; Fowler and 32, 40, 77; Heming at 8, 133, 147, 166, 168, 178, 222, 226, 300; location 37; murder weapon found at 32, 60, 143, 170, 179; survival of 311; William Barnett acquires 172, 182, 247

Church Lane, Oddingley 9, 18, 36, 37, 39, 61, 63, 78, 79, 98, 104, 105, 109, 125, 161

Churchill, Clement 86, 110, 156, 160, 246

Clark, Daniel 2, 256

Clewes, Thomas 3, 50, 53, 76, 128, 133, 197; appearance 37; arrest 226, 227, 284; background 37; bankruptcy 181–2; Banks and 239, 240, 241, 296–306; Barnett and 241, 242, 243, 245, 246, 298, 299, 300; Burton and 192–3; calls on Parker 77–8; character 38; charged with Heming murder 251; confessions 229–43, 244–9, 253, 254, 258, 259, 275–7, 281–3, 285–8, 295–306; court cases with Parker 49; damns name of Parker 8, 19, 77, 140, 203, 213; day of Parker's murder 7–8, 93, 109, 110–11, 148, 222, 225; death 308; Easter meeting and 55, 56; enclosure and 66; Evans and 133, 239, 240–1, 242; heard debating the shooting of Parker 8, 49, 156, 214, 222, 225, 275, 278; Heming and 116, 126, 172–3, 177, 203, 212, 221, 224, 225, 226, 241–2; inquest into Heming death/ Smith investigation and 203, 207, 208, 212, 213–14, 216, 217–19, 220, 221–2, 223, 224, 225, 226, 227, 248, 249; jail 229–39, 260; landlord of pub 313, 314; Netherwood Farm tenure ends 192–3, 197; offers £50 to have Parker shot 78, 213, 274–5; Pershore Fair 166, 287, 298, 299, 303; Pigeon House meeting 74–5; press depictions of 217–18, 253, 255, 294–5; Pyndar's investigation into Parker

murder and 169, 172–3, 174;
released from jail 292;
'should be glad to find a
dead parson in Oddingley
when he came back' 8, 156,
214, 222, 225, 275, 278; social
standing 38; spoils tithe milk
53; stands trial for Heming
murder 261, 265, 266, 267,
268, 269, 270–91; Taylor and
240, 241, 242; threats against
Parker 77–8, 140; tithe and
28; vestry meeting and 43
Clewes, Diana 37, 38
Clewes, John 38, 55
Clifton, Reverend Robert:
  Clewes confession and 229,
  233–5, 236, 237–8, 244, 275–6,
  282, 283–6, 287, 305, 306;
  Heming inquest and 226;
  Heming murder trial and
  283, 283–6, 287
Cole, Pennell 134–5, 137, 139,
  280–1, 307
Colley, Joseph 116, 122, 156, 160,
  221–2, 278
Colley, William 27, 49, 120
Collins, John 133, 220, 224, 225,
  230, 231, 287
Colwell, Thomas 113, 114, 115,
  122, 123, 139, 168, 223, 279
Commeline, Reverend Samuel
  21–2, 23–4, 28, 45
constables 42, 236, 269; Barnett
  as 42, 136, 137, 140, 247;

election of 42; Heming
  inquest and 223, 226, 229;
  Heming skeleton and 196,
  197; in London 152; powers
  of arrest 101; Pyndar's
  investigation and 122, 123,
  136, 137, 139, 140, 146, 164,
  173; search Church Farm
  179; search Heming's home
  139; in Worcester 108
Cooper, Reverend Sterry 314,
  315, 316
Corder, William 252, 317
Crockett, Richard 214, 225–6
Crowle 5, 8, 9, 30, 60, 66, 78,
  110, 154, 155, 167, 168, 206,
  310
Crown Inn, Worcester,
  meeting of magistrates at
  157–8, 160–3, 166, 262
Cumin, Dr 215–16
Curwood, John 271, 272, 274–5,
  276, 278, 281, 282, 284, 285,
  286, 287, 288, 290–1, 295, 304

Davis of Dunhampstead, Mr
  74, 75, 87, 94
Davis, Marta 231
Day, George 105, 107–8, 115,
  123, 137, 207, 213
death penalty 183–4
Dickens, Charles 2, 85, 87, 91,
  100, 119, 146, 189, 276
Dream of Eugene Aram, The
  (Hood) 256

Droitwich Spa: appearance and
    nature of 126, 127–8; Clewes
    and 38, 221, 225, 226, 280;
    country fairs at 7; Evans
    and 34, 37, 128–33, 171, 185–7,
    188, 190, 312, 313; Heming,
    search for in 117, 118, 119,
    122, 123, 125, 139, 147, 151, 155,
    159, 164, 172, 173, 175, 176,
    177; industry 126–7, 128;
    location 15; taverns 19
Droitwich Road 56, 77, 107

Earl of Surrey, later, Duke of
    Norfolk 19–22, 24, 25, 28
Easter Meeting, Tibberton,
    1806 55–61, 87
ecclesiastical courts 48–9
Eldon, Lord 267
Elstree murder, 1823 254
Emsley, Clive 130
enclosure acts 66–7
Evans, Captain Samuel 3, 37,
    111, 134; appearance 33;
    arrives at Church Farm 85;
    background 33, 80–5, 129;
    Banks and 41, 172, 186–8,
    189–90, 297, 304, 305; Barnett
    and 148, 149, 157, 161, 162–3,
    226; challenges Elizabeth
    Fowler to drink toast
    against Parker 77, 89–91;
    character 33–4, 85; Clewes
    confessions and 239–42,
    244–5, 246, 287, 288, 289,

299, 300, 301, 302, 304, 305,
    306; coins 'Bonaparte of
    Oddingley' nickname for
    Parker 50, 52; confronts
    Parker 60, 78–9; court cases
    with Parker 49; damns
    Parker 49, 54, 55, 56, 57–8,
    59–60, 74, 77, 86–8, 226, 227,
    299; day of Parker's murder
    8, 105, 109–10, 111, 147–9,
    160–4; death 186–90, 227,
    254–8, 293, 308; drinks left-
    handed toast to Parker at
    Plough 55–6, 57, 58, 59–60;
    Droitwich and 128–31; Easter
    meeting and 55, 56, 57–8,
    59–60; Evans and 148, 149,
    161, 162–3, 226; grave 312–13;
    Heming and 61, 118, 147–9,
    157, 162, 164–5, 207, 210, 212,
    225, 239–42, 244–5, 246, 287,
    288, 289, 304, 305, 306, 307,
    308, 309, 312–14; inquest into
    Parker's murder and 138,
    140, 141; intimidates people
    into silence 168; leads
    opposition to Parker 19; life
    after Parker murder
    investigation 185–90;
    magistrates, summoned
    before 160, 161, 162–3, 176;
    murder weapon and 60–1;
    New House, moves to 171;
    offers £50 to shoot Parker
    246; Perkins and 54, 57–60;

Pigeon House meeting and 74; press depictions of 251, 253, 254–8, 306–7; Pyndar's investigation into Parker murder and 147–9, 155–60, 161, 162–3, 164–5, 168, 169; retires as a farmer 171–2; secures deeds of Church Farm 36; Smith's investigation Heming murder and 205; social standing 38, 85–6; Taylor and 301, 303; 'there was no more harm in shooting the parson than in shooting a dog' 49, 54, 155–6; throws weight behind search for Heming 160; tithe and 28, 43, 45, 53, 54, 85; vestry meeting 41, 42, 78

Feckenham Forest 30, 35, 36, 127
Fir Tree Inn, Dunhampstead 313, 314
Foley, Lord Thomas 7, 17, 18, 22, 24, 28, 33, 36, 39, 182, 184, 190, 193
Footman 218
footpads 29, 40, 60, 152
Fowler, Elizabeth: day of Parker's murder 8; discovers murder weapon 32, 40, 41, 60, 143, 179, 246, 279; Evans asks to drink a toast against Parker 77, 89, 90, 91;

Heming inquest and 246; Heming murder trial and 279; Parker inquest and 132, 133, 140, 141; search for Heming and 166–7
Fox, Charles 20, 58, 71, 72, 73
France: Revolution 28–9, 49–50, 59; wars with, Napoleonic 1, 17, 28–31, 50–3, 67–8, 181

Galton, John Howard 184, 193
Georgian era/society: architecture 63, 264; deathbed and 189; end of 182–3, 257; literary representations of 2–3; lost nature of 2; personal honour in 89; politics 28–31, 49–53; underworld 30, 119
Giles, Thomas: day of Parker's murder 9–13, 95–6, 98, 102, 103, 108, 113, 114, 122; Parker inquest and 134, 138–9, 204–5, 213
Gillray, James 51, 58, 71, 72, 73
God Speed the Plough, Tibberton 55–6, 88, 132, 169, 226, 241, 280
Godson, Richard 286
Godson, Stephen 261
Great Expectations (Dickens) 2, 91, 119, 146
Green, Thomas 109, 110, 148, 149, 161, 163, 226

Grenville, Lord 71
Grose, Francis 43
Guildhall, Worcester 264–5,
    268, 269, 290, 291, 295 314

Hadzor 9, 25, 99, 102, 172, 177
Halberd, Henry 222, 300
Hardcourt, Edward 28, 39, 54,
    58, 91, 93, 109, 138, 140, 184,
    214–15, 222, 278, 311
Hardy, Thomas 2, 7, 90, 317
Heming (née Burton; later,
    Newbury), Elizabeth:
    background 118; belief that
    farmers were hiding
    something about
    disappearance of husband
    177–9; Burton and 118, 192;
    Heming murder trial and
    277–8; house searched 122,
    123; Pyndar interviews 164,
    165; Richard Heming and
    118; Smith's investigation /
    Heming inquest and 204,
    209–10, 211, 213, 227
Heming, Richard 3; appearance
    60, 113; background 60,
    116–18, 144; Barnett and see
    Barnett, John; character
    116–20; claims shotgun 60–1;
    Clewes and 116, 126, 172–3,
    177, 203, 212, 219, 221, 224,
    225, 226, 239–43, 244–5; day
    of Parker's murder 8, 114–15,
    122, 139, 144–5, 210; Evans

and see Evans, Captain
    Samuel; inquest into killing
    of 206–28, 236–7, 246–50;
    motive for Parker murder
    144–5; murder of 239–319;
    murder trial 274–91; Pyndar's
    investigation into Parker's
    murder and 132–3, 145, 147,
    148, 164–5, 174, 176; reward
    for 158, 169, 172; search for
    113–24, 125–6, 132–3, 137,
    146–7, 149–54, 157, 158, 160,
    164–70, 172–3, 176–80, 280;
    skeleton analysis and
    identification 202–3, 209–12,
    268, 278, 281; skeleton
    discovered 193–205, 217, 281,
    311, 312; as suspect in Parker
    murder 113–24, 140, 145
Hemmus, Mr 102, 103, 157, 215
Herefordshire Journal, The 217
Hill, Thomas 115, 280
Home Office 146, 201, 202, 235,
    305
home secretary 152, 158, 159,
    184, 199, 200, 202, 220, 221,
    233, 235, 237, 286 see also
    under individual home
    secretary name
Hooper, James 242, 281, 282–3,
    286
Household Words 126–7
hue and cry 100–2, 137, 158
Hue and Cry and Police Gazette,
    The 152, 159

inflation 1, 43, 44, 67, 70, 181
inquests: Heming 206–28, 236–43, 246–50; Parker 134–41
Ipswich Journal 2, 255

Jackson's Oxford Journal 151, 306
Johnson, Dr Samuel 86–7, 121, 141
Jones, George Gilbert 75–6, 246
Jones, Samuel 39, 91, 94, 97, 138, 140, 184, 239, 312
justice of the peace 25, 104, 137

Kendall, Joseph 79, 154–6
Knight, William 94

Langford, Thomas 8, 98, 133, 226
Lavender, Mr 230, 238, 281–2, 293
Lee, Valentine 278, 279
Leicester Chronicle 251–2
Lench, John: day of Parker's murder 9–11, 12, 95–6, 97, 98, 102, 103, 108, 113, 122; Heming inquest and 213, 223; Heming murder trial and 279; Parker inquest and 134, 138–9, 148, 160, 161, 204–5
Littledale, Justice Joseph: background and appearance 266–7, 270; enters Worcester 262; Heming murder trial and 262, 265–7, 269, 270, 270, 271, 272, 273–4, 275, 279, 283, 284, 286–7, 288, 289, 290, 291, 294, 295, 313
Lloyd, George 75, 122, 139
Lloyd, Sarah 74, 75, 78, 87, 91, 94, 95, 122, 140, 141, 155, 278–9
Lloyd, Thomas 48, 214
London Medical Gazette 211, 215
Ludlow, Ebenezer 272, 273, 274, 275, 276, 277, 278, 279, 280, 281–2, 283, 284, 286, 288–9, 295

magistrates: Clewes confession and 233, 234, 238, 242, 248, 249, 276, 282, 283, 298; Crown Inn meeting of 157–8, 160–4, 176; Evans as 34, 59, 86, 130, 131, 132, 138, 148, 171, 185, 188, 190; Heming murder trial and 276, 282, 283, 285, 286; Parker murder investigation and 2, 3, 103–4, 105, 122, 135, 137, 138, 140, 141, 142–3, 145, 149, 157–8, 159, 160, 161, 162, 163, 165, 167, 174, 175, 176, 179; Smith's inquest 202, 220, 226; system of policing and 103–4, 145–6
Marshall, John 39, 91, 109, 138, 140, 184
Marshall, Sarah 98
Marten, Maria 252–3

Maul and the Pear Tree, The
    (James/Critchley) 136
Mayor of Casterbridge, The
    (Hardy) 7, 90, 91–2
Miles, Richard 46–7
Miller, Hugh 127, 128
Morning Chronicle 2, 17, 62, 191,
    227–8, 247–8, 251, 254, 258,
    260, 263, 269, 279
Morris, Mrs 172–3
murder, Georgian society and
    141–4

Nash, William 214, 239
Nelson, Admiral Lord 29, 57,
    308
Netherwood Farm, Oddingley
    5; Clewes and 7, 19, 28, 37, 38,
    49, 74–5, 133, 182, 192, 203, 214,
    218, 219, 220, 222, 241–2, 253,
    261, 287, 301, 302; day of the
    Parker's murder 110–11, 123,
    133, 218, 222, 241–2, 254, 267,
    301; Heming's skeleton
    discovered at 191–9, 203–4,
    205, 206, 208, 212, 214, 218,
    219, 220, 222, 224, 253, 277, 277,
    278; location and appearance
    of 37–8, 192, 277; Parker
    avoids 78; plan of 207; present
    day 310–12, 319; Waterson and
    192–3, 194–5, 196, 197, 212–13
newspaper sensation,
    Oddingley murders as a 1, 2;
    Clewes and 217–18, 244, 245,
    251–4, 262, 279, 294–5;
    discovery of Heming
    skeleton and 203–4, 211,
    215–16, 217–18, 227–8; Evans
    and 188–9, 251, 253, 254–8,
    306–7; Heming inquest and
    215–16, 217–18, 227–8, 235,
    244, 245, 249–54; Heming
    search and 151, 158, 164,
    169–70; Heming murder trial
    and 262, 287, 292–6; report
    Parker's murder 141–4
Noake, John 180–1

oaths 89–92
Oddingley, Worcestershire:
    alcohol and 56; areas of
    36–7; changing nature of
    early 19th century 65–8;
    farming calendar 16–17;
    history of 35–6; leading men
    of 17; location and
    appearance 15, 16; migration
    from 1, 66; name 35;
    reputation 3
Oddingley Lane 36, 95, 125
Oddingley Lane Farm 8, 39, 93,
    94, 102
Oddingley Rectory 62–4, 68,
    98, 118, 134, 141, 172
Oliver Twist (Dickens) 100

Page, Richard 114–15, 279, 280
Pardoe, John 25, 94, 123, 137,
    156, 226

Park Farm, Oddingley 37, 182, 311, 315

Parker, Reverend George 3; accounts of 25–7; appearance of 17–18, *18*; arrival in Oddingley 18–19, 21–4; as Devil 92; background 19–22; 'Bonaparte of Oddingley' nickname 50–2, 92, 116, 221; character 20, 21, 24–8; Clewes confession and 239, 242, 245; conciliatory offer from farmers and 31, 53–4; conflict with farmers *see under individual farmer name*; coroner's inquest 134–49, 151, 262; court cases with Barnett 19, 48, 49, 53; day of murder 9–13, 95, 96, 97, 98, 101, 103, 105; Dorking curacy 21; education 20, 21; election agent 20; Evans and *see* Evans, Captain Samuel; finances/financial ambition 27, 43–9; funeral 154; haughtiness 27–8; Heming and *see* Heming, Richard; Heming inquest and 213–15, 218, 221, 222, 223, 224–5, 226, 246, 247; Heming murder trial and 262, 265, 266, 267, 268, 271–3, 289–90; Howard family and 20–2; life at Oddingley Rectory 62–3; man out of time 70; name damned 8, 19, 49, 53, 53–61, 74–5, 76, 77, 86–92, 140, 203, 213, 226, 227, 246, 299; newspaper depictions of 251; night-time disturbances at home 62–4, 71, 227; parish records and *23*, 24–5; politics and feud with farmers 28–31; reaction to curses and provocation 88–9; refusal to approve annual accounts 42–3; stone 312; tithe and 28, 43, 44–9, 52–4, 68, 73; toasts drunk damning 55–61, 74–5, 88, 278; vanity 27; vestry meeting 42–3, 78

Parker, Mary (daughter of George Parker) 9, 25, 62–3, 99

Parker, Mary (wife of George Parker) 79; background 64–5; Barnett refuses to visit 160–1; death 307; Heming inquest and 227; husband's murder and 113, 136, 140, 164; inquest into husband's killing and 136, 140; meets and marries George Parker 25; night-time disturbances at rectory and 62–3; Perkins and 94

Patch, Richard 2, 142–4

Peel, Robert: appointed home secretary 184; Clewes

confession and 202, 209, 212, 216, 220–1, 233–5, 236, 237, 238, 305, 306; Clifton writes to 233–5, 236, 237, 238, 305, 306; early life 200; Heming inquest and 202, 209, 212, 216, 220–1, 233–5, 236, 237, 238, 305, 306; ignores request for royal pardon 202, 209, 212, 216, 220–1, 233–5, 236, 237, 238, 305, 306; last prime minister not to be photographed 316; police force and 201; reforms law 184; Smith writes to 199–202, 220–1

Perkins, Betty 94, 102, 157, 226
Perkins, John 159, 166, 167, 312; background 39, 43; Banks and 169; day of Parker's murder 8, 93, 94, 95, 99, 100, 106, 109, 113, 116, 123, 126,; deputised constable 137, 173; Easter meeting and 57–8, 59–60, 137, 226; Evans and 57–8, 59–60, 85, 87, 155–6; forced back into labouring ranks 181; friendship with Parker 28, 43, 54, 57–8, 59–60, 76, 87, 91, 94; Heming murder trial and 280, 312; Parker inquest and 140; Parker's funeral and 154; Pigeon House meeting and 87; search for Heming and

147; Smith investigation 204; vestry meeting and 54, 57–8, 59–60
Petty, Lord Henry 71–2
Pickwick Papers (Dickens) 189
Pierpoint, Matthew 196, 197, 198, 199, 202–3, 208–9, 210, 211, 216, 247–8, 258, 277, 300, 303
Pigeon House, Oddingley 74–5, 76, 87, 88, 94, 140, 278, 312
Pigeon House Field, Oddingley 97, 98
Pineapple Farm, Oddingley 39, 98, 125, 311
Pitt the Younger, William 1, 50, 57, 69, 71, 89
Political Register 71
Pound Farm, Oddingley: Barnett and 8, 19, 28, 38–9, 48, 49, 64, 76, 79, 137, 138, 149, 161, 246; day of Parker murder 9, 10, 11, 95, 76, 78, 79, 95, 96, 97, 99, 102, 103, 105, 122, 137, 138, 161; Heming and 115, 120; 1930s 315, 316; Park Farm and 182; Parker and 48, 49, 53, 78, 246; present day 311; Surman and 8
press gangs 81, 82–3
Priestley, Joseph 86
Pritchard (farmhand) 5, 123
Pyndar, Mary 318–19
Pyndar, Reverend Reginald: appoints deputised

constables 137; day of
Parker's murder 99–100, 102,
103, 104, 105, 109, 114; death
307; Heming and 114, 122,
123, 125–6, 132–3, 151, 153–4,
159, 165–9; magistrates
meetings and 157–8, 160–5;
omitted from Parker inquest
140; Parker and 25, 154;
Parker murder investigation
99–100, 102, 103, 104, 105,
109, 114, 122, 125, 132, 137,
140, 145–8, 151, 152, 153, 154,
155, 156–7, 158, 159, 160, 161,
162, 163, 164–5, 167, 169, 172,
173, 174, 175, 176, 178, 179,
200, 204, 215, 220, 234, 237,
262, 279, 299, 300, 318;
Parker's funeral and 154;
Read and 152–3; Smith
investigation and 279

Ratcliffe Highway murders,
1811 136, 138, 317
Raven, Droitwich Road 77, 87,
246
Red Barn Murder, 1827 2, 252,
317
Red Lion, Driotwich 38, 56,
116, 119, 126, 128, 156, 173,
221, 225, 278, 280
Reed, Thomas 77
Rogers, William 178, 222
Rowe, John 173, 174, 175–6, 179,
204, 237, 242, 300

Sale Green village 77, 125, 194,
213
Sanders, Benjamin 25–7, 322
Sequel to the Oddingley Murders
(Sherwood) 294
Sherwood, Mary 3, 33–4, 84,
180, 260, 294
Sketches By Boz (Dickens) 85, 276
Skinner, Reverend John 69–70,
71
Smite Hill 9, 125, 196
Smith, William: first hears of
discovery of Heming
skeleton 195–6, 197; Heming
murder trial and 261, 262,
267, 268, 272–3, 281–2, 286,
287; initial Investigation into
Heming murder 195–6, 197,
199, 200–1, 202, 203, 204–5,
277; inquest into Heming
murder 206, 207–8, 209–10,
211, 212, 214, 215, 216, 217,
220–3, 224, 233, 234, 236–7,
238–9, 242, 247, 248, 249–50
Southey, Robert 16, 29, 56
Spencer, Earl 158, 159–60, 200
St James' Church, Oddingley 5,
36, 53, 156, 180, 291, 308, 311
statute, 1702: 'no accessory can
be convicted or suffer
punishment where the
principal is not attained' 165,
184; repealed, 1826 184,
261–2, 271
Stephens, Edward 123, 137, 156

Surman, Susan: day of
     Parker's murder 7–8, 9, 96,
     96, 99, 102, 103, 104, 105, 122,
     137, 140, 144, 214–15, 222;
     Heming inquest and 214–15,
     216, 218; Heming murder
     trial and 278; Heming
     sightings in weeks before
     Parker murder 120; on
     Barnett on the day of
     Parker's murder 104, 105,
     148; overhears Clewes say he
     'should be glad to find a
     dead parson in Oddingley
     when he came back' 9;
     Parker inquest and 140, 141

Taunton, William 271, 272, 295
Taylor, James: appearance 173;
     character 175–6; Clewes
     confession and 240–3, 244,
     251, 254, 258, 296–7, 296–7,
     300, 301, 302–3, 305; day of
     Parker's murder 173, 174,
     175–6, 254; Heming inquest
     and 237, 238, 240, 242, 243;
     Heming murder trial and
     283, 287, 293
Taylor, Joseph 130, 237
Taylor, Susannah 237, 238
tenant farm system 39
thief-takers 153, 166
Thurtell, John 254, 317
Tibberton 9, 32, 52, 55–61, 113,
     114, 147, 169, 182, 206, 226

Times, The 244
tithe 1; as motive for Parker's
     murder 157, 293; as
     opportunity to knit
     community together 69;
     avoidance of 52; Butt and
     172; Clewes spoils tithe milk
     53; commissions, 1840s 316;
     dispute, Parker's 73, 76, 79,
     80, 85, 101, 157, 251, 254, 281,
     293, 314, 315, 317; disputes
     become common 69, 184–5,
     227–8; farmers' offer to
     renegotiate with Parker 31,
     53–4; history of 43; modus
     45; Parker assaulted by
     Barnett collecting 48; Parker
     haughtiness in collecting 28;
     Parker raises 44, 45–6, 47;
     Parker's tithe men 48, 53,
     207, 213; payment in kind
     47–8, 49, 54, 59, 68, 76–7;
     Sanders forfeit of 27;
     Skinner and 69, 70; vestry
     meeting and 43
Tithe Commutation Act, 1836
     293, 315
toasts drunk damning Parker
     55–61, 74–5, 88, 278
Tookey, Reverend Charles 184,
     292
Trench Wood 15, 30–1, 36, 37,
     45, 62, 76, 119, 125, 160, 168,
     182, 192, 194, 204, 218, 224,
     225, 231, 300, 312, 314, 315, 319

trial, Heming murder 262–3, 264–91

Tustin, James: day of Parker's murder 8, 9, 10, 11–12, 94–5, 96–7, 98, 102–3, 104, 105, 122, 157, 160, 161; Heming inquest and 207, 215; Heming murder trial and 293; Heming pursuit and 102–3, 157, 160, 161, 215; Parker inquest and 134, 137, 139

vestry meeting, Oddingley, 1806 41–3, 48, 55, 78, 79, 247, 293

Virgin Tavern, Newtown 114–15, 218, 279, 280

Ward, Richard 153, 177

Waterson, Henry/Waterson family 246, 258; Clewes and 192–3, 194–5, 196, 197, 204, 242; Heming inquest and 212–13, 218–20

weapon, Parker murder 2, 32, 40–1, 60, 103, 122, 134, 140, 179, 210, 213, 220, 279

Whateley, William 286

Wilberforce, William 46

woodcuts, Oddingley murder 258, 316

Woodforde, Reverend James 68–9, 70, 174n

Worcester: appearance and location of 4, 15–17, 106, 107, 183; bad harvests and 16–17, 169, 181; City Gaol, Castle Street 226, 229–43, 248, 292, 298; Clewes confession in 229–43; Crown Inn meeting of magistrates 157–8, 160–5; fair days 7; food riots, 1790s 44; Guildhall, Heming murder trial at 264–91; Heming inquest in 205–28; Heming murder trial in 264–91; industry 15–16, 107; Napoleonic Wars, attitude towards within 17, 67; Nelson visits 29; River Severn breaks banks at, 1806 32; Sadler's 'aerial voyage' and, 1785 65; Sanders and Parker in 25–6; search for Heming and 107–8, 114–15, 123, 124, 125–6, 127

Worcester Herald: Evans and 187, 188; Heming inquest and 211, 214, 221, 235, 253, 260; Heming murder trial and 262, 270, 296, 298; Heming search and 150, 167, 168–9; Napoleonic wars and 17, 29, 30–1

Worcestershire 3, 62, 65; character and appearance of 15–16; fair days 7; farming in 67–8; food supplies, scarcity of 1, 50, 181; harvests 1, 5, 6, 8, 12, 16–17, 31, 50, 56, 65, 67, 73, 76, 78, 79, 93, 94, 111, 120,

144, 169, 170, 179, 181, 197, 225; industry in 65–6; map of, 1804 4; nature of early 19th century 16; Napoleonic wars and 28, 29, 181; Oddingley *see* Oddingley; Oddingley murders story, legacy of within 318–19; seasons and 5, 6, 62, 111, 121; tithe in 47, 68 *see also* tithe; *see also under individual town or area name*